THE REVELS PLAYS

Former general editors
Clifford Leech
F. David Hoeniger
E. A. J. Honigmann
Eugene M. Waith

General editors
David Bevington, Richard Dutton, Alison Findlay,
J. R. Mulryne and Helen Ostovich

THE DUCHESS OF MALFI

Manchester University Press

THE REVELS PLAYS

THE REVELS PLAYS

THE DUCHESS OF MALFI

JOHN WEBSTER

Second edition
edited by John Russell Brown

MANCHESTER
UNIVERSITY PRESS

Manchester and New York

*distributed in the United States exclusively
by Palgrave Macmillan*

Introduction, critical apparatus, etc.
© John Russell Brown 1963, 1974, 2009

The right of John Russell Brown to be identified as the editor of
this work has been asserted by him in accordance with the
Copyright, Designs and Patents Act 1988.

First edition published 1963 by Methuen
Published by Manchester University Press 1974
Reprinted 1976, 1977, 1981, 1984

This edition published by Manchester University Press
Oxford Road, Manchester M13 9NR, UK
and Room 400, 175 Fifth Avenue, New York, NY 10010, USA
www.manchesteruniversitypress.co.uk

Distributed in the United States exclusively by
Palgrave Macmillan, 175 Fifth Avenue, New York,
NY 10010, USA

Distributed in Canada exclusively by
UBC Press, University of British Columbia, 2029 West Mall,
Vancouver, BC, Canada V6T 1Z2

British Library Cataloguing-in-Publication Data
A catalogue record for this book is available from
the British Library

Library of Congress Cataloging-in-Publication Data applied for

ISBN 978 0 7190 7518 6 *paperback*

This edition published 2009

18 17 16 15 14 13 12 11 10 09   10 9 8 7 6 5 4 3 2 1

The publisher has no responsibility for the persistence or accuracy
of URLs for external or any third-party internet websites referred
to in this book, and does not guarantee that any content on such
websites is, or will remain, accurate or appropriate.

Typeset in Plantin
by SNP Best-set Typesetter Ltd., Hong Kong
Printed in Great Britain
by Bell & Bain Ltd, Glasgow

To
PAUL HARMAN
GEOFFREY HUTCHINGS
and
ROSEMARY KERNAN

Contents

General Editors' Preface

Clifford Leech conceived of the Revels Plays as a series in the mid-1950s, modelling the project on the New Arden Shakespeare. The aim, as he wrote in 1958, was 'to apply to Shakespeare's predecessors, contemporaries and successors the methods that are now used in Shakespeare's editing'. The plays chosen were to include well-known works from the early Tudor period to about 1700, as well as others less familiar but of literary and theatrical merit: 'the plays included', Leech wrote, 'should be such as to deserve and indeed demand performance'. We owe it to Clifford Leech that the idea became reality. He set the high standards of the series, ensuring that editors of individual volumes produced work of lasting merit, equally useful for teachers and students, theatre directors and actors. Clifford Leech remained General Editor until 1971, and was succeeded by F. David Hoeniger, who retired in 1985.

From 1985 the Revels Plays were under the direction of four General Editors: initially David Bevington, E. A. J. Honigmann, J. R. Mulryne and E. M. Waith. E. A. J. Honigmann retired in 2000 and was succeeded by Richard Dutton. E. M. Waith retired in 2003 and was succeeded by Alison Findlay and Helen Ostovich. Published originally by Methuen, the series is now published by Manchester University Press, embodying essentially the same format, scholarly character and high editorial standards of the series as first conceived. The series concentrates on plays from the period 1558–1642, and includes a small number of non-dramatic works of interest to students of drama. Some slight changes have been made: for example, in editions from 1978 onward, notes to the introduction are placed together at the end, not at the foot of the page. Collation and commentary notes continue, however, to appear on the relevant pages.

The text of each Revels play, in accordance with established practice in the series, is edited afresh from the original text of best authority (in a few instances, texts), but spelling and punctuation are modernised and speech headings are silently made consistent. Elisions in the original are also silently regularised, except where metre would be affected by the change; since 1968 the '-ed' form is used for non-syllabic terminations in past tenses and past participles

('-'d'earlier), and '-èd' for syllabic ('-ed' earlier). The editor emends, as distinct from modernises, the original only in instances where error is patent, or at least very probable, and correction persuasive. Act division are given only if they appear in the original or if the structure of the play clearly points to them. Those act and scene divisions not in the original are provided in small type. Square brackets are also used for any other additions to or changes in the stage directions of the original.

Revels Plays do not provide a variorum collation, but only those variants which require the critical attention of serious textual students. All departures of substance from 'copy-text' are listed, including any relineation and those changes in punctuation which involve to any degree a decision between alternative interpretations; but not such accidentals as turned letters, nor necessary additions to stage directions whose editorial nature is already made clear by the use of brackets. Press corrections in the 'copy-text' are likewise collated. Of later emendations of the text, only those are given which as alternative readings still deserve attention.

One of the hallmarks of the Revels Plays is the thoroughness of their annotations. Besides explaining the meaning of difficult words and passages, the editor provides comments on customs or usage, text or stage-business – indeed, on anything judged pertinent and helpful. Each volume contains an Index to the Commentary, in which particular attention is drawn to meanings for words not listed in *OED*, and (starting in 1996) an indexing of proper names and topics in the Introduction and Commentary.

The introduction to a Revels play assesses the authority of the 'copy-text' on which it is based, and discusses the editorial methods employed in dealing with it; the editor also considers the play's date and (where relevant) sources, together with its place in the work of the author and in the theatre of its time. Stage history is offered, and in the case of a play by an author not previously represented in the series a brief biography is given.

It is our hope that plays edited in this fashion will promote further scholarly and theatrical investigation of one of the richest periods in theatrical history.

DAVID BEVINGTON
RICHARD DUTTON
ALISON FINDLAY
J. R. MULRYNE
HELEN OSTOVICH

Preface to the First Edition

This Revels Plays edition of *The Duchess of Malfi* is planned as a companion to *The White Devil* in the same series.

As a student of Webster I have been helped in many ways, by Professor F. P. Wilson, under whom I first started to work, by my colleagues, students, and friends at Birmingham and Stratford-upon-Avon, and by Dr Gunnar Boklund, Professor Fredson Bowers, Mr John Crow, Professor G. B. Howarth, Dr George Hunter, Professor F. W. Sternfeld, Professor R. K. Turner, Jr, and Mr Patrick Wymark. Three debts are specifically concerned with preparing this book: to Mr David Greer for the Appendix on the music; to my wife, Hilary, for much of the work on Appendix I and for help with the proofs; and to the General Editor of the Revels Plays, Professor Clifford Leech, for his forbearance and most generous and scrupulous criticism at all times. The pleasures of my studies have been greatly increased by this co-operation; I shall always be grateful.

The opportunity to direct a production of *The Duchess of Malfi* I owe to the Guild Theatre Group of Birmingham University: for this, as for many other opportunities of working in a theatre, I am most grateful to the Group and appreciative of its talents, enthusiasm, and capacity for taking pains.

JOHN RUSSELL BROWN
Birmingham, 1963

Preface to the Second Edition

This second edition thoroughly revises the introduction and annotations of the first in the light of further studies and new editions by others as well as myself. In particular it draws on the Revels Student edition of 1996 and my experience of recent productions of the play. Further insights have come from exploratory work with actors of New Fortune Theatre and graduate students at Middlesex University. I am most grateful for these opportunities and for the support of Matthew Frost of Manchester University Press, and Nathanial Nesmith, my research assistant in North America.

During the printing and proofing of my book, members of the production team at Manchester University Press, especially Rachel Armstrong and Reena Jugnarain, have patiently and skilfully supported me. John Banks identified problems during the final stages of this process and expertly contributed in many ways to ease my task as well as improve the text. For all this help I am greatly indebted and grateful.

I have been greatly indebted to Alison Findlay, General Editor of Revels Plays, at every stage from the conception of a revised edition onwards. We have considered many questions together and her notes on my drafts have improved both the Introduction and Annotations. To record every instance would encumber the text with references to our exchanges that would be of little advantage to a reader. This general account of our collaboration must stand as record of my debt and grateful thanks although it gives no detail of our agreements and disagreements, suggestions gladly accepted or declined. The final version of this revised edition, which I completed in 2007, is, of course, my responsibility, not least in its inevitable shortcomings as a presentation of Webster's extraordinary tragedy that can engage deep feelings and awaken a piercing sense of uncertainty. Ongoing critical debate over the play is restimony to these qualities.

JOHN RUSSELL BROWN
London, 2009

Introduction

John Webster would have been well known in theatrical circles when *The Duchess of Malfi* was first performed, some time before the death on 16 December 1614 of William Ostler, its first Antonio. In his early twenties, Webster had been among the writers who, in groups of three, four or more, had supplied new plays for Philip Henslowe, theatre owner and company manager. The plays he worked on are now lost but Webster's name occurs repeatedly in Henslowe's surviving account book from 22 May 1602 until March 1603 when regular entries ceased. Antony Munday, Thomas Middleton, Michael Drayton, Thomas Dekker, Thomas Heywood, Wentworth Smith and Henry Chettle were among his co-authors working on a busy and, no doubt, hectic schedule (Foakes, pp. 210–12, 218–19). With fewer collaborators, other work followed. In 1604 Webster contributed a prologue and additions to John Marston's *Malcontent* for its revival by the King's Men. In the same year, with Dekker, he wrote *Westward Ho*, a comedy for a company of boy-actors, the Children of Paul's, and followed this the next year with *Northward Ho*, after other authors and another company had produced a rival play, *Eastward Ho*. He may have started work on another play if he was author of a manuscript fragment of 144 lines of dialogue about Alessandro de' Medici that has been found in Derbyshire (see Hammond and DelVecchio in Cambridge edition). After this busy and mostly collaborative start, *The White Devil* of 1612 was the first play known to have been performed that was entirely his own.

In a prefatory note 'To the Reader', Webster confessed that he had been a 'long time in finishing' this tragedy and, we may add, it was in marked contrast to his earlier work. His preface also says that this lengthy and ambitious play had been performed in 'so dull a time of winter' and at a theatre, the Red Bull, that was 'so open and black', that it had lacked a 'full and understanding auditory'. Those who patronised this theatre, he added, resembled 'ignorant asses' who paid no regard to good writing. He asked that the play might now be read by the 'light' of the best of his fellow playwrights, among whom he included Beaumont and Fletcher, Jonson and Shakespeare, none of whom had been among his collaborators.

But Webster's *White Devil* found approval despite disappointing performances. Its text was published almost at once and, no more than two years later, his second play written alone was staged by the King's Men, the country's leading company that played frequently at Court as well as at the recently rebuilt Globe Theatre on Bankside and the more expensive, indoor playhouse at Blackfriars in the City. Some time before 16 December, 1614, *The Duchess of Malfi* had its first performance and Webster, the playwright, might truly be said to have arrived. He had found success on his own terms. In subject matter, vocabulary, dialogue, spectacle and the demands they make upon actors, his two tragedies are much alike. Both show that Webster possessed an active, wide-ranging imagination, and was a keen observer of himself and those among whom he lived. He also had read many books from which he wrote down passages for subsequent use in his own plays. He was probably a loner for, while collaboration had given him direct contact with writers and theatre people, his writings show him to be very much his own man, independent in mind and uncompromisingly ambitious.

Although born and bred in the city, he made some acquaintance with influential persons at Court, the established seat of power and government in the land. His main contact was Thomas Overbury who had been knighted in 1608 for serving as secretary to the King's favourite, Robert Carr, a young Scotsman who in 1611 was created Viscount Rochester and, in 1613, the Earl of Somerset. Towards the end of 1612, while working on *The Duchess*, Webster made time to write *A Monumental Column* that was published the following year in commemoration of the death of Henry Prince of Wales. Overbury's role was much like Flamineo's in *The White Devil* who, in his own words, is the 'poor secretary' to 'a great duke' (IV.ii.60); as Carr prospered at Court, so Overbury's influence increased rapidly. But he incurred the 'great displeasure' of the king when he became involved with the scandals and jealousies aroused by Carr's plans to marry Frances Howard who was then married to the Earl of Essex. When offered an overseas ambassadorial appointment that would have removed him from Carr his refusal was considered a 'matter of high contempt': he was imprisoned in the Tower of London and died shortly afterwards, almost certainly poisoned by the Countess of Essex (see Lindley).

Webster had experienced at first hand the ruthless ambition of these two courtiers and their intimate personal relationship. He dedicated his elegy for Prince Henry to 'the Right Honourable Sir Robert Carr, Viscount Rochester', addressing him as 'My right Noble Lord', and signing himself, 'Your honour's truly devoted servant'. Later he contributed to a collection of 'Characters' that were added to a posthumous publication of Overbury's poem 'The Wife'. The title page says that these additions were 'written by himself and other learned gentlemen his friends' but no ascriptions were provided and Overbury's authorship of any of them is doubtful. Coinciding with the high-profile Essex divorce, this publication was in demand and a sixth edition of 1615 seems to have been overseen by Webster, as possibly were earlier ones; his former collaborator, Thomas Dekker, probably contributed six items to the edition of 1616. Webster himself appears to be author of thirty-two characters in the eleventh edition of 1622; he may have known Overbury sufficiently well to act as if he were literary executor supervising each of the book's many posthumous editions (so Forker, pp. 120–2).

But the playwright's upbringing had been in the City and there he lived and was closely connected throughout his life. While his two tragedies are set in Italian Courts and, by this means, strangely and sensationally mirror the Court of King James, Webster's own life as a citizen of London was a significant influence throughout his writing career. His father, John Webster senior, was a coach-maker who had been made free of the Merchant Taylors' Company of the City on 10 December 1571; he also took an active role in local affairs. By supplying a growing demand for transport in the over-crowded and rapidly expanding capital his trade was profitable and highly visible. He hired out coaches, as well as making them, and could supply wagons for the annual Lord Mayor show, hearses for funerals, and carts to take criminals on their way to public hanging at Tyburn. A younger son, Edward, was apprenticed to the trade and eventually took over the business but, in view of the elder son's meagre literary output and lawyer's training, it is likely that John, too, was actively employed in the family firm and thereby gained a reasonable income (so Bradbrook, p. 4). On 18 March 1606, he married Sara, the sixteen-year-old daughter of Simon Peniall, a master in the allied craft of saddler, and two months later John, their first-born, was baptised. In 1615, after his father's death, the playwright claimed an elder son's right to membership of the Merchant Taylors.

Born some time around 1578–1580, the future dramatist is likely to have been a pupil at the Merchant Taylors' School that was run by his father's guild and, in the opinion of many, provided the best education in London: Edmund Spenser, Thomas Lodge and Thomas Kyd were among earlier pupils. He may well have been the John Webster who, after some time at the New Inn, was admitted in 1598 to study law at the Middle Temple where he could train for the administrative and litigious side of his father's business. After study at Queen's College, Oxford, Thomas Overbury also became a member in 1598. Other fellow students were John Marston the future dramatist, resident from the mid-1590s until 1606, and possibly John Ford who entered in 1602. At the Middle Temple Webster belonged to an institution that functioned as a university and community for young men who would later become courtiers, public servants and authors.

The family business and two tragedies, together with some occasional poems and an independent and painstaking nature, would account for the satirical verses by Henry Fitzjeffrey – also of the Middle Temple – that were headed 'Crabbed *Websterio*, the Playwright, Cartwright', and published in *Certain Elegies done by Sundry Excellent Wits* of 1618:

Was ever man so mangl'd with a poem?
See how he draws his mouth awry of late;
How he scrubs, wrings his wrists, scratches his pate.
'A Midwife! Help!' By his brain's coitus,
Some centaur strange, some huge Bucephalus
Or Pallas, sure, engend'red in his brain:
Strike Vulcan with thy hammer once again.

    This is the critic that, of all the rest,
I'd not have view me, yet I fear him least.
Here's not a word cursively I have writ
But he'll industriously examine it,
And in some twelve months hence, or thereabout,
Set in a shameful sheet my errors out.
But what care I? It will be so obscure
That none shall understand him, I am sure.   (F6v–F7r)

Webster who sought 'weighty and perspicuous comment' would rate this critic as one among 'the ignorant scorners of the Muses' of his time (*Duchess*, Dedication). The congratulatory poems prefacing *The Duchess of Malfi* provide a very different contemporary judgement: here the dramatist is 'well-deserver' and 'friend', his *Duchess* judged unsurpassed as a masterpiece by any poet in Rome or Greece. Webster's life was split in three ways: between theatre, City and, at one time, the royal Court. Writing of Edward the Black Prince in *The Monumental Column*, he seems to be aware of this diversity and makes what appears to be a joke about his tradesman's life as a provider for funerals:

> it was his trade
> To fashion death-beds, and hath often made
> Horror look lovely.... (ll. 84–6)

Fitzjeffrey described a troubled and industrious writer who would be incapable of making jokes, even though they are far from lacking in his two great tragedies. This is not surprising because Webster has continued to divide opinion; only towards the end of the twentieth century was *The Duchess of Malfi* generally recognized as one of the very greatest of tragedies written in English and its central character acknowledged as the most sensitively written, demanding, and rewarding of female roles from the age of Shakespeare.

The two tragedies stand apart from Webster's other works although a reference to '*Guise*' in his dedication to *The Devil's Law Case* (1623) probably refers to another tragedy that no longer survives. This new play, completed some time between late 1616 and early 1619, is best described as a tragi-comedy and, although set in Italy and frequently echoing its two precursors, it is chiefly peopled by merchants, lawyers with their servants and dependants who all talk much about trade, money, voyages and the Exchange or Bourse, as if they were Webster's fellow citizens in London. From now on Webster's plays would be written in collaboration and mirror his tradesman's way of life, not that of the Court: *Anything for a Quiet Life* (c. 1621), with Middleton; the lost *Keep the Widow Waking* or *A Late Murder of the Son upon the Mother* (1624), with Dekker, Ford, and Rowley, its story now known from records of a current law case; *A Cure for a Cuckold* (1624–25), with Rowley; *The Fair Maid of the Inn* (1625–26), written by John Fletcher and completed by Webster, Ford and Massinger. The odd one out, being set firmly in ancient Rome, was *Appius and Virginia* (? 1625–27), written with Thomas Heywood.

In 1624 Webster wrote a very elaborate and expensive Lord Mayor's Pageant, *Monuments of Honour*, for the Merchant Taylor's Company. The title page of the published version suggests, in the grandest possible terms, the ideals that underlay and could have inspired Webster's City life:

Monuments of Honour

Derived from remarkable antiquity, and celebrated in the honourable City of London, at the sole munificent charge and expenses of the right worthy and worshipful Fraternity of the eminent Merchant Taylors; Directed in their most affectionate love, at the confirmation of their right worthy brother, John Gore, in the high office of His Majesty's Lieutenant over this his royal chamber [i.e. the City of London, the king's place of residence];

Expressing in a magnificent triumph, all the pageants, chariots of Glory, temples of Honour, besides a spacious and goodly sea triumph, as well particularly to the honour of the City, as generally to the glory of this our kingdom.

Invented and written by John Webster, Merchant Taylor.

– Non norunt hæc monumenta mori

The Latin tag, which is to be found in the *Aeneid*, could mean that Webster had never been engaged in a less noble task: if so, it affirms the loyalty he maintained to his worshipful city brothers whose way of life had so often been in his mind.

We do not know for sure when and where Webster died, although an allusion to him by John Hemings of the King's Men implies a date after 1632. The register of St James, Clerkenwell, records the burial on 3 March 1638 of a 'John Webster', who might have been the dramatist. This parish lies next to St Sepulchre's where, in 1606, Webster and his young family had lived in Nag's Head Alley, not far from Cow Lane. Both Dekker and Rowley were buried in St James's and Webster in his last years might well have been 'living close to friends and colleagues of many years' standing' (Gunby; Cambridge ed., p. 14)

THE PLAY: PRESENTATION

Origins

By 1612, when Webster was writing The *Duchess of Malfi*, the King's Men were actively exploring the resources of their new indoor theatre, the Blackfriars, and staging the plays of John Fletcher and

Francis Beaument. Fletcher, like Webster, was some fifteen years younger than Shakespeare, and Francis Beaumont twenty years younger. Their backgrounds, however, were quite different, Fletcher being the son of a well-connected clergyman who was briefly Bishop of London, and Beaumont a country gentleman and part-time lawyer. Today their plays might be called experimental: characters and action were, for the most part, surprising and unlikely, sentiment tended to be emotionally demanding, and elegant rhetoric was an almost constant feature. When Webster chose to dramatise a real-life story for the King's Men (as he had in the less-than-successful *White Devil*), he was setting himself apart from these new colleagues but, in the way he presented action on stage, he too would be creating a new kind of play while exploring some of theatre's newly available resources.

In 1490, Giovanna d'Aragona, who had been married when twelve years old to the Duke of Amalfi, was left a widow at nineteen or twenty. About five years later she fell in love with her chief steward, Antonio Bologna, and married him. Knowing that a low-born husband would outrage and anger her two brothers, the elder a cardinal and the younger inheriting the family's title, she kept the relationship secret until rumours of the birth of a second child reached them. To avoid confrontation the husband and then the mother went into exile and subsequently, deserted by servants and pursued by the two brothers, the young family sought refuge together in Ancona. When the Cardinal arranged that the papal Legate should banish Antonio, they fled to Sienna, whereupon the Cardinal persuaded the city authorities to banish Antonio once again. As they were leaving this second refuge, they were intercepted by soldiers who took the mother and two children to Milan after which nothing more was heard of them. Antonio had escaped with the elder boy, a child aged about six, only to be assassinated in October of the following year, 1513. Matteo Bandello had told this story in his *Novelle* (1554) and this account, augmented and moralized, was translated into French by François de Belleforest for the second volume of his *Histoires Tragiques* (1565). From this version, William Painter made an English translation for inclusion in volume ii of his *Palace of Pleasure* (1575), adding his own observations on its events. And here Webster had found it.

As he carefully adapted this version of the story to his own purposes, Webster used details from both the first and second editions of 1567 and *c.* 1575, as echoes from both in the play's dialogue show (see Appendix I, collation). He changed some of the names found in Painter and invented others but gave no name to either the Duchess or her cardinal brother, while changing that of their brother. Webster's industry might well be called 'copious' (*W.D.*, Preface, 1. 41) because a comparison of *The Duchess* and Painter's telling of her story shows that he made many changes, adding characters, inventing incidents of madness, torture, intrigue, insecurity, deception, devotion, ambition, sexual encounter. He picked up suggestions from a wide reading and frequent play-going (see Boklund, pp. 24–36) but the only undoubted and regular source for changes to the narrative was his own *White Devil*. With active invention. Webster has reconsidered and re-imagined the motives of all the principal characters and presented then so skilfully and subtly that they seem to change before the eyes of an audience when mental guards drop or opposition reveals hitherto hidden resources of thought and feeling.

Action

In outline, the story remained much the same and on more than forty occasions Painter's words became part of Webster's dialogue (see Appendix I, footnotes) but, in myriads of small as well major ways, every element was made to serve his own purposes. At the very start one addition marks his intentions unmistakably. Antonio has returned from France and his friend Delio is there to identify what is happening by his statement and question: 'You have been long in France. . . . How do you like the French court?' (1.i.2–4). For Antonio's answer Webster borrowed a passage from Sir Thomas Elyot's *Image of Governance* (1541) declaring that a king's court should be purged of all 'dissolute persons' and be an example to his entire country. This implanted speech reflects on the action that immediately follows as Bosola, the 'only court-gall', enters and speaks of corruption in high places, implicating the Cardinal in covert crime and machination. By a sequence of question-and-answers Webster then defined his major characters in relation to each other and awakened current ideas about political power and religion, poverty and ambition, private and public life, effects of the passing of time and much else. To these general ideas found in Elyot with regard to France, Webster added a highly topical and English relevance. In this first extended speech, he had Antonio allude to the prolonged and increasingly entrenched argument between King James I and the House of Commons of Parliament in London:

And what is't makes this blessèd government,
But a most provident council, who dare freely
Inform him the corruption of the times?
Though some o' th' court hold it presumption
To instruct princes what they ought to do,
It is a noble duty to inform them
What they ought to foresee.   (I.i.16–22)

Instruct and *inform*, *duty* and *corruption* are the very words with which the Commons insisted that they had the right to tell James how he should rule the country and conduct the affairs of his Court (see *Commons Journal*, i, 479–501). They were not thanked for their *presumption* in drawing attention to the political deadlock that within comparatively few years would lead the country back towards civil war and forward to the beheading of James's son, Charles I.

This long speech at the start of the play is by no means necessary to its plot or narrative and comes oddly from the mouth of a steward, who has no personal involvement in politics at this point of the story, but it serves to ground the action of the play in the affairs of England in Webster's time by raising issues that challenge authority and will underlie much that follows. It is only the first in a series of alterations whereby the events and persons in Italy at the beginning of the previous century were made relevant to the lives and concerns of the play's first audiences. The foreign subject matter allowed Webster to represent topical and political matters that, if shown within an English setting, would have had the play banned and its author imprisoned.

Webster's alteration of the original story involved more than added dialogue and episodes or modified speeches, characters or incidents. He was intent on altering what he would call the play's 'action' – by which he meant what happens on stage, moment by moment; the shape of narrative and changing dramatic focus; the placing of uncertainty, revelation, crisis, and resolution and the ever-changing dramatic energy expressed through the varying phrasing and the weight, speed, and force of the words that are spoken. In the preface 'To the Judicious Reader' of *The Devil's Law Case* (1623), Webster gave own account of this kind of playwriting that he had made his own:

A great part of the grace of this (I confess) lay in action; yet can no action ever be gracious where the decency of the language and ingenious structure of the scæne arrive not to make up a perfect harmony.

These terms provide a means of analysing *The Duchess*. 'Fitness to purpose and circumstance' were the current meanings of 'decency' with regard to speech (*O.E.D.*, 1. a); today we might say that Webster wanted grace, subtlety and lifelikeness in stage dialogue. From the late 1590s to the end of the next century the word *scene* or *scæne* was used of stage 'representation' or 'performance' (*O.E.D.*, 3) so Webster was asking that spoken dialogue should function in harmony with a succession of aural, visual and other sensuous impressions that derive from on-stage action. If the 'greater part of the grace of [all] this' – that is its attractiveness, virtue, excellence, source of power (see *O.E.D.*, I and II) – depends on action and performance, it is no accident that the positive reassessments of Webster made since the mid twentieth century have coincided with the return of his two tragedies to the stage (see below, pp. 60–4).

The most influential and sustained addition to the action ensures that the Duchess dominates attention throughout Act IV and other persons are almost entirely presented in relation to her. None of this is in Painter and the same is true of almost all the incidents of the final Act: besides the Echo scene (v.iii), the more notable additions here are Julia's encounters with Pescara, Bosola and the Cardinal, Ferdinand's madness and death, the Cardinal's fearful end, and the increasing role of Bosola and the accidental way in which he kills Antonio ('such a mistake as I have often seen / In a play', v.v.95–6). Bosola becomes a leading player in events: in soliloquy he says he will strike with 'the sword of justice' and he acts as if the Duchess 'haunts' him (v.ii.342–6); when the other principal characters are dead, his last extended speeches will command total attention as he re-values all that has happened and his own part in it.

After the death of the Duchess, the action very noticeably widens to include the outcome of earlier events but from the start of the play Webster added incidents that establish a full context for the central story: the arrival of the Cardinal and Ferdinand at Malfi in Act I to warn their sister against marriage; in Act II, the eating of apricots and consequent discovery of the birth of the Duchess's third child; in Act III, Ferdinand's entry to her private chamber to give her their father's poniard, the 'pretended' pilgrimage to Loretto, and the Cardinal's transformation into a soldier. In the first three Acts, Delio, Julia, Castruchio, and the Old Lady are almost wholly Webster's invention, together with many incidental details of dialogue and action (see Appendix I and its footnotes).

Structure

We cannot be sure why Webster made the many changes to his source but we are able to observe how they helped to make the 'structure of the scene' into a harmonious whole. Most obviously, the action has been divided into five Acts separated from each other by an interval of time, the one between Acts II and III being sufficient for the birth of 'two children more' (III.i.6–7). They all begin with a question that identifies and locates the action: at the start of Acts I, II, III and IV, the audience is introduced to the political and personal situation at the Court of Malfi; at the start of the last Act, the Court has dispersed and attention is directed to Milan and the consequences of earlier action. By this means Webster established his widest themes at the start of each Act (see pp. 38–40, below) and placed the tragedy's most exceptional and intense moments within a context that his audience could recognize as belonging to their own time and world. In contrast, at the end of each Act Webster focused attention on the Duchess who is both the heart and unifying element of the entire play. But this culminating emphasis is sharply varied: she concludes Act I by leading her new husband to bed, watched by a pitying Cariola; at the end of Act II she is present only in Ferdinand's fervid words as he breaks into 'a cold sweat'; she leaves Act III as a captive; at the end of Act IV, in which she has been the dominant presence, her corpse is lifted and carried from the stage; not actually present in Act V, only echoes of her remain in the ghostly voice of an echo and in the echo of her physical presence that is seen in her young son who stands silently centre stage at the end.

This double focus on the Duchess and on her Court is established further by a series of 'presence chamber' scenes (see I.i.82, II.i.120, IV.ii.169). Physical enactment will create visual images that reflect and meaningfully vary each other: the first hundred and forty-seven lines of Act I build expectation for the Duchess's entry and then, surrounded by courtiers and seated in state, she is the centre of attention until she leaves after some seventy lines: for the first sixty lines she is on stage, the Duchess is a silent figure, saying nothing audible. Act II starts in a similar way, slowly building towards the Duchess giving a formal audience that lasts from her entry at line 107 until fifty lines later when, calling for 'lights', she leaves hurriedly to give birth to her first child. Act III starts with the much briefer formality of 'the Lord Ferdinand . . . going to bed' (ll. 37–56) but, after he has entered and left her private chamber, the Duchess

calls her officers about her and gives a second protracted and informal 'presence', no longer sitting 'in state' as she had done in Acts
I and II. A prison is the setting for the whole of Act IV but the
Duchess is told by Bosola that this is her 'last presence-chamber'
(IV.ii.169) and, spanning two scenes, it is the longest continuous
action in the play. In the dark, she is again attended by Ferdinand
who gives her a '*dead man's hand*' to kiss (IV.i.43, S.D.) and then
reveals wax figures of her husband and children to make her believe
that they are dead. In the second scene, before she is strangled, she
is presented formally with a masque of madmen and '*a coffin, cords
and a bell*' (IV.ii.163, S.D.). In Act V the only presence scene is the
appearance of the Duchess's son, to whom everyone present will
probably kneel to formally 'establish [him] . . . in's mother's right'
(V.v.111–13).

The repeated action of kneeling to the royal presence marks the
political authority of the Duchess that will slowly ebb following her
secret marriage to the lowborn Antonio. In contrast, her personal
authority is not diminished but becomes progressively more apparent towards the end of Act IV as she keeps her sanity – 'I am not
mad yet' – and endures her brothers' tyranny: she is 'Duchess of
Malfi still' in her own mind (IV.ii.24, 60, 141) and in death and after
death continues to affect the play's action.

The structural harmony of the action is made more evident by
way the persons of the play are used to define each other. From the
start Ferdinand and his brother Cardinal are set in contrast to their
sister:

> You never fix'd your eye on three fair medals,
> Cast in one figure, of so different temper . . .   (I.i.188–9)

The contrast between the two brothers becomes progressively clear
and, by the end of Act II, is specified in the dialogue;

> *Ferd.*   Have not you
>   My palsy?
> *Card.*   Yes – I can be angry
>   Without this rupture . . .   (II.v.54–6)

Elsewhere contrasts and similarities between persons register without
being identified in the dialogue so that the structural balance seems
to arise naturally from the action. Those between the Duchess and
the other women in the play are notable examples: the old woman

who, according to Bosola, paints over the 'deep ruts' on her face (II.i.21–40) and Cariola who panics, lies, and 'bites and scratches' as she faces death (IV.ii.250).

Julia's words and actions are surprisingly similar to those of the Duchess and in performance may be more noticeable and puzzling than on the page. Like the Duchess, she dies without flinching and she tells the man who murders her, 'I forgive you', as the Duchess had told her executioners (v.ii.280 and IV.ii.205). After Julia is dead, Bosola carries her body off stage as he had done for the Duchess. Differences are also significant: Julia speaks remarkably little of herself as she dies – ''Tis weakness, / Too much to think what should have been done' – whereas at this point the Duchess has to resolve to 'put off my last woman's fault, / I'd not be tedious to you' (v.ii.285–6 and IV.ii.224–5). At the moment of death, Julia knows, like Vittoria in *The White Devil* (v.vi.248–9), 'I go / I know not whither' but, unlike both of them, the Duchess expects to meet 'excellent company / In th' other world' (v.ii.286–7 and IV.ii.209–10). Annotations to this edition note numerous echoes in Julia's last scene from elsewhere in the Duchess's story, especially her intimate scene with Antonio in Act III, scene ii. In Julia, Webster may have sought to awaken memories of the Duchess and encouraged contrasts with her in order to compensate for the heroine's long absence from the last Act.

The introduction of Bosola helped Webster to dramatise Painter's story by providing a commentator as the action unfolds: see, especially his ironic comments on the Duchess's marriage that foresee revolutionary social changes arising from its precedent (see III.ii.280–98) but his words and actions also provide contrasts with Antonio that help to establish the social context. Both are lowborn servants in a world belonging to the great and noble, in which one of them gains advancement because he is an 'upright' steward (I.i.372) and beloved by the Duchess, and the other because he is determined to 'thrive . . . in hard weather' and willing, if need be, to cut a 'throat' (I.i.37–8 and 249). At the beginning of Act II when both have received 'preferment', one as a spy, the other as the Duchess's husband, Webster brings them together to probe each other's 'inside' and exchange half-concealed insults. But a greater difference between them is shown when the Duchess falls into labour: Antonio is 'lost in amazement' and speaks of his own danger (II.i.173 and II.ii.70) while Bosola is ready with one 'trick' after another to serve his master (II.ii.24–5). When Bosola brings Ferdinand's threatening letter to the family who have been banished from Ancona, Antonio's thoughts are again of his danger, not his wife's; thinking of himself, he leaves her to the mercy of 'the tiger':

> My heart is turn'd to a heavy lump of lead,
> With which I sound my danger; fare you well.   (III.v.91–2)
>   *Exit [with his elder Son].*

Bosola's comment rings true – 'Every small thing draws a base mind to fear' (1. 54) – and Antonio's 'base mind', not his fear, is apparent again in Act V, scene i, when he goes to Milan in hope of reconciling himself with his wife's brothers and so receiving part of her estate. In this Act he is foolishly rash and when he hears his wife's echo from her grave he fails to take her advice. Bosola, in contrast, grows in stature, courage and honesty after he has carried out Ferdinand's revenge: 'What would I do, were this to do again? . . .' (IV.ii.336ff.). A change of 'heart' may start as early as his response when the Duchess confesses that Antonio is her husband and asks for his help: 'the secret of my prince . . . I will wear on th' inside of my heart' (III.ii.301–2). In Act V his sympathy with the Duchess is unquestioned – 'still methinks the duchess / Haunts me'; in contrast to Antonio, he vows 'penitence' and is prepared to 'die / In so good a quarrel' (v.ii.343–4 and v.v.99–100).

The contrasts and similarities between Antonio, Bosola, Julia and the Duchess give a sense of coherence and inevitability to the tragedy that is likely to prove more powerful than anything that is said to that effect. They are also in accord with another structural characteristic of the play that leads an audience towards a progressively truer and more inward view of the principal persons of the drama. In the very first scene of *The White Devil* Lodovico enunciates what proves to be a principal feature of Webster's tragic vision:

>   affliction
> Expresseth virtue, fully, whether true,
> Or else adulterate.   (I.i.49–51)

Similarly, soon after the start of *The Duchess*, Ferdinand warns his sister:

> Your darkest actions – nay, your privat'st thoughts –
> Will come to light.   (I.i.315–16)

Dramatic dialogue speaks for a play's characters, not for its playwright, but the preface to *The Devil's Law Case*, where Webster

would later write of the qualities he sought in a tragi-comedy, was
not a suitable place to explain how he structured a tragedy. The
device of handling narrative, action and dialogue so that characters
are revealed slowly and by degrees can be confirmed only in rehearsal
or performance and by a close examination of the texts of his
tragedies over the course of the entire plays. Progressively, Webster
leads readers and audiences to become aware of the 'true' nature of
the persons in the play – a quality of being that Antonio calls their
'inside' or 'inward character' (II.i.82 and I.i.156) which at first is
hidden, obscure or, at best, elusive.

Characters

Early in the opening scene, before Duke Ferdinand has said much
and nothing in private, Antonio describes him as:

> a most perverse, and turbulent nature:
> What appears in him mirth, is merely outside;
> If he laugh heartily, it is to laugh
> All honesty out of fashion.   (I.i.169–72)

Alone with Bosola and intending to hire him as an 'intelligencer' to
spy on his sister, Ferdinand abruptly stops proceedings:

>   she's a young widow –
> I would not have her marry again.
> *Bos.*   No, sir?
> *Ferd.* Do not you ask the reason: but be satisfied,
> I say I would not.   (I.i.255–8)

Ferdinand's feelings towards his sister will prove to be responsible
for his own 'darkest action' and the 'privat'st thoughts' that eventually 'come to light' in the way, he is about to say, that hers will do
(ll. 315–16).

Ferdinand is torn between desire and fear, mixed with pride and
self-assertion, but these thoughts are not spoken openly at this stage
in the play: his actions are left unexplained until his very last
moments:

> My sister! O! my sister! there's the cause on't:
> Whether we fall by ambition, blood, or lust,
> Like diamonds, we are cut with our own dust.   (v.v.71–3)

Much will depend on how the role is performed. An actor could
make Ferdinand sex-crazed from the outset, emphasizing double

meanings, fondling his poniard, feeding his gaze whenever possible on his sister, impatient in other matters. But actors have seldom followed such an obvious way: a far more rewarding response is to maintain a courtly, intelligent, sensitive 'outside' and use Webster's means of showing how feeling is at first hidden and only 'lightens' into action as it gathers strength and eventually fills the whole being, even at the cost of Ferdinand's life. As soon as his sister is dead, he vows to fix his eye 'constantly' on her and yet, almost at once, calls out, in such tensely phrased the words that they seem to be wrung out of him: 'Cover her face: mine eyes dazzle: she died young' (IV.ii.258–62). Moments later he asks to 'see her face again' only to blame Bosola for not standing with his drawn sword between 'her innocence and my revenge':

> I bade thee, when I was distracted of my wits,
> Go kill my dearest friend, and thou hast done't.

Ferdinand is driven by his intelligence and need to understand, as well as by wonder, love, and lust:

> For let me but examine well the cause:
> What was the meanness of her match to me? . . .

Then follows the clearest acknowledgement so far of his helplessness and pain:

>   her marriage! –
> That drew a stream of gall, quite through my heart.

His meaning is unmistakable but the syntax is broken and strained, calling on the actor to sustain the sense of the words with a performance that is strong both physically and imaginatively. From being 'distracted', Ferdinand eventually becomes dangerously mad, even as he understands and accepts the danger he had foreseen:

> He that can compass me, and know my drifts,
> May say he hath put a girdle 'bout the world
> And sounded all her quicksands.   (III.i.84–6)

Bosola is at hand when Ferdinand dies and says what should ensure that the actor does not play him now as if he were 'out of his wits' but, rather so that he 'seems to come to himself, / Now he's so near the bottom' (v.ii.289 and v.v.69–70).

As already shown, the two 'Aragonian brethren' are presented as a pair (V.i.2) who are repeatedly contrasted from the start of the play until their inward natures are finally revealed. On their first entries, Ferdinand speaks to numerous people but the Cardinal keeps alone and is almost inscrutable, speaking only when he must and then saying very little (see 1.i.29ff. and 87ff.), and yet, when the two brothers warn their sister against a second marriage, they chime so regularly with each other that, she tells them, their speech seems 'studied, / It came so roundly off' (1.i.329–30). Again Ferdinand is the more explicit and he stays longer, ominously showing his 'father's poniard' and speaking unmistakably about his sister's sexual nature and experience. The Cardinal says much less but foresees what will happen in words that will prove more accurate than he can know: she will 'privately be married' and will enter 'into some prison'. His warning that 'Wisdom begins at the end' will prove true for all three of them (ll. 316–18, 324–5 and 327–8). Staying away from Malfi, the Cardinal's entry with Julia as his mistress at the start of Act II, scene iv, comes as a complete surprise to an audience; when he asks to be kissed, perhaps several times (see note, ll. 32–6), a physical intimacy is required that, in Webster's day, was rare in scenes between an adult and a very young male actor (see pp. 51–2, below). His self-control and knowledge of his own feelings that repeatedly mark him apart from his brother (see II.v.1–2 and 66) encourage an audience to search for signs of what is not said. Having kept away from Milan, he is transformed from cardinal to soldier in the public ceremony of Act III, scene iv, without any words to reveal what he is thinking.

The 'wisdom' that the Cardinal foresaw comes at the end for himself in a characteristically reasonable way. Although he poisons Julia rapidly and seemingly without a second thought, the Cardinal's own death is protracted over eighty-three lines of dialogue. At the start of the play's last scene he enters alone and reading a book about hell but almost at once he lays the book aside to acknowledge his own 'guilty conscience' and a nightmare vision of 'a thing, arm'd with a rake / That seems to strike at me' (v.v.1–7) that again proves prophetic when at this moment Bosola enters intent on revenging the Duchess. The Cardinal's ingenious device to conceal Julia's murder fails to work and his cries for 'rescue' only serve to keep help away: the courtiers, who could have intervened, laugh at him and think that he counterfeits. Before he strikes a deathblow, Bosola tells him:

Now it seems thy greatness was only outward;
For thou fall'st faster of thy self, than calamity
Can drive thee.   (v.v.42–4)

And so it proves for, although he falls and receives further wounds
from his brother, he maintains self-control until the end, unlike
Ferdinand. Acknowledging that 'Justice' has been done he asks to
be 'laid by, and never thought of' (ll. 53–5 and 89–90): he knows
that his life is worthless.

The Duchess, who is at the centre of the play's narrative from the
start, is the play's most provocative and puzzling character. At the
beginning of Act IV Bosola describes her in a series of paradoxes:
she bears her recent imprisonment as

> . . . one long us'd to't; and she seems
> Rather to welcome the end of misery
> Than shun it: – a behaviour so noble
> As gives a majesty to adversity;
> You may discern the shape of loveliness
> More perfect in her tears, than in her smiles;
> She will muse four hours together, and her silence,
> Methinks, expresseth more than if she spake.   (IV.i.3–10)

Despite numerous other eulogies delivered in course of the play, her
character remains the least knowable. Antonio, Delio says, plays 'the
wire-drawer with her commendations' (I.i.187–209); Cariola, at the
end of the first Act, remains on stage to voice uncertainty:

> Whether the spirit of greatness or of woman
> Reign most in her, I know not, but it shows
> A fearful madness; I owe her much of pity.

The Duchess, herself, throws doubt over what is about to happen
when she tells her new husband that they may 'Lay a naked sword
between us, keep us chaste' (I.i.501). She considers many responses
to torture in the first scene of Act IV, from suicide to weary forbearance, from praying to cursing (see IV.i.65–76 and 87–94; 95 and
96–108); she leaves the stage saying only, 'I long to bleed: / It is
some mercy, when men kill with speed' (ll. 109–10). In the second
prison scene, she is on stage continuously as she faces each new
presentation in this 'last presence-chamber' (l. 169), alternately
controlled and impatient.[1]

When other characters die Webster gave them few words and
little freedom of action so that the 'truth' when at last revealed is

witnessed only for a moment and its impact will depend greatly on the actor and the reactions of audience or reader. For the death of the Duchess, however, comparatively little is left in doubt: attention is held remorselessly during the long preparation and, after her death, by the contrast of a frenzied Cariola and the reactions of Ferdinand and Bosola. How the actor has embodied the character and given scope to each variation in both scenes of Act IV will affect the reception of her final moments but, when she kneels and accepts strangulation, both her courage and submission are inescapably and affectingly present in simple actions. After that is achieved, her last reference to her brothers again depends greatly on the actor, as if an instinctive and spontaneous lifelikeness was still a principal concern of the playwright:

> Go tell my brothers, when I am laid out,
> They then may feed in quiet.   *They strangle her.*

Is she mocking those responsible for her murder or does she care about their 'quiet'? Does she imply that she is being 'laid out' only for their satisfaction or that their kinship has previously brought only disquiet? Are her very last moments marked by her response to great physical pain or does the smooth progress of her words imply an amazing calm? As these questions are resolved in performance and the actor finds the 'truth' of the moment, the emotion, eloquence and intellectual challenges of the tragedy will have an inescapable touch of the uncertainties of actual life.

One of the commendatory verses that accompanied the play on publication praises the experience of *seeing* the Duchess 'live, and die' and another that of *seeing* her 'lively body'd' in the play. The same could be true of a modern production because the sight of the heroine at centre stage in a varied succession of scenes may well be what an audience most remember. In the first four Acts Webster's handling of action and dialogue seem designed to give her a life-like presence but in the fifth Act she is only inter- mittently on stage as a shadowy or imminent being and the play continues in another dimension as other persons hold centre stage and their stories are presented. The third and last commendatory poem by John Ford seems to take this into account when it claims that, 'whiles words and matter change, and men / Act one another', these all 'took life' from what Webster had written: in other words, the life-giving achievement of this tragedy was not restricted to the Duchess, but as wide as the world that it presented.

Language

Research has shown that Webster kept a commonplace book from which he borrowed freely as he wrote his plays, and the annotations to this edition show in detail how he re-used the ideas, comparisons, words and phrases taken from other writers. This dependency is so frequent that it might indicate mere bookishness or lack of self-confidence but that would not account for the very careful way in which Webster made the words and sentiments of other writers into those of his characters. The index in Appendix III shows where a specific author was uppermost in his mind and a study of individual borrowings gives a uniquely close and detailed view of the creative processes of a dramatist: how his mind moved quickly and could splinter into several distinct fragments, how deft was his sense of phrasing, syntax, vocabulary, pitch and tone, as he turned and tuned what he borrowed to the precise and changing demands of the drama.

The variety of Webster's dialogue is as remarkable as its subtlety, as may be seen in a single speech, for example:

> What would it pleasure me to have my throat cut
> With diamonds? or to be smothered
> With cassia? or to be shot to death with pearls?
> I know death hath ten thousand several doors
> For men to take their exits; and 'tis found
> They go on such strange geometrical hinges,
> You may open them both ways: – any way, for heaven-sake,
> So I were out of your whispering: – tell my brothers
> That I perceive death, now I am well awake,
> Best gift is they can give, or I can take.   (IV.ii.214–23)

Variety of phrasing and rhythm, alternating broken and flowing verse-lines, together with verbs that evoke palpable sense-experiences – *pleasure, smothered, shot* – changing to others that give intellectual definitions – *know, take, found* – or imply a simple action – *cut, go, open* – followed by an interjection that has no verb and the accent of everyday but highly charged impatience – 'any way, for heaven-sake'. This cry is linked with an acute awareness of other persons present on stage that, in 'whispering', has an edge of sarcasm and reproof. A brief order and shift of focus then introduce the composed yet sharply phrased conclusion to this engagement with her torturer.

Those last two lines of this passage exemplify Webster's reshaping of what he borrowed from other writers. The words derive from William Alexander's *Alexandrean Tragedy* where the heroine welcomes a sword, cord and poison as:

> Fit gifts for her to give, for me to take,
> Since she exceeds in hate, and I in grief.

Her husband has been murdered and she is being offered the means to kill herself. In Webster's riddle-like version, a willingness to 'take' action herself concludes the speech and yet the possibility of suicide is nowhere explicit. The words 'death' and 'I am well awake' will govern the actor's performance and hold the attention of an audience or reader. Then the restlessness of Webster's imagination is evident once more as the mood is broken by a more commonplace, proverbial thought, here charged with ironic self-assertion: 'I would fain put off my last women's fault, / I'd not be tedious to you'.

The far and often strange reach of Webster's imagination, fantasy, intellect and invention is especially apparent in prose speeches where the compact images of the verse are exchanged for elaborate descriptions and similes that often give rise to alternative and sharply contrasting reactions. The same precise, exploratory and restless intelligence lies behind the dialogue in prose and verse evoking a world full of diverse purposes and properties. The activity of animals and birds are prominent and the opposition between health and disease, riches and poverty, gentleness and brutality, the normal and the disordered, a conscious performance as opposed to instinctive and fully engaged participation. Active verbs often suggest that this teeming world has a palpable presence in Webster's imagination. Comparatively few passages can exemplify all these qualities:

> He, and his brother, are like plum-trees, that grow crooked over standing pools; they are rich, and o'erladen with fruit, but none but crows, pies, and caterpillars feed on them: could I be one of their flattering panders, I would hang on their ears like a horse-leech till I were full, and then drop off . . .   (I.i.48–53)

> I would sooner eat a dead pigeon, taken from the soles of the feet of one sick of the plague, than kiss one of you fasting.   (II.i.38–40)

> Till I know who leaps my sister, I'll not stir:
> That known, I'll find scorpions to string my whips,
> And fix her in a general eclipse.   (II.v.77–9)

I'll go hunt the badger, by owl-light:
'Tis a deed of darkness.   (IV.ii.332–3)

In a mist: I know not how –
Such a mistake as I have often seen
In a play: – O, I am gone! –
We are only like dead walls, or vaulted graves,
That ruin'd, yields no echo.   (V.v.94–8)

The last of those quotations shows how phrases of great simplicity – 'O, I am gone!' – will sometimes offset the pressure of imagistic invention. Such interventions can be sweet, ironic, cruel, unfeeling, or whatever sensation can represent an inward and instinctive response to the dramatic moment. They often need to be heard or read in context if they are to reveal any adequate meaning or force: for example, 'Die then, *quickly*', or 'This good one that you speak of, *is my husband*', or 'Do, and *be happy*' (III.ii.71 and 275 and V.ii.143).

A strange image is sometimes fused with simple utterance: for example, in Ferdinand's response to news of his sister's first child, 'I have this night digg'd up a mandrake . . . And I *am grown mad* with't', or his comment on seeing her murdered children, 'The death / Of young wolves is never *to be pitied*' (II.v.1–2 and IV.ii.256–7). When the Duchess speaks in this way it can seem as if she is both deeply and unconsciously involved: for example, 'So, now the *ground's broke*', or 'O *bless'd comfort*! / This deadly air is purg'd', or 'My laurel is *all withered*', or, among a sequence of such phrases in her last speech before being killed, '*Pull*, and *pull strongly*, for your able strength / Must pull down heaven upon me' (I.i.428, III.i.55–6, III.v.93 and IV.ii.228–9).

Awareness of unspoken thoughts, pressures, and instincts under-lies and sustains the obvious artifice of Webster's dialogue and invites actors and readers to share in this subtextual activity. Here is a principal source of that 'inward life' which, for his contempo-raries and ourselves, seems to animate his characters in perfor-mance. Although naturally obscure, the unspoken can suddenly lighten into consciousness, expressed by ambiguity, imprecision, double meaning, joke, unnecessary repetition, glimmer of disbelief or sudden change of subject matter. So sexual awareness and desire emerge in talk about political, routine or religious matters and the other way about. These devices are commonly present in Ferdinand's speeches and in exchanges between Antonio and the

Duchess. The effect can seem entirely unforced and natural in performance but the annotations to this edition show that a reader will often need to be mentally alert and aware of Jacobean social and linguistic usages.

As if he knew that his writing would make severe demands on audiences and readers, Webster included short proverbial, axiomatic and generalized passages that simplify the dramatic and intellectual issues that arise in performance so that they may be readily understood. In this he and fellow dramatists were following the rhetorical practice of using *sententiae*, or sentences, to summarize and clinch arguments, a device favoured by preachers and pamphleteers at a time when reading was not a universal practice. To a reader, these short passages can seem like self-contained insertions but, to avoid holding back the action in performance at moments of high dramatic expectation, they were often expressed in verse couplets that give a compensating energy and decisiveness.[2] For audiences drawn from many sections of society, such as those at the Globe theatre, Webster's *sententiae* probably brought welcome moments of clarification to offset the intellectual brilliance and sensuous subtlety on which much of his reputation now rests.

THE PLAY: CONTEXTS AND ARGUMENTS

The Court

The royal Court of Malfi is the principal context in which the Duchess is seen. The play starts with an eye-catching demonstration of its wealth and power as two princes join the courtiers over whom their sister is presiding at the conclusion of costly 'triumphs' and 'sportive action' (I.i.365 and 90). Despite this public show of accord and dynastic unity, Antonio's first speech is a warning that the 'fixed order' intended to provide stability, harmony and blessed contentment could be swept away by 'poison' near its head (I.i.5–23 and pp. 8–9, above). Almost at once Bosola declares that the two royal brothers are 'crooked' and corrupt and, later, Ferdinand warns his sister that the court at Malfi is a 'rank pasture' (I.i.48–53 and 306). Disruption soon follows and the very air becomes 'deadly' (III.i.56). Bosola, the 'court-gall', is present throughout and sees through the pretensions and lies of courtiers (see above and, especially, III.ii.228–41) but, according to Antonio, he is as corrupt as the world he castigates:

> ... he rails at those things which he wants,
> Would be as lecherous, covetous, or proud,
> Bloody, or envious, as any man,
> If he had means to be so.   (I.i.25–8)

No one at Court is concerned with the welfare of the state beyond occasional references to the 'common rabble' (III.i.25) or general problems that occur anywhere, such as unemployment, poverty, old age, the plague and other misfortunes. At Court, the only 'reward / Of doing well, is the doing of it' (I.i.31–2).

In the London of 1614 such a world could seem both real and topical. James I's Court was the 'only mart of preferment and honour: a gulf of gain' (Gabriel Harvey, *Marginalia*, ed. 1913, p. 142) and so courtiers vied with each other for influence with the King. Immediately before the dissolution of parliament in June 1614, the *Commons Journal* records many angry complaints about favourites, pensioners and 'misinformations' (vol. i, 497–581). Only a few in Webster's audience would actually have been to Court but in the absence of newspapers or television, curiosity eagerly fed upon rumour. A pamphlet, published soon after the Overbury scandal (see above, p. 3), gives a sketch of a successful courtier:

> If he chance to come into the eye of the world, he then creeps into the favour of some great personage, in feeding whose humours (to relieve his wants) he makes intrusion into some heritage and matcheth not according to his birth, but to the increase of his fortune, and by that means, by hook or crook, he attaineth to some place in the Court. Then begins he with gifts to win hearts, by feigned humility to avoid hatred, by offices of friendship to bind his equals, by cunning insinuations to work his superiors, by which means he is held to be worthily a statesman. Being grown to this step higher, the authority likes him not without the style, wherein if any cross him, look for poison in his cup or conspiracy in his walks; yea so pestilent is his nature that (like fire raked up in embers) he never showeth but to consume, both himself and others. (*The Just Downfall of Ambition, Adultery, and Murder* (1616), A3v–B1)

Bosola gives a more lurid account of the same phenomena when speaking of 'rogues' who envied Antonio's advancement and:

> But to have waited on his fortune, could have wish'd
> His dirty stirrup riveted through their noses,
> And follow'd after's mule, like a bear in a ring;
> Would have prostituted their daughters to his lust;
> Made their first-born intelligencers; thought none happy

But such as were born under his bless'd planet,
And wore his livery; and do these lice drop off now?
(III.ii.229–35)

Many echoes of the ambition and intrigue found at James I's
Court are present in Webster's play. For example, Bosola's private
conferences with Ferdinand near the beginning of Acts I and II
('Places and riches oft are bribes of shame . . . I never gave pension
but to flatterers . . .') and Antonio's response to the Duchess's
wooing ('Ambition, madam, is a great man's madness . . .') voice
dangers that would be recognized by any insider. The verbal sparring of Bosola and Antonio near the beginning of Act II ('You would
not seem to appear to the world puffed up with your preferment . . .'
and 'I look no higher than I can reach . . . when a man's mind rides
faster than his horse can gallop, they quickly both tire') exemplifies
the competitive relationships of courtiers. Delio is likely to surprise
a present-day audience when, as one of Julia's 'old suitors', he
comes to Rome with money to buy her favours (II.iv.46–83) but the
matter-of-fact revelation marks the callous acceptance of prostitu-
tion at Court. The Cardinal's treatment of courtiers in Act V and
their obedience to his strange request would be implausible outside
a court where personal advantage is paramount and the whims of
great men followed obsequiously.

A major difference between the courts of King James and
Webster's Malfi is that, in the latter, a woman is the prince. The
Duchess's lowborn sexual preference and the secrecy this required
were not, however, very far from the consequences of King James's
attachments to a succession of handsome young men in his entourage and the ennoblement of some of them. And in both courts
marriages were a cause of concern as agents of change; when *The
Duchess* was first performed, Lady Arabella Stuart was in prison for
marrying Lord William Seymour, a man who would strengthen her
claim to the English throne.

In *The Duchess* two 'tales' hold up the narrative to mark unmistakably the processes and risks of a royal court. The first is Ferdinand's
account of Reputation, Love, and Death in which Love would not
be found at Court, but:

'mongst unambitious shepherds,
Where dowries were not talk'd of, and sometimes
'Mongst quiet kindred that had nothing left
By their dead parents.

'Stay', interjects Reputation:

> 'Do not forsake me; for it is my nature
> If I once I part from any man I meet
> I am never found again'.   (III.ii.127–33)

Before being led off to prison the Duchess takes time to recount the 'sad tale' of a dog-fish who rebukes a salmon as 'no eminent courtier':

> 'O', quoth the salmon, 'sister be at peace:
> Thank Jupiter we both have pass'd the net!
> Our value never can be truly known
> Till in the fisher's basket we be shown;
> I' th' market then my price may be the higher,
> Even when I am nearest to the cook and fire.'
> So, to great men, the moral may be stretched:
> *Men oft are valued high, when th' are most wretched.*
>   (III.v.134–41)

By means of this tale, as action is drawn forward at the conclusion of the third Act, Webster focuses attention on life at Court, the source of power throughout the country, and on the presumption of those who value status above inward peace of mind. This moment does not stand alone in the play. When the Duchess speaks of being 'nearest to the cook and fire', she is thinking of a final judgement when affliction will express virtue fully, 'whether true or else adulterate'. Her words are in tune with a principle that underlies the structure of the entire play.

The City

With the action taking place in palaces and, for individual scenes, in a shrine, prison, ruined church and open country, Webster's life in the City of London is reflected only occasionally but establishes an alternative perspective and further basis for judgement. When the Duchess woos Antonio she tells him

> You were ill to sell yourself –
> This dark'ning of your worth is not like that
> Which tradesmen use i'th' city; their false lights
> Are to rid bad wares off.   (I.i.431–4)

The two fishes in her story at the end of Act III are shown to the world only when in 'the fisher's basket' and brought to 'market'. In both instances, the City's mercantile standards are founded solely on individual worth, not on status or successful enterprise.

For Ferdinand, the world outside the Court is threatening: in his jealousy he imagines his sister's 'shameful act of sin' with:

> some strong thigh'd bargeman;
> Or one o'th' wood-yard, that can quoit the sledge,
> Or toss the bar, or else some lovely squire
> That carries coals up to her privy lodgings. (II.v.42–5)

In his madness, he thinks of 'flaying off his doctor's skin to cover one of the 'anatomies this rogue hath set i'th'cold yonder, in Barber-Chirurgeons' Hall' (v.ii.76–8). Only the madmen who are let loose to torment the Duchess consistently represent the life Webster knew in the City; obsessed with their own appetites and their professions of Astrologer, Priest, Doctor and Lawyer, they are both comic and threatening; an active, uncontrollable other world, for most of the play out of sight.

Family and Home

Another occasional but more consistent influence on Webster's writing was his domestic life and experience as a husband and father. *The Duchess* offers insights into the daily affairs of its characters that in other tragedies of the time are extremely rare, moments in *Romeo and Juliet* and the second short scene of *Coriolanus* being well-known exceptions. Webster repeatedly brings home life into focus. As the heroine awaits execution, she asks:

> I pray thee, look thou giv'st my little boy
> Some syrup for his cold, and let the girl
> Say her prayers, ere she sleep. (IV.ii.201–3)

This is not an untypical thought introduced to awaken sentiment at a crucial moment but one in a succession of references that cast shafts of everyday light on the courtly and ominous events of the play.

When he started to write *The Duchess*, Webster was in his early thirties and had been married for six years; Sara his wife was then twenty-two years of age and had borne him several children. His house would be noisy with 'little ones' and he might well watch his son 'ride a-cock-horse / Upon a painted stick, [and] hear him chatter / Like a taught starling'; he would know, too, how children could make sweetmeats last a long time, being 'fearful to devour

them too soon', and how a 'little infant that breeds its teeth . . .
would cry out' in the night (I.i.401–3, 466–7, and IV.ii.138–40).

The Duchess, of course, is no City wife but of royal blood and,
as a widow, the regent of an independent state. Being 'born great',
she knows she is not expected to marry out of her own class or to
please only herself (I.i.441–2). After she has broken these taboos
that protected the purity of royal blood and rights of inheritance,
and when she has taken flight from Malfi and is almost alone in
open countryside, the same thought is still with her, but now intensi-
fied, sustained, and sensuously realized:

> The birds that live i'th' field
> On the wild benefit of nature, live
> Happier than we; for they may choose their mates,
> And carol their sweet pleasures to the spring.   (III.v.18–21)

Webster's handling of the Duchess's marriage is consistently
sympathetic but its validity, legally and ecclesiastically, is equivocal
(see, for example, Callaghan, pp. 14–15). Those among early audiences who were knowledgeable about these matters would realize
that a contract '*per verba de presenti*' was *not* 'absolute marriage',
despite what Duchess says, and that a private betrothal had to follow
a fixed form of words and afterwards be ratified by the church,
despite her rhetorical question that seems to deny this (I.i.478–9 and
491). To be binding in civil law, two witnesses were necessary and
so Cariola's presence would not ensure that Antonio's son would be
'heir' to his mother's possessions or rights (as assumed at V.v.107–8
and 122–3). Whether widows should marry again was much debated
at the time and on this point Webster gives both views, the Duchess
boldly following her inclinations and Ferdinand condemning her as
'most luxurious' for wedding twice. That these ambiguities and
conflicting responses are at the very heart of the play's action can
be no accident coming from an author trained in law at the Middle
Temple. On numerous occasions before the Duchess is summoned
to die, Webster must have intended to awaken his audience to question the relative strengths of her personal feelings or willfulness and
her sense of royal or wifely responsibilities.

The Church

Religion is a strong strand in the action of the tragedy, visually
present whenever the Cardinal is on stage or the two pilgrims and

mad priest; there may also have been some physical indication of a grave in the ruins of a church (see below, p. 55). But its influence is pervasive because all the principal persons speak about religion either to curse or pray, to remember blessed souls and angels or think of devils and the souls of the damned. They can imagine the fire in hell 'that never goes out' or the 'heaven o'er my head' (IV.ii.77–9 and 25). The scene being Italy, the Church is Roman Catholic and the Pope its ultimate authority, both circumstances being an advantage to Webster (and fellow dramatists) by greatly reducing the risk of censorship and imprisonment for dealing with 'matters of religion', which were proscribed, as were 'affairs of state' from which, at the time, they could hardly be separated. By adopting the outward form of Catholicism, Webster could give religion a significant part in his play and reflect some of the religious ideas and daily practices of his audience.

For much of the previous hundred years the Church of Rome had been feared, demonized and satirized, attitudes that seemed fully justified when in 1605 Catholics were involved in the Gunpowder Plot and its failed attempt to destroy both king and parliament. *The Duchess of Malfi* reflects (and would tend to enflame) current political and religious feelings when the Cardinal is said to be responsible for a 'notorious murder' and is seen to have an adulterous and long-standing affair with Julia, when a religious ceremony transforms him into a soldier and when he interferes in the political affairs of Ancona to procure the banishment of the Duchess and her family. In 1618, Orazio Busino, Chaplain to the Venetian Embassy, gave an account of a play that is almost certainly *The Duchess* but sufficiently inaccurate to make it likely that he was relying on scandalized rumour rather than visiting the playhouse himself. English actors, he wrote:

> never put on any public show whatever, be it tragedy or satire or comedy, into which they do not insert some Catholic churchman's vices and wickednesses, making mock and scorn of him, according to their taste, but to the dismay of good men. . . . [On one occasion] they showed a cardinal in all his grandeur, in the formal robes appropriate to his station, splendid and rich, with his train in attendance, having an altar erected on the stage, where he pretended to make a prayer, organizing a procession; and then they produced him in public with a harlot on his knee. They showed him giving poison to one of his sisters, in a question of honour. Moreover he goes to war, first laying down his cardinal's habit on the altar; . . . and all this was acted in condemnation of the grandeur of the Church, which

they despise and which in this kingdom they hate to the death. (Hunter, pp. 31–2; the fullest available English translation)

Less sensationally, the Cardinal assumes that church practices are corrupt when he tells Bosola to 'inquire out / Delio's confessor, and see if you can bribe / Him to reveal' Antonio's whereabouts (v.ii.133–5). Even this small detail would bring *The Duchess* into current controversy when King James was trying to repair relations with the Catholic country that had sent an armada against Elizabeth's Protestant England and was seeking a Spanish bride for his son.

Alongside this view of a powerful and corrupt church, Webster gave his heroine an instinctive Christian piety:

Her days are practis'd in such noble virtue
That sure her nights – nay more, her very sleeps –
Are more in heaven than other ladies' shrifts.   (i.i.201–3)

So Antonio praises the Duchess in the first moments of the play and, when they pledge themselves as husband and wife, her first words are 'Bless, heaven, this sacred Gordian, which let violence / Never untwine' (i.i.480–1). Having been banished from Ancona and about to be separated from her husband, the Duchess hopes for reunion in the 'eternal church', as a good Christian would, and she weeps a moment later as she recognizes that she is being chastised by heaven's 'heavy hand' (iii.v.71–81). In prison, she veers between fortitude and submission and between prayers and curses (see iv.i.1–12 and 95–110). She knows she is on the brink of madness and despair, yet retains memories of freedom and a sense, in Old Testament terms, of impending judgement (see iv.ii.20–34 and notes). Weeping, she sees no way of escape – 'Fortune seems only to have her eyesight / To behold my tragedy' (iv.ii.35–6) – and it is at this moment that her trials escalate, with the entry of madmen and then of her coffin.

In her last 'adversity' (see p. 26, above), which brings the certainty of death, the Duchess finds a new strength: having forgiven her executioners, she reverts to more religious language and unexpectedly takes charge of proceedings:

Pull, and pull strongly, for your able strength
Must pull down heaven upon me: –
Yet stay; heaven-gates are not so highly arch'd
As princes' palaces; they that enter there
Must go upon their knees. . . .   (iv.ii.228–32)

As Ferdinand had warned – but in a manner he could not foresee – her 'privat'st thoughts' seem to 'come to light' (I.i.315–16) when she accepts death and kneels in humility before heaven.

The action of kneeling is significant in the play from the moment in the first Act when the Duchess kneels with Antonio to commit herself to marriage as if in a church and it accumulates more significance when, having '*presented*' herself and the entire family at the shrine of our Lady of Loretto, she kneels 'To pay her vow of pilgrimage' (III.iv, S.D. and 5–6). Whereas in the presence chamber scenes of Acts I and II, the courtiers will kneel to approach their sovereign, she now kneels with other anonymous pilgrims to a statue of the Virgin. (In early performances the statue could either have been a large stage property or an imaginary one that is 'seen' by all the actors at a distance from the stage and above the heads of the audience.) This silent act of devotion might well be the most thoughtful, and certainly the most sustained, expression of the Duchess's piety so far in the play, its effect magnified by a 'noble ceremony' sufficiently grand to draw the attention of a Venetian chaplain (l. 7 and see above, p. 29). The 'violence' with which the Cardinal takes the wedding ring off her finger destroys all reverence by breaking up the silent religious tableau and clearly sets the Duchess in opposition to a dignitary of the established Church, as she is to her brother princes of the Aragonian state.

The shrine at Loretto was famous throughout Europe as Mary's very own humble home that had been miraculously transported from Galilee to Italy and was now filled with treasures. Its most famous and dominating feature was a statue of the Virgin which was said to be a miraculously true likeness and before which pilgrims would kneel in reverence and offer rich gifts. The Prince of Transylvania, for example, had donated a further image of 'Our Blessed Lady' some two feet high; made of solid silver, it was 'of excellent workmanship and curiously inlaid with gold' and at its feet the donor was portrayed in full armour as if praying (O. Torsellino, *History of Our B. Lady of Loretto*, tr. 1608, K3). Pilgrims would honour the Virgin as foremost of all the saints and ask for her help and, through her intercession, for mercy:

> Christ, who in justice might condemn the human race to hell, will be merciful because he has been human and knows our weakness. Since Mary gave him his flesh, her intercession recalls his humanity and thus evokes his mercy. (*Oxford Companion to Christian Thought* (2000), pp. 414–15)

A *Litany of Loretto* was approved by Pope Sixtus V in 1581 and again by Clement VIII in 1601.

In *The White Devil*, Webster had staged an elaborate papal election and subsequently used the assembled ambassadors in their ceremonial and holy regalia to witness the wedding of Vittoria to Duke Bracciano and to return in the last scene when dead bodies that were its consequence were lying on the stage (see *W.D.*, III.i.64–78, III.ii.0, S.D., IV.iii.5–14 and V.vi.281, S.D.). In his second tragedy, having staged the ceremonies at Loretto, he gave the Duchess an after-life that echoes the holiness and benefits accredited to our Lady. When she awakes from apparent death, Webster was probably indebted to Shakespeare's Desdemona who also wakes after being left for dead and whose murder also takes a long time against current theatrical practice when the victim was a woman. But, unlike Desdemona, when the Duchess returns to life she offers Bosola hope of divine forgiveness:

> her eye opes,
> And heaven in it seems to ope, that late was shut,
> To take me up to mercy.   (IV.ii.345–7)

When he falsely tells her that Antonio is alive, the only word she speaks is 'Mercy'.

In the fifth Act, the Duchess continues to offer hope and mercy. When Bosola resolves to seek 'a most just revenge', she 'haunts' him as a hallucination (V.ii.341–5). As an echo and 'a face folded in sorrow', she appears and speaks to Antonio, warning him to 'fly your fate' (V.iii.45 and 35). Finally, her likeness is represented in her young son whom Delio brings on stage to accept homage and prompt a fresh start.

By all these means the Duchess becomes associated with the Virgin Mary but not entirely so and only in her death and subsequent appearances. Her instinctive piety did not give immunity from despair or near madness, nor did it exclude an instinct for revenge. She was ready to quote the teaching of the established church to express her hatred and then to support a suicidal resolve: 'You violate a sacrament o' th' church / Shall make you howl in hell for't'; and, again, 'The church enjoins fasting: / I'll starve myself to death' (IV.i.39–40 and 75–6). Even her submission to death by execution is followed immediately by self-aware irony, perhaps vindictiveness (see above, pp. 19–20). While an audience cannot doubt her sense of the wrongs she has suffered or the strength of her instinctive piety, it may not know at the end of the play which spirit may 'Reign most in her' (I.i.504–6) – holy acceptance or passionate resistance. Last judgement will depend on the actor's performance and the audience's beliefs and engagement throughout the play.

Blood and passion

Desire, a word used variously in Webster's time, will serve to identify a mysterious and powerful impulse that motivates all the principal characters in *The Duchess* and operates throughout the play. Variously called love, affection, wantonness, longing, wilfulness, passion, blood, it is sometimes present without words to describe the experience. In all these manifestations, sexual desire is shown to be either a blessing or a curse. Its most crude, stupid, crazed, obsessed and unmanageable elements are brought on stage when the Madmen are 'let loose' to torment the Duchess in prison, a 'tyranny' that she feels 'chain'd to endure' in silence (IV.ii.59–60).

On her first entrance, Antonio credits the Duchess with a life-giving presence and control:

> whilst she speaks,
> She throws upon a man so sweet a look,
> That it were able raise one to a galliard
> That lay in a dead palsy, and to dote
> On that sweet countenance. . . .

But she can arrest sexual desire as well as awaken it:

> but in that look,
> There speaketh so divine a continence
> As cuts off all lascivious, and vain hope. (I.i.194–200)

Ferdinand soon gives another view: for him she is a 'lusty widow' who knows already 'what man is' (I.i.340 and 294).

In this play, desire is shown in many forms. Antonio becomes silent with fear when the Duchess confesses that she loves him:

> You do tremble:
> Make not your heart so dead a piece of flesh
> To fear, more than to love me: sir, be confident –
> What is't distracts you? This is flesh, and blood, sir;
> 'Tis not the figure cut in alabaster
> Kneels at my husband's tomb. Awake, awake, man!

As Antonio hesitates, she responds physically as well as verbally: her princely status has no relevance now:

> I do here put off all vain ceremony,
> And only do appear to you a young widow
> That claims you for her husband, and like a widow,
> I use but half a blush in't.   (I.i.450–9)

Sexual desire is inherent in much that the Duchess says and does in her encounters with Antonio. Even when speaking before the assembled Court or excusing his sudden departure to her officers, her words carry sexual implications. In the privacy of her own chamber, desire is tangibly represented in performance by kisses, physical closeness, delays, repetitions, laughter and silent pleasure, as well as words: 'I'll stop your mouth', she says; when they have kissed, he complains, 'Nay that's but one ... I must have another'. After a string of mythological allusions and sexual banter, she asks. 'When were we so merry?' and almost at once Antonio plays another game by slipping from the room with Cariola, saying 'I love to see her angry', a desire to gaze on her being uppermost in his mind (III.ii.20–2, 53 and 57). In Elizabethan and Jacobean theatres where boys or very young men performed the women's parts, words were the most reliable way for a dramatist to suggest sexual desire and activity (see, for example, Brown, 1997) and in this tragedy Webster repeatedly uses them, together with hesitation and silence, to draw attention to a lover's 'flesh and blood' (I.i.453).

In his sister's presence Ferdinand's words are charged with sexual implications and later, away from Malfi and hearing that she has a lover, the 'wild fire' of his rage seems to carry him on 'violent whirlwinds', as if he were 'stark mad' (II.v.47–66). Back at Malfi, he is seen at first to 'bear himself right dangerously' and later, convinced that 'witchcraft lies in her rank blood', he enters her bedchamber unannounced and gives her their father's poniard saying, 'Die then, quickly', his 'action' implying that she should use it on herself; he leaves denouncing her as a witch and vowing 'I will never see thee more' (III.i.20 and 78; III.ii.71, 150–2 and 141). Sending a masque of madmen to torment his sister implies that he is aware of what sexuality can become when out of reason's control. In all these ways, Webster has staged the potential power, danger and pain of Ferdinand's unsatisfied sexual longings. A 'List of Actors' printed in the first edition told readers that the role was originally played by Richard Burbage, the most famous actor of the time who was then at the height of his mature powers (see also p. 50).

Understated in words, complicated in nature and developing slowly, the Duchess's effect on Bosola will make a stronger impression in performance than in reading. A crucial moment that is sure to register comes immediately after her death and leads to unexpected and perhaps shocking action. Ferdinand, now 'distracted', has disowned the murder and left Bosola alone with time and freedom to realize that he would not, 'for all the wealth of Europe', do again what he has done. At this moment the Duchess returns to life and a spring seems to be released within Bosola: calling for her 'fair soul' to return, he touches her and so discovers that 'she's warm, she breathes'. Perhaps excusing his intimacy or eagerness, he immediately resolves, 'Upon thy pale lips I will melt my heart, / To store them with fresh colour' (IV.ii.342–3). That impulse from his 'heart', the seat of passion, which he thinks likely to 'melt' in contact with her lips, will be in part physical and in part holy. The kissing of a dead body is bound to draw special and possibly shocked attention, especially since Bosola, after 'seven years in the galleys' (I.i.69), is physically strong and has repeatedly spoken with a precisely sensual consciousness – recently, for example, 'Send her a penitential garment to put on / Next to her delicate skin' and talk of a mouse sleeping 'in a cat's ear' (IV.i.119–20 and IV.ii.137–8). A mutual attraction between Bosola and the Duchess has been signaled earlier: when taking his advice she asks him to 'lead me by the hand' and moments later he boasts of having worked 'in a lady's chamber' (III.i.312–13 and 325–6). In prison he speaks of seeing the 'shape of loveliness' in her tears and of her passionate apprehension of 'those pleasures she's kept from': moments later he offers his service, 'Come, be of comfort, I will save your life' (IV.i.7–8, 12–15 and 86).

The Court is a 'rank pasture', says Ferdinand, warning his sister against a second marriage (I.i.306), and so it is shown to be on stage, most surprisingly in the adultery of Julia and the Cardinal. With his 'cross, hat, robes and ring' signifying that he is wedded to Christ (III.iv.7, S.D.), he probably takes her 'on his knee' (see p. 29, above) as he tells her:

> When thou wast with thy husband, thou wast watch'd
> Like a tame elephant: – still you are to thank me –
> Thou hadst only kisses from him, and high feeding,
> But what delight was that? 'twas just like one
> That hath a little fing'ring on the lute,
> Yet cannot tune it.   (II.iv.31ff.)

Although elsewhere Delio is characterized as Antonio's reliable friend, when he arrives in Rome he goes straight to visit Julia who recognizes him as 'one of my old suitors' and soon is offered gold in return for her favours. Earlier Webster had Bosola tell the Old Lady that some women 'give entertainment for pure love; but more, for more precious reward'.

The most sustained and powerful expression of sexuality is Ferdinand's struggle with his fantasies and subsequent madness: it leads to murder and death. As he tells his brother, it can put him 'in a cold sweat' and destroy all self-confidence and the will to live:

> I could kill her now,
> In you, or in myself, for I do think
> It is some sin in us, heaven doth revenge
> By her.   (II.v.76 and 63–6)

Revenge and justice

The tragic action springs from the blood relationship of the Duchess and her two brothers and from their sexuality, ambition, fear, and pride: in Ferdinand's dying words.

> Whether we fall by ambition, blood, or lust,
> Like diamonds we are cut with our own dust'   (v.v.72–3).

For Webster's contemporaries the word *blood* had several connotations. Life-blood supplied by the heart was its primary meaning and hence it was also used for sexuality because the heart was believed to be the bodily organ where passion and affection had their origin. It was also used of the blood that members of a family have in common and bound them together, hence their parentage and kinship. All three usages are crucial for understanding the action of this tragedy. Sometimes they merge into each other as, for example, in Ferdinand's reply when Bosola tries to restrain his cruelty and lead the Duchess towards Christian penitence:

> Damn her! that body of hers,
> While that my blood ran pure in't, was more worth
> Than that which thou wouldst comfort, call'd a soul.
> (IV.i.121–3)

When Ferdinand's princely honour is stained, bloody revenge becomes his ruling purpose but he does not attempt to kill either the Duchess or Antonio with his own hands. When executioners have strangled her, he still seeks to shed other blood, condemning

himself to 'go hunt the badger; by owl-light' (IV.ii.332). On return-
ing to the stage, he is haunted by his own shadow and thoughts
of his sister's death: 'strangling', he says, 'is a very quiet death'
(V.ii.31–43 and V.iv.34). On his next and final appearance, in his
deranged mind he is still seeking some form of bloody revenge:
imagining that he is fighting an entire army, he wounds both his
brother and Bosola.

In contrast, after the Duchess's death the Cardinal has taken up
a book of Christian theology but, laying it aside, acknowledges that
a nightmare image of 'a thing, arm'd with a rake' seems to strike at
him, as if he were already tormented in hell's fire. But soon he pays
in blood for what he has done and, when his brother wounds him,
accepts the punishment:

> O Justice!
> I suffer now, for what hath former been.
> Sorrow is held the eldest child of sin.   (V.v.53–5)

In this tragedy, murder is paid for in blood: giving Ferdinand his
death blow, Bosola knows his 'revenge is perfect' and claims that
'the last part of my life / Hath done me best service' (V.v.63–5).

Fate plays an increasing part in punishing wrong-doing as the
story reaches its final stages. To many it may seem that all happens
'in a mist', as Bosola says at one point, or by accident, the death of
Antonio being 'such a mistake as I have often seen / In a play'
(V.v.94–6); events are sometimes so contrived that an audience may
laugh uneasily at the absurdity. But much of the later action has an
underlying drive towards judgement and punishment for wrong-
doing that seems unstoppable. The force producing this is spoken
of in many ways: as an impersonal Fate or man-made 'revenge'; or
as an inevitable 'Justice' or 'fortune'; or as an irresistible 'calamity'
(V.v.81–4; 40–1 and 53; 54–9; 43–4). Sometimes the process is said
to be the work of 'Heaven', 'the heaven' or, very occasionally, 'the
devil' (III.v.78–81 and V.iv.27–8); on one occasion, the force producing judgement is called 'Nature' (V.v.118–19).

One of the most extraordinary features of *The Duchess* is its complicated and often fortuitous action. The plot-line raises so many
questions that we may believe Webster intended to draw an audience's attention to the mysterious ways in which Fate or some
supernatural force controls events, beyond the will of any person in
the play. Contrivance is sometimes so absurdly contrived that an
audience laughs uneasily, unsure who or what is responsible, the

characters or the author. Unexpected and significant choices are left unexplained: why does Ferdinand not kill his sister himself, as he said he could, and why is her blood not shed when he orders her death, as he had anticipated (II.v.63 and 47–8)? Why does he fail to discover that it is Antonio in the next room when he is talking to him? The reasons for the Cardinal 'turning soldier' are left very vague and no adequate explanation is given for devising such a complicated way of concealing Julia's death, which in the event proves ineffective and a source of laughter? Why does the Duchess not run to embrace the wax figures of her family, when moments later she says she longs to do just this? Is Bosola following Ferdinand's instructions when he takes so many disguises in which to torture the Duchess, or are they his own choice? All these unexplained details have been taken as faults in Webster as a playwright but they are so numerous and so dispersed throughout the play that, together, they must represent a determined choice.

Similar 'faults' were introduced where less depends on them. Why should Lord Silvio enter in the first scene only to go to Milan and why should the Duchess leave the stage to 'bring [him] down to the haven' (I.i.219–23)? A 'Servant' enters in the first prison scene to say nothing until questioned and then briefly says that he is 'One that wishes you long life' (IV.i.92). Delio's overture to Julia is totally unexpected and leaves no trace elsewhere in the play. Antonio has a horoscope drawn up for his firstborn's birth and then carelessly drops it. When his son arrives on stage in the last scene, nothing in the text suggests that he will suffer the 'violent death' that is foretold (II.iii.55–64); the Duchess's eldest son by her first marriage is forgotten at this stage in the action, although he is her legal heir. Perhaps the most puzzling fault of all is leaving the legality and sanctity of the Duchess's marriage open to question (see above, p. 28): what advantage could be gained by obscuring the validity of this ceremony that is of crucial importance to the Duchess and from which so many other actions stem?

Webster's purpose may become more explicable if the plotting of the play is seen to be in keeping with the many ambiguities and uncertainties of meaning and intention that are found in its language. Throughout the play an audience is encouraged by many means to listen and look carefully as the inner nature of each person is progressively revealed (see pp. 14–15, above) and, finally, the nature of the society in which they live. Gradually it becomes increasingly clear that that these persons and this society may not exist alone;

individuals are responsible for their acts but some other compulsion is also involved in their fate. Although this force is called many names and sometimes is scarcely believable, the Duchess's influence after death, which has no rational explanation, and the fortuitous way in which 'sorrow' follows wrong-doing combine to suggest that some controlling influence has ensured that what has happened is closely connected with how these men and women have lived together.

An audience watches a seemingly inevitable process during which Bosola is 'an actor in the main of all' and, consequently, 'a wretched thing of blood', but he also repeatedly alerts spectators to purpose and deception. In soliloquy he comments on himself and weeps 'penitent' tears as he confronts the dead body of the Duchess whom he has killed: after this he knows 'That we cannot be suffer'd / To do good when we have a mind to it!' (v.v.85, 92 and iv.ii.357–65). His last words take survey of all the play:

> In what a shadow, or deep pit of darkness,
> Doth womanish and fearful mankind live!
> Let worthy minds ne'er stagger in distrust
> To suffer death, or shame for what is just –
> Mine is another voyage. (v.v.101–5)

Bosola has shared his thoughts so often while standing back from the action that now his words might be intended to represent the dramatist's own judgement. But at this point, Delio returns to the stage and, by speaking of what happens after death, concludes the tragedy with a more positive statement:

> Nature doth nothing so great, for great men,
> As when she's pleas'd to make them lords of truth:
> Integrity of life is fame's best friend,
> Which nobly, beyond death, shall crown the end.

The continuing influence of the Duchess after her death, which is Webster's addition to his source, suggests that Delio, even more clearly than Bosola, is here speaking the author's mind about 'worthy minds' and 'integrity of life'; he is very much Webster's creature, having had only a small part in the action and even smaller in the source for the play.

Certainly Webster wanted his play to show the darkness in which men and women live and the effects of lust, ambition, corruption, murder and revenge. These are common motifs in other tragedies of the time and more remarkable in *The Duchess* is its emphasis on 'integrity of life', which implies that truth, steadfastness and love emerge from the action and lighten the darkness. All these elements in the action interact in a process that leads towards death and appears to be inevitable. But while Fate, Fortune or the heavens are variously blamed for the disasters and suffering in the play, the motive for action lies within each individual and is the gift of what Delio calls 'Nature'. That idea and others that arise from the action of the closing Acts are borrowed from Sir Philip Sidney's *Arcadia* (see Appendix III), an influence suggesting that Webster had become more concerned with the fall-out from disaster than with a hero's moment of death. This emphasis is strongly expressed in the very structure of the tragedy that presents the death of its titular character in Act IV and a complex interweaving of individual stories in Act V. Among the sensationalism of numerous episodes and the revealing intensity and deep feeling of others that have proved to be the tragedy's most memorable features, this wider perspective is responsible for a sense of hard-won understanding that an audience can progressively experience as the tragedy moves towards its conclusion.

We may believe that Webster was determined to present all that experience had taught him about the inwardness of life, its passions and suffering: in that sense it is a traditional tragedy based on an acutely sensitive life-experience. He was also declaring the value of possessing a 'worthy mind' and recognizing a 'truth' that could ennoble and outlast life.

THE QUARTO TEXT OF 1623

The Duchess of Malfi was first published in a quarto dated 1623, and this edition was obviously authoritative. It was furnished with commendatory verses by three dramatists, a list of actors who had played in the original production and in a revival, and a dedication by Webster himself to a nobleman who had family connections with the King's Men. Unlike any other play from the same printer or publisher between 1615 and 1625, its title page was given a motto, which was in Latin and ascribed to Horace. This quotation in its full form would have been pretentious ('If you know wiser precepts than these of mine, kindly tell me; if you do not, practise these with me'), and being shortened is obscure as well. Undoubtedly it was placed there by the author, rather than publisher, printer or some other. And above this exhortation the title page advertised 'The perfect and exact Coppy, with diuerse things Printed, that the length of the Play would not beare in the Presentment'. A discriminating purchaser would also have noted that the volume was thicker than usual – only three dramatic quartos first printed between 1615 and 1625 come within a dozen of the 104 pages of *The Duchess* – and turning over its leaves he would have found clear divisions into acts and scenes, and character-names assembled together at the head of each scene in the manner approved for learned drama. He might have been assured that this was 'the book of the play' that the King's Men had performed, in a complete, authentic, and formal version.

By studying six copies of this quarto (and photographs of twelve more) and by comparing other works by Webster and other plays from the same printing-house, a bibliographer can now confirm this general impression and attempt a more precise judgement (see also Brown, 1954, 1956, and 1962).

Printing and correcting

It is now known that two compositors set the book in Nicholas Okes's shop, dividing the work thus:

Compositor A A1–4^v, B3–C2^v, D3–E2^v, F3–G2^v, H3–I2^v,
K3–L2^v, M3–N2^v
Compositor B B1–2^v, C3–D2^v, E3–F2^v, G3–H2^v, I3–K2^v,
L3–M2^v, N3–4

This means that, excluding prefatory matter on sheet A, the first four pages of each gathering of eight were set by one man, and the second four by the other; and that A and B alternated regularly. Press-correction cannot have been through or regular, for some nonsense words and obvious errors have been left, especially in sheets D, E and K. Compositor A was the less efficient. He was more apt to substitute one short word for another or to set one or two wrong letters in a word; and he alone made obvious errors or omissions in the speech-prefixes. He was slightly more prone to omit short words, but A and B were equally liable to omit single letters from the ends of words. So much the obvious errors can betray, and variations in punctuation – on A's pages there are two, three or, at the beginning, four times the number of colons found on B's – suggest that one or both compositors altered the punctuation of their copy. But, in comparison with errors and variations in other quarto plays of the time, these blemishes are slight, and we may judge that the compositors worked from a very clear copy and provided a clean text – or, possibly, in view of Webster's idiosyncratic writing elsewhere, an over-clear and over-clean text.

Indeed, it was set so regularly that it is difficult to trace the work of the two compositors in other books from Okes's shop. Their preferred spellings are most evident in Samuel Daniel's *Cleopatra* and *Queen's Arcadia*, two plays reprinted by Okes in 1623, the year of the *Duchess* quarto. A few pages of *Cleopatra*, reprinted from an edition of 1601, may be assigned to them individually with some confidence.[3] Here Compositor A was responsible for some errors similar to his obvious ones in *The Duchess*, and we can see that he introduced minor changes in the punctuation, making it heavier at the end of a line, adding or omitting commas, substituting a comma for a colon. However, the two Daniel plays show that both workmen were generally faithful to the elision of their copy and surpassed others who had reprinted these plays in scrupulously retaining peculiarities like the indentations marking Daniel's verse-pargraphs. They followed (and sometimes regularized) their copy's use of italics for proper names, but occasionally modified its capitalization. Changes like *beene* to *bin*, *trueth* to *truth*, *of* to *off*, occur sporadically throughout the plays. Thus a study of these reprints confirms the differentiations between the two compositors of *The Duchess* and, in many respects, shows them to be conservative and careful workmen.

However, a study of the press-work of *The Duchess* complicates this view, proving that both compositors introduced changes in punctuation and the arrangement of the text to suit their own convenience. Nicholas Okes had only one printing press in 1623 (Jackson, 1957, p. 158) and limited quantities of type, so his compositors, working simultaneously on *The Duchess*, did not set the pages in the order in which they are read, but the inner-forme page before the outer-forme. Each sheet was probably set in this order: 1^v and 2 with 3^v and 4; and then, 1 and 2^v with 3 and 4^v. This means that, if the pages of a gathering are numbered 1 to 8, one compositor would set pages 2 and 3 before 1 and 4, while the other set 6 and 7 before 5 and 8. They used two skeleton formes (the 'furniture' for holding the type in the press and including running titles) so that the pages of the inner forme of each sheet could be machined while those of its outer forme were still being set. (This procedure reduced the demands on the type, for there would be fewer pages waiting for machining at any one time; as soon as the first four of any gathering were ready, machining could start. Setting in the order of reading, on the other hand, would mean that machining could not start until 7 out of 8 were set, and then another complete forme of 4 pages would be ready almost at once.) In order to work in this way the printer's copy had to be 'cast off', that is, marked so that compositors knew in advance of composition the amount of text to be accommodated on each page; only so could they know how much to leave for page number 1 when starting to set a new gathering with page number 2, and so on. And here alterations to their copy became almost inevitable, for manuscript copy could be cast off accurately only by taking great care and, as work proceeded, there would be many miscalculations. On the first pages set in each sheet or gathering these could be rectified easily by printing more or less than was marked off, but errors on subsequent pages (especially, 1, 2^v, 3 and 4^v) forced compositors to compress or extend the text to fit the text-space of the page assigned to it in the casting-off. For these purposes compositors would save a line of type by printing a half verse-line at the end of a speech with the preceding line as if all were one line, or they would gain an extra line by splitting one verse-line and printing it as two separate lines. Adjustments of these kinds were made in *The Duchess* and, excepting the few occasions where two or three words were misplaced without altering the number of lines of text, all the obvious mislineations (those which both Lucas and McIlwraith correct in their editions) can be accounted for in this way. And possible mislineations are often better judged when considered, in conjunction with the obvious ones, as similar accommodations of the cast-off copy to the available text-space.

Simultaneous composition by formes did not wholly prevent type-shortage: sometimes italic type was used for roman, and *vice versa*; and, more important editorially, there are indications that the compositors were occasionally forced to depart from their copy because colons, semi-colons, hyphens and brackets were in short supply. Bibliographers cannot trace changes of punctuation so precisely as those of verse-lining, but at least they know where they are most likely to occur. Colons seem to have been in short supply on L1, 2, and 4^v; hyphens on K3 and 4^v, L1, 1^v and 2 and M2^v; brackets on K3 and 4^v, L3, 4 and 4^v, and M1 and 2^v.

A comparison of eighteen copies of the quarto has disclosed the presence of variant readings on ten formes, (see Brown, 1956, pp. 117–19) and so proved that some attempt at press-correction must have been made after a number of sheets had been printed off. Seven of the ten formes have three variants or fewer, and all these correct obvious errors and imply no more authority than a corrector's sense of what is fitting; most are obviously right, as 'remembre' to 'remember' on I2 (IV.i.74), but three, 'did' and 'pleadon' to 'died' and 'pardon' on B2 (I.i.56–7) and 'too' to 'go' on M4 (V.iii.28), may give a plausible rather than a correct reading. The first sign that the corrector consulted the copy or some other authority is the addition of a stage-direction on the inner forme of Sheet F (III.ii.71); and here the change from 'approbation' to 'apprehention' (III.ii.41) and the correction of two proper names may also have been authorized. The next variant forme, G outer, is in three states, implying two phases of correction, and again in the second of these some kind of authority must have been invoked: here spellings are altered rather than corrected, as 'doombe' to 'doome' and '*Bermoothes*' to '*Bermootha's*' (III.ii.238 and 266), while the change from 'Pewterers' to 'Painters' on G4ᵛ (III.iii.20) is the first that cannot have been suggested by an obvious error in the proof-sheet, for both readings make good sense; and this one is unlikely to have been made after reference to the copy, for if that had read 'Painters' it is hard to see how 'Pewterers' could have been set originally. Variants in Sheet H indicate the probable authority for these corrections. Here '*order*' was changed to '*habit*' and '*Hymne*' to '*Ditty*', the heading 'The Hymne' was excised and a note 'The Author disclaims this Ditty to be his' was added, all on H1ᵛ and 2 (III.iv.8–11). None of these modifications corrects an obvious error, none would appear necessary to a printer or his workman, and none could have been made after reference to the copy. They prove that Webster himself was helping with proof-correction at this stage, and that he might have done so for the two preceding sheets. A new stage-direction on H4 (III.v.95), the supply of a 'sir' and two indefinite articles on H2 and 4 (III.iv.30 and III.v.94 and 111), and the addition of '*in dumbe-shew*' on H1ᵛ (III.iv.7.5) may also have been Webster's alterations, for these likewise do not correct obvious errors. Webster had visited the press to help correct *The White Devil* (see Revels, *W.D.*, p. lxviii) and variants show that he gave the same attention to one, two or, perhaps, three formes of *The Duchess*.

With this play, however, his last-minute alterations were probably more extensive than press-variants alone suggest. Besides entries at the head of scenes, a dumb-show, and simple exits, there are only sixteen stage-directions in the whole book: two were additions during press-correction and there is evidence for believing that at least six of the others were not in the printer's copy but were added at the last minute. Three of these occur on, or contiguous to, pages where new speeches are set in line with the conclusion of earlier ones, thus reversing a rule followed on all preceding sheets and saving sufficient space for adding the directions (IV.i.55.1–2, IV.ii.60.2 and 114.1–2); another is on a page with thirty-eight instead of the normal thirty-seven lines of type, and this is the only direction to have a single line of type to itself (III.ii.141.1); another is out of alignment with the rest of the type on the page (IV.i.43.1) and another uses an italic *B* where these were not available for the text itself (IV.ii.166–8). All these irregularities would be accounted for if the six directions had been added after the original typesetting. They occur in the work of both compositors and after Sheet F where Webster's presence in the printing-shop has first been suspected. The six directions therefore, like the two among the variants, may have been added on Webster's instructions after the text had been set up from the printer's copy, but before any sheets had been printed off. Possibly all the others were added in this way, for none occurs in the formes showing authorial press-variants; only '*he kneeles*' on C3^v (I.i.415) would be an oddity, occurring three sheets before any more obvious sign of Webster's changes to the type as set from the printer's copy.

The printer's copy

The copy from which the compositors of *The Duchess of Malfi* worked was specially prepared for readers. No manuscript intended for use in a theatre would have the character-names together at the head of each scene, rather than where they enter individually; and very few would be so inadequately furnished with stage-directions. These features of *The Duchess* and the clarity and regularity of its text imply that its copy was a good, professional transcript.

It was probably prepared by Ralph Crane, an expert scrivener associated with the King's Men from before 1621: the arrangement of entries, some spellings and devices of presentation, the elided forms and punctuation, all indicate his hand. The unusual arrangement of almost all the prose in unjustified lines, with a capital letter at the beginning of each, is probably due to Crane's frequent practice of beginning both verse and prose lines with lower-case letters so that the two kinds of dialogue are not readily distinguished. In *The Duchess*, verse lines begin with lower-case letters at I.i.233 and 235.

Crane can be relied on for careful work, but the 'perfect and exact coppy' advertised on the title page of the quarto must have been far from the author's manuscript in stage-directions, arrangement, orthography, elision and punctuation. Besides re-arranging entries and pruning stage-directions, the scribe probably regularized character-names and speech-prefixes (*The White Devil* has several variations in these) and generally tidied up the text in accordance with his own notions of propriety. A comparison of Crane's transcripts of *A Game at Chess* with those made by the author or copied faithfully from his papers shows how he rephrased the stage-directions and substituted *you would* for *you'de*, *they are* for *they're*, *I am* for *Ime*, and so forth, and *hath* and *doth* for *has* and *does*. He also introduced capitals for emphasis and provided fuller and more careful punctuation – though he would modify his practice for special purposes, as in the light punctuation for the formal address of the Prince of Orange in *Barnavelt* (ll. 1823ff.). Moreover, while all Crane's manuscripts are of fine workmanship, they are sometimes ambiguous in minor details: in three of them '?' is not distinguished from '!'; L, M, N, W and Y are not always different from l, m, n, w and y; occasionally word-divisions are not clear, as in 'gentle woman' or 'gentlewoman'. Errors corrected by modern editors of his transcripts show that Crane was sometimes responsible for small inaccuracies: the most prevalent of these are the wrong number of minim strokes in words containing a sequence of them, misplaced apostrophes in abbreviations, and omissions or errors involving the final letter of a word, especially when this was an 'e'. Such modifications and practices must be taken into account when assessing the quality of the quarto text of *The Duchess*.

The general authority of the text will, of course, depend on the kind of manuscript from which Crane prepared the printer's copy. But of this the regularizing efficiency of the transcription has left no clear evidence. The inclusion of a song which the author 'disclaimed' to be his (III.iv) suggests that the scribe was working from a theatrical manuscript with additions to the author's text; but the song fits its context precisely and may thus have been taken by Webster from some source, or commissioned by him from a writer who was primarily a musician. The direction at the head of v.iii, '*Antonio, Delio, Eccho, (from the Dutchesse Graue.)*' is readily explained as a rephrasing of a note in the author's fair copy, for a prompter would hardly use these words to remind himself that the actor of the Duchess was to speak the Echo; but author's directions were sometimes retained in theatrical manuscripts, and here the scribe may have adapted one of two notes in the manuscript from which he was working. The claim on the title page that the text includes '*diuerse things . . . that the length of the Play would not beare in the Presentment*' again suggests an author's copy; but cuts were usually marked in prompt-books so that the full text would still be legible. More important is the naming of 'Forobosco' as played by '*N. Towley*' in the list of actors prefacing the text; this character does not appear in the play itself, beyond a passing reference to him as keeping the key of the park gate (II.ii.32), so it might be argued that a scene was omitted after the first performance and that the copy must be dependent on a prompt-book in which the cut was marked. Yet on further consideration even this argument is insecure. The list of actors was probably drawn up by another hand than that responsible for the printer's copy, and may therefore have different authority. Only here are there variations in the names of characters, 'the Marquesse of Pescara' instead of 'Pescara' and 'The Cardinals Mis' instead of 'Julia'; Roderigo, Grisolan, Castruchio and the Old Lady are all omitted. Possibly the list was written out by Webster from memory ten years after the first performance, and he included Forobosco because he had once intended to give him some significance; so this name would be like one of the 'ghost characters' in *The White Devil* which are known only from stage directions. Or perhaps there were two versions of *The Duchess*, the play described by Orazio Busino (see above, pp. 29–30) being the version, including a Forobosco scene, which is now lost. Or again, '*N. Towley*' might have been intended to appear opposite 'Malateste' on the next line, to whom no actor is assigned; this error would be similar to the obvious one of placing '*R. Pallant*' opposite 'Cariola' and the 'Court Officers' instead of 'The Doctor' and 'Cariola'. Commas following the latter pair may indicate that the compositor intended to place the bracket correctly; 'Officers' is followed by a full stop like 'Malateste', '*Children*' and '*Pilgrime*', all of which are without an actor's name.

The closest definition of the authority of the quarto text is that it was printed from a transcript in which no clear signs of its origins survived; the most reassuring fact is that its publication was under the aegis of Webster himself.

Censorship

In *The Duchess of Malfi*, the word *god* occurs only twice, in reference to Pluto (III.ii.243–6), and the word *heaven* or *heavens* thirty times.

A table setting out the number of occurrences shows a marked contrast to *The White Devil* that has been taken to indicate that the text has been purged of profanities:

	White Devil	Duchess
God	16	0
god	1	2
Abbreviations for God (as in 'Ud's death')	7	0
Lord (for God)	3	0
heaven, heavens	11	30

Because the censor required the removal of the word *God* from play-scripts, in accordance with a statute of 1606, many scholars have deduced from these figures that the text from which Crane transcribed the play had already been censored for performance. This view has been taken by many editors (including the present editor in first Revels Plays edition) and led the more recent Cambridge editors to emend *Heaven* to *God* wherever they found reason for thinking that censorship had altered what Webster wrote. But it is by no means certain that he would have used *God* in this play as freely as he had done in *The White Devil* or that Crane worked from a theatrical manuscript from which all reference to God had been removed. In two instances 'God' would indeed make a better and more meaningful contrast with 'Devil' than the Quarto's 'heaven' (I.i.275–7 and III.v.100) but there is little other evidence to show that Crane worked from a prompt-book in which another hand might have made changes.

It remains possible, or even probable, that Webster avoided the word *God* in *The Duchess* for his own reasons. It is also absent from *The Devil's Law Case* which seems to have been printed from an autograph manuscript or a transcript of one (so Brown, 1954, pp. 122–3 and Cambridge ed., pp. 62–4). Moreover *The Duchess* has nineteen passages where *God* is not a possible reading for *heaven* – almost twice the number in *The White Devil*. An absence of definite and assured references to the almighty and personal God of Christian theology may well have been Webster's own and well-considered choice. Such a decision would suit well with the hidden motivations and textual ambiguities of *The Duchess* that seem designed to create uncertainty or scepticism in readers and audiences. Other important issues are similarly treated: the duties of the Duchess as regent are only vaguely suggested and confusion remains about the inheritance of the son of her earlier marriage and the legality of her second marriage (see note on v.v.113 and above, p. 28). In accord with the textual absence of God, Bosola imagines mankind to be living in a 'shadow or deep pit of darkness', not in a world watched over and illuminated by the Almighty; and Delio, concluding the tragedy, says that it is 'Nature' that ennobles 'great men' in the course of their lives. If the avoidance of *God* and the use of *heaven* and *the heavens* were Webster's own choices that decision would also have avoided censorship and the likelihood that another hand would alter what he had written and wanted to be read and spoken on stage.

EARLY PERFORMANCES

The first performance of *The Duchess* must have been earlier than 16 December 1614, because William Ostler, who first acted Antonio, died on that day. But it is likely that writing continued throughout 1613 because unmistakable borrowings from Sideny's *Arcadia* from III.ii onwards are likely to follow the reprinting of this Elizabethan work in 1613 after a nine-year interval. Moreover, some ideas for the Madmen of IV.ii may have come from the masques performed for the marriage of James I's daughter, Elizabeth, to the Elector Palatine in February 1613. These had included for the first time comic characters who, in Campion's *Lords' Masque* and Beaumont's *Masque of the Inner Temple and Gray's Inn*, were described on entry, one by one, like Webster's Madmen.

When *The Duchess of Malfi* was published in 1623, the title page announced that it had been 'presented privately at the Blackfriars and publicly at the Globe, by the King's Majesty's Servants'. The change from the Queen's Men who had presented Webster's earlier tragedy represented a considerable gain in prestige. The King's Men were popular at Court, the Chamber of Accounts showing that they gave 109 performances there between the autumn of 1609 and the spring of 1616, when all the other companies together were responsible for only seventy-two.

The membership of the King's Men when *The Duchess of Malfi* was performed has been fairly well established from records and information about individual actors (see Gurr, 2004, pp. 217–46). The list of 'Actors' Names' prefixed to the first edition can be interpreted with some precision. Of John Lowin, who leads as Bosola, James Wright has left a record which dates from after 1630: at that time he 'used to act with mighty applause, Falstaff; Morose; Vulpone; and Mammon in the *Alchemist*; Melancius in the *Maid's Tragedy*', (*Historia Histronica*, 1699). He also played the title role in *Henry VIII* and, according to Downes's *Roscius Anglicanus* (1709), 'had his Instructions from Mr Shakespeare himself'. In 1604, he acted in Webster's Induction to *The Malcontent* and, in a revival of *The Wild Goose Chase* of 1632, the part of 'Belleur . . . of a stout blunt humour' was said to have been 'most naturally acted by Mr. John Lowin' (Bentley, II, 499–506). When *The Duchess* was first performed he was thirty-seven or thirty-eight years of age.

For Ferdinand, the Cardinal and Antonio, the list of actors gives two performers, each numbered 1 and 2, and, since it includes Ostler who died in December 1614, the first cast is probably that of early performances. Richard Burbage, who created Ferdinand, was the foremost actor of his time. His repute is attested in many allusion and verses, and in his starring roles, as Jeronimo in *The Spanish Tragedy*, Richard III, Othello, Lear and Malevole in *The Malcontent*. His portrait at Dulwich College suggests that he had the refinement and sensibility to act Hamlet, while his roles of Lear and Othello imply vocal and physical strength as well. An Elegy of 1619 praises the 'just weight' of his delivery and 'Inchaunting toung', and also gives grounds for believing that he could bring to Ferdinand's passion and madness an illusion of reality: he could act:

> . . . a sadd Lover, with so true an Eye
> That theer I would have sworne, he meant to dye.

He brought a mature art to Ferdinand – in fiction, the twin of a boy-actor's Duchess – for he was then at least forty years old.

Of Condell, the first Cardinal, Underwood the Delio, Tooley, who appears opposite Forobosco, perhaps in error for Malateste, and of Ostler, little is known except that Ostler was called 'the Roscius of these times' by John Davies in his *Scourge of Folly* (*c.* 1611), and that Tooley had been apprenticed to Burbage, and his roles included Ananias in *The Alchemist* and Corvino in *Volpone*. Except for Condell, these were of a younger generation.

At least two of the cast named in the first edition can hardly have appeared in the first production. John Rice, the Pescaro, was only a boy in the company in 1610, when he played a nymph in a pageant. By 1611 he had left to join Lady Elizabeth's Men and there is no certain evidence that he rejoined his earlier company before 1619. In any event, an actor in his teens would have been too slight for the 'noble old fellow' Pescaro (v.i.60) in a cast that included Burbage, Lowin and Condell. Thomas Pollard, the Silvio, did not join the King's Men until within a year or two of 1615 when he was about twenty; so this actor, who was later to gain considerable success in comic roles, was probably a young Silvio in some revival of *The Duchess*, and named in the printed cast for the sake of his later reputation.

Richard Sharp, the only actor assigned to the rôle of the Duchess, is known to have played young romantic leads from 1625 until his death in January 1632. If he was then in his twenties, he must have been about eleven or twelve when *The Duchess* was first performed, and possibly too young for such a large part. At that time Richard Robinson was the leading boy-actor of the company and would have been the obvious choice; perhaps his name was omitted for the part because he had already figured in the list as the actor who later took over the Cardinal from Condell. Numerous references to Robinson in female roles have survived from 1611 to 1616, whereas the earliest to Sharp, if the cast list of *The Duchess* is discounted, dates from 1616. The talents of 'Dick Robinson' have been described by Ben Jonson in *The Devil Is an Ass* (1616), telling the story of a masquerade in real life as a lawyer's wife:

> to see him behaue it;
> And lay the law; and carue; and drinke vnto 'hem;
> And then talke baudy: and send frolicks! O!
>
> (II.vii.71–3)

Robinson is named in the 1623 Folio of Shakespeare's works, among the 'Principall Actors in all these Playes'. Of Sharp little is known beyond the names of his later male roles which included romantic leads.

While Sharp's assignment to the Duchess probably refers to a revival close to the date of publication, John Thompson's to Julia must certainly do so. Not until 1621 did this boy-actor start to play a series of female roles in Fletcher's plays, and he was still in skirts ten years later. Roger Pallant, 'the younger', who seems to have played both Cariola and the doctor (see p. 47 above), was just nine years old in September 1614, so while he might possibly have been an inexperienced Cariola in the first performance, he could not have played the doctor. Perhaps he played both roles in a revival of 1621 or 1622 when he was sixteen or seventeen.

We know very little about Jacobean cross-gender performances but we may be sure that they were accepted as part of the play's illusion of life created on stage.[4] Two members of early audiences have testified in their commendatory verses that the impersonal and transient art of a boy-actor had made the greatest effect in *The Duchess of Malfi*. For Middleton and Rowley, the enactment of the Duchess herself was the pathetic and eloquent centre of the play, and proof of Webster's genius.

While scholars differ about the size and facilities of the Globe Theatre where the Quarto's title page says performances of the play were given, its basic shape will be familiar to readers of this edition through illustrations, models and functional replicas. It was a traditional building, reminiscent of inn yards and bearbaiting arenas, and basically similar to the Curtain or Red Bull where *The White Devil* had been produced. But it was larger, and, especially after rebuilding in 1613, finer and more elaborately equipped. Above two thousand spectators could be accommodated on three or four sides of the stage; some sat in the 'lords' rooms' and galleries while many more stood in the yard which was unroofed. On a stage some forty feet wide and thirty deep, there was plenty of space for processions, crowd scenes, 'shows' and battles. Yet the encircling audience could also give an effect of concentration or intensity, as described by Webster himself in the *Character* of 'An Excellent Actor' (1615):

> sit in a full Theater, and you will thinke you see so many lines drawne from the circumference of so many eares whiles the *Actor* is the *Center*.

The Globe's stage had an upper terrace or balcony, a curtained recess or enclosure, at least two doors opening from the tiring house, one on each side, and one or more trapdoors in the main stage. An actor could be lowered mechanically from the 'heavens' or 'roof', which covered most of the acting area.

The Blackfriars 'private' theatre differed from the Globe in important ways. It was located in an enclosed hall, measuring only sixty-six by forty-four feet. A full audience probably numbered six or seven hundred, all of whom were seated in the pit or galleries, with a few on the stage itself. This stage seems to have been a smaller version of the Globe's, but it was lit by torches and candles. The auditorium could be darkened by covering its windows.

The King's Men had first used the Blackfriars in 1609 and started to develop an up-market repertoire for a new and more select audience (see Sturgess, 1996, Chapters 3, 4 and 6, and Gurr, 2004, p. 159). There are several indications that *The Duchess of Malfi* was written with its special opportunities in mind. Although the presence-chamber scenes and the dumb show of III.iv are similar to episodes in *The White Devil*, there are passages of action and dialogue which are more intimate, still, or quiet than anything in the earlier play, and more appropriate to a small, enclosed auditorium in which spectators were comfortably seated. Silence is used several times to intensify pathos or terror; a notable example is the scene in the Duchess's private chamber when at one moment she is thoughtfully brushing her hair and the next facing the 'terrible' and silent 'apparition' of Ferdinand's entry holding their father's poniard (III.ii.147 and 142). In the next scene, when Bosola enters to tell Ferdinand that Antonio is his sister's lover, the audience hears nothing of their talk but two courtiers watch at a distance and comment:

> *Pes.* The Lord Ferdinand laughs.
> *Delio.*   Like a deadly cannon
>   That lightens ere it smokes.
> *Pes.* These are your true pangs of death,
>   The pangs of life that struggled with great statesmen –
> *Delio.* In such a deformed silence, witches whisper
>   Their charms.   (III.iii.54–9)

Sharp gaps in time and action are the clearest indication that Webster wrote specifically for performance at the Blackfriars where it was a regular custom to play music in breaks between Acts. Whereas *The White Devil* calls for continuous performance with, perhaps, a single pause between Acts IV and V, *The Duchess* requires a pause between all five Acts. The longest and most obvious narrative break is between Acts II and III in which time Antonio has fathered 'two children more' (III.i.7). Without a pause for music as at the Blackfriars, the explanation given of these births in the dialogue would be so curt that it would sound like a last minute and obvious cover-up for clumsy playwriting. It is far more likely to be just one of the four action-breaks that enhance the narrative by clarifying the passage of time throughout the play. What Webster would later call the 'ingenious structure of the scene' (*Devil's Law Case*, Preface) depends upon the short musical interludes that were the custom at the Blackfriars. Reviews of present-day productions of *The Duchess* are likely to find fault with Webster's playwriting if some equally efficient way has not been found for marking the narrative's forward movement between the Acts.

A third characteristic suggesting that performance at the Blackfriars was in Webster's mind is a repeated and occasionally special use of darkness. Scenes acted at night or in darkness were common in plays belonging to the King's Men long before they performed in their new theatre. Professor R. B. Graves has recently argued that the scene in which Ferdinand asks for lights to be removed before visiting his sister and offering her a dead man's hand that she 'affectionately' kisses would have been more 'suspenseful' in performance on the open-air stage of the Globe where the audience could see all that happens and would therefore be fully aware of the trick as it was about to terrify its victim: he could have entered with the false hand covered by his sleeve (Graves, 1999, pp. 220–33). On the other hand David Carnegie reports that 'The dead hand scene has on more than one occasion been successfully played in a total blackout' (Cambridge ed., p. 414). Whatever may be surmised about the effect in both theatres, the text has much to say about the removal and return of lights that in the Blackfriars could have been some of the many that had lit the stage from the beginning of the play. At the Globe special lights would have to be lit and brought on stage beforehand at some convenient moment, and then removed, and then brought on once more; they would probably be taken off stage a second time to remove an on-stage obstacle and the need to take care of the burning lights when no longer needed. The text has a broken, quick rhythm and taut syntax at the crucial moment, which might well have been more effective in the smaller theatre:

> Take hence the lights: he's come
> > *Where are you?*
> > > Here sir: –
> *This darkness suits you well.*
> I would ask you pardon: –
> > *You have it;…*

After she realises that she has kissed a dead man's hand, the duologue is still more abrupt: 'Hah! lights! – O, horrible!' – 'Let her have lights enough' (IV.i.29–31 and 53).

In the Echo scene of Act V a special lighting effect is required when Antonio hears his wife's voice as *'from the Duchess' Grave'* and then exclaims, 'on the sudden, a clear light / Presented me a face folded in sorrow' (v.iii.entry and 44–5). For this surprise Webster could have been relying on a mechanical stage device previously used by the King's Men in *The Second Maiden's Tragedy* in 1611 and probably at the Blackfriars (see ed. Lancashire, p. 54):

> On a sodayne in a kinde of Noyse like a Wynde, the dores clattering, the Toombstone flies open, and a great light appears in the midst of the Toombe; His Lady as went owt, standing iust before hym all in white . . .

Ben Jonson's *Catiline*, also staged by the King's Men in 1611, has the stage-direction '*A darkness comes over the place*' and six lines later, '*A fiery light appears*' (i.i.312–20). A special light might also have accompanied or announced the vision that Bosola has of the Duchess in Act V: 'still methinks the duchess / Haunts me: there, there! –' (v.ii.343–4).

The Quarto title page carries a note, unique at the time, saying that the text was 'The perfect and exact copy, with diverse things printed, that the length of the play would not bear in the present-ment'; more usually texts were advertised as 'augmented' for pub-lication or performance. *The Duchess* is among the very longest plays and contains a number of detachable and expendable 'things' – meaning, perhaps, episodes rather than speeches or passages of dialogue. The whole of the echo scene could easily be omitted, and the episode of the dead man's hand, the Madmen's song and dance and several other incidents in Act IV. The 'tales' of Reputation, Love and Death (iii.ii.122–33) and of the Salmon and Dogfish (iii.v.125–41) could also be deleted without further alteration; with only a little re-writing, so could Bosola's encounter with Castruchio and the Old Woman at the start of Act II and much of the talk of courtiers at the start of Act I and Act III, scene iii. Julia's involve-ment in Act V, scene ii can take several large cuts. With the omission of a short passage in the preceding scene and possibly a few words in the following, the dumb-show at Loretto of the Cardinal's inves-titure as a solider and his banishment of the Duchess and her family is entirely expendable, although at considerable loss to the religious context of the play and the character of the Cardinal. None of these omissions would have been particularly appropriate for either theatre except possibly the last, if it had proved impractical to stage its elaborate ceremonies on the smaller Blackfriars stage.

The Quarto's title page gives priority to the Blackfriars but that may reflect its social status rather than imply that the first perfor-mance was given there. What can be inferred from the information and tone of the title page and from its motto in Latin is that Webster was a determinedly ambitious playwright who wrote at greater length than was expected or found to be practicable while in his tragedy he exploited a number of staging possibilities and repeatedly kept his audiences alert by ambiguities, hidden purposes, surprise and suspense.

The play was revived at least once before publication in 1623. If the Spanish chaplain was referring to *The Duchess* in his report of 7 February 1618 (see p. 29 above), that would be the first of which we have record. The list of Actors' Names in the Quarto points to a later revival sometime after 1619 because Joseph Taylor who took over Ferdinand did not join the company until after Burbage's death on 13 March 1619; other records of John Thompson, who is the only actor assigned to Julia, do not begin until 1621. A further revival is recorded before the King at the new Cockpit Theatre in Whitehall on 26 December 1630 (Bentley, i, 27–8).

THEATRE PRODUCTIONS

At the Restoration, *The Duchess* was one of the pre-war plays allotted to Davenant and there are records of performances in 1662, 1668 and, at Court, in 1686. From the Quarto edition of 1678, 'As it is now acted at the Duke's Theatre', we know that Betterton played Bosola, Mrs Betterton the Duchess, and Harris played Ferdinand. In 1662, Pepys judged the play 'well performed, but Betterton and Ianthe [Mary Saunderson, later Mrs Betterton], to admiration', and John Downes noted in *Roscius Anglicanus*:

> This Play was so exceedingly Excellently Acted in Parts: chiefly, Duke Ferdinand and Bosola: It fill'd the House 8 Days Successively, it proving one of the Best of Stock Tragedies.

There was a revival, under the new title, *The Unfortunate Duchess of Malfy, or The Unnatural Brothers: a tragedy*, at the Haymarket on 22 July 1707. As we have seen, cast and text were printed in the 1708 quarto: Mrs Porter as the Duchess, Verbruggen as Ferdinand, and Mills as Bosola. Numerous cuts reduced playing time: the pilgrim scene (III.iv) is gone and both the Reputation and Salmon stories marked for omission. The narrative was tidied up by omitting the reference to the Duchess's son by her first marriage (III.ii.100) while rephrasing regularized the metre, modernized vocabulary and made the play more respectable: for example, 'lecher' becomes 'lover' and 'I pour it in your bosom' is omitted (III.ii.100 and III.i.52). The text is useful today as the earliest to provide adequate stage directions.

In 1735, *The Fatal Secret* by Lewis Theobald was published. This was an adaptation of *The Duchess* that had been performed at the Theatre Royal: the Duchess and Antonio are reunited at the end together with a twelve-year-old son; the scene is Malfi throughout and the action starts after the marriage. Julia is omitted.

In the nineteenth century, *The Duchess* was usually produced in a version by R. H. Horne. He had made it as regular and respectable as possible; there is no Julia and the Duchess, now called Marina, is strangled off-stage. The tragedy became a star-vehicle for actresses: Miss Isabella Glyn at Sadler's Wells in 1850 and many subsequent tours; Mrs Emma Waller at the Broadway, New York, in 1858, and subsequent tours; Miss Mariott at the Sadler's Wells in 1864; and Miss Glyn in a new production under her 'immediate Direction', at the Standard, Shoreditch, in 1868. *The Lady's Newspaper* of 23 November 1850, commented:

> Miss Glynne's performance of the duchess is one of the most striking achievements of that rising actress. The scenes, intrinsically coarse, in which she makes love to her steward, were admirably softened by the playful spirit of coquetry which she infused into them. The soft passages of sorrow stole with mournful effect upon the naturally mirthful temperament, and, when her wrongs aroused her alike to a sense of pain and dignity, her denunciations were terrific. . . .

The only other role, in this group of revivals, to be particularly noted was Bosola as portrayed by George Bennett at Sadler's Wells. Westland Marston recorded in *Our Recent Actors*, ii (1888), that it:

> was one of his most impressive characters. In the appalling scene with the Duchess, where, as an old man, he prepares her for her approaching murder, there was something in his servile appearance, in his deep, sepulchral tones, slow movements, and watchful, deliberate revelation of coming horror, that seemed as if he himself had had such near commerce with Death as to be the fit representative of his terrors to the living. (p. 61)

At the end of the century, in October 1892, the Independent Theatre Society gave two performances in a new version by William Poel, directed by Poel at the Opéra Comique. Irving lent costumes and scenery. There was no Julia but a 'Dance of Death'; Sidney Barraclough was Ferdinand, Murray Carson was Bosola, and Mary Rorke the Duchess.

The years after the Second World War saw more frequent productions and a greater reliance on Webster's text, although always heavily cut:

1919 Lyric, Hammersmith (two performances only)	*Duchess*, Cathleen Nesbitt; *Ferd.*, R. Farquharson; *Bos.*, W. Rea. *Julia* was restored, played by Edith Evans. Director was Allan Wade.
1933 Embassy Theatre	*Duchess*, Joyce Bland; *Ferd.*, John Laurie; *Bos.*, R. Graham. There was no Julia. Director was John Fernald.
1937 Gate, Dublin	*Duchess*, Jean Anderson; *Ferd.*, Norman Scase; *Bos.*, Ben Gifford. Director was Peter Powell.
1945 Haymarket, London	*Duchess*, Peggy Ashcroft; *Ferd.*, John Gielgud; *Bos.*, Cecil Trouncer. Director was George Rylands.
1946 Ethel Barrymore, New York	*Duchess*, Elisabeth Bergner; *Ferd.*, David Eccles; *Bos.*, Canada Lee. Adapted by W. H. Auden; director was G. Rylands; music by Benjamin Britten.
1957 Phoenix, New York	*Duchess*, Jacqueline Brookes; *Ferd.*, J. Wiseman; *Bos.*, P. Roberts. Director was Jack Landau.
1960 Shakespeare Memorial Theatre and Alwych, London	*Duchess*, Peggy Ashcroft; *Ferd.*, Eric Porter; *Bos.*, Patrick Wymark. Director was Donald McWhinnie.

At first directors were shy of the horrors. The critic of *The Times* in 1919 excused the audience's 'tittering . . . towards the close' and the next production of 1935 played safe: 'horror was absent altogether. The masque of madmen was turned into a sort of ballet' (*Daily Telegraph*); 'The dead-hand scene is produced in a pleasant amber light and the pallor of human flesh is hidden by a glove' (*New Statesman*); the director 'cannot put Elizabethan ferocity into the hearts of his actors' (*Times*).

Peggy Ashcroft twice played the Duchess, and Ferdinand and Bosola returned to pre-Restoration power and prominence. Even in the tame 1935 production, 'John Laurie's ... epileptic frenzy', as Ferdinand was 'genuinely terrible and his ranting [had] a ghastly perverse sincerity'. In this part the chief laurels were Gielgud's: fifteen years after his performance, Kenneth Tynan remembered the 'thrill of finality' he gave to 'I will never see thee more' (Observer, 18 Dec. 1960) and Harold Hobson his 'torment of spirit that still excites the imagination' (Sunday Times, 18 Dec. 1960). Gielgud had accepted the indications of incestuous desire and they seemed so up-to-date that he was praised for an originality that is properly Webster's.

William Rea's Bosola of 1919 exploited the character's isolation, playing him 'with an air of melancholy reverie and aloofness which gave him immense distinction' (Times). Cecil Trouncer, in 1945, risked consistency to give a full interpretation: in The Sunday Times, James Agate called it 'a grand exhibition. I am not quite sure the actor knew what to do with this mixture of Enobarbus and Thersites; to watch him do it was nevertheless a rich experience'. The Times praised his 'vital study, of ... a murderer of fortune prematurely aged in the galleys', as the 'supreme attraction of the revival'.

The constant problem has been the shape and effect of the play as a whole. The fifth Act has often been called 'irredeemable'. According to The Hartford Courant (10 Jan. 1946), Auden's adaptation was chiefly confined to Acts IV and V, but:

> Early in the play an interpolated passage. ... establishes the Duke's concern for his sister as born of affection, if perhaps a little incestuous, while the Duke's original confession that he merely sought to secure her estates is saddled on the Cardinal.

But still Rosamund Gilder, in Theatre Arts (Dec. 1946), called the production laboured, lacking 'intensity and lurid beauty'. Productions have often been praised for isolated 'moments': Theatre Arts said the play at the Phoenix was 'curiously episodic, and the episodes are somehow not cumulative'; Harold Hobson, at the Aldwych, found The Duchess had 'no drive, no force, no continuity', as if the director had decided that 'it is in single lines, that the genius of Webster lies'. The roles of the Duchess, Bosola and Ferdinand had been variously and effectively realized in performance but the structure of the play had yet to be vindicated. At the Aldwych, the five-act structure was ignored; there was no presence-chamber; among the lines cut were Bosola's concluding:

> Let worthy minds ne'er stagger in distrust
> To suffer death, or shame, for what is just.

While such neglect was possible, and such disbelief in Webster's action and argument, the tragedy had not yet been given a fair chance in the theatre.

By the beginning of the twenty-first century much had changed. During the 1950s *The Duchess* became a text increasingly studied in higher education and, as its text was read with closer attention, students became increasingly concerned with the world of the play and the predicament of the Duchess in a male-dominated society. Although difficult to understand and perform, the text spoke directly to the younger generation. While actors and critics had long been aware of the power of certain of its lines in the theatre, now students were finding them both relevant and mesmerizing. Webster was a 'revelation' to Harold Pinter at school in his teens: on walks with his teacher and friends:

> we would declare into the wind, at the passing trolley-buses or indeed to the passers-by, nuggets of Webster, such as. . . . 'Cover her face; mine eyes dazzle; she died young'. (quoted in *Times*, 11 March 1995)

Increasingly, directors and actors learned to trust the dialogue, finding that it reflected the concerns of the moment, the traumas of an inwardly stressed existence and the violence underlying an appearance of political stability. It also drew upon the skills that actors and directors had developed for performance of contemporary plays.

Peter Gill's production at the Royal Court Theatre in 1971 was starkly set on a small stage with only doors for scenery and a few chairs for furnishing. Instead of a fully fledged and splendid Court, a chorus of actors, uniformly and simply dressed, remained on stage throughout to mark the changing location and circumstance, as well as playing many of the smaller characters. This treatment exposed some inadequate casting but the Duchess of Judy Parfitt was seen not only for her courage and strength of mind but also as a person deeply engaged in the unavoidable and pervasive pressures of her social situation. The production started a trend and audiences, as well as students, were to become increasingly concerned with Webster's view of a hierarchical and power-seeking society.

In 1985 at the National Theatre, *The Duchess* was given an atmospheric and impressive production by the designer and director Philip Prowse. Ian McKellan was a sharp-minded Bosola and Eleanor Bron a splendid and sensitive Duchess but little excitement or argument was aroused, critics finding the play underpowered. But then. against all precedent and what was unthinkable a few years earlier, in the season of 1995–1996 one production of *The Duchess* followed another into Wyndhams, one of the smaller commercial theatres in London's West End. When his production for the Cheek by Jowl company opened in town after an international tour, Declan Donnellan reported that:

> In country after country, people have told us how clever we were to choose such a timely play. But that's because a very rich stew builds up. It's about the supernatural. It's about sex. It's about politics. It's about redemption. It's about spirituality. Webster's characters are everywhere. (Interview, *Times*, 29 December 1995)

As well as Blackpool, Cheltenham, Coventry and Oxford in England, this production visited the principal cities of eleven countries around the world and everywhere it was acclaimed, from Hong Kong and Botoga to Mexico City and New York. Never had so many and so very different people seen Webster's Duchess of Malfi 'lively bodied' on a stage.

Philip Franks, an actor recently turned director, was the first to bring a production into Wyndhams, following its opening at the Greenwich Theatre. On tour, performances had been refined and the production paced and tuned to hold attention (see Brown, 1998, pp. 319–26, 335n. 7), and now, with a small cast and simple set, individual characters dominated the audience's experience. Juliet Stevenson, as the Duchess, took time to realize sexual interplay and subtextual thought in her scenes with Antonio. Performances occasionally had a finesse more usual in film than theatre which slowed down the action, and that seemed to encourage Simon Russell Beale to express Ferdinand's desire for his sister in an overtly sexual and infantile manner. The play as a whole suffered from this loss of pace: major cuts had to be made, including the Loretto scene and Julia's wooing of Bosola (III.iv and v.ii). Many incidental similes, illustrative images and verbal elaborations were also cut, from which Bosola suffered most: his trenchant irony and the energy of his restless mind had little chance of making their mark. But, in an intimate theatre and with small scenic resources, the narrative gripped the audience's attention and almost silenced the usual complaints of reviewers about Webster's lack of theatrical judgement.

Reinstatement of the dramatist as a master of theatre was confirmed when the second production by Cheek by Jowl hit town. This company has often lived up to its adventurous and bare-faced name and its *Duchess* was distinguished from its predecessors by the freedom with which the director had encouraged actors to find their own ways to bring the characters to life, introducing stage business and speaking the dialogue to suit their own imaginations and temperaments. Anastasia Hille played the Duchess with a commanding and often cynical intelligence: she was, in turn, restless, aggressive, dismissive; she would laugh harshly or nervously and then, suddenly, speak with unaffected simplicity. Scott Handy's Ferdinand was a badly behaved boy-man, alternately given to fighting and hugging his sister. The director, it seems, had encouraged his actors to be as dynamic and varied as possible. In Act III scene ii, when the Duchess confesses 'I pray sir, hear me: I am married' (l. 82), she takes Ferdinand off guard, brings him to the floor, gets astride him, and brandishes the dagger at him. During his subsequent rant, she goes on drinking whisky. When he touches a deeper note of pain:

> And thou hast ta'en that massy sheet of lead
> That hid thy husband's bones, and folded it
> About my heart,

she replies loudly and sarcastically, 'Mine bleeds for it' (III.ii.112–14) and breaks off into coarse laughter. By the time Ferdinand starts to tell the story of 'Reputation, Love, and Death' (ll. 119–35), both are near exhaustion and sitting side by side on the floor, like children after a game that had become too rough. He then regains his energy and, crying out 'I will never see you more', clasps hand over eyes and, rushing from the stage, trips over a chair as he exits.

As in Peter Gill's production more than twenty years earlier, a small but physically varied group of actors kept the audience alert to the changing context of the main action and replaced individual characters with nameless courtiers, officers, acolytes, soldiers and torturers. They often used eye-catching stage business; for example, many doctors struggled to tame Ferdinand's lycanthropia in Act V, not the single one required by the text; in formal scenes, they stood around, stiff and unmoving. The end of the play was given a greater sense of cohesion than the text warrants when all the principals rose from death to pose, as if for a family photograph. The strong individualism evident in both direction and acting regained for the play widespread approval that has been absent in reviews since its early stage history (see Brown, 1998, 326–32).

At times Cheek by Jowl's production, like the earlier one at the same theatre, drew a close and quiet attention from its audience but it had a stronger and more obvious energy running throughout. The sense of committal and competition between the actors led to confident and outgoing performances that might have suited the large outdoor stage of the original performances at the Globe Theatre. An open and adventurous rehearsal process that continued during its long tour (see interview, *New York Times*, 3 December 1995) had encouraged actors to improvise in performance, much as the large and daily-changing repertoire of the King's Men might have done, whether playing at the Globe or at the more intimate Blackfriars.

A far more costly and elaborate production by Phyllida Lloyd opened on the wide Lyttelton stage of the National Theatre on 23 January 2003. Costumed in smart modern dress and following the lead of many productions on tighter budgets, the action took place within a small area, here seen in front of long rows of steps on which the assembled cast waited and watched: Ferdinand was provided with a table and lamp so that he could note all that happened as his scheming changed and unfolded. When individual characters died in the last Act, they stood and addressed their final speeches to the theatre audience. These innovations signalled the director's intention to present the tragedy in a political and judgemental context but they often meant that dramatic focus lacked intensity. Webster's carefully nurtured and varied atmosphere and the play's occasional impression of domestic actuality both suffered and made what happened on stage seem distant and pre-meditated. This effect was accentuated by the use of video recording to give disembodied impressions of crazed behaviour on a large screen in place of the actual presence of madmen. The production made its audience think about the consequences of action but did not trust the means that Webster had used to give the tragedy life on stage. Ignoring the composure of the Duchess's speech during her last moments, her death was a struggle against brute violence, as if she had no resource other than her weaker physical strength and inchoate cries of pain and protest. This production was another failure to establish a tragic view of existence, nor did it offer a coherent view of a dysfunctional society such as academic study has found in the text and towards which a number of productions with fewer resources have made notable progress.

The foregoing account of British productions since the Second World War draws upon first-hand experience of performances but the present editor has had no opportunity to sample productions of the play elsewhere. What follows is a list of the few North American productions that, according to press reviews, made strong impressions on their audiences.

| 1971 Stratford Festival Ontario | *Duchess*, Pat Galloway; *Ferd.*, Roland Hewgill; *Bos.*, Powys Thomas. Designed by Desmond Heeley; directed by Jean Gascon. |
| 1976 Mark Taper Forum, Los Angeles | *Duchess*, Eileen Atkins; *Ferd.*, Robin Gammell; *Bos.*, Henry Hoffman. Designed by Paul Sylbert; directed by Howard Sackler. |

CRITICISM AND SCHOLARSHIP

During the first decades of the twentieth century, *The Duchess* was principally valued for its occasional poetry, dark 'atmosphere' of menace, and sympathetic portrayal of its heroine alongside the complicated intrigue and sensational villainy that surrounded her. In 1913 the poet Rupert Brooke won a Fellowship at King's College, Cambridge, with a dissertation on Webster that was published in 1916. He found 'childishnesses and blunders' in the two major tragedies but an 'extraordinarily sure touch' in their dialogue: while characters appeared as 'writhing grubs in an immense night,' at times their words had a 'flash from the thundercloud of wrath or passion' with occasionally 'a certain quietude in darkness; but not very much' (pp. 156–8). T. S. Eliot's poem 'Whispers of Immortality' (1919) celebrated this view of Webster:

> Webster was much possessed by death
> And saw the skull beneath the skin; . . .
> He knew that thought clings round dead limbs
> Tightening its lusts and luxuries.

Rupert Brooke also noted that 'several little irrelevant scenes of satire' contributed to the two plays' peculiar atmosphere: these are 'incessant' and their topics 'the ordinary ones, the painting of women, the ingratitude of princes, the swaggering of blusterers, the cowardice of pseudo-soldiers' (p. 121).

In 1927, F. L. Lucas, also of King's College, Cambridge, published a scrupulous, old-spelling edition of Webster's *Complete Works* and in the Introduction eloquently represents current views of *The Duchess*. After marking the play's defects, especially 'the plot's obvious weaknesses', this edition praises:

> [its] picture of a spirit that faces the cold shining of the stars with none of Pascal's terror before their infinite silence, and the mopping and mowing of the demented world around it with a calm that prosperity could not give, nor disaster take away. (vol. ii, 25).

The editor's copious annotations remain valuable for placing Webster in a cultural context as wide as classical learning and an eager mind could reach.

By the mid twentieth century, when leading actors and directors were re-discovering the hold that *The Duchess* can exert over audiences, issues that had long been neglected or harshly judged began to receive closer attention. 'The most serious error that critics of Webster have committed' wrote Irving Ribner, 'has been to regard him as a dramatist lacking moral vision' (1962, p. 99). But a search for this did not immediately bring agreement. According to Ribner, Antonio's death proves 'the nobility of his endurance' (1962, p. 121) but Robert Ornstein judged his death to be 'contemptible' (1960, p. 144). Una Ellis-Fermor thought that the Cardinal 'redeems himself at the last' (1936, p. 180) but Gunnar Bokund argued that death revealed him to be a 'coward', without 'even the redeeming feature of bravado' (1962, pp. 133–4). Some critics found the courtship of Antonio by the Duchess to be 'a charming idyll' but Clifford Leech argued that 'the more we consider the Duchess, the more hints of guilt seem to appear' (1951, p. 75). Bosola was said to be a chorus rather than a character and, on the other hand, a person who, against his own will, develops from illusion to self-knowledge, from spying and cutting throats to penitence and moral purpose. Ferdinand's madness was variously 'convincing' and 'unconvincing', his motivation 'sexual', 'emblematic', 'routine', 'muddled'. Whether critics looked for consistent characterisation or a 'moral vision' in the play, they seldom agreed and often doubted their own judgement. After some ten years, Professor Leech had reconsidered the play's 'inconsistencies' with regard to the Duchess and changed his mind: 'in this compound of attitudes I now think we have Webster's chief claim to major status in this play' (1963, p. 49).

The dramatic form of the tragedy was reappraised in the light of comparative and historical scholarship. Travis Bogard saw Webster's 'tragic satire' as a thoughtful fusion of dramatic modes (1955) and, in an article that was to be frequently reprinted, Inga-Stina Ekeblad took a hint from T. S. Eliot and claimed that Webster had very consciously created an 'impure art' and followed no single pattern or mode (1958). She showed how the tortures endured by the Duchess are not an indulgent accumulation of horrors with no better purpose than to thrill an audience but a carefully modified Court masque that demonstrated both the predicament of the Duchess and the dangerous fantasies of Ferdinand. Song and dance, mad antics, obsessive speech and representative characters served to draw an audience's attention to the contrasting silence of the Duchess, her suffering expressed physically in her constant presence.

The wide perspective of Michael Neill's *Issues of Death: Mortality and Identity in English Renaissance Tragedy* (1997) gave a clearer view of the structural importance of the recurrent images of graves and monuments in *The Duchess*, the sustained focus on the heroine in Act IV, the continuation of the tragedy for another Act and, especially, the seeming reappearance of the Duchess in the Echo scene (v.iii). Professor Neill argued that 'the full significance of the Duchess's death is hardly comprehensible outside the context created by the fifth act' in which Bosola emerges as 'the tragedy's second protagonist' and its action as 'a dramatized pageant of Fame' (pp. 330–1). He supported his argument by quoting Webster's elegy for Prince Henry, the dedication and commendatory poems printed with *The Duchess*, plays by Middleton, Marlowe, Shakespeare and Ford, and inscriptions and figures on monuments erected in memory of famous lives.

The full range of criticism that was being developed to study Shakespeare was employed on Webster's plays. Following major studies of 'Shakespeare's Imagery', verbal and visual images in the two tragedies were scrutinized with more methodical care. In 1955 an influential article by Hereward T. Price distinguished the 'resolute consistency with which Webster elaborates an extended sequence of diverse but interrelated images' as a unique mark of his tragedies (1955). The cultural and materialist study of Shakespeare, epitomized in Jonathan Dollimore's *Radical Tragedy: Religion, Ideology, and Power in the Drama of Shakespeare and His Contemporaries* (1984), has left a wide wake in Webster studies. For example, Dena Goldberg's *Between Worlds* (1987) explores Webster's radical attitudes to the law and authority. Frank Whigham's account of 'Sexual and Social Mobility in *The Duchess of Malfi*' sees Ferdinand 'as a threatened aristocrat, frightened by the contamination of his ascriptive social rank, and obsessively preoccupied with its defense' (1985; 1996, p. 191). M. C. Bradbrook's *John Webster* had for its subtitle '*Citizen and Dramatist*', indicating that by 1980 the social and political context in which the dramatist wrote had already become a major subject of study, as well as literary influences and associations.

Feminist critics have examined the Duchess's sexuality, gender and status in society as wife, widow, mother, lover, sister and prince: these are very obvious features of her role in the play that have now been given a more careful and questioning attention. The 'New Casebook' on *The Duchess of Malfi* (Callaghan, 2000) reprints articles previously scattered in journals and anthologies that are representative of 'gender-conscious criticism' and demonstrate its width and originality, ranging from Jacobean public controversy to the institution of marriage and rights of widows, from conventions of courtship to the silent power of female presence. The play figures frequently in the numerous books that consider feminist issues in tragedies throughout the Jacobean period. For example, Albert H. Triconi's *Reading Tudor-Stuart Texts through Cultural Historicism* (1996), considering the 'mothering body' of the Duchess, finds theatrical and thematic importance when wax figures of her husband and children are revealed to her in prison: by wishing to be bound to the 'lifeless trunk . . . and freeze to death' (IV.i.68–9), she identifies self with family, and so the spectacle:

> releases a core anxiety – that the inexplicable enmity of the world, the all-powerful Other, will destroy every member of our family unity, leaving us bereft, without support love, or safety. (pp. 145–6)

By citing the power structures of Jacobean times, these studies may search out issues that are not treated explicitly in the play-text. Lisa Jardine's *Still Harping on Daughters: Women and Drama in the Age of Shakespeare* (1983), considering Church and Common Law, argues that:

> [the Duchess] lost her princely immunity through forfeiture of her dower – the forfeiture being because she proved herself 'loose' by marrying

without her brothers' consent 'so mean a person as Antonio.... From this moment she is not, despite her own protests to the contrary, "Duchess of Malfi still." (p. 91)

In the twenty-first century a student of Webster has many guides to consult that are almost as various in method and opinion as those who write about Shakespeare. But almost every aspect of *The Duchess of Malfi* both draws and frustrates precise enquiry, perhaps more than any Shakespeare play. The rite and rights of marriage are of crucial importance in the action but Webster has avoided any accepted form of words or ceremony so that nothing in the play is of general validity or everyday importance. The political power and personal independence of widows were often debated but those of the Duchess are not put to any expected or everyday test. The authority of priests and the schisms in Christianity were matters of grave and political concern but Webster's treatment of saints and devils, the sacraments and theology, seems purposefully ambiguous, even while religion's footprints in the text and stage action are plain for all to see. The new forms of criticism, viewed against earlier ones, have made notable steps forward. First, we now know that Webster was scrupulously concerned to present on stage the society and culture in which he lived at the same time as 'being much possessed by death', showing the power of unspoken thoughts and feelings, and creating a moving and remarkable tragedy. In keeping with his own restless, pragmatic and ingenious mind, his choice of a heroine, rather than hero, seems calculated to intensify enquiry and puzzlement rather than simplify or settle opinion. These decisions are well served by the subtlety and life likeness of the dialogue and the unusual and challenging distribution of action into five contrasting Acts; indeed, these features of the text seem made for each other.

Stage histories and the study of performances, well-established for Shakespeare, have been increasingly used for Webster. For instance, Keith Sturgess's *Jacobean Private Theatre* (1987) has a chapter on 'A perspective that shows us Hell: *The Duchess of Malfi* at the Blackfriars' and Peter Thomson (1970) has considered how present-day actors can find an appropriate style for Jacobean dramas and Webster's tragedies in particular. Lois Potter (1975) discussed the problems of staging a play that stylistically varied between 'realism and nightmare'. Richard Cave's volume for the 'Text and Performance' series (1988) gives accounts of outstanding productions and performances that are mindful of their critical implications.

David Carnegie's 'Theatrical Introduction' to the Cambridge old-spelling edition (1995) provides a twentieth-century stage history that includes professional productions in Dublin, Manchester, New York, Oxford, Pitlochry, Sheffield and Stratford, Ontario, as well as Stratford, England, and London: although lacking space for full appraisals, its considered judgements and, in many cases, first-hand experiences of performance provide a wide basis for comparisons. Taken a little later, as in the necessarily brief account of recent productions in this edition, such a stage history would show *The Duchess* to be unusually open to varying performances of the play's characters and crucial moments in its action. This is especially evident in rehearsal and workshop conditions; Peter Gill had experimented freely with the play's text and action before making his production of *The Duchess*, in a way that he was to find unproductive when he turned to a production of Shakespeare (see Burgess, 2008, pp. 95–6).

Also in common with Shakespeare, a number of anthologies allow comparative study of Webster criticism. Brian Morris's 'Mermaid Critical Commentary' (1970) prints especially commissioned articles and so is able to give a comprehensive view. Other anthologies edited by G. K. and S. K. Hunter (1969), R. V. Holdsworth (1975) and Dympna Callaghan (2000), the last of these including only feminist criticism, bring together previously published articles that are often hard to find elsewhere. Don Moore's survey of criticism from 1617 to 1964 is useful as a survey but does not include details of reprints (1956).

THIS EDITION AND ITS PREDECESSORS

Three quarto editions of *The Duchess of Malfi* followed the first, in 1640, 1678 and 1708. They were all straight reprints, correcting some obvious errors, introducing some new ones and occasionally simplifying difficult passages. The Quarto of 1708 includes stage directions from performances 'at the Queen's Theatre in the Haymarket'. Numerous cuts reduce playing time: the pilgrim scene (III.iv) is gone and both the Reputation and Salmon stories marked for omission. The narrative was tidied up by omitting the references to the Duchess's son by her first marriage (III.ii.100) and the text rephrased to regularize metre and modernize vocabulary. The play is also made more respectable: for example, 'lecher' becomes 'lover' and 'I pour it in your bosom' is omitted (III.ii.100 and III.i.52). This text is useful today as the earliest that provided adequate stage directions.

The present text is that of the first quarto (which I shall call Q), emended where desirable and modernized in spelling. Its punctuation is changed in the interest of readability and some of the irregularities and obscurities introduced by Okes's compositors are removed. All emendations (other than the correction of technical slips such as turned letters, and obvious errors where there is no doubt of the required reading) are noted in the collation, together with those substantive readings from later editions which, in my opinion, might be correct or are of special textual interest. I have normally followed each reading with only its first known authority. Words quoted in the collation from this text are in the type in which they occur in the text. Other readings are quoted in the original spelling but in the same type as the relevant quotation from this text; where more than one authority is given for such a reading, the spelling is that of the first authority quoted.

Act- and scene-divisions are reproduced from Q without the customary indication of the location of the action: this is discussed, in terms of Jacobean and modern staging, in the annotations. I have replaced Q's collective entries at the head of each scene with directions at the appropriate places for individual entries, but the form of Q's entry is always recorded in the collation. I have retained all the stage-directions of the copy-text and have supplied new ones which are the briefest that can make on-stage action clear to a reader; all additions, including each entry after an earlier exit in the same scene, are printed within square brackets. The collation records the authority or for additions or changes to Q's directions and act- and scene-divisions, but I have standardized the manner of marking exits without notification of changes from Q, unless there is some ambiguity (as at III.ii.322).

Because Crane sometimes used italics and capitals at his own discretion, and because the compositors sometimes regularized the one and modified the other, I have followed normal modern practice in these respects, collating changes only where the sense is affected or where Q's italics indicate quotation or song. I have, however, made an exception for sententious statements which are clearly marked as such in Q. Unlike those who set *The White Devil*, both compositors of *The Duchess* marked *sententice* throughout the play,

B with quotation marks (and once with both italic type and inset-ting) and A with italic type (occasionally inset) or with quotation marks. Moreover, a press-variant shows that one such notation was added during press-correction (III.v.75), thus indicating a concern for such detail in the printing-shop; and, being on the inner forme of Sheet H, this may have been introduced by Webster himself. I have used italic type without insetting in order to mark these pas-sages, noting Q's arrangement in the collation. I have also followed the use of roman type for salient words in the generally italicized dedication; Q's usage here is not paralleled in the text of the play and may represent that of Webster's autograph dedication.

Knowledge about the setting of Q from cast-off copy has been used to judge suspected mislineation. I have also borne in mind Webster's undoubted employment, in this play and *The White Devil*, of incomplete verse-lines and short passages of prose for dramatic effects: see, for example, I.i.496 and IV.i.108, and Revels *W.D.*, pp. lxx–lxxi. However, the proper arrangement of some passages remains uncertain (as at II.iv.51–5 and 72–4, and III.ii.33–5, 61, 160, 235 and 246–7) and so I have made it a rule to collate all modifications of Q's verse-lining and to record Q's precise arrangements wherever there is some doubt whether a speech, or part of a speech, which I have printed as prose should be so, or whether a new paragraph should be marked in a prose speech. I have printed the beginning of each new speech on a new line, judging that Q's variations from this rule in a few sheets were introduced to save text-space. Where the end of one speech and the beginning of the next clearly make up one verse-line I have indicated this by insetting the second half-line. Where two arrangements seemed possible (as at v.ii.99–100) I have taken dramatic effectiveness into account as well as the metre. Where the proper arrangement remained in doubt (as at I.i.311–12) I have printed both consecutive half-lines without insetting. Modi-fications of Q's placing of the first lines of speeches are not recorded in the collation.

The only departures from modern spelling in this text are a few archaic forms where a rhyme or a primary sense would be lost by the modern form; in such cases, and where an archaic form *might* be preferred, the collation records the authority for the text's spell-ing and notes one or more alternative spellings. All contractions have been expanded, changes being collated only where the correct form is debatable. Where the metre clearly demands elision within a word, Q has been modified if necessary – this rule is particularly expedient in view of Crane's known habits as a transcriber – and the usual modern elided form used. These changes are not recorded but, where the metre suggests elision involving more than one word, Q's form has usually been retained and any change collated. In prose Q's elisions are not retained except between words or where emphasis in speaking seems to be affected (as in 'o'erladen' instead of 'overladen' at 1.i.49). Changes in elision in prose are not collated.

The original punctuation of the play – the pointing of the lines suggested by Webster's fair copy – can never be recovered. This text has therefore been re-punctuated throughout, using as a guide the lively pointing of the first quarto of *The White Devil*, which was probably set from an autograph copy, as well as what is known of the influences that affected the printing of Q. The dash is used more frequently than is usual to supplement a colon, full stop or comma and, sometimes, to replace other punctuation or to indicate that speech is broken off unexpectedly. The result is dialogue punctuated to indicate underlying shifts of attention, thought and feeling, as well as grammatical structure. The collation does not record these changes from Q unless they affect the sense or clearly modify dramatic emphasis in delivery.

For collating the 1640 quarto I have used the copy in the British Museum with the press-mark 644 f. 73. The following is a list of editions collated and of symbols used to refer to them:

Q   First Quarto of 1623; variant readings due to proof-correction during printing are distinguished by 'Q^a' for the uncorrected state, 'Q^b' and 'Q^c' for successive corrected states.
Q2   Second Quarto of 1640.
Q3   Third Quarto of 1678.
Q4   Fourth Quarto of 1708.
Scott   Walter Scott, *Ancient British Drama* (1810), III.
Dyce i   A. Dyce, *The Works of John Webster* (1830), I.
Dyce ii   A. Dyce, *The Works of John Webster* (1857).
Haz   W. Hazlitt, *The Dramatic Works of John Webster* (1857), II.
Kel   J. S. Keltie, *The Works of the British Dramatists* (Edinburgh, 1870).
Samp   M. W. Sampson, *The White Devil and The Duchess of Malfi* (Boston and London, 1904).
Thorn   A. H. Thorndike, *Webster & Tourneur* (New York, 1922).

Luc i   F. L. Lucas, *The Complete Works of John Webster* (1927), II.

Har   G. B. Harrison, *Selected Plays of Webster and Ford* (1933).

McIl   A. K. McIlwraith, *Five Stuart Tragedies* (1953).

Luc ii   F. L. Lucas, *The Duchess of Malfi* (1958).

Bren   Elizabeth Brennan, *The Duchess of Malfi* (1964).

Cam   David Gunby *et al.*, *The Works of John Webster*, Cambridge edition, vol. i (1995).

Brown ii   John Russell Brown, *The Duchess of Malfi* (1997).

Brown iii   This edition, *The Duchess of Malfi*, The Revels second edition.

NOTES

1 Her inconsistencies exemplify Catherine Belsey's thesis that early modern women lack 'any single position that they can identify as theirs' so that in tragedies they display an '"inconstancy" which is typically feminine' (p. 149).

2 See, for example, III.i.92–3; III.ii.297–8, 321–2, 330–1; III.iv.43–4; III. v.10–1, 30–1, 51–2, 74–5, 136–41, 143–4. It is notable that the couplets are more frequent in the final scene of the Act, making a strong final impression before the break in action and change of location.

3 A is clearest on Ss1–3, 4^v, 8^v, and Tt1–2^v, 3^v–4; for B on Ss5^v–6, 8.

4 Orgel, 1996, gives a fair and full account of recent scholarship on this subject.

THE
TRAGEDY

OF THE DVTCHESSE
Of Malfy.

As it was Preſented priuatly, at the Black-
Friers; and publiquely at the Globe, By the
Kings Maieſties Seruants.

The perfect and exact Coppy, with diuerſe
things Printed, that the length of the Play would
not beare in the Preſentment.

VVritten by *John Webſter.*

Flora.——— *Si quid*----
——— *Candidus Imperti ſi non his vtere mecum.*

Jo: yatos .

Printed by NICHOLAS OKES, for IOHN
WATERSON, and are to be ſold at the
ſigne of the Crowne, in *Paules*
Church-yard, 1623.

THE DUCHESS OF MALFI

[Dedication]

To the Right Honourable, George Harding, Baron Berkeley
of Berkeley Castle, and Knight of the Order of the Bath to
the Illustrious Prince Charles.

My Noble Lord,

That I may present my excuse why, being a stranger to your   5
lordship, I offer this poem to your patronage, I plead this
warrant: men who never saw the sea, yet desire to behold that
regiment of waters, choose some eminent river to guide them
thither, and make that, as it were, their conduct or *postilion*;
by the like ingenious means has your *fame* arrived at my   10
knowledge, receiving it from some of worth who both in *con-*
templation and *practice* owe to your *Honour* their clearest
service. I do not altogether look up at your *title*, the ancientest
nobility being but a *relic* of time past, and the truest *honour*

4–31.] *italicized Q.*   9. etc. *postilion, fame*, etc.] *roman Q.*

---

1. *George Harding*] Son of Sir Thomas Berkeley by Elizabeth Carey
(daughter of George, Lord Hunsdon), he was born 7 Oct. 1601. In 1619 he
was entered as canon-commoner at Christ Church, Oxford. He travelled
widely and died in 1658. While still at Oxford he received the dedication
of Burton's *Anatomy* (1621); and gave the author the living of Seagrave,
Leics., in 1630. Some years after Webster's dedication he received those of
Massinger's *Renegado* (1630) and Shirley's *Young Admiral* (1637).

7–9. *men ... thither*] found in Erasmus, *Adagia* (from Plautus, *Poenulus*, III.
iii): '*Viam qui nescit, qua deveniat ad mare, / Eum oportet amnem quaerere comitem*
sibi'. See also Tilley R137: 'Follow the river and you'll get to the sea'.

9. *conduct*] conductor, escort.

postilion] guide, forerunner; a word introduced into English at the end
of the 16th century, and still restricted to these meanings (cf. *O.E.D.*).

11–12. *some ... service*] perhaps the King's Men, who as the Chamber-
lain's Men had 'served' Lord Hunsdon (see l. 1, note above); *clearest* =
unqualified, most entire.

13. *look up*] The sense of 'feel respect' is first recorded by *O.E.D.* in
Bacon, *New Atlantis* (1626).

13–14. *ancientest ... past*] Cf. *D.L.C.*, I.i.40–1: 'Gentrie ... [is] nought
else / But a superstitous relique of time past': both passages echo Overbury's
The Wife (1614), xx.3.

indeed being for a man to confer *honour* on himself, which   15
your *learning* strives to propagate and shall make you arrive
at the *dignity* of a great *example*. I am confident this work is
not unworthy your *Honour*'s perusal; for by such *poems* as this,
poets have kissed the hands of *great princes* and drawn their
gentle eyes to look down upon their sheets of paper when the   20
poets themselves were bound up in their winding sheets. The
like courtesy from your *Lordship* shall make you live in your
grave and *laurel* spring out of it, when the ignorant scorners
of the *Muses* (that like worms in *libraries* seem to live only to
destroy *learning*) shall wither, neglected and forgotten. This   25
work and myself I humbly present to your approved censure,
it being the utmost of my wishes to have your Honourable
self my weighty and perspicuous comment: which grace so
done me, shall ever be acknowledged

By your Lordship's   30
in all duty and observance,
John Webster.

---

32. *John Webster*] roman *Q.*

18–20. *by . . . paper*] Cf. Dedication, *D.L.C.*: 'I present this humbly . . .
knowing the greatest of Caesars, haue cheerfully entertain'd lesse Poems
then this', which Dent paralleled in Warner's dedication of *The Continuance
of Albion's England* (1606).
    26. *approved censure*] tested judgement.
    28. *perspicuous*] perhaps 'discerning' rather than, more properly, 'lucid'.

[Commendatory Verses]

In the just worth of that well-deserver, Mr. John Webster, and
upon this masterpiece of tragedy.

> In this thou imitat'st one rich, and wise,
> That sees his good deeds done before he dies;
> As he by works, thou by this work of fame,   5
> Hast well provided for thy living name.
> To trust to others' honourings is worth's crime –
> Thy monument is rais'd in thy life-time;
> And 'tis most just; for every worthy man
> Is his own marble, and his merit can   10
> Cut him to any figure and express
> More art than Death's cathedral palaces,
> Where royal ashes keep their court. Thy note
> Be ever plainness, 'tis the richest coat:
> Thy epitaph only the title be –   15
> Write, 'Duchess', that will fetch a tear for thee,
> For who e'er saw this duchess live, and die,
> That could get off under a bleeding eye?

> *In Tragœdiam.*

> *Ut lux ex tenebris ictu percussa Tonantis,*   20
> *Illa, ruina malis, claris fit vita poetis.*
> > Thomas Middletonus,
> > *Poeta & Chron. Londinensis.*

VERSES] Ford was later to commend plays by Massinger, Shirley and
Brome, but Middleton and Rowley never performed this service for another
play.

19–21.] 'To Tragedy: As light from darkness springs at the Thunderer's
stroke, / So she brings ruin to the wicked and life to the poet'.

22. *Middletonus*] Thomas Middleton collaborated with Webster during
their earlier days (cf. Revels *W.D.*, pp. xvii–xviii) and again for *A.Q.L.*,
performed by the King's Men in 1621 (cf. *Works*, Cambridge, i, p. 12). He
frequently collaborated with Rowley, here his fellow commender, in the years
around 1620. He was appointed City Chronologer, 6 Sept. 1620.

To his friend, Mr. John Webster, upon his *Duchess of Malfi*.

I never saw thy duchess till the day 25
That she was lively body'd in thy play;
Howe'er she answer'd her low-rated love,
Her brothers' anger did so fatal prove,
Yet my opinion is, she might speak more,
But never, in her life, so well before. 30

Wil. Rowley.

To the reader of the author, and his *Duchess of Malfi*.

Crown him a poet, whom nor Rome, nor Greece,
Transcend in all theirs, for a masterpiece:
In which, whiles words and matter change, and men 35
Act one another, he, from whose clear pen
They all took life, to memory hath lent
A lasting fame, to raise his monument.

John Ford.

---

26. *body'd*] embodied.
27. *answer'd*] justified.
28. *Her...prove*] i.e., 'Which her...'.
29. *Yet*] still, now as always.
31. Rowley] actor and dramatist (c. 1585–1625/6): he collaborated with Webster twice in 1624–25 (cf. Revels *W.D.*, p. xxv).
35–6. *whiles...another*] i.e., 'while literature has its fashions and the theatre continues to exist'; *words and matter* was a common phrase, opposing the style and substance of writing.
37. *all*] i.e., words, substance, and character.
39.] John Ford (1586–?1639) may have commenced dramatist, like Webster, under Dekker's tutelage (so Bentley): he collaborated with Webster (and Dekker and Rowley) in the lost *Late Murder in Whitechapel* (1624).

The Actors' Names

[as given in the first edition].

Bosola, *J. Lowin.*
Ferdinand, 1. *R. Burbidge.* 2. *J. Taylor.*
Cardinal, 1. *H. Cundaile.* 2. *R. Robinson.*
Antonio, 1. *W. Ostler.* 2. *R. Benfield.*
Delio, *J. Underwood.*   5
Forobosco, *N. Towley.*
Malateste.
The Marquis of Pescara, *J. Rice.*
Silvio, *T. Pollard.*
The several madmen, *N. Towley, J. Underwood, etc.*   10
The Duchess, *R. Sharpe.*
The Cardinal's Mistress, *J. Tomson.*
The Doctor, ⎫
Cariola,   ⎬ *R. Pallant.*
                ⎭
Court Officers.   15
Three young children.
Two Pilgrims.

[Dramatis Personae

FERDINAND, *Duke of Calabria, twin brother to the Duchess.*
The Cardinal, *their brother.*

1–17.] *before dedication, A₂ᵛ, Q.*   13–14.] *bracket so Luc ii; bracket opposite*
Cariola *and* Court Officers *Q. Dramatis Personae....]* so this ed.

Actors' Names] *The Duchess* is the earliest English play to be published
with a list of actors assigned to individual roles; this innovation was not
copied until 1629, in plays by the courtier Carlell, and Massinger and
Shirley. For the casting, see Intro., pp. 49–51.
   Dramatis personae were often printed before plays. Here Bosola has been
given unprecedented prominence at the head of the list; characters were
usually placed in order of rank and status, with males first. Webster may have
been responsible for this (cf. Intro., pp. 44–5), thus expressing his view of
the play's dramatic structure and the relative importance of its characters.
   6. *Forobosco*] Cf. Intro., p. 47.

DANIEL DE BOSOLA, *returned from imprisonment in the galleys*
following service for the Cardinal; later the Provisor of Horse
to the Duchess, and in the pay of Ferdinand.   5
ANTONIO BOLOGNA, *Steward of the Household to the Duchess;*
later her husband.
DELIO, *his friend; a courtier.*
CASTRUCHIO, *an old lord; husband of Julia.*
Marquis of PESCARA, *a soldier.*   10
Count MALATESTE, *a courtier at Rome.*
SILVIO, *a courtier at Malfi and Rome.*
RODERIGO }
GRISOLAN } *courtiers at Malfi.*
Doctor.   15

The Duchess of Malfi, *a young widow; later wife of Antonio;*
sister to the Cardinal and twin sister to Ferdinand.
CARIOLA, *her waiting-woman.*
JULIA, *wife of Castruchio and mistress of the Cardinal.*   20
Old Lady, *a midwife.*

Two Pilgrims.
Eight Madmen, *being an Astrologer, Lawyer, Priest, Doctor,*
English Tailor, Gentleman Usher, Farmer, and Broker.
Court Officers; Servants; Guards; Executioners; Attendants;   25
Churchmen.
Ladies-in-Waiting.

SCENE: *Malfi, Rome, Loretto, the countryside near Ancona,*
and Milan.]

The Duchess of Malfi
Act I

Enter ANTONIO *and* DELIO.

Delio. You are welcome to your country, dear Antonio –
　　You have been long in France, and you return
　　A very formal Frenchman in your habit.
　　How do you like the French court?
Ant. 　　　　　　　　　　　　I admire it –
　　In seeking to reduce both state and people　　　　　5
　　To a fix'd order, their judicious king

1.i.0.1.] *Q4; Antonio, and Delio, Bosola, Cardinall Q.*

Actus . . . Prima] Ralph Crane (cf. Intro., pp. 45–6) followed a common practice in using Latin for marking act- and scene-divisions. But he may have represented his author's wishes here, for *D.L.C.* (a literary, rather than theatrical, text) also has Latin divisions. The first ed. of *W.D.* has no divisions.

　　2. *long in France*] Cf. Painter; App. I, pp. 245–50.
　　3. *formal*] precise, punctilious.
　　habit] dress.
　　5–15.] probably from Elyot, *Image of Governance* (1541), viii: Mammen, mother of Alexander Severus, 'with good reson perswaded to hym, that he coulde neuer wel stablyshe his astate Imperyall, but onely by reducynge of the senate and people into their prystinate order, whyche coulde neuer be brought to passe, except that fyrste his own palaice were cleane purged of personages corrupted with vices, . . . consydering that the princis palaice is lyke a common fountayne or sprynge to his citie or countrey, wherby the people by the cleannes therof longe preserued in honestie, or by the impurenes therof, are with sundry vyces corrupted. And vntylle the fountain be purged, there can neuer be any sure hope of remedy. / Wherefore Alexander immediatly after that he had receiued of the senate and people the name of Augustus, . . . fyrste he dyscharged all mynysters, . . . banyshing also out of his palaice, al such as he mought by any meanes knowe, to be persones infamed, semblably flatterers, . . .' The passage can be paralleled in many Renaissance books on policy, but Webster is indebted to Elyot at 1.i.398–403. For the dramatic and topical importance of this speech, see Intro., pp. 8–9 and 11.
　　5. *reduce*] bring, restore.
　　state] ruling body, grand council; cf. Elyot's 'senate and people'.

Begins at home: quits first his royal palace
Of flatt'ring sycophants, of dissolute
And infamous persons – which he sweetly terms
His Master's masterpiece, the work of heaven –   10
Consid'ring duly, that a prince's court
Is like a common fountain, whence should flow
Pure silver drops in general: but if't chance
Some curs'd example poison 't near the head,
Death, and diseases through the whole land spread.   15
And what is't makes this blessed government,
But a most provident Council, who dare freely
Inform him the corruption of the times?
Though some o'th' court hold it presumption
To instruct princes what they ought to do,   20
It is a noble duty to inform them
What they ought to foresee: –

Enter BOSOLA.

                                    Here comes Bosola,
The only court-gall: – yet I observe his railing
Is not for simple love of piety;
Indeed he rails at those things which he wants,   25
Would be as lecherous, covetous, or proud,

15.] *italicized this ed.*; "Death . . . Q.   22. S.D.] *so this ed.*; *at l. o.1 Q; after
l. 28 ('. . . Bosola, Cardinal') Q4.*

---

12. *fountain*] spring of water.
13. *in general*] everywhere.
14. *head*] (1) source, (2) chief person, ruler.
16–22. *And . . . foresee*] Dent compared Painter, *Palace*, II (1567), xiii,
p. 87: the Senate addresses Trajan, 'sith you wrote unto us the maner and
order what we ought to do: reason it is that we write to you againe what you
ought to foresee . . . Princes oftentimes be negligent of many things, not for
that they will not foresee the same, but rather for want of one that dare tel
them what they ought to doe.'
23. *court-gall*] court-scourge. Primarily, *gall* = 'sore, produced by chafing',
and hence 'harasser, tormenter'. But *gall* also = 'bile' and, hence, 'asperity,
bitterness of spirit', and something of this is implied by 'rail' of ll. 23 and
25. Shakespeare often associated *gall* = 'bile' with railing; cf. *Troil.*, I.iii.193:
'whose gall coins slanders like a mint'.
25–8. *he rails . . . so*] from *A.T.*, v.ii.2932–4: 'We what we wish for most,
seeme to mislike: / And oft of others doe the course disproue, / Whilst we
want nought but meanes to doe the like'.

Bloody, or envious, as any man,
If he had means to be so: –

Enter Cardinal.

Here's the cardinal.
Bos. I do haunt you still.
Card.   So.
Bos.   I have done you
Better service than to be slighted thus: –   30
Miserable age, where only the reward
Of doing well, is the doing of it.
Card. You enforce your merit too much.
Bos. I fell into the galleys in your service, where for two years
together, I wore two towels instead of a shirt, with a knot   35
on the shoulder, after the fashion of a Roman mantle: –
slighted thus? I will thrive some way: blackbirds fatten
best in hard weather; why not I, in these dog-days?
Card. Would you could become honest.
Bos. With all your divinity, do but direct me the way to it –   40
[*Exit* Cardinal.] I have known many travel far for it, and

---

28. S.D.] *so this ed; at l. o.1 Q; at end of line* ('. . . *Bosola, Cardinal') Q4.*
29–32. I have . . .] *so Q; as prose Dyce i.*   41. S.D.] *so this ed.; after them,*
l. 44 Dyce i.

---

27. *envious*] Envy, like pride, wrath, etc., was a deally sin.
29. *haunt*] follow after; or, perhaps, 'search for' (cf. *W.D.*, II.i.175,
note).
31–2.] probably taken from Florio (there derived from Seneca and Cicero),
II. xvi: 'The reward of wel doing, is the doing, & the fruit of our duty, is our
dutie'; the idea was proverbial, as 'Virtue is its own reward' (Tilley V81).
Cf. Bosola's last couplet, v.v.103–4.
35–6. *I . . . mantle*] Cf. 1HIV, IV.ii.44–51. Sarcastically, Bosola gives a
mock dignity to poverty.
37–8. *blackbirds . . . weather*] Dent compared Hall, *Epistles* (1611), VI.vii:
'growne wealthy with warre, like those Fowles which fatten with hard
weather . . .' The particularization of '*black*-birds' may be Webster's
independent colouring to show Bosola's cast of mind; perhaps he is dressed
in black as a melancholic (see ll. 74, 81 and 278) or poor scholar (see
III.iii.41–7).
38. *dog-days*] days during the Heliacal rising of the Dog-star, renowned
as the hottest and most unwholesome time of the year; usually reckoned as
the forty days following II August.
41. S.D.] An early exit seems preferable: so the Cardinal does not appear
to wait on Bosola's words, and Bosola's tendency towards soliloquy, or

yet return as arrant knaves as they went forth, because
they carried themselves always along with them; – Are
you gone? Some fellows, they say, are possessed with the
devil, but this great fellow were able to possess the great-   45
est devil, and make him worse.

Ant. He hath denied thee some suit?

Bos. He, and his brother, are like plum-trees, that grow
crooked over standing pools; they are rich, and o'erladen
with fruit, but none but crows, pies, and caterpillars feed   50
on them; could I be one of their flattering panders, I
would hang on their ears like a horse-leech till I were full,
and then drop off: – I pray leave me.

Who would rely upon these miserable dependences, in
expectation to be advanced tomorrow? what creature   55
ever fed worse than hoping Tantalus? nor ever died any
man more fearfully than he that hoped for a pardon.

---

54. and] *Q2*; an *Q*.   54–61.] *4, out of 6, lines justified as prose (exceptionally)
in Q*.   54. dependences] *Q*; dependencies *Dyce i*.   56. died] *Q^b*; did *Q^a*.
57. pardon] *Q^b*; pleadon *Q^a*.

'contemplation' (cf. II.i.76), is established at the outset. 'Are you gone?', a
few lines later, implies that the Cardinal has already left the stage and that
Bosola has not watched him for some time.

41–3. *I . . . them*] Cf. Florio, I.xxxviii: 'It was told Socrates, that one was
no whit amended by his travell: I beleeve it well (saide he) for he carried
himselfe with him'.

48–51. *like . . . them*] a common simile, usually of fig trees growing on
steep mountains; Dent found one example with fig trees 'growing ouer deepe
Waters, full of Fruite, but the Iayes eate them: Ruffians, Harlots, vicious
Companions enjoy those Graces, that might honour God', in T. Adams,
Gallant's Burden (1612), F2.

standing = stagnant; cf. Tilley P465: 'Standing pools gather filth'.

crows, pies, and *caterpillars* were frequently used of inhuman men: feeding
on carrion; wily (magpies); and rapacious.

52. *horse-leech*] i.e., blood-sucker; cf. *W.D.*, v.vi.166.

55–6. *what . . . Tantalus*] from Whetstone, *Heptameron* (1582), I2^v: ' . . . no
man dyneth worse, then hoping Tantalus'.

Tantalus was a proverbial figure of the hoping and disappointed man; the
Eng. vb 'tantalize' is derived from his name. He was said to have been pun-
ished in Hades by perpetual thirst and by being placed in the middle of a
lake of water which receded whenever he tried to drink; fruit hung above
him which always eluded his grasp; and a huge rock over his head was always
threatening to fall.

There are rewards for hawks, and dogs, when they have
done us service; but for a soldier, that hazards his limbs
in a battle, nothing but a kind of geometry is his last   60
supportation.

Delio. Geometry?

Bos. Ay, to hang in a fair pair of slings, take his latter swing
in the world upon an honourable pair of crutches, from
hospital to hospital – fare ye well sir. And yet do not you   65
scorn us, for places in the court are but like beds in the
hospital, where this man's head lies at that man's foot,
and so lower, and lower.   [*Exit.*]

---

58. dogs,] *Q2*; dogges, and *Q*; dogs, and horses, *conj. Luc i*; dogs, and
whores, *conj. this ed.*   68. Exit] *Q4*.

---

58. *dogs,*] Q's 'dogges, and' may be due to the erroneous repetition of the
preceding 'and'. But *service* is not particularly appropriate to either *dogs* or
hawks, and an omission may be suspected. But more evidence must be
considered. First, 'dogges, and' is at the end of a line of text in Q and followed by a space sufficient for three to five pieces of type; this is remarkable
in that the three previous lines and the one following have been 'justified'
to run to the full width of the text-space, as usual in setting prose but unique
in this book (see Intro., p. 45). Perhaps a gap in the prose was intentional
and represented the compositor's copy where Webster had indicated a
missing word, *whores* being left to the actor to suggest.

Lucas suggested that 'horses' had dropped out, and then warned that
reward as a technical term of the chase is suitable only to *dogs* and *hawks*.
Dent, however, supported this conjecture by quoting Florio who compared
man's treatment of men with his treatment of horses and then of *dogs* and
hawks: 'The men that serve vs, doe it better cheape, and for a less curious
and favourable entreating, than we use vnto birds, vnto horses, and vnto
dogges . . . We share the fruites of our prey with our dogges and hawkes, as
a meede of their paine and reward for their industry' (II.xii).

Further evidence is Webster's use of *reward* elsewhere: at II.ii.15–18,
Bosola speaks of 'reward' for women's 'entertainment'; and in *W.D.* Vittoria,
having blamed Bracciano for treating her as a whore, makes her last reproach,
'Your dog or hawk should be *rewarded* better / Than I have been' (IV.ii.107–
19, 136, 145 and 190–1). If a word is missing in association with *reward*,
hawks and *dogs*, it may well be 'whores'. The following *service*, *limbs* and
supportation also have associations fitting to 'whores'.

60. *geometry*] 'Hang by geometry' (i.e., goes on crutches) was a proverbial
phrase; see Tilley G82 who quotes *Match at Midnight* by Webster's friend
Rowley: 'Look you, here's Jarvis, hangs by geometry'.

63. *swing*] quibblingly: (1) 'forcible movement', as on crutches, and
(2) 'fling' ('to *take* one's *swing*' was to indulge oneself, as with mod.
'fling').

Delio. I knew this fellow seven years in the galleys
    For a notorious murder, and 'twas thought   70
    The cardinal suborn'd it: he was releas'd
    By the French general, Gaston de Foix,
    When he recover'd Naples.
Ant.   'Tis great pity
    He should be thus neglected – I have heard
    He's very valiant: this foul melancholy   75
    Will poison all his goodness, for – I'll tell you –
    If too immoderate sleep be truly said
    To be an inward rust unto the soul,
    It then doth follow want of action
    Breeds all black malcontents, and their close rearing,   80
    Like moths in cloth, do hurt for want of wearing.

---

72. Foix] *Q2* (Foyx); Foux *Q*. 81.1.] *Samp; Scena II. / Antonio, Delio, Ferdinand, Cardinall, Dutchesse, Castruchio, Siluio. Rodocico, Grisolan, Bosola, Iulia, Cariola Q; Exeunt. / Scena II. / Enter Antonio, Delio, Ferdinand, Castruchio, Sylvio Q4; not in Dyce ii.*

---

72. *Foix*] Webster probably wrote thus, and not 'Foux' as in Q, for the name derives from Painter (see App. I, p. 249); extant MSS. by Crane occasionally have too many minims in a word. Foix was too young to have had a part in the relief of Naples in 1501.

75. *melancholy*] This was both a mental disease (thought to be due to an excess of 'black bile'; cf. T. Bright's *Treatise of Melancholy*, 1586) and an affectation. In Renaissance Italy, partly on the authority of Marsilio Ficino, the disease was regarded as the infirmity of great minds, and so it became fashionable to affect it; 'malcontents', disappointed by their fortunes or opposed to an established regime, were especially given to this pose. In the 1580s the fashion spread to England. Ferdinand assumes that Bosola only affects melancholy, as a 'garb' (l.278).

Malcontents were 'usually black-suited and dishevelled, unsociable, asperous, morosely meditative, taciturn yet prone to occasional railing' (L. Babb, *Elizabethan Malady* (1957), p. 75).

77–81.] Cf. *W.D.*, v.vi.274, and T. Coghan, *Haven of Health* (1584), Hhi^v: 'immoderate sleepe maketh the bodie slowe, and vnapt to honest exercises, and subiect to manie diseases, and the witte dull and vnable either to conceiue or to retaine'.

80. *close*] secret, solitary.

81. *do*] Strictly 'close rearing' is its subject, but this verb is in the plural influenced by 'malcontents' and 'moths'; cf. Abbott §412.

81. S.D.] Following other modern editions, rather than Q, in printing Act I as one single scene is in keeping with the continuous on-stage action. See Intro., p. 45, for Crane's rearrangement of entry directions.

Enter SILVIO, CASTRUCHIO, JULIA, RODERIGO, *and* GRISOLAN.

Delio. The presence 'gins to fill – you promis'd me
To make me the partaker of the natures
Of some of your great courtiers.
Ant.   The Lord Cardinal's
And other strangers', that are now in court?   85
I shall: –

Enter FERDINAND.

Here comes the great Calabrian duke.
Ferd. Who took the ring oftenest?
Sil. Antonio Bologna, my lord.
Ferd. Our sister duchess' great master of her household? Give
him the jewel: – When shall we leave this sportive action,   90
and fall to action indeed?
Cast. Methinks, my lord, you should not desire to go to war
in person.

---

86. S.D.] *so this ed.; at l. 81.1 Q, Q4; at end of line Dyce ii. Ferdinand Q;
Ferdinand, Castruccio, Silvio, Roderigo, Grisolan and Attendants Dyce ii, Ferdinand, with Attendants conj. this ed.*

---

82. *presence*] presence-chamber; the central throne, or 'state', will remain
empty until the Duchess enters at l. 147 (so Cambridge ed.).
87. *ring*] Riding at the *ring*, to carry it away on a lance, was a common
form of jousting.
Webster may have intended Ferdinand to speak with (unintentional)
irony: (1) his abrupt manner of speech on his first, elaborate entry gives
unusual emphasis to the phrase; (2) Antonio 'takes the *ring*' at the end
of this act (ll. 404–15) and in prison Ferdinand gives the Duchess a 'ring'
(iv.i.44–51); and, perhaps, the cord which strangles her is a further echo, for
Cariola's is called her 'wedding ring' (iv.ii.247); and (3) *ring* may have an
(unintentional) undertone that is sexual; it was a common word in sexual
jokes (see, e.g., *Mer.V.*, v.i.304–7) and is here followed by 'jewel' (also
common in bawdy) which in *W.D.*, i.ii.221–8 Webster used for a series of
suggestive puns (and cf. *D.L.C.*, ii.i.296); sexual undertones may be continued in '*fall* to action' (l. 91) and are certainly present by ll. 104 (see note)
and iii–13.
89. *great*] chief.
92–103.] Cf. *W.D.*, ii.i.116–23, and note. Webster is probably indebted
here (as at ll.16–22 above) to Painter, *Palace*, ii (1567), xiii, p. 84: 'Truly it
liketh me wel, that from the degree of Captains men be aduanced to be
Emperors, but I thinke it not good, that Emperours do descend to be Captains, considering that the realme shal neuer be in quiet, when the Prince is
to great a warrior' (so Dent).

Ferd. Now for some gravity! – why, my lord?

Cast. It is fitting a soldier arise to be a prince, but not neces-   95
sary a prince descend to be a captain.

Ferd. No?

Cast. No, my lord, he were far better do it by a deputy.

Ferd. Why should he not as well sleep, or eat, by a deputy?
This might take idle, offensive, and base office from him,   100
whereas the other deprives him of honour.

Cast. Believe my experience: that realm is never long in quiet,
where the ruler is a soldier.

Ferd. Thou told'st me thy wife could not endure fighting.

Cast. True, my lord.   105

Ferd. And of a jest she broke, of a captain she met full of
wounds: – I have forgot it.

Cast. She told him, my lord, he was a pitiful fellow, to lie,
like the children of Israel, all in tents.

Ferd. Why, there's a wit were able to undo all the chirurgeons   110
o' the city, for although gallants should quarrel, and had
drawn their weapons, and were ready to go to it, yet her
persuasions would make them put up.

Cast. That she would, my lord –

Ferd. How do you like my Spanish jennet?   115

---

109. Israel] *Brown iii, conj. Brennan; Ismael Q.*   115. Ferd. How . . .] *conj.*
Samp, this ed.; How . . . *(separate line and inset) Q.*

---

104. *fighting*] with a *double entendre*: the implication is that Castruchio's
'realm', or marriage, is '*un*quiet'.

109. *Israel*] Q's 'Ismael' is an unusual spelling for *Ishmael* and is likely to
be an error. The *O.T.* reports several times that 'the children of Israel' lived
in tents (so Brennan).

tents] (1) ordinary sense, (2) 'surgical dressings', and, possibly, (3) 'intentions' (cf. *O.E.D.*, *sb.* 2). The third meaning is clearer in Middleton, *More
Dissemblers* (?1615), II.iii, where Aurelia complains of a soldier's talk immediately before making the same jest: 'All his discourse [is] out of the Book
of Surgery, / Cere-cloth and salve, and lies you all in tents, / Like your
camp-vic'lers'.

110. *chirurgeons*] surgeons.

111–13. *although* . . .] with *doubles entendres*, especially on *drawn their
weapons* and *put up*.

115. Ferd.] The separate line 'How . . . jennet' is inset in Q as if Compositor B had placed a space in his composing-stick intending to set a
speech-prefix and had then forgotten to add it. Compositor A inset a line in
this way at v.iii.35 where a prefix is clearly omitted.

Rod. He is all fire.

Ferd. I am of Pliny's opinion, I think he was begot by the
wind; he runs as if he were ballasted with quicksilver.

Sil. True, my lord, he reels from the tilt often.

Rod., Gris. Ha, ha, ha!   120

Ferd. Why do you laugh? Methinks you that are courtiers
should be my touch-wood, taken fire, when I given fire;
that is, laugh when I laugh, were the subject never so
witty –

Cast. True, my lord, I myself have heard a very good jest, and   125
have scorned to seem to have so silly a wit as to understand it.

Ferd. But I can laugh at your fool, my lord.

---

123. laugh when] *Q*; Not laugh but when *Q4*; laugh but when *Dyce i.*

A *jennet* is a light, sporting horse (cf. Painter; App. I, p. 253) and quite
inappropriate to the old Castruchio (cf. II.iv.44–5 and 53–6). Moreover,
Ferdinand alone introduces new topics of conversation in this small-talk with
sycophantic courtiers. Lucas, who followed most editors in giving the question to Castruchio, argued that the jest at l.119 would be too audacious to
apply to Ferdinand's horse. But this is probably the reason why Webster
included the passage: he thus demonstrated Ferdinand's power in his quench-
ing of laughter suddenly – always an effective theatrical device for centring
attention on someone's ability to control others. Moreover, the incident
illustrates the precarious life of attendance at Court: Silvio had relaxed sufficiently to forget propriety and the rising enjoyment is rebuked at once.

117. *Pliny's opinion*] Cf. *Natural History* (tr. 1601), xlii: 'In Portugall,
along the river Tagus, and about Lisbon, certaine it is, that when the West
wind bloweth, the mares set up their tailes, and turne them full against it,
and so conceive that genitall aire in steed of naturall seed: in such sort, as
they become great withall, and quicken in their time, and bring foorth foles
as swift as the wind . . .'

118. *ballasted with quicksilver*] The point is, probably, that the ballast that
should slow the horse down is itself *quick* and valuable.

119. *reels . . . tilt*] quibblingly: (1) the ballast rights the *tilt* (as of a boat),
and (2) the horse jibs (as in jousting). Possibly, Roderigo and Grisolan laugh
so noticeably because they sense the common bawdy meaning of *tilt* (cf.
W.D., III.i.16 and note, and 66–73); Bosola's laughter is indicated in the
same way on talk of a codpiece (II.ii.41).

If Ferdinand silences bawdy laughter and yet speaks bawdily himself, his
sexual awareness will seem the more private and dangerous to an
audience.

122. *touch-wood*] tinder.

123. *when I laugh*] i.e., and only then.

126–29. *so silly . . . faces*] Congenital imbeciles were kept as 'fools' in great
households: Castruchio's was a dumb idiot.

Cast. He cannot speak, you know, but he makes faces – my
lady cannot abide him.   130

Ferd. No?

Cast. Nor endure to be in merry company: for she says too
much laughing, and too much company, fills her too full
of the wrinkle.

Ferd. I would then have a mathematical instrument made for   135
her face, that she might not laugh out of compass: – I
shall shortly visit you at Milan, Lord Silvio.

Sil. Your grace shall arrive most welcome.

Ferd. You are a good horseman, Antonio – you have excellent riders in France; what do you think of good   140
horsemanship?

Ant. Nobly, my lord – as out of the Grecian horse issued
many famous princes, so, out of brave horsemanship,
arise the first sparks of growing resolution, that raise the
mind to noble action.   145

Ferd. You have bespoke it worthily.

> *Enter* Cardinal, Duchess, CARIOLA [*with* Attendants].

Sil. Your brother, the Lord Cardinal, and sister Duchess.

Card. Are the galleys come about?

Gris. They are, my lord.

Ferd. Here's the Lord Silvio, is come to take his leave.   150

Delio. Now sir, your promise: what's that cardinal?
I mean his temper? they say he's a brave fellow,
Will play his five thousand crowns at tennis, dance,
Court ladies, and one that hath fought single combats.

146.1. *with Attendants*] *This ed.; and Bosola Q4; and Julia Dyce i.*

---

136. *out of compass*] immoderately, beyond due limits; with a pun on
compass as a 'mathematical instrument' (l. 135).

139. *You . . . Antonio*] Cf. Painter; App. I, p. 249.

138–40. *excellent . . . France*] The French were commonly held to be good
riders; cf. *W.D.*, IV.iii.96. The Trojan horse was filled with Greek soldiers.

148–9.] This exchange is never developed in narrative or in the relationship between the two men: it is a brief, but theatrically effective, device for
suggesting the alert and independent intrigues behind the façade of formal
Court-life.

150.] With the Duchess seated in her state, 'Silvio approaches and bends
the knee. . . . the formal leave-taking becomes in effect a dumb show on
which Antonio and Delio comment' (Cambridge ed.).

153. *Will . . . tennis*] Cf. *W.D.*, II.i.182, and note.

Ant. Some such flashes superficially hang on him, for form;   155
but observe his inward character: – he is a melancholy
churchman; the spring in his face is nothing but the
engendering of toads; where he is jealous of any man, he
lays worse plots for them than ever was imposed on
Hercules, for he strews in his way flatterers, panders,   160
intelligencers, atheists, and a thousand such political
monsters. He should have been Pope; but instead of
coming to it by the primitive decency of the church, he
did bestow bribes so largely, and so impudently, as if he
would have carried it away without heaven's knowledge.   165
Some good he hath done.

Delio. You have given too much of him: what's his brother?

Ant. The duke there? a most perverse, and turbulent
nature:
What appears in him mirth, is merely outside;   170
If he laugh heartily, it is to laugh
All honesty out of fashion.

Delio.   Twins?

Ant.   In quality: –

---

159. them] *Q;* him *Haz.*   160. flatterers] *Q3;* Flatters *Q.*

155. *form*] merely outward appearances; cf. *W.D.*, IV.iii.144–9 where the
form is modesty, rather than *flashes* of youthful bravery. *O.E.D.* first records
flash = 'ostentation, éclat' in 1674, but = 'showy talk' in Jonson's character
'Sir Petronell Flash' in *Eastward Ho* (1605).

157–8. *spring...toads*] Cf. Chapman, *Bussy* (1604), III.ii.363–5: '...thy
gall/Turns all thy blood to poison, which is cause / Of that toad-pool that
stands in thy complexion'; see also *Mer.V.*, I.i.88–9, and *Oth.*, IV.ii.59–64
(so Lucas).

158. *jealous*] suspicious (a common meaning).

161. *intelligencers*] informers, spies.

atheists] commonly used, in a general sense, for impious or wicked
persons.

political] shrewd, scheming.

162–5. *He...*] perhaps from Hall, *Characters* (1608), 'Ambitious': 'His
wit so contriues the likely plots of his promotion, as if hee would steale it
away without Gods knowledge'.

171–2. *If...fashion*] another possible debt to Hall, *Characters*, 'Profane':
'Euery vertue hath his slander and his iest to laugh it out of fashion'.

172. *Twins?*] Webster probably intended the two brothers and sister to
look alike in appearance and age; Ferdinand later says that he and the
duchess are twins (IV.ii.265). See also I.i.188–9.

He speaks with other's tongues, and hears men's suits
With others' ears; will seem to sleep o'th' bench
Only to entrap offenders in their answers;   175
Dooms men to death by information,
Rewards by hearsay.
Delio.   Then the law to him
Is like a foul black cobweb to a spider –
He makes it his dwelling, and a prison
To entangle those shall feed him.
Ant.   Most true: 180
He ne'er pays debts, unless they be shrewd turns,
And those he will confess that he doth owe.
Last, for his brother, there, the cardinal –
They that do flatter him most say oracles
Hang at his lips: and verily I believe them;   185
For the devil speaks in them.
But for their sister, the right noble duchess –
You never fix'd your eye on three fair medals,
Cast in one figure, of so different temper:
For her discourse, it is so full of rapture   190

181. shrewd] *Q2;* shewed *Q.*   188. your] *Q2;* you *Q.*

173–7. *He . . . hearsay*] from *A.T.*, II.i.570–8: 'Whilst he that rulde still
needing to be rulde, / Spake but with others tongues, heard with their eares.
/ . . . / That of himselfe cannot discerne a crime: / But doomes by information
men to death'.
    information = 'reported intelligence' or 'accusation'.
    177–80. *law . . . him*] Webster has adapted the common proverb, 'the
law, like a cobweb, traps the little and allows the great to escape' (Tilley
L116): Dyce, however, compared Field, *Woman Is a Weathercock* (1612),
II.i.316–19; law 'is a Spiders web / Made to entangle the poore helplesse flies,
/ Whilst the great Spiders that did make it first, / And rule it, sit i' th midst
secure and laugh . . .'
    181–2.] Muriel Bradbrook (*M.L.R.*, 1947) compared Chapman, *Penitential
Psalms* (1612), 'A Great Man': 'Paies neuer debt, but what he should not ow'.
    shrewd turns = 'acts of ill will, injuries' (the opposite to a 'good turn').
    184–5. *They . . . lips*] Cf. Hall, *Characters* (1608), 'Flatterer': 'He hangs
vpon the lips which he admireth, as if they could let fall nothing but
oracles . . .'
    189. *figure*] (1) bodily shape, (2) representation (*O.E.D.*, 4 and 9–10).
    190–205. *For . . . her*] from Pettie, II.241–2: 'her talke and discourses are so
delightfull, that you wyll only then beginne to bee sory, when shee endeth to
speake: and wishe that shee woulde bee no more weary to speake, then you
are to heare . . . She wyll also in talke cast oft times upon a man such a sweete

You only will begin then to be sorry
When she doth end her speech; and wish, in wonder,
She held it less vain-glory to talk much,
Than you penance to hear her: whilst she speaks,
She throws upon a man so sweet a look,   195
That it were able raise one to a galliard
That lay in a dead palsy, and to dote
On that sweet countenance: but in that look,
There speaketh so divine a continence
As cuts off all lascivious, and vain hope.   200
Her days are practis'd in such noble virtue
That sure her nights – nay more, her very sleeps –
Are more in heaven than other ladies' shrifts.
Let all sweet ladies break their flatt'ring glasses,
And dress themselves in her.
Delio.   Fie Antonio,   205
You play the wire-drawer with her commendations.
Ant. I'll case the picture up: – only thus much –
All her particular worth grows to this sum:
She stains the time past, lights the time to come.

194. Than] *Q2;* Then *Q.* you] *Anderson;* your *Q.* 196. able] *Q;* able to
Q3.

***

smyle, that it were enough to bryng him into a fooles Paradise, but that her
countenance couteineth such continencie in it, as is sufficient to cut off all fond
hope . . . I cannot sufficientlye set foorth unto you the graces and perfections
of this perfect peece, but for conclusion I will say, that shee may well bee set
for an example, whereto other women ought to conforme them selves . . .'
   In noting this source, Marcia Anderson (cited by Dent) untangled the
confusion due to Q's 'your' at l. 194.
   196. *galliard*] a lively dance; Davies (*Orchestra*) called it 'gallant . . . / With
lofty turns and capriols in the air'.
   197. *palsy*] paralysis.
   198–9. *countenance . . . continence*] a quibble: both words are derived from
L. *continentia,* and in the 16th century were confused in spelling.
   201–3.] Perhaps suggested by Donne, *Progress of the Soul* (1612), ll. 463–4:
'Whose twilights were more cleare, then our mid-day; / Who dreamt devout-
lier, then most use to pray' (so Lucas).
   nay . . . sleeps alludes to the notion that dreams 'are certaine signes of ye
affections of ye minde . . . : the fearfull dreame that they flye daunger: the
couetous yt they imbrace riches', etc. (Bartholomeous, *De Proprietatibus
Rerum* (tr. 1582), VI.xxvii).
   206. *play the wire-drawer*] spin out your words, make much of little.
   207. *case*] close, cover; cf. III.ii.139.
   209.] from *A.T.,* III.ii.1319: 'Staine of times past, and light of times to
come'.

Cari. You must attend my lady, in the gallery,   210
   Some half an hour hence.
Ant. I shall.
Ferd. Sister, I have a suit to you: –
Duch.   To me, sir?
Ferd. A gentleman here, Daniel de Bosola;
   One that was in the galleys.
Duch.   Yes, I know him: –   215
Ferd. A worthy fellow h' is: pray let me entreat for
   The provisorship of your horse.
Duch.   Your knowledge of him
   Commends him, and prefers him.
Ferd.   Call him hither –
                      [*Exit* Attendant.]
   We now are upon parting: good Lord Silvio,
   Do us commend to all our noble friends   220
   At the leaguer.
Sil.   Sir, I shall.
Duch.   You are for Milan?
Sil. I am: –
Duch. Bring the caroches: we'll bring you down to the haven.
                [*Exeunt all except* Cardinal *and* FERDINAND.]
Card. Be sure you entertain that Bosola
   For your intelligence: I would not be seen in't;   225
   And therefore many times I have slighted him
   When he did court our furtherance, as this morning.

---

212. shall] *Q;* shall. *Ex. Ant. Delio Q4.*   216. for] *Q;* for him *conj. Luc i.*
218.1.] *Dyce i.*   219. now are] *McIl;* now *Q;* are now *Q4.*   221. leaguer] *Q2;*
Leagues *Q. Duch.*] *Samp; Ferd. Q.*   223.1.] *Dyce i subs.*

---

   stains = 'eclipses, puts in the shade' (a common sense in Webster's
day).
   221. *leaguer*] military camp.
   Duch.] The speech can hardly be Ferdinand's (as in Q) because he obviously knows Silvio's destination (cf. his previous speech and l. 150, above)
and would have no motive for uttering it as a statement rather than a question (question marks are found in Q for exclamations or full-stops); moreover, the Duchess's next speech would be too curiously abrupt without this
preparation. Compositor A confused speech-prefixes on at least one other
occasion (cf. III.v.105).
   223. *caroches*] coaches (of a stately kind).
   bring] accompany.

Ferd. Antonio, the great master of her household
       Had been far fitter: –
Card.   You are deceiv'd in him,

               Enter BOSOLA.

       His nature is too honest for such business –   230
       He comes: I'll leave you.   [*Exit.*]
Bos.   I was lur'd to you.
Ferd. My brother here, the cardinal, could never
       Abide you.
Bos.   Never since he was in my debt.
Ferd. May be some oblique character in you face
       Made him suspect you!
Bos.   Doth he study physiognomy?   235
       There's no more credit to be given to th' face
       Than to a sick man's urine, which some call
       The physician's whore, because she cozens him: –
       He did suspect me wrongfully.
Ferd.   For that
       You must give great men leave to take their times: 240
       Distrust doth cause us seldom be deceiv'd; –
       You see, the oft shaking of the cedar-tree
       Fastens it more at root.
Bos.   Yet take heed:
       For to suspect a friend unworthily

229.1.] *so this ed.; at l. 81.1 Q; at l. 146 Q4; after* leave you, *l. 230 Dyce i.*
231. Exit] *Dyce i.*

229.1.] By marking Bosola's entrance thus early, the irony of the brothers'
talk is enhanced. And Bosola and Antonio are clearly linked elsewhere as
two men with similar opportunities for advancement (e.g. II.i.84–107).
    In the first three Acts other early entries are effective in similar ways; cf.
II.i.107.1, note, and III.ii.62.1.
    241.] Cf. the proverb, 'He who trusts not is not deceived' (Tilley
T559).
    242–3. *oft . . . root*] Dent compared Hall, *Epistles* (1608), IV.vi: 'the oft-
shaking of the tree, fastens it more at the roote'; he noted that the more
common 'sentence' expressed the opposite, that shrubs are safe when great
trees perish in a storm (see Tilley C208).
    The *cedar* was a symbol of greatness; cf. *Cymb.*, v.v.453.
    244–6. *to . . . you*] The idea is in Florio, III.ix; but, as Dent shows,
Webster seems closer to the original Seneca (*Epist.*, III.3).
    next = 'nearest'.

Instructs him the next way to suspect you,   245
  And prompts him to deceive you.
Ferd.   There's gold.
Bos.   So:
  What follows? Never rain'd such show'rs as these
  Without thunderbolts in the tail of them;
  Whose throat must I cut?
Ferd. Your inclination to shed blood rides post   250
  Before my occasion to use you: – I give you that
  To live i'th' court, here; and observe the duchess,
  To note all the particulars of her 'haviour;
  What suitors do solicit her for marriage
  And whom she best affects: she's a young widow –   255
  I would not have her marry again.
Bos.   No, sir?
Ferd. Do not you ask the reason: but be satisfied,
  I say I would not.
Bos.   It seems you would create me
  One of your familiars.
Ferd.   Familiar! what's that?
Bos. Why, a very quaint invisible devil, in flesh: 260
  An intelligencer.
Ferd.   Such a kind of thriving thing
  I would wish thee: and ere long, thou mayst arrive
  At a higher place by't.

248–9.] *so this ed.; one line Q.*   248. in the] *This ed.;* i'th *Q.*

247–9.] an allusion to the shower of gold, in which form Jupiter visited
the imprisoned Danäe.

248–9.] These words are only just accommodated in the third line of type
from the foot of the last page of Sheet B: Compositor A probably altered
the lining of his copy and elided *in the* so that he could complete the text
cast-off for his page. See Intro., pp. 42–3.

250. *post*] in haste.

259. *familiars*] (1) 'members of household', (2) 'intimate friends', and (3)
'familiar spirits' (supposed to attend at a call). Lucas suggested that a Jacobean audience might recall *familiar* = 'Officer of the Inquisition, chiefly
employed in arresting and imprisoning' (*O.E.D.*).

260. *quaint*] skilful, cunning.

263–4. *devils . . . angels*] In Webster's time there was a gold coin with St
Michael stamped on it (the noble) which was commonly called an *angel*.

Bos.   Take your devils
　　Which hell calls angels: these curs'd gifts would make
　　You a corrupter, me an impudent traitor,   265
　　And should I take these they'd take me to hell.
Ferd. Sir, I'll take nothing from you that I have given: –
　　There is a place that I procur'd for you
　　This morning: the provisorship o'th' horse –
　　Have you heard on't?
Bos.   No.
Ferd.   'Tis yours – is't not worth thanks?   270
Bos. I would have you curse yourself now, that your
　　　　bounty,
　　Which makes men truly noble, e'er should make
　　Me a villain: O, that to avoid ingratitude
　　For the good deed you have done me, I must do
　　All the ill man can invent! Thus the devil   275
　　Candies all sins o'er; and what heaven terms vile,
　　That names he complimental.
Ferd.   Be yourself:
　　Keep your old garb of melancholy; 'twill express
　　You envy those that stand above your reach,
　　Yet strive not to come near 'em: this will gain   280
　　Access to private lodgings, where youself
　　May, like a politic dormouse –
Bos.   As I have seen some
　　Feed in a lord's dish, half asleep, not seeming

---

266. to] *Q4; not in Q.*   270. on't] *Q2* (ont); out *Q.*   276. o'er] *Q2* (ore);
are *Q.*

264–6. *these...*] probably from *A.T.,* v.i.2791–8: 'I tolde, that such a
summe but seru'd, to make / Him a corrupter, me corrupted thought: / And
foule for him to giue, for me to take,...'
　　275–6. *devil...o'er*] Cf. *W.D.,* v.vi.58–60. *Candies* = 'sugars'.
　　277. *complimental*] i.e., a polite accomplishment, or refinement; cf. *Troil.,*
III.i.42.
　　282. *dormouse*] Cf. III.i.22. Pliny's *Natural History* (tr. 1601) tells how
dormice 'renue their age every yeare, by sleeping all Winter: for they lie by
it close, snug all the while, and are not to be seene. But come the Summer
once, they bee young and fresh againe' (VIII.lvii).
　　283. *Feed...dish*] dine at a lord's table; the usage is not recorded in
O.E.D., but cf. Marston, *Malcontent* (1604), II.iii: 'Lay one into his breast
shall sleepe with him, / Feede in the same dish,.../ Who may discover any
shape of danger...'

To listen to any talk; and yet these rogues
Have cut his throat in a dream: – what's my place?   285
The provisorship o'th' horse? say then, my corruption
Grew out of horse-dung: I am your creature.
Ferd. Away.
Bos. Let good men, for good deeds, covet good fame,
Since place and riches oft are bribes of shame –   290
Sometimes the devil doth preach.   *Exit.*

[*Enter* Duchess *and* Cardinal.]

Card. We are to part from you: and your own discretion
Must now be your director.
Ferd.   You are a widow:
You know already what man is; and therefore
Let not youth, high promotion, eloquence –   295
Card. No, nor anything without the addition, honour,
Sway your high blood.

288. Away] *Q; Away. Exit Samp.* 291.1.] *This ed.;... and Cariola Dyce i;
Scene ii. /... / Enter Cardinal, Ferdinand, Duchess, and Cariola Samp;... and
Ferdinand conj. this ed.* 296.] *so Q;* No, / Nor... *Dyce i.*

291. *Sometimes... preach*] Cf. the proverbs: 'The devil can cite scripture
for his purpose' and 'The devil sometimes speaks truth' (Tilley D230 and
D266).
    291. S.D.] Possibly Ferdinand should leave the stage on 'Away' (l. 288)
to re-enter here with the Cardinal and Duchess; thus the change of location
to 'the gallery' (l. 210) would be clearly indicated. Such an arrangement would
also (1) suggest that the family conference is in a less public place than the
presence chamber of the first part of Act I; (2) avoid the possible awkward-
ness of Ferdinand suddenly breaking into an intimate duologue (at l. 293)
without the fact being remarked upon (the three could enter already talking
together); and (3) give Bosola a clear stage (and concentrated attention) for
his couplet-soliloquy and comment upon it. However, if Crane transcribed
the printer's copy from a MS. which had directions for Ferdinand's exit and
re-entry, he would normally have marked a new scene after l. 291.
    In a Jacobean theatre the curtains of some kind of inner-stage could be
closed before Antonio's entry at l. 361 (perhaps concealing the thrones
appropriate to the 'presence') and thus Webster's audience could easily
accept the fiction of a change of place by the time it is undoubtedly required
by the text; these curtains could be the 'arras' of l. 357. The action of
W.D., IV.ii moves from outside to inside the House of Convertites without
exit and re-entry.
    297. *high blood*] noble lineage; Ferdinand seems to take *blood* = 'passion,
sensual appetite' (cf. *W.D.*, I.ii.292 and note).
    luxurious] lecherous, unchaste.

Ferd.   Marry! they are most luxurious
    Will wed twice.
Card.   O fie!
Ferd.   Their livers are more spotted
    Than Laban's sheep.
Duch.   Diamonds are of most value
    They say, that have pass'd through most jewellers'
        hands.   300
Ferd. Whores, by that rule, are precious: –
Duch.   Will you hear me?
    I'll never marry: –
Card.   So most widows say:
    But commonly that motion lasts no longer
    Than the turning of an hour-glass – the funeral sermon
    And it, end both together.
Ferd.   Now hear me: 305
    You live in a rank pasture here, i'th' court –
    There is a kind of honey-dew that's deadly:
    'Twill poison your fame; look to't: be not cunning:
    For they whose faces do belie their hearts
    Are witches, ere they arrive at twenty years –   310
    Ay: and give the devil suck.
Duch. This is terrible good counsel: –
Ferd. Hypocrisy is woven of a fine small thread,

---

298. *livers*] The liver was thought to be the seat of love and violent passions: cf. *A.Y.L.*, III.ii.441–4, where Rosalind promises 'to wash your liver
as clean as a sound sheep's heart, that there shall not be one spot of
love in't'.

298–9. *more...sheep*] Cf. *Genesis*, xxx.31–43; Webster probably found
the phrase in Whetstone *Heptameron* (1582), C3ᵛ: 'a company as spotted as
Labans Sheepe', applied to members of the Church of Rome who have taken
but broken a vow of chastity (so Dent).

299–301. *Diamonds...precious*] Contrast 'A Virtuous Widow', *Characters* (1614): '...as one Diamond fashions another, so is she wrought into
works of charity, with the dust or ashes of her husband' (*Works*, ed. Lucas,
iv, 38–9).

303. *motion*] resolve.

307. *honey-dew*] a sweet, sticky substance found on leaves, etc., being
excreted by aphides; formerly it was supposed to be a kind of dew
(so *O.E.D.*).

313.] probably from Ariosto, *Satires*, tr. R. Tofte (1608), III: 'Hypocrisie
is wouen of fine thrid'; it may be proverbial.

Subtler than Vulcan's engine: yet, believe 't,
Your darkest actions – nay, your privat'st thoughts –   315
Will come to light.
Card.   You may flatter yourself,
And take your own choice: privately be married
Under the eaves of night.
Ferd.   Think 't the best voyage
That e'er you made; like the irregular crab,
Which though 't goes backward, thinks that it goes
     right,   320
Because it goes its own way: but observe,
Such weddings may more properly be said
To be executed, than celebrated.
Card. The marriage night
Is the entrance into some prison.
Ferd.   And those joys,   325
Those lustful pleasures, are like heavy sleeps
Which do fore-run man's mischief –
Card.   Fare you well.
Wisdom begins at the end: remember it.   [*Exit.*]
Duch. I think this speech between you both was studied,
It came so roundly off.
Ferd.   You are my sister –   330
This was my father's poniard: do you see?
I'd be loth to see 't look rusty, 'cause 'twas his: –

---

328. *Exit*] Q4.

314. *Vulcan's engine*] the net of very fine thread (cf. l. 313) in which he
caught Mars and Venus in adultery.
318. *eaves*] overhanging shelter, cover.
319–21. *like . . . way*] The crab's sideways motion is often alluded to, as
in Sidney's *Arcadia*, II.iii (*Wks*, I.164): it 'looks one way and goes another';
but its illusion of normality may well be Webster's addition.
323. *executed*] Meanings ranged from 'carried out' (practically or legally)
to 'put to death'; the word-play turns on the accepted meaning 'celebrated'
(of ceremonies and rites).
328. *Wisdom . . . end*] a counsel of prudence and a *memento mori*: cf. the
proverbs 'Think on the end before you begin' and 'Remember the end'
(Tilley E125 and E128).
330. *roundly*] (1) fluently, (2) bluntly, forcefully.
331. *poniard*] short, stabbing weapon; perhaps the start of phallic innuendo that becomes obvious at ll. 336ff. (Cambridge ed.).

I would have you to give o'er these chargeable revels;
A visor and a mask are whispering-rooms
That were ne'er built for goodness: fare ye well: –   335
And women like that part which, like the lamprey,
Hath ne'er a bone in't.

Duch.   Fie sir!

Ferd.   Nay,
I mean the tongue: variety of courtship; –
What cannot a neat knave with a smooth tale
Make a woman believe? Farewell, lusty widow.   [*Exit.*]   340

Duch. Shall this move me? If all my royal kindred
Lay in my way unto this marriage,
I'd make them my low footsteps: and even now,
Even in this hate, as men in some great battles,
By apprehending danger, have achiev'd   345
Almost impossible actions – I have heard soldiers say
    so –
So I, through frights, and threat'nings, will assay
This dangerous venture: let old wives report
I wink'd and chose a husband. Cariola,

---

333. to] *Q; not in Q2.* 340. *Exit*] *Q4.* 349.1.] *This ed.*

---

333. *chargeable*] burdensome, costly.

334. *whispering-rooms*] intimate, private closets, as at III.ii.257; these are the only occurrences of the word recorded in *O.E.D.*

336. *lamprey*] This eel-like fish with sucker mouth 'swimmeth all whole in flexible sort, and all alike bending hir bodie' (J. Maplet, *Green Forest* (1567), N3ᵛ).

339–40. *What ... believe*] Cf. Overbury, *Characters* (1614), 'A Good Woman': 'Shee leaues the neat youth telling his lushious tales' (so Lucas). *neat* = 'fine, elegant', or, in mod. slang, 'smooth'; cf. the description of Jack Donne as '*neat*', but not 'dissolute'. Following ll. 336–7, there is an equivocation centring on *tale* for 'tail' (or penis); this was a common quibble (see, e.g., *Rom.*, II.iv.99–106).

343. *footsteps*] steps (as before an altar or throne; rungs of a ladder).

349. *I ... chose*] 'I chose with my eyes shut'; a proverbial phrase first noted by Tilley in 1621 (W501). However, here there may be a quibble suggesting a premonition of moral condemnation, for to *wink* = 'to close one's eyes', and also 'to shut one's eyes to wrong, to be complaisant'.

349.1.] Some editors direct Cariola to enter with her mistress at l. 291.1; but a later entrance has the advantage of Ferdinand and the Duchess being alone when he says (ll. 330ff.) what he seems to have restrained until the Cardinal's departure. It also makes it credible that Cariola, and not her mistress, should know that Antonio is waiting (cf. l. 356).

[*Enter* CARIOLA.]

To thy known secrecy I have given up   350
More than my life, my fame: –
Cari.   Both shall be safe:
For I'll conceal this secret from the world
As warily as those that trade in poison
Keep poison from their children.
Duch.   Thy protestation
Is ingenious and hearty: I believe it.   355
Is Antonio come?
Cari.   He attends you: –
Duch.   Good dear soul,
Leave me: but place thyself behind the arras,
Where thou mayst overhear us: – wish me good speed
For I am going into a wilderness,
Where I shall find nor path nor friendly clew   360
To be my guide.   [*Cariola withdraws behind the arras.*]

[*Enter* ANTONIO.]

I sent for you – sit down:
Take pen and ink, and write: are you ready?
Ant.   Yes: –
Duch. What did I say?
Ant.   That I should write somewhat.

355. ingenious] *Q;* ingenuous *Q3.* 361. *Cariola . . .*] *Dyce i subs.; Exit Car.*
Q4 (after l. 357), Samp (after l. 358). Enter Antonio] *Q4 (at l. 358), Dyce i (as*
here).

355. *ingenious*] intelligent, sagacious (in opposition to 'hearty'); but the
word was often used for 'ingenuous', and this sense may also be required
here. Cf. the ambiguous use in *W.D.*, III.iii.70.
360. *clew*] perhaps a reference to the ball of thread whereby Theseus
entered the Minotaur's labyrinth and destroyed it, so winning Ariadne for
his bride.
361. Cariola . . . arras] If Cariola has to open a door for Antonio as well
as withdraw, the stage movement may be clumsy and involve a pause not
indicated by the metre or words. Probably the Duchess lets the steward in
herself; this would explain his initial silence, and add to his surprise when
Cariola discloses her presence at l. 475. Possibly, Cariola should leave at the
end of l. 358; this would entail the addition of heavy punctuation after 'speed'
and the Duchess speaking the next two and a half lines as soliloquy (gaining
closer attention from the audience and perhaps making her courage and
dignity appear studied).

Duch. O, I remember: –
    After these triumphs, and this large expense,   365
    It's fit, like thrifty husbands, we inquire
    What's laid up for tomorrow.
Ant. So please your beauteous excellence.
Duch.   Beauteous?
    Indeed I thank you: I look young for your sake.
    You have ta'en my cares upon you.
Ant.   I'll fetch your grace   370
    The particulars of your revenue, and expense.
Duch. O, you are an upright treasurer: but you mistook,
    For when I said I meant to make inquiry
    What's laid up for tomorrow, I did mean
    What's laid up yonder for me.
Ant.   Where?
Duch.   In heaven –   375
    I am making my will (as 'tis fit princes should,
    In perfect memory), and I pray sir, tell me
    Were not one better make it smiling, thus,
    Than in deep groans, and terrible ghastly looks,
    As if the gifts we parted with procur'd   380
    That violent distraction?
Ant.   O, much better.
Duch. If I had a husband now, this care were quit:
    But I intend to make you overseer; –
    What good deed shall we first remember? say.
Ant. Begin with that first good deed began i'th' world   385
    After man's creation, the sacrament of marriage –

---

365. these] *Dyce i; this Q.*   368–9. *Beauteous...*] *so Dyce i; one line Q.*
370–1. *I'll ...*] *so Dyce i; ...* the / Particulars *... Q.*   372.] *so Q; ...* are /
An *... Dyce i.*   378. thus,] *Q3; thus? Q.*   381. distraction] *Q3; distruction*
Q.

---

    365. *triumphs*] festivities.
    366. *husbands*] husbanders, heads of households.
    369. *for ... sake*] (1) 'thanks to you', and (2) 'for love of you' (cf. *O.E.D.*,
sake, 6 and 6b).
    372. *upright treasurer*] a pun, if Antonio is now standing to obey the
Duchess's order (so Cambridge ed.).
    383. *overseer*] person appointed by a testator to supervise or assist the
executors of the will.

I'd have you first provide for a good husband,
Give him all.
Duch.   All?
Ant.   Yes, your excellent self.
Duch. In a winding sheet?
Ant.   In a couple.
Duch. Saint Winifred, that were a strange will!   390
Ant. 'Twere strange if there were no will in you
To marry again.
Duch.   What do you think of marriage?
Ant. I take 't, as those that deny purgatory –
It locally contains, or heaven, or hell;
There's no third place in't.
Duch.   How do you affect it?   395
Ant. My banishment, feeding my melancholy,
Would often reason thus . . .
Duch.   Pray let's hear it.
Ant. Say a man never marry, nor have children,
What takes that from him? only the bare name
Of being a father, or the weak delight   400

---

390. Winifred] *Dyce   i;* Winfrid *Q.* 391–2. 'Twere . . . again] *so   Q; . . .*
strange / If . . . *Luc i.* 391. strange] *Q;* stranger *Dyce ii.*

389. *In . . . sheet*] i.e., fit to accompany her dead husband.
couple] i.e., of sheets; but with a quibble, for *couple* also meant both
'wedlock' and 'copulation'.
390. *Saint Winifred*] a 7th-century Welsh saint; her head was struck off
by Caradoc ap Alauc whose love she had refused, but she was restored to
life by St Bruno. Her shrine at Holywell, north-east Wales, has been a centre
of pilgrimage, especially popular in Webster's lifetime when Flintshire was
a recusant stronghold. The saint was regarded as a helper of women who
wanted children. (So *N & Q,* 45 (1998), pp. 33–4)
391. *strange*] Emendation is unnecessary and the metre satisfactory if *no*
and *will* are both stressed.
will] Besides the obvious quibble on 'testament' and 'desire, inclination',
there may be an allusion to *will* = 'carnal desire, passion' (as at III.i.73).
392–5. *What . . . in't*] Dent has shown that the usual maxim called marriage purgatory or hell, *or* heaven or hell; Webster seems to have responded
to both forms in finding his own idiosyncratic 'sentence'.
395. *affect*] fancy, feel towards.
398–403. *Say . . . starling*] from Elyot, *Image of Governance* (1541), P1ᵛ:
'. . . sterilitie can no more hurte me, but onely take from me the name of a
father, or the dotynge pleasure to se my lytell sonne ryde on a cokhorse, or
to here hymn chatter and speake lyke a wanton'.

To see the little wanton ride a-cock-horse
Upon a painted stick, or hear him chatter
Like a taught starling.
Duch.   Fie, fie, what's all this?
One of your eyes is blood-shot – use my ring to't,
That say 'tis very sovereign – 'twas my wedding ring,   405
And I did vow never to part with it,
But to my second husband.
Ant. You have parted with it now.
Duch. Yes, to help your eyesight.
Ant. You have made me stark blind.   410
Duch. How?
Ant. There is a saucy, and ambitious devil
Is dancing in this circle.
Duch.   Remove him.
Ant.   How?
Duch. There needs small conjuration, when your finger
May do it: thus – is it fit?
                    [*She puts her ring upon his finger:*] *he kneels.*
Ant.   What said you?
Duch   Sir,   415
This goodly roof of yours is too low built,
I cannot stand upright in't, nor discourse,
Without I raise it higher: raise yourself,
Or if you please, my hand to help you: so. [*Raises him.*]
Ant. Ambition, madam, is a great man's madness,   420
That is not kept in chains, and close-pent rooms,
But in fair lightsome lodgings, and is girt

---

415. *She...finger*] *Dyce i (subs.). he kneels*] so *Q2; after* you *Q.*
419. S.D.] *Dyce ii.*

404–7. The exchange of rings was a ritual used in betrothals (see Cressy,
p. 267).
sovereign] efficacious, powerful.
412–13. *devil...circle*] Magicians when raising spirits either protected
themselves with a magic circle or confined the spirit within one; the latter
practice is alluded to in *W.Ho*, IV.ii.
416.] Lucas compared Hall, *Characters*, 'Humble Man': 'He is...a
rich stone set in lead; and lastly, a true Temple of God built with a low
roofe'.
421. *close-pent*] (1) securely shut, (2) secret.

With the wild noise of prattling visitants,
Which makes it lunatic, beyond all cure –
Conceive not I am so stupid but I aim   425
Whereto your favours tend: but he's a fool
That, being a-cold, would thrust his hands i'th' fire
To warm them.
Duch.   So, now the ground's broke,
You may discover what a wealthy mine
I make you lord of.
Ant.   O, my unworthiness!   430
Duch. You were ill to sell yourself –
This dark'ning of your worth is not like that
Which tradesmen use i'th' city; their false lights
Are to rid bad wares off: and I must tell you
If you will know where breathes a complete man –   435
I speak it without flattery – turn your eyes
And progress through yourself.
Ant. Were there nor heaven nor hell,
I should be honest: I have long serv'd virtue,
And ne'er ta'en wages of her.
Duch.   Now she pays it!   440
The misery of us that are born great –
We are forc'd to woo, because none dare woo us:
And as a tyrant doubles with his words,
And fearfully equivocates, so we
Are forc'd to express our violent passions   445
In riddles, and in dreams, and leave the path

---

435. will] *Q;* would *Q2.*

---

423. *prattling*] could be used in Webster's time of prating, or small-talk,
without suggesting childishness; Antonio pictures a great man surrounded
by courtiers who appear to speak about nothing, but are hoping to forward
their individual suits.
   433. *false*] weak, deceptive.
   437. *progress*] make a royal progress, or journey in state; i.e. 'you are the
ruler of such a man'.
   438–40.] from Hall, 'Honest Man': '. . . if there were no heauen, yet he
would be vertuous', and, possibly, Hall, *Epistles* (1611), VI.x: 'Serue honestie
euer, though without apparant wages: shee will pay sure, if slow'. *pays* =
'repays, rewards'.
   442. *woo . . . woo*] a pun, introduced by *misery* of the previous line; cf.
Rom., III.v.120: 'Ere he that should be Husband comes to woe' (Q2) and
Kökeritz, p. 85. For the sentiment, see Painter; App. I, p. 183.

Of simple virtue, which was never made
To seem the thing it is not. Go, go brag
You have left me heartless – mine is in your bosom,
I hope 'twill multiply love there. You do tremble: 450
Make not your heart so dead a piece of flesh
To fear, more than to love me: sir, be confident –
What is't distracts you? This is flesh, and blood, sir;
'Tis not the figure cut in alabaster
Kneels at my husband's tomb. Awake, awake, man!   455
I do here put off all vain ceremony,
And only do appear to you a young widow
That claims you for her husband, and like a widow,
I use but half a blush in't.

Ant.   Truth speak for me:
I will remain the constant sanctuary   460
Of your good name.

Duch.   I thank you, gentle love,
And 'cause you shall not come to me in debt,
Being now my steward, here upon your lips
I sign your *Quietus est*: –   [*Kisses him.*]
This you should have begg'd now –   465
I have seen children oft eat sweetmeats thus,
As fearful to devour them too soon.

Ant. But for your brothers?

Duch.   Do not think of them –
All discord, without this circumference,

464–5.] *so this ed.; one line Q.*   464. S.D.] *This ed.*

451–2. *Make . . . me*] possibly from Hall, *Characters*, 'Profane': 'To matter
of Religion his heart is a peece of dead flesh, without feeling of loue, of
feare . . .'
453. *flesh, and blood*] Cf. the proverb, 'To be flesh and blood as others
are' (Tilley F367).
464. Quietus est] 'He is discharged, or acquitted of payment due'; the
phrase was also used of the 'release' of death, as in *Ham.*, III.i.75 (and cf.
Tilley Q16). There is a sequence of allusions to death in this duologue; cf.
ll. 375–81, 389, 451, 454–5.
469. *without . . . circumference*] outside these bounds. They have probably
taken each other's hands in the usual ritual for becoming betrothed or
'handfast' (as it was often called; see Cressy, p. 269); by now they may also
have embraced. Alternatively, she may refer to her ring on his finger (see
ll. 404–7).

Is only to be pitied, and not fear'd: 470
Yet, should they know it, time will easily
Scatter the tempest.
Ant.   These words should be mine,
And all the parts you have spoke, if some part of it
Would not have savour'd flattery.
Duch. Kneel.   [CARIOLA *comes from behind the arras.*]   475
Ant. Hah?
Duch. Be not amaz'd, this woman's of my counsel –
I have heard lawyers say, a contract in a chamber
Per verba de presenti is absolute marriage: –
Bless, heaven, this sacred Gordian, which let violence   480
Never untwine.
Ant. And may our sweet affections, like the spheres,
Be still in motion.

---

475. S.D.] *Dyce i; Enter Cariola (after l. 474) Q4.*   479. *de*] *Samp; not in
Q.*   marriage] *Q; marriage. (She and Antonio kneel Dyce ii.*

---

473. *parts*] 'part' in the same line suggests that this is used quibblingly:
(1) 'parts of speech' (cf. 'words', l. 472), and (2) 'matter, particulars' (see
O.E.D., sb. 2, a and c).

479. *Per ... presenti*] When a couple declared that they were man and
wife (with or without a witness, and without a deposition in writing), they
were legally married. The church's official attitude was that these mariages
were valid and binding, but also sinful and forbidden; offenders had to sol-
emnize their marriage *in facie ecclesiae.* The consummation of such unions
before public solemnizing was regarded as fornication and a deadly sin. In
practice, however, sexual intercourse before the final religious ceremony was
accepted behaviour for such contracted couples, despite the disapproval of
puritans and some clergy. (See Cressy, pp. 316–18, which quotes contemporary English authorities.)

480. *Gordian*] Gordius, king of Gordium in Phrygia, tied a knot in the
yoke of the oxen that pulled his chariot when he was chosen king: the oracle
declared that whoever loosened it would rule Asia. Alexander the Great cut
through the knot with his sword.

482–4.] The relevant properties of the planetary *spheres* are described in
Florio's Montaigne, I.xxii; perpetual movement (*still* = 'continuously,
always'), touching (*Quickening* = 'stimulating, exciting'), and unheard music
(*soft*, or appropriate to the pleasures of a secret marriage) are all mentioned:
'Philosophers deeme of the celestiall musicke ... that the bodies of it's
circles, being solid smooth, and in their rowling motion, touching and
rubbing one against another, must of necessitie produce a wonderfull har-
monie ... But that universally the hearing senses of these low world's creatures ... cannot sensibly perceive or distinguish the same.'

Duch.   Quickening, and make
   The like soft music.
Ant. That we may imitate the loving palms,   485
   Best emblem of a peaceful marriage,
   That ne'er bore fruit, divided.
Duch. What can the church force more?
Ant. That Fortune may not know an accident,
   Either of joy or sorrow, to divide   490
   Our fixed wishes.
Duch.   How can the church bind faster?
   We now are man and wife, and 'tis the church
   That must but echo this: – maid, stand apart –
   I now am blind.
Ant.   What's your conceit in this?
Duch. I would have you lead your fortune by the hand,   495
   Unto your marriage bed: –

---

491. bind] *This ed.;* build *Q.*

485–7.] The idea was common, being found in Pliny's *Natural History* and
often quoted as an *emblem* of marriage (see Dent). James Maxwell's *Monument of Remembrance* (1613) used it of the marriage of Princess Elizabeth
(Sig. C4):

> . . . wise Nature doth vs show
> In the *Palme-trees*, which being set asunder
> From mutuall sight, no fruit is seene to grow
> Of either kinde; but faint, as if some thunder
>   Had blasted both; they pine and droope as dead,
>   And haue no heart once to hold up their head . . .

485, 489. *That . . .*] Antonio (but not the Duchess), in praying to 'heaven',
introduces new petitions with *That*, as in the Litany of the Church of
England.

488. *force*] enforce (of a law or regulation); or, possibly, 'care for' (cf.
O.E.D., s.v., 14), or 'urge'.

491. *bind*] Q's 'build' is not meaningful, whereas *bind* is in keeping with
associations of 'contract . . . Gordian . . . like . . . divided . . . divide . . . faster . . .
man and wife'. Crane occasionally used too many minim strokes, so 'build'
may be the compositor's attempt to make sense of four minims between a 'b'
and 'd' in his copy. Professor Leech compared *Spanish Gipsy* (1623), v.iii: '– He
is not married to thee. – In his faith / He is; and faith and troth I hope bind
faster / Than any other ceremonies can.' *faster* = more firmly, more securely.

494. *blind*] as Fortune; see l. 489, and l. 495 (where the primary sense is
probably 'good fortune').

conceit] idea, fancy.

496.] The incomplete verse-line probably indicates a silence in which
Antonio takes the Duchess in his arms. However, it would be possible for

(You speak in me this, for we now are one)
We'll only lie, and talk together, and plot
T'appease my humorous kindred; and if you please,
Like the old tale, in 'Alexander and Lodowick',   500
Lay a naked sword between us, keep us chaste: –
O, let me shroud my blushes in your bosom,
Since 'tis the treasury of all my secrets.
                              [*Exeunt* Duchess *and* ANTONIO.]
Cari. Whether the spirit of greatness or of woman
Reign most in her, I know not, but it shows   505
A fearful madness; I owe her much of pity.   *Exit.*

503.1.] *Dyce i.*   506. *Exit*] *Dyce i; Exeunt Q.*

---

him to hesitate and remain kneeling, or at least apart from his wife, until
after the very last words she speaks in this scene.

499. *humorous*] ill-humoured; or, possibly, with irony, 'capricious'.

500–1.] The Admiral's Men performed a (now lost) play with this title in
1597. The story was told in *The Seven Sages of Rome* and in a ballad to the
tune of *Flying Fame: The Two Faithful Friends*: 'the pleasant history of Alexander and Lodowicke, who were so like one another, that none could know
them asunder: wherin is declared how Lodwike married the Princesse of
Hungaria in Alexander's name and how each night he layd a naked sword
betweene him and the Princesse, because he would not wrong his friend'
(reprinted, *Pepys Ballads*, ed. H. E. Rollins (1929), I, pp. 136ff.).

502. *shroud*] (1) conceal; (2) treat them as dead.

503.1 S.D.] Since Antonio leaves without saying a further word, a great
freedom is allowed to the actors in showing the characters' mutual feelings
and physical relationship at this moment. Perhaps the clearest clue to what
Webster imagined is Cariola's recognition of what seems – from her point
of view – to be 'madness' – in the Duchess's behaviour. More certainly, the
frequent changes of thought, rhythm and mode of address in her last speech
do not suggest any great confidence or stability. At this moment, Antonio
is a cipher on the page and he might be played that way on the stage, with
consequences for the audience's response to the Duchess.

504. *spirit . . . madness*] In Cariola's opinion, the spirit of a 'great man'
(see l. 240, above, and *W.D.*, v.vi.261–2) is not that of a woman.

504–6.] Lucas compared the 'gloomy anticipations' in Webster's source
at this point; see App. I, pp. 257–8, 263.

505–6. *shows . . . woman*] either 'the madness is terrible to witness' or 'the
madness appears to be the result of the Duchess's fears'.

Act II

Actus II, Scena I.

Enter BOSOLA *and* CASTRUCHIO.

Bos. You say you would fain be taken for an eminent courtier?

Cast. 'Tis the very main of my ambition.

Bos. Let me see, you have a reasonable good face for't already,
and your night-cap expresses your ears sufficient largely
– I would have you learn to twirl the strings of your band   5
with a good grace; and in a set speech, at th' end of every
sentence, to hum, three or four times, or blow your nose

II.i.o.i.] *Q4; Bosola, Castruchio, an Old Lady, Antonio, Delio, Duchesse, Rodorico, Grisolan Q.* 4. sufficient] *Q;* sufficiently *McIl.*

II.i.] The preparatory entries without specific motivation, the casual talk as if waiting for something else, Bosola's bringing of a gift in expectation of presenting it, the Duchess's address to Antonio and Bosola as if she expected them to be in attendance, and her reference to etiquette and 'the presence' (l. 120) all show that this is a formal presence-chamber scene, like I.i. Webster has repeated an effect with differences that clarify the story: *now* the Duchess is not attended by her brothers, and the formality ends in disorder.

1. *courtier*] member of a law court; this unusual sense mocks the old man's presence among the young and ambitious *courtiers* of the Duchess's entourage.

2. *main*] aim, purpose (perhaps originating as a term of archery).

4. *your . . . largely*] Cf. *W.Ho*, I.i.213–14: 'put case this night-cap be to little for my eares or forehead, can any man tell mee where my Night-cap wringes me, except I be such an asse to proclaime it', and *W.D.*, I.ii.87–9. Bosola implies that Castruchio has the long ears of an ass.

In *W.Ho* and *W.D.* the wearers are cuckolds, and so is Castruchio. But he is also a would-be lawyer (cf. l. 9) and Webster used *night-cap* elsewhere of a lawyer's white coif or skull-cap (so Sykes.): cf. *A.V.*, IV.i.121, and *D.L.C.*, IV.i.66–70: Bosola mocks Castruchio as a lawyer and, perhaps, as a husband.

5. *band*] neck-band; here, probably, a lawyer's white tabs (so Lucas). But, possibly, there is a reference to a growing fashion among courtiers, in the early 17th century in England, for elaborate bands; in Jonson's *Cynthia's Revels*, v.iv.158, the frenchified Amorphus makes an 'accost' which includes some 'solemne' play with his 'band string'.

till it smart again, to recover your memory; when you
come to be a president in criminal causes, if you smile
upon a prisoner, hang him, but if you frown upon him   10
and threaten him, let him be sure to 'scape the gallows.
Cast. I would be a very merry president –
Bos. Do not sup o'nights, 'twill beget you an admirable wit.
Cast. Rather it would make me have a good stomach to
quarrel, for they say your roaring boys eat meat seldom,   15
and that makes them so valiant. But how shall I know
whether the people take me for an eminent fellow?
Bos. I will teach a trick to know it: give out you lie a-dying,
and if you hear the common people curse you, be sure
you are taken for one of the prime night-caps –   20

Enter an Old Lady.

You come from painting now?
Old Lady. From what?
Bos. Why, from your scurvy face-physic – to behold thee not
painted inclines somewhat near a miracle: these, in thy
face here, were deep ruts and foul sloughs the last pro-   25
gress. There was a lady in France, that having had the
smallpox, flayed the skin off her face to make it more
level; and whereas before she looked like a nutmeg-grater,
after she resembled an abortive hedgehog.
Old Lady. Do you call this painting?   30
Bos. No, no, but careening of an old morphewed lady, to
make her disembogue again – there's rough-cast phrase
to your plastic.

20.1.] *so Dyce i; at l. o.1 Q.*   24. these,] *McIl;* These *Q;* These . . . *Luc i;*
these dimples *conj. Luc i.*   31. but] *McIl;* but you call *Q;* but you call it *Q3;*
but I call *Luc i.*

---

15. *roaring boys*] slang for 'rowdies'.
20. *night-caps*] lawyers; cf. *D.L.C.,* II.i.43. *O.E.D.* glosses 'nocturnal
bullies', but quotes Webster only.
20.1.] She is to act as midwife; see II.ii.3.1, note.
26–8. *lady . . . level*] probably from Florio, I.xl: 'Who hath not heard of
hir at Paris, which onely to get a fresher hew of a new skinne, endured to
have hir face flead all over'.
31. *but*] Q is obviously corrupt, and McIlwraith's emendation is probably
the most satisfactory; some memory, or sight, of 'you call' immediately above
caused the error.

Old Lady. It seems you are well acquainted with my closet.

Bos. One would suspect it for a shop of witchcraft, to find in   35
it the fat of serpents, spawn of snakes, Jews' spittle, and
their young children's ordure – and all these for the face:
I would sooner eat a dead pigeon, taken from the soles
of the feet of one sick of the plague, than kiss one of you
fasting. Here are two of you, whose sin of your youth is   40
the very patrimony of the physician, makes him renew
his footcloth with the spring and change his high-prized
courtezan with the fall of the leaf: I do wonder you do
not loathe yourselves – observe my meditation now:
What thing is in this outward form of man   45
To be belov'd? we account it ominous
If nature do produce a colt, or lamb,
A fawn, or goat, in any limb resembling
A man; and fly from't as a prodigy.
Man stands amaz'd to see his deformity   50
In any other creature but himself.

---

37. children's ordure] *Q2*; children ordures *Q*; children's ordures *Luc i.*
42. high-prized] *Q* (-priz'd); high-priced *Dyce i.*

31–2. *careening ... again*] i.e., 'scraping clean an old scurfy lady, as if she
were the hull of a ship, so that she can look for new adventures, like a ship
leaving harbour for sea again'.

32–3. *rough-cast ... plastic*] coarse (harsh, brutal) plaster ... (fine, artis-
tic) modelling.

34–7.] probably from Ariosto, *Satires*, tr. Tofte (1608), IV: 'He knowes
not, did he know it he would spewe, / That paintings made with spettle of
a Iewe, / (For they the best sell) nor that loathsome smell, / (Though mixt
with muske and amber nere so well), / Can they with all their cunning take
away / The fleame and snot so ranke in it doth stay. / Little thinks he that
with the filthy doung, / Of their small circumcised infants young, / The fat
of hideous serpents, spaune of snakes, / Which slaues from out their poisonous bodies takes.'

38–9. *dead ... plague*] A broadsheet of *Remedies Against the Plague* told
how the rump of a cock, pullet or chicken should be bared and held to the
plague-sore until the creature died; this should be repeated 'so long as any
doe die', for when all the poison is 'drawn foorth' the bird will live; 'This
Medicine is necessarie to driue the venome from the heart' (reproduced in
F. P. Wilson, *The Plague* (1927), p. 8).

42. *footcloth*] a rich cloth laid over the back of a horse to protect the rider
from mud and dust; it was a sign of dignity and rank.

44. *observe ... now*] follow [take part in] my formal act of [quasi-
religious] meditation [on the vanity of human wishes].

But in our own flesh, though we bear diseases
Which have their true names only ta'en from beasts,
As the most ulcerous wolf, and swinish measle;
Though we are eaten up of lice and worms,   55
And though continually we bear about us
A rotten and dead body, we delight
To hide it in rich tissue: all our fear –
Nay, all our terror – is lest our physician
Should put us in the ground, to be made sweet.   60
Your wife's gone to Rome: you two couple, and get you
to the wells at Lucca, to recover your aches.
                    [*Exeunt* CASTRUCHIO *and* Old Lady.]
I have other work on foot: – I observe our duchess
Is sick o' days, she pukes, her stomach seethes,
The fins of her eyelids look most teeming blue,   65
She wanes i'th' cheek, and waxes fat i'th' flank;
And (contrary to our Italian fashion)
Wears a loose-body'd gown – there's somewhat in't!
I have a trick may chance discover it,
A pretty one: I have bought some apricocks,   70
The first our spring yields.

61–2.] *so Dyce i;* ... you / To ... *Q.*   62.1.] *Dyce i.*   71. S.D. *Enter* ...
Delio] *so Q4; at l. 0.1 Q.   talking apart*] *Samp subs.*

53–4.] Cf. Topsell, *History of Four-Footed Beasts* (1607), sig. Xxx I[v]: 'There
is a disease called a wolfe, because it consumeth and eateth vp the flesh in
the bodie next the sore, and must euery day be fed with fresh meat, as
Lambes, Pigeons, and such other things wherein is bloode, or else it consumeth al the flesh of the body, leauing not so much as the skin to couer
the bones'.
    Webster says that the common human disease of measles (earlier used in
the singular) was given the name of a skin disease in swine caused by tape-
worm; according to *O.E.D.*, both human and *swinish* measle were confused
with 'mesel' (leper, leprous).
    57. *dead*] i.e., dying (see *O.E.D.*, 4).
    62. *Lucca*] The town was famous as a spa in the 16th and 17th
centuries.
    65. *fins*] probably 'eyelids' (so *O.E.D.*, 2b, quoting Marston), and so
tautologous here.
    68. *loose-body'd gown*] In Webster's England loose, unwaisted gowns were
worn 'by older women' (Cunningham, *English Costume in 16th Century*
(1954), p. 167), as well as by pregnant women.

Enter ANTONIO *and* DELIO[, *talking apart*].

Delio.   And so long since married?
     You amaze me.
Ant.   Let me seal your lips for ever,
     For did I think that anything but th' air
     Could carry these words from you, I should wish
     You had no breath at all: –   75
     [*To Bosola*] Now sir, in your contemplation? You are
     studying to become a great wise fellow?
Bos. O sir, the opinion of wisdom is a foul tetter that runs all
     over a man's body: if simplicity direct us to have no evil,
     it directs us to a happy being; for the subtlest folly proceeds 80
     from the subtlest wisdom: let me be simply honest.
Ant. I do understand your inside.
Bos. Do you so?
Ant. Because you would not seem to appear to the world
     puffed up with your preferment, you continue this out-   85
     of-fashion melancholy – leave it, leave it.
Bos. Give me leave to be honest in any phrase, in any compli-
     ment whatsoever – shall I confess myself to you? I look

75–7.] *so this ed.;* ... contemplation / You ... (*two lines*) *Q.*   76. S.D.] *Luc
i.*   84–6.] *as prose this ed.;* ... world / Puff'd ... continue / This ... *Q.*

76–107.] This small-talk – opinionated, ironic and complimental – presents two ambitious men sparring for advantage. Bosola out-plays Antonio
by pretending at one point to reveal all (l. 88) and then turning defence into
attack.
     78–81. *opinion ... wisdom*] from three or four pages of Florio, II.xii: 'The
opinion of Wisedome is the plague of man ... Whence proceeds the
subtilest follie, but from the subtilest wisdome? ... I say therefore, that if
simplicitie directeth vs to have no evil, it also addresseth vs, according to
our condition to a most happy estate.' *tetter* = 'sore'.
     85–6. *out-of-fashion melancholy*] Cf. I.i.76, note. Bosola's *melancholy* is
out-of-fashion now because he has got preferment.
     L. Babb has suggested that this is a topical allusion, the affectation of
melancholy becoming less popular after the first decade of the 17th century
(*Eliz. Malady* (1951), pp. 83–4); but Webster can hardly have intended this,
for the malcontent was still a recognizable type-character delineated in
Overbury's *Characters* (1614) and A. Nixon, *Strange Foot-Post* (1613), and
other writings.
     88–9. *I ... reach*] Cf. the proverbs 'Things that are above us are nothing
to us' and 'One may look at a star, but not reach at it' (Tilley T206 and
S825).

no higher than I can reach: they are the gods that must
ride on winged horses; a lawyer's mule of a slow pace will   90
both suit my disposition and business: for mark me, when
a man's mind rides faster than his horse can gallop, they
quickly both tire.

Ant. You would look up to heaven, but I think
The devil, that rules i'th' air, stands in your light.   95

Bos. O sir, you are lord of the ascendant, chief man with the
duchess, a duke was your cousin-german removed: – say
you were lineally descended from King Pepin, or he
himself, what of this? search the heads of the greatest
rivers in the world, you shall find them but bubbles of   100
water. Some would think the souls of princes were

89–90. *they . . . horses*] from Florio, I.xlii: 'Al the true commodities that
Princes have, are common vnto them with men of meane fortune. It is for
Gods to mount winged horses, and to feed on Ambrosia.'

91. *mark me*] talk of horsemanship also points the generalizations at
Antonio (cf. I.i.139–46).

95.] Cf. *Ephesians*, ii.2: the devil 'ruleth in the ayre' (Bishops' Bible);
Webster links this with the proverbial criticism of men who 'stand in their
own light' (Tilley L276).

96. *lord . . . ascendant*] Astrologers divided the heavens into 12 'houses'
(shaped like sections of an orange by imaginary lines drawn through the
north and south points of the horizon). The 'first house', or 'house of
the ascendant', is that section of the sky which is at the moment rising in the
east, extending from 5° above to 25° below the horizon. The *lord of the
ascendant* was any planet within the first house.

Bosola speaks with (unintentional) irony in so calling Antonio, for the *lord
of the ascendant* was supposed to have a special influence upon the life of a
child then born and Antonio's son is born in the next scene; cf. the dramatic
irony at I.i.88.

97. *cousin-german removed*] first cousin once removed.

98. *King Pepin*] King of the Franks, who died in 768; in *W.D.* (v.vi.107–
12) Webster ranked him with great rulers like Alexander and Caesar.

99–101. *search . . . water*] probably from Florio, II.xii: laws 'swell, and
grow greater and greater, as do our rivers: follow them vpward, vnto their
sourse, & you shall find them but a bubble of water, scarse to be discerned,
which in gliding-on sewelleth so proud, & gathers so much strength'.

101–7. *Some . . . cannon*] from Florio, II.xii: 'The soules of Emperours
and Coblers are all cast in one same mold. Considering the importance of
Princes actions, and their weight, wee perswade our selves, they are brought
forth by some as weighty and important causes; we are deceived: They are
mooved, stirred and remooved in their motions, by the same springs and
wardes, that we are in ours. The same reason that makes vs chide and braule,
and fall out with anie of our neighbours, causeth a warre to follow between

brought forth by some more weighty cause than those of
meaner persons – they are deceived, there's the same
hand to them: the like passions sway them, the same
reason that makes a vicar go to law for a tithe-pig and   105
undo his neighbours, makes them spoil a whole province,
and batter down goodly cities with the cannon.

        Enter Duchess [*with* Attendants *and* Ladies.]

Duch. Your arm Antonio – do I not grow fat?
   I am exceeding short-winded: – Bosola,
   I would have you, sir, provide for me a litter,   110
   Such a one as the Duchess of Florence rode in.
Bos. The duchess us'd one when she was great with child.
Duch. I think she did: – Come hither, mend my ruff –
   Here, when? thou art such a tedious lady; and
   Thy breath smells of lemon pills – would thou hadst done –   115
   Shall I swoon under thy fingers? I am
   So troubled with the mother.
Bos. [*Aside*]   I fear too much.

107.1. *Enter Duchess*] so *Q4; at l. o.1 Q; after* water, *l. 101 conj. this ed.   with
. . . Ladies*] *This ed.; Ladies Q4   115. pills*] *Q3; pils Q; peel Q4; peels
Thorn.*   116. swoon] *Dyce i.* sound *Q;* swound *Q2.*   117. *Aside*] *Dyce ii.*

Princes; The same reason that makes vs whippe or beate a lackey, maketh
a Prince (if he apprehend it) to spoyle and waste a whole Province.'
   105. *tithe-pig*] the tenth pig of a litter, paid by a rural householder to the
parish priest to represent a tenth of his yearly produce, in accordance with
Mosaic law.
   107.1. *Attendants*] suitable for a presence-chamber; see note on the
scene-heading above. The entry of the Duchess *enceinte* for the first time
should, perhaps, be marked earlier, as Bosola comments, 'some would
think . . . the like passions sway them'; this would given an effect comparable
to Vittoria's entry during Flamineo's speech in *W.D.,* I.ii.113. See, also,
I.i.229.1, note.
   111. *Duchess of Florence*] Editors have been unable to suggest any particular reference; cf. IV.i.112–14, note on 'Lauriola'.
   114. *tedious*] troublesome, dilatory (cf. *O.E.D.,* 2 and 4).
   115. *pills*] rinds, peel.
   116. *swoon*] Q's 'sound' was a common form, and (with 'under your
fingers') implies a secondary meaning of 'sounding' (as a musical
instrument).
   117. *the mother*] hysteria; the pun is common.

Duch. I have heard you say that the French courtiers
    Wear their hats on 'fore the king.
Ant.   I have seen it.
Duch. In the presence?   120
Ant. Yes: –
Duch.   Why should not we bring up that fashion?
    'Tis ceremony more than duty, that consists
    In the removing of a piece of felt:
    Be you the example to the rest o'th' court,
    Put on your hat first
Ant.   You must pardon me: 125
    I have seen, in colder countries than in France,
    Nobles stand bare to th' prince; and the distinction
    Methought show'd reverently.
Bos. I have a present for your grace.
Duch.   For me sir?
Bos. Apricocks, madam.
Duch.   O sir, where are they?   130
    I have heard of none to-year.
Bos. [*Aside*]   Good, her colour rises.
Duch. Indeed I thank you; they are wondrous fair ones:
    What an unskilful fellow is our gardener!
    We shall have none this month.
Bos. Will not your grace pare them?   135

---

121. *Duch.*] *Q4; not in Q.*   131. *Aside*] *Dyce ii.*

118–19 *hats*] a much debated question at the time (see Boklund, pp. 35–
6): cf. Florio, I.xliii: 'Our Kings have the power to addresse all these
externall reformations . . . "Whatsoever Princes doe, that they seeme to
command". The rest of France takes the modell of the court as a rule unto
it selfe to follow. [So,] against our forefathers manner and the particular
libertie of our French nobilitie, we should stand bare-headed, aloofe-off from
them, wheresoever they be.'
    In its context, this is not casual talk. The Duchess is teasing Antonio and
wants the private excitement of seeing him with his hat on before the rest
of the court put on theirs, as if he were publicly acknowledged to be her
equal. Antonio turns the secret jest, saying that he has seen 'Nobles *stand
bare* to th' prince' (meaning himself standing naked before the Duchess, his
'prince'). See ll. 142–3, note, below, and III.ii.5 where the Duchess clearly
talks of Antonio as a 'nobleman'.
    126. *colder countries*] Lucas suggested an allusion to English loyalty.
    131. *to-year*] this year (like 'today').

Duch. No, they taste of musk, methinks; indeed they do: –
Bos. I know not: yet I wish your grace had par'd 'em: –
Duch. Why?
Bos.   I forgot to tell you the knave gard'ner
       (Only to raise his profit by them the sooner)
       Did ripen them in horse-dung.
Duch.   O you jest: –   140
       You shall judge; pray taste one.
Ant.   Indeed madam,
       I do not love the fruit.
Duch.   Sir, you are loth
       To rob us of our dainties: – 'tis a delicate fruit,
       They say they are restorative.
Bos.   'Tis a pretty art,
       This grafting.
Dunch.   'Tis so: a bettering of nature.   145
Bos. To make a pippin grow upon a crab,
       A damson on a blackthorn: – [*Aside*] how greedily she
          eats them!
       A whirlwind strike off these bawd farthingales,
       For, but for that, and the loose-body'd gown,

144–5. 'Tis . . . grafting] *so Dyce i;* . . . pretty / Art . . . *Q.*   147. Aside] *Q4*
(*at end of line*).

142–3. *you . . . dainties*] another *double entendre*: *dainties* = (1) 'choice
foods', and (2) 'things delighted in, luxuries'. In *A.Q.L.*, III.i.147–8,
'Tastes . . . of the daintiest Dish' is used with an unmistakable sexual innuendo; see also Marston, *Sophonisba* (1606), 1 (*Wks*, II.17): 'These dainties,
this first fruits of nuptials'.

144–5. *'Tis . . . grafting*] Lucas compared the *double entendre* in Florio,
II.xii, the page from which Webster borrowed for ll. 99–101 above: 'graft the
forked tree'.

146–7. *pippin . . . blackthorn*] Dent illustrated Webster's choice of trees
from Breton, *Will of Wit* (1606), Il: 'is not the Damson tree to be accounted
off, aboue the Blackthorne tree? is not the Pippin tree to be esteemed aboue
the crabtree? the Abricock aboue the common plum?'

Webster probably gave prominence to *pippin* to echo 'Pepin' (an alternative spelling) of l. 98; he so punned on the king's name in *W.D.*

148. *bawd*] deceiving (for sexual, illicit purposes): an unusual
adjectival use.

farthingales] hooped petticoats.

I should have discover'd apparently   150
     The young springal cutting a caper in her belly.
Duch. I thank you, Bosola, they were right good ones –
     If they do not make me sick.
Ant.   How now madam?
Duch. This green fruit and my stomach are not friends –
     How they swell me!
Bos. [*Aside*]   Nay, you are too much swell'd already.   155
Duch. O, I am in an extreme cold sweat!
Bos. I am very sorry: –
Duch. Lights to my chamber: O good Antonio,
     I fear I am undone.   *Exit.*
Delio.   Lights there, lights!
               [*Exeunt all except* ANTONIO *and* DELIO.]
Ant. O my most trusty Delio, we are lost!   160
     I fear she's fall'n in labour; and there's left
     No time for her remove.
Delio.   Have you prepar'd
     Those ladies to attend her? and procur'd
     That politic safe conveyance for the midwife
     Your duchess plotted?   165
Ant. I have: –
Delio.   Make use then of this forc'd occasion:
     Give out that Bosola hath poison'd her
     With these apricocks; that will give some colour
     For her keeping close.
Ant.   Fie, fie, the physicians
     Will then flock to her.
Delio.   For that you may pretend   170
     She'll use some prepar'd antidote of her own,
     Lest the physicians should re-poison her.
Ant. I am lost in amazement: I know not what to think on't.
                                             Exeunt.

---

155. *Aside*] *Q4.*   157. sorry:] *Q*; sorry. *Exit. Q4.*   159.1] *Q4 subs.*

110. *apparently*] manifestly, visibly.
151. *springal … caper*] stripling dancing.
166. *forc'd*] enforced, unsought.
168. *colour*] pretext.

SCENA II.

Enter BOSOLA.

Bos. So, so: there's no question but her tetchiness and most
vulturous eating of the apricocks are apparent signs of
breeding –

Enter Old Lady.

Now?
Old Lady. I am in haste, sir.   5
Bos. There was a young waiting-woman had a monstrous
desire to see the glass-house.
Old Lady. Nay, pray let me go: –
Bos. And it was only to know what strange instrument it
was should swell up a glass to the fashion of a woman's   10
belly.
Old Lady. I will hear no more of the glass-house – you are
still abusing women!
Bos. Who I? no, only (by the way now and then) mention
your frailties. The orange tree bears ripe and green fruit,   15
and blossoms all together: and some of you give entertainment for pure love; but more, for more precious
reward. The lusty spring smells well; but drooping

II.ii.0.1.] *Dyce i; Bosola, old Lady, Antonio, Rodorigo, Grisolan: seruants, Delio,
Cariola Q; Enter Bosola, Lady Q4.* 3.1.] *so Dyce i; at l. 0.1 Q, Q4.*
13. women!] *Kel;* woemen? *Q;* women. *Haz.* 15. bears] *Q3;* beare *Q.*
16. all together] *Dyce ii;* altogether *Q.*

II.ii.1. *tetchiness*] irritability, testiness; *O.E.D.* first records the word in
1623, but 'tetchy' is known earlier (e.g. *Rom.*, I.iii.32).

3.1.] She is 'in haste' (l.5) to act as midwife (cf. II.i.164 and l. 25, below);
she may carry some parcel or bag to make this clear to Bosola and the
audience.

12. *glass-house*] glass-factory; there was one near the Blackfriars theatre.

15–22. *orange ... them*] i.e., some women make love in youth and for
'pure love's' sake, others (like the 'Old Lady') when they are *drooping*, for
the sake of the *reward*.

For the *orange tree*, cf. J. Maplet, *Green Forest* (1567), H7ᵛ: 'This tree is at
all seasons of ye yeare fruit bearing or fruitfull: insomuch that it is neuer
found without fruit, ... for when the first of their fruit is mellow, and readie
ripe: then the second you shall espie greene and sower: and the thirde newe
blossoming and in flower'.

For *Danäes*, see I.i.247–9, note.

autumn tastes well: if we have the same golden showers
that rained in the time of Jupiter the Thunderer, you have   20
the same Danäes still, to hold up their laps to receive
them: – didst thou never study the mathematics?
Old Lady. What's that, sir?
Bos. Why, to know the trick how to make a many lines meet
in one centre: – go, go; give your foster-daughters good   25
counsel: tell them that the devil takes delight to hang at
a woman's girdle, like a false rusty watch, that she cannot
discern how the time passes.   [*Exit* Old Lady.]

  Enter ANTONIO, DELIO, RODERIGO, GRISOLAN.

Ant. Shut up the court gates: –
Rod.   Why sir? what's the danger?
Ant. Shut up the posterns presently: and call   30
  All the officers o' th' court.
Gris.   I shall instantly.   [*Exit.*]
Ant. Who keeps the key o' th' park gate?
Rod.   Forobosco.
Ant. Let him bring 't presently.

  Enter [GRISOLAN *with*] Officers.

1st. Off. O, gentlemen o'th' court, the foulest treason!
Bos. [*Aside*] If that these apricocks should be poison'd now,   35
  Without my knowledge!
1st. Off. There was taken even now a Switzer in the duchess'
  bedchamber.

---

21. Danäes] *Q4*; Danes *Q.*   28. S.D.] *Dyce i.*   28.1.] *so Dyce i; at l. o.1 Q;*
after gates, *l. 29 Q4.*   31. *Exit*] *Dyce i.*   33.1.] *so Dyce i; at l. o.1 Q.*   *Grisolan*
with] *Dyce i subs.*   34ff. *1st. Off.*] *This ed.; Seru. Q subs.*   35. *Aside*] *Q4.*
37–8.] *so Dyce i;* ... Switzer / In ... *Q;* ... now / A ... *Luc i.*

24–5. *many* ... *centre*] proverbial, usually in the form, 'many ways meet
in one town' (Tilley W176); for the *double entendre* Lucas compared Florio,
III.v: 'All the worlds motions bend and yeelde to this [sexual] coniunction:
it is a matter euery-where infused; and a Centre whereto all lines come, all
things looke'.

 30. *presently*] at once.

 32. *Forobosco*] See Intro., p. 47.

 37–49.] from Nashe, *Unfortunate Traveller* (1594), *Wks*, II.223, of a Switzer
captain whom Wilton duped: 'after hee was throughly searched; ... the
molds of his buttons they turned out, to see if they were not bullets couered

2nd. Off. A Switzer?
1st. Off. With a pistol in his great cod-piece.   40
Bos. Ha, ha, ha!
1st. Off. The cod-piece was the case for't.
2nd. Off. There was a cunning traitor. Who would have
    searched his cod-piece?
1st. Off. True, if he had kept out of the ladies' chambers: –   45
    and all the moulds of his buttons were leaden bullets.
2nd. Off. O, wicked cannibal! a fire-lock in's cod-piece!
1st. Off. 'Twas a French plot, upon my life.
2nd. Off. To see what the devil can do!
Ant. All the officers here?   50
Off. We are: –
Ant. Gentlemen,
    We have lost much plate you know; and but this evening
    Jewels, to the value of four thousand ducats
    Are missing in the duchess' cabinet –   55
    Are the gates shut?
Off.   Yes.

39ff. *2nd. Off.*] *This ed.; 2. Seru. Q subs.*   43–6.] *so Dyce i;* ... traitor, /
Who ... cod-piece? / *Seru* ... chambers: / And ... Q, *Luc i.*   50. All] Q;
Are all *Q4.*   officers] *Q2*; Offices *Q.*   51, 56. *Off.*] *This ed.; Seru. Q subs.*

---

ouer with thred; the cod-peece in his diuels breeches (for they wer then in
fashion) they said plainly was a case for a pistol . . .'
    Switzer = Swiss mercenary; these were frequently used in feuds between
Italian noblemen. A *cod-piece* was a necessary accessory of close-fitting hose
or breeches; it was often enlarged and ornamented (cf. *W.D.*, v.iii.99–101),
and sometimes used as a pocket for handkerchief, purse or even oranges.
But cod-pieces were discarded by the fashionable in England in the 1590s
(see Nashe's parenthesis), and by all soon after 1600.
    41.] This is bawdy laughter; Bosola probably hears a pun on pizzle
(= penis), for the 'current colloquial pronunciation of *pistol* [was] without
the medial *t* as in castle' (H. Kökeritz, *Shakespeare's Pronunciation* (1953),
p. 135). There is a pun on Pistol's name in *2H4*.
    47–8.] 'French disease', 'cannibal' and 'fire' were all used as slang for
syphilis: see, for example, John Cooke, *Greene's Tu Quoque* (1614), Hiv,
'May the French Canniball eate into they flesch, / And picke thy bones'
(Cambridge, citing *O.E.D.*).
    fire-lock] firing mechanism of a pistol; hence, here, source of semen or
sexual drive.
    52. *plate*] gold or silver money.
    54. *cabinet*] private apartment, boudoir.

Ant.   'Tis the duchess' pleasure
Each officer be lock'd into his chamber
Till the sun-rising; and to send the keys
Of all their chests, and of their outward doors,
Into her bedchamber: – she is very sick.   60
Rod. At her pleasure.
Ant. She entreats you take 't not ill: the innocent
Shall be the more approv'd by it.
Bos. Gentleman o'th' wood-yard, where's your Switzer now?
1st. Off. By this hand, 'twas credibly reported by one o' the   65
black guard.   [*Exeunt all except* ANTONIO *and* DELIO.]
Delio. How fares it with the duchess?
Ant.   She's expos'd
Unto the worst of torture, pain, and fear: –
Delio. Speak to her all happy comfort.
Ant. How I do play the fool with mine own danger!   70
You are this night, dear friend, to post to Rome;
My life lies in your service.
Delio.   Do not doubt me –
Ant. O, 'tis far from me: and yet fear presents me
Somewhat that looks like danger.
Delio.   Believe it,
'Tis but the shadow of your fear, no more: 75
How superstitiously we mind our evils!
The throwing down salt, or crossing of a hare,

---

66. S.D.] *Dyce i subs.*

---

63. *Gentleman o'th' wood-yard*] Bosola mocks the 'Gentleman o'th' court'
(cf. l. 34, above). The 'wood-yard' in London was an outlying and disrepu-
table part of Whitehall between the Tilt-yard and the Thames, used for
cutting and storing fuel for heating the palace.
66. *black guard*] lowest menials of a noble household.
71. *post*] speed; ride on post horses.
76–80. *How . . . us*] Cf. Florio, II.xii, on a page used for II.i.99–101: 'A
gust of contrarie winds, the croking of a flight of Ravens, the false pase of a
Horse, the casuall flight of an Eagle, a dreame . . . are enough to overthrow,
sufficient to overwhelme, and able to pul him [man] to the ground'.
Crossing of a hare boded disordered senses (so Lucas, quoting Fletcher's
Wit at Several Weapons, II.iii), or the presence of a witch (cf. G. Giffard,
Dialogue concerning Witches (1593), B1: 'I am afraide, for I see nowe and then
a Hare; which my conscience giueth me is a witch, or some witches spirite').
For *bleeding nose*, see II.iii.41–6. A *stumbling horse* and *singing cricket* boded
death (cf. *R3*, III.iv.86–8, and *W.D.*, v.iv.85–7).

Bleeding at nose, the stumbling of a horse,
Or singing of a cricket, are of pow'r
To daunt whole man in us. Sir, fare you well: 80
I wish you all the joys of a bless'd father;
And, for my faith, lay this unto your breast –
Old friends, like old swords, still are trusted best.

[Exit.]

Enter CARIOLA.

Cari. Sir, you are the happy father of a son –
Your wife commends him to you.
Ant.   Blessed comfort: 85
For heaven-sake tend her well; I'll presently
Go set a figure for's nativity.   *Exeunt.*

SCENA III.

Enter BOSOLA[, *with a dark lantern*].

Bos. Sure I did hear a woman shriek: list, hah?
And the sound came, if I receiv'd it right,
From the duchess' lodgings: there's some stratagem
In the confining all our courtiers
To their several wards: I must have part of it,   5
My intelligence will freeze else: – list again!

83. *Exit*] Dyce i.   83.1.] *so* Dyce i; *at l. 0.1* Q; *Enter Cariola with a Child*
Q4.

II.iii.0.1.] *Q4; Bosola, Antonio* Q.

---

80. *whole man*] Cf. *W.D.*, I.i.45: 'Have a full man within you' (be fully
fortified and resolved).

83.] a rephrasing of the proverbial 'Old friends and old wine are best'
(Tilley F755); see also Tilley F321 and W740.

86. *presently*] immediately, at once.

87. *set ... nativity*] cast a horoscope, calculate the aspects of the astrological houses (see II.i.96, note), for the time of the child's birth. Such
practice was common despite satirical attacks upon it: e.g. Henry IV of
France summoned an astrologer at the moment of Louis XIII's birth.

II.iii.0.1. *dark lantern*] a lantern with an arrangement for concealing its
light (cf. l. 54, below); *O.E.D.* first records the phrase in 1650 but one is
mentioned in *D.M.* at v.iv.43.

5. *wards*] places of guard (cf. mod. 'action stations;' an emergency has
been declared). See, however, l. 24, below.

part] i.e. some function in, or some understanding.

6. *freeze*] *O.E.D.* does not record a similar figurative usage.

It may be 'twas the melancholy bird,
Best friend of silence and of solitariness,
The owl, that scream'd so: –

Enter ANTONIO.

                  hah? Antonio!
Ant. I heard some noise: who's there? what art thou? speak.   10
Bos. Antonio? Put not your face nor body
    To such a forc'd expression of fear –
    I am Bosola; your friend.
Ant.   Bosola! –
    [*Aside*] This mole does undermine me – [*To him*] heard
        you not
    A noise even now?
Bos.   From whence?
Ant.   From the duchess' lodging.   15
Bos. Not I: did you?
Ant.   I did: or else I dream'd.
Bos. Let's walk towards it.
Ant.   No: it may be 'twas
    But the rising of the wind: –
Bos.   Very likely.
    Methinks 'tis very cold, and yet you sweat:
    You look wildly.
Ant.   I have been setting a figure   20
    For the duchess' jewels: –
Bos.   Ah: and how falls your question?
    Do you find it radical?
Ant.   What's that to you?
    'Tis rather to be question'd what design,

---

9. S.D.] *so this ed.; at l. 0.1 Q; at end of line Q4; Enter Antonio, with a Candle his Sword drawn Q4.* 14. S.D.s] *Dyce ii subs.;* This . . . me *within brackets Q.*

---

9. *owl*] also a portent of death.
20–1. *setting . . . jewels*] i.e., casting a horoscope to inquire about the recovery of the stolen goods; so, it was said, thieves could be identified, hiding places revealed, and the course of recovery or final loss foretold.
22. *radical*] *O.E.D.* quoted (*adj.* 6) Lilly, *Christian Astrology* (1647), p. 121: 'The question then shall be taken for radicall, or fit to be judged, when as the Lord of the hour at the time of proposing the question . . . and the Lord of the Ascendant . . ., are of one Triplicity [i.e., in one group of three houses] or be one'; its earliest quotation is from Burton (1621).

When all men were commanded to their lodgings,
Makes you a night-walker.

Bos.   In sooth I'll tell you: 25
Now all the court's asleep, I thought the devil
Had least to do here; I came to say my prayers –
And if it do offend you I do so,
You are a fine courtier.

Ant. [*Aside*]   This fellow will undo me: –
[*To him*] You gave the duchess apricocks today,   30
Pray heaven they were not poison'd!

Bos.   Poison'd! a Spanish fig
For the imputation.

Ant.   Traitors are ever confident,
Till they are discover'd: – there were jewels stol'n too –
In my conceit, none are to be suspected
More than yourself.

Bos.   You are a false steward.   35

Ant. Saucy slave! I'll pull thee up by the roots; –

Bos. May be the ruin will crush you to pieces.
You are an impudent snake indeed, sir.
Are you scarce warm, and do you show your sting?

29–30. S.D.s] *Q4 subs.*   38. You] *Brown ii; Ant.* You *Q, Q2.*

---

25. *night-walker*] commonly used of thieves, rogues etc.

31. *Spanish fig*] According to Nashe, those who 'swallow Spanish figs' are men who 'deuoure anie hooke baited for them' (*Wks*, II.299). The phrase was doubly appropriate, for a *Spanish fig* was also a synonym for the poison supposed to be administered with it (cf. *W.D.*, IV.ii.61).

Lucas suggested that Bosola 'gave the fig' on saying this (i.e., thrust his thumb between the first and middle finger with a phallic implication; this was a common offensive gesture).

34. *conceit*] opinion.

37. *ruin*] falling down (cf. *O.E.D.*, 1 and 1b).

38. *You are ...*] Two consecutive prefixes for Antonio in Q could imply that a further speech for Bosola is missing (so Lucas). But ll. 38–9 might well belong to Bosola, continuing his speech of l. 37 and referring, like l. 35, to Antonio, the upstart ('fine courtier') who is a threatening ('I'll pull thee up ...' l. 36) and strangely prosperous ('snake') steward. In Webster's day, *snake* was used of a needy person or drudge (*O.E.D*, 3, a and b); in Aesop's fable, the snake was treacherous. Compositor A might have anticipated the next speech-prefix for Antonio and, not realizing his error, set it again at the correct place; he certainly confused and omitted prefixes elsewhere in Q.

39. *scarce warm*] just out of hibernation; i.e., only recently having obtained preferment.

Ant. You libel well, sir.

Bos.   No sir, copy it out,   40
      And I will set my hand to't.

Ant. [*Aside*]   My nose bleeds:
      One that were superstitious would count
      This ominous; – when it merely comes by chance.
      Two letters, that are wrought here for my name,
      Are drown'd in blood!   45
      Mere accident: – [*To him*] for you, sir, I'll take order:
      I'th' morn you shall be safe: – [*Aside*] 'tis that must
          colour
      Her lying-in: – [*To him*] sir, this door you pass not:
      I do not hold it fit that you come near
      The duchess' lodgings, till you have quit yourself.   50
      [*Aside*] *The great are like the base – nay, they are the same –*
      When they seek shameful ways, to avoid shame.   *Exit.*

Bos. Antonio hereabout did drop a paper –
      Some of your help, false friend – O, here it is:
      What's here? a child's nativity calculated!   55
      [*Reads*] *The duchess was delivered of a son, 'tween the hours*

---

40. *Ant.*] *Q; not in Q2.* 40–1. No ... to't] *Dyce i; ... sir,) / Copy ...
Q. 41–51. S.Ds.] *Dyce ii subs.* 41–2. My ... count] *so Dyce i; one line Q.*
44. wrought] *Q;* wrote *Q3.* 45–6.] *so Dyce i; one line Q.* 46. order:] *Q;*
order *Dyce i.* 50. quit] *Q3;* quite *Q.* 51–2.] *italicized Q.* 56. Reads] *Dyce
ii.* 56–64.] *so italicized Q4 subs.; all italicized except Latin words Q.*

---

40. *copy it out*] i.e., the supposed 'libel'.
41. *set ... to't*] sign it.
41–3. *My ...*] Cf. II.ii.76–80, and note.
44. *wrought*] i.e., on a handkerchief; busied with this, he drops the copy
of the horoscope.
47. *colour*] disguise.
50. *quit*] acquitted.
54. *false friend*] i.e., his dark lantern.
56–64.] J. Parr (*Tamburlaine's Malady* (1953), pp. 94–100) has shown that
the configurations described never occurred in the early years of the 16th
century. The horoscope was probably invented by Webster (or a professional
astrologer) to prognosticate a violent death as clearly as possible. 'combust'
= 'burnt up', signifying that a planet is positioned within $8\frac{1}{2}°$ of the sun; this
implies that its benign influence is almost destroyed.
   Parr has shown that for 19 Dec. in any year, Capricorn must be the sign
in the first house (cf. II.i.96, note), and that Saturn is the ruler of
Capricorn.

twelve and one, in the night: Anno Dom. 1504, – that's this
year – *decimo nono Decembris,* – that's this night – *taken
according to the meridian of Malfi* – that's our duchess:
happy discovery! – *The lord of the first house, being combust*   60
in the ascendant, signifies short life: and Mars being in
a human sign, joined to the tail of the Dragon, in the
eighth house, doth threaten a violent death; caetera non
scrutantur.

Why now 'tis most apparent: this precise fellow   65
Is the duchess' bawd: – I have it to my wish;
This is a parcel of intelligency
Our courtiers were cas'd up for! It needs must follow
That I must be committed on pretence
Of poisoning her; which I'll endure, and laugh at: –   70
If one could find the father now! but that
Time will discover. Old Castruchio
I'th' morning posts to Rome; by him I'll send
A letter, that shall make her brothers' galls
O'erflow their livers – this was a thrifty way.   75
Though lust do mask in ne'er so strange disguise,
She's oft found witty, but is never wise.   [*Exit.*]

---

68. cas'd] *Q2;* caside *Q.*   76–7.] *italicized Q (and indented).*   76. mask] *Q4;*
masque *Q.*   ne'er] *Q3 (ne're); nea'r Q.*   77. Exit] *Q4.*

The 'human signs' of the zodiac are Gemini, Virgo, Sagittarius and
Aquarius. The 'tail of the Dragon' is the point in the heavens where the
moon crosses the sun's ecliptic in its descent into southern latitude; it was
thought to exert a sinister influence.

Ironically, the son whose nativity is calculated here is the one child surviving at the end of the play from the marriage of the Duchess and Antonio.
An astrologer would suspect that some benevolent influence, as of Jupiter
or Venus, was exerted before the 'combustion' and so delayed the disaster;
by adding *caetera non scrutantur* Webster made it clear that the horoscope
was not fully investigated.

65. *precise*] scrupulous, correct.

67. *parcel*] item, piece.

68. *cas'd*] III.ii.139 suggests that it is unnecessary to look further for an
explanation of Q's 'caside'.

75. *livers*] The liver was thought to be the source of sexual passion.
thrifty] profitable.

76–7.] Only the second line is likely to have been proverbial (so Dent).

76. *mask*] 'Masque' and *mask* were not differentiated in spelling.

SCENA IV.

Enter Cardinal *and* JULIA.

Card. Sit: thou art my best of wishes – prithee tell me
    What trick didst thou invent to come to Rome
    Without thy husband.
Julia.   Why, my lord, I told him
    I came to visit an old anchorite
    Here, for devotion.
Card.   Thou art a witty false one: –   5
    I mean to him.
Julia.   You have prevail'd with me
    Beyond my strongest thoughts: I would not now
    Find you inconstant.
Card.   Do not put thyself
    To such a voluntary torture, which proceeds
    Out of your own guilt.
Julia.   How, my lord?
Card.   You fear   10
    My constancy, because you have approv'd
    Those giddy and wild turnings in yourself.
Julia. Did you e'er find them?
Card.   Sooth, generally for women:
    A man might strive to make glass malleable,
    Ere he should make them fixed.
Julia.   So, my lord –   15
Card. We had need go borrow that fantastic glass
    Invented by Galileo the Florentine,
    To view another spacious world i'th' moon
    And look to find a constant woman there.

II.iv.o.1.] *Q4; Cardinall, and Iulia, Seruant, and Delio Q.*   10–11. You . . .] *so
Dyce i; one line Q.*   12. turnings] *Q3; turning Q.*   13. generally] *Q; generally; Haz.* women:] *Q; women, Dyce i, Haz.*

II.iv.5. *devotion*] The same quibble is found in *W.D.*, II.i.150.
witty] This echoes the 'sentence' at the end of the previous scene.
16–19.] Cf. Donne, *Ignatius His Conclave* (1611), pp. 116–17: 'I will write
to the Bishop of Rome: he shall call Galilaeo the Florentine to him; who by
this time hath throughly instructed himselfe of all the hills, woods, and Cities
in the new world, the Moone. And since he effected so much with his first
Glasses, . . . he may draw the Moone . . . as neere the earth as he will' (so
Marcia Anderson, *ap.* Dent).

Julia. This is very well, my lord.
Card.   Why do you weep?   20
    Are tears your justification? the self-same tears
    Will fall into your husband's bosom, lady,
    With a loud protestation, that you love him
    Above the world: – come, I'll love you wisely,
    That's jealously, since I am very certain   25
    You cannot me make cuckold.
Julia.   I'll go home
    To my husband.
Card.   You may thank me, lady,
    I have taken you off your melancholy perch,
    Bore you upon my fist, and show'd you game,
    And let you fly at it: – I pray thee kiss me –   30
    When thou wast with thy husband, thou wast watch'd
    Like a tame elephant: – still you are to thank me –
    Thou hadst only kisses from him, and high feeding,
    But what delight was that? 'twas just like one
    That hath a little fing'ring on the lute,   35
    Yet cannot tune it: – still you are to thank me.
Julia. You told me of a piteous wound i'th' heart,
    And a sick liver, when you woo'd me first,
    And spake like one in physic.

26. me make] *Q;* make me *Q2.*

---

25. *jealously*] probably, 'ardently' or 'solicitously' (cf. *O.E.D.*, 1 and 3, and *Jealous, a,* 1–3); he is assuring her that love is better without marriage. There may be an ironic quibble on the more usual meaning of *jealously.*
    28–30. *perch...fist...game...fly*] terms of falconry.
    31–2. *watch'd...elephant*] Cf. *A.Q.L.,* I.i.158–60: 'she rail'd vpon me when I should sleep, / And that's, you know, intollerable; for indeed / 'Twill tame an Elephant'. The huge and, in Webster's day, almost fabulous animal was proverbially unmanageable. *watch'd* = (1) 'kept awake' (cf. *O.E.D.,* 2 and 13), and, perhaps, (2) 'kept in sight'.
    32–6. *Still...Still...me*] 'I pray thee, kiss me' (l. 30), following soon after 'You may thank me, lady' (l. 27) suggests that the Cardinal was asking for kisses at that point. Now he does so again, for the second and third times. Under the Cardinal's coaxing, Julia's mood has changed very noticeably in her next speech, from blunt rejection to intimacy and a teasing reproof. Such prolonged and intimate physical contact is rarely called for in Jacobean theatres which used young male actors for all women's roles.
    33. *high feeding*] lavish, luxurious food.
    38. *liver*] Cf. I.i.298, note.
    39. *in physic*] under a doctor's care.

Card.   Who's that? –
Rest firm: for my affection to thee,   40
Lightning moves slow to't.

Enter Servant.

Serv.   Madam, a gentleman,
That's come post from Malfi, desires to see you.
Card. Let him enter, I'll withdraw.   *Exit.*
Serv.   He says,
Your husband, old Castruchio, is come to Rome,
Most pitifully tir'd with riding post.   [*Exit.*]   45

Enter DELIO.

Julia. [*Aside*] Signior Delio! 'tis one of my old suitors.
Delio. I was bold to come and see you.
Julia.   Sir, you are welcome.
Delio. Do you lie here?
Julia.   Sure, your own experience
Will satisfy you, no – our Roman prelates
Do not keep lodging for ladies.
Delio.   Very well: 50
I have brought you no commendations from your
    husband,
For I know none by him.
Julia.   I hear he's come to Rome?
Delio. I never knew man and beast, of a horse and a knight,
So weary of each other – if he had had a good back,
He would have undertook to have borne his horse,   55
His breech was so pitifully sore.

41. S.D.] *so this ed.; at l. 0.1 Q; after l. 39 Dyce i.*   45. *Exit*] *Dyce i.*   45.1.] *so Q4; at l. 0.1. Q.*   46. *Aside*] *Dyce ii.*   47. you are] *Q2;* your are *Q;* you're *conj. this ed.*   52. Rome ?] *Q;* Rome. *Q2.*   53. of] *Q;* or *conj. Leeck.*

40–1. *Rest ... to't*] The comparison was not unusual, but normally it illustrated love's impermanence or destruction: cf., e.g., *Bussy,* v.i.177–8: 'O what a lightning / Is man's delight in women! what a bubble, ...' *to't* = 'in comparison with it'.
    53. *of*] Emending to 'or' would give better grammar, but the stiff sentence structure may be appropriate to Delio's careful approach.
    54. *had ... back*] implying that he is impotent as well as weak; cf. II.v.73 and *W.D.,* I.ii.33–4.

Julia.   Your laughter
     Is my pity.
Delio.   Lady, I know not whether
     You want money, but I have brought you some.
Julia. From my husband?
Delio.   No, from mine own allowance.
Julia. I must hear the condition, ere I be bound to take it.   60
Delio. Look on't, 'tis gold – hath it not a fine colour?
Julia. I have a bird more beautiful.
Delio. Try the sound on't.
Julia.   A lute-string far exceeds it;
     It hath no smell, like cassia or civet,
     Nor is it physical, though some fond doctors   65
     Persuade us seethe 't in cullises – I'll tell you,
     This is a creature bred by . . .

                    [*Enter* Servant.]

Serv.   Your husband's come,
     Hath deliver'd a letter to the Duke of Calabria,
     That, to my thinking, hath put him out of his wits.
                                        [*Exit.*]
Julia. Sir, you hear –   70
     Pray let me know your business and your suit,
     As briefly as can be.
Delio.   With good speed – I would wish you
     (At such time as you are non-resident
     With your husband) my mistress.

---

67. S.D.] *Q4* (*at end of line*). 68–9.] *so* Dyce *i;* . . . that, / To . . . *Q.*
69. *Exit*] *Q4 subs.*

---

64. *cassia*] properly, an inferior kind of cinnamon; but, influenced by the
Bible (e.g., *Psalms*, xlv.8) and perhaps Virgil and Ovid, poets often used it
for a plant of great fragrance (so *O.E.D.*, 1 and 3).
     65. *physical*] medicinal.
     66. *cullises*] broths.
     67. *This . . . by*] Cf. *Characters* (1615), 'A Devillish Usurer': 'He puts his
money to the vnnaturall Act of Generation'; Julia is about to say that gold
is 'a breed for barren metal' (*Mer. V.*, I.iii.135).
     71. *suit*] petition; Julia speaks as if she were a 'great man' giving a hurried
audience.
     74. *my mistress*] Lucas suggested that Delio intended to use Julia as a
means of gaining information about Antonio's enemies (as Bosola does later,

Julia. Sir, I'll go ask my husband if I shall,   75
And straight return your answer.   *Exit.*
Delio.   Very fine!
Is this her wit or honesty that speaks thus?
I heard one say the duke was highly mov'd
With a letter sent from Malfi: – I do fear
Antonio is betray'd. How fearfully   80
Shows his ambition now! unfortunate fortune!
They pass through whirlpools and deep woes do shun,
Who the event weigh, ere the action's done.   *Exit.*

SCENA V.

Enter Cardinal, *and* FERDINAND *with a letter.*

Ferd. I have this night digg'd up a mandrake.
Card.   .   Say you?

82–3.] *italicized Q4;* "They . . . Q.
II.v.o.1.] *Q4 subs.; Cardinall,* . . . Q.   I.   digg'd] Q^b (dig'd); dig Q^a.

and Francisco uses Zanche in *W.D.*); but this notion is nowhere stated or developed.

Perhaps Webster purposely avoided an 'explanation' or 'development' of this incident, and so used it to aggravate the audience's sense of a growing web of intrigue and an increasing complexity of character; the concluding 'sentence' would support such a response.

II.v.1–2. *I . . . with't*] A *mandrake* (i.e., mandragora) is a poisonous plant formerly used medicinally for its narcotic and emetic properties. When forked its root can look like a caricature of the human form. Gerarde's *Hertball* (1597), S4^v–5, recounts some 'ridiculous tales' about it, and in his two main tragedies Webster alludes to several of these: it was said to utter a shriek when pulled from the ground (cf. *W.D.*, v.vi.67), to feed on blood (cf. *W.D.*, III.iii.114–15), and to have the power to madden by its shriek any who pulled it up (see this passage). Webster also mentions its poisonous qualities (cf. *W.D.*, III.i.50–2). He once calls it 'mandragora' when he alludes to its narcotic properties (cf. *D.M.*, IV.ii.233).

But Ferdinand's cry is still puzzling. That he feels himself *grown mad* could have been said simply: the *mandrake* establishes at once a sense of fantasy, vivid sensation, and disfigured, naked bodies. Webster's substitution of *digged*, for an expected 'pulled', adds a suggestion of extreme physical effort.

Ferdinand's reaction to the news of the birth of his sister's son is not due wholly to thwarted political intrigue as he says later (cf. IV.ii.280–4), or to outraged honour and pride of family as he implied in Act I; the cry shows, at the beginning of this crucial scene, which is the climax of Act II, that his reaction involves, in some fantastic way, horror, violence and sexuality.

Ferd. And I am grown mad with't.

Card.   What's the prodigy?

Ferd. Read there – a sister damn'd; she's loose i'th' hilts:
   Grown a notorious strumpet.

Card.   Speak lower.

Ferd.   Lower?
   Rogues do not whisper 't now, but seek to publish 't   5
   (As servants do the bounty of their lords)
   Aloud; and with a covetous searching eye
   To mark who note them: – O confusion seize her!
   She hath had most cunning bawds to serve her turn,
   And more secure conveyances for lust   10
   Than towns of garrison for service.

Card.   Is't possible?
   Can this be certain?

Ferd.   Rhubarb, O for rhubarb
   To purge this choler! here's the cursed day
   To prompt my memory, and here 't shall stick
   Till of her bleeding heart I make a sponge   15
   To wipe it out.

---

3. *loose . . . hilts*] (1) unreliable, (2) open to any man. A *hilt* is the handle of a sword or dagger.

7. *covetous*] because they hope to be paid for future silence, or further information.

9. *serve her turn*] be useful to her, answer her purpose. The phrase could be used with sexual innuendo; cf. *Tit.*, II.i.95–6.

11. *service*] 'supplies' (cf. *O.E.D.*, *sb*¹., 23); and, quibblingly, 'sexual indulgence' (cf. *O.E.D.*, *serve, v.*, 52).

12–13. *rhubarb . . . choler*] *choler*, or 'bile', was considered to be one of the 'four humours' contributing to the 'complexion' or temperament of a person; *rhubarb* was a common prescription for dealing with an excess of it.
P. Charron, *Of Wisdom* (tr. 1608), G4, says *choler* 'stirreth vp furious vapors in our spirits, which blinde vs and cast vs headlong to whatsoeuer may satisfie the desire which we haue of reuenge'.

13. *here's*] Lucas suggested that Ferdinand refers to the horoscope which Bosola has sent to Rome, and at 'here 't shall stick' thrusts it back into his bosom. But this gesture might be too difficult for an actor to effect quickly enough for this 'wild' scene. Ferdinand's following words are highly figurative – 'Till of her bleeding heart I make a sponge' – and he may be speaking so already: like Hamlet, he may allude to the 'table of his memory' and the 'book and volume of his brain' (*Ham.*, I.v.97–104). This would fittingly indicate the ineradicable nature of his sensations, and the mingling of fact and fiction.

Card.   Why do you make yourself
So wild a tempest?
Ferd.   Would I could be one,
That I might toss her palace 'bout her ears,
Root up her goodly forests, blast her meads,
And lay her general territory as waste   20
As she hath done her honours.
Card.   Shall our blood,
The royal blood of Aragon and Castile,
Be thus attainted?
Ferd.   Apply desperate physic:
We must not now use balsamum, but fire,
The smarting cupping-glass, for that's the mean   25
To purge infected blood, such blood as hers: –
There is a kind of pity in mine eye,
I'll give it to my handkercher; and now 'tis here,
I'll bequeath this to her bastard.
Card.   What to do?
Ferd. Why, to make soft lint for his mother's wounds,   30
When I have hew'd her to pieces.
Card.   Curs'd creature!
Unequal nature, to place women's hearts
So far upon the left side!
Ferd.   Foolish men,
That e'er will trust their honour in a bark

---

28. handkercher] *Q;* handkerchief *Q3.*   30. mother's] *Q2;* mother *Q.*

---

23. *attainted*] The Cardinal seems to use the word legally, as 'held to be
stained or corrupted' (*O.E.D.*, 6); Ferdinand to understand it more physically, as 'infected' (cf. l. 26), and he speaks of 'her' blood rather than 'our
blood'. For the cardinal, *blood* = 'noble lineage'; and for Ferdinand, 'life-
blood' or 'passion, sensual appetite' (cf. i.i.297, note, and i.i.453).
    24. *balsamum*] balm, aromatic resin mixed with oils.
    25. *cupping-glass*] surgical vessel in which a vacuum is created by the
application of heat, and then is used to draw off blood.
    32–3. *place . . . side*] Cf. Matthieu, *History of Louis XI* (1614), V2ᵛf.: 'The
hearts of men lie on the left side; they are full of deceit; Truth, freedome
and loyalty are rare, vnknowne and exiled qualities'; and in the margin,
'Aristotle . . . saith that man onely hath his hart on the left side, and all beasts
haue it in the middest of their brests' (so Dent). See also Painter, where the
Duchess's brother says that women 'seem to be procreated and borne against
all order of nature, . . .' (App. I, p. 274). *Unequal* = 'unjust'.

Made of so slight, weak bulrush as is woman,   35
Apt every minute to sink it!
Card. Thus ignorance, when it hath purchas'd honour,
It cannot wield it.
Ferd.   Methinks I see her laughing –
Excellent hyena! – talk to me somewhat, quickly,
Or my imagination will carry me   40
To see her, in the shameful act of sin.
Card. With whom?
Ferd.   Happily with some strong thigh'd bargeman;
Or one o'th' wood-yard, that can quoit the sledge,
Or toss the bar, or else some lovely squire
That carries coals up to her privy lodgings.   45
Card. You fly beyond your reason.
Ferd.   Go to, mistress!
'Tis not your whore's milk that shall quench my
     wild-fire,
But your whore's blood.

37.] *so Samp;* Thus / Ignorance ... *Q.*   43. o'th'] *Q3;* th' *Q.*

37–8. *Thus ... it*] Cf. Hall, *Characters*, 'The Truly Noble': 'He so studies,
as one that knows ignorance can neither purchase honour, nor wield it'.
purchas'd = 'obtained' (as often).

38–9. *Methinks ... hyena*] The cry of a *hyena* sounds like a laugh.
Topsell's *Four-Footed Beasts* (1607), pp. 435–42, distinguishes four kinds of
hyena. The 'first and vulgar kind' cannot 'see one quarter so perfectly in the
day as in the night; ... the female is far more subtill then the male, and
therefore more seldome taken ...' She can kill a sleeping man 'with ... some
secret worke of nature by stretching her body vpon him'. So the animal
became a type of treachery, especially in woman.
   But since Ferdinand seems to see and hear the Duchess as if she were
present, Topsell's second kind of *hyena* may be alluded to: 'their voices are
so shrill and sounding, that although they be very remote and farre off, yet
do men heare them as if they were hard by ... they barke onely in the night
time'.

42. *Happily*] commonly used as 'haply'.

43. *wood-yard*] Cf. II.ii.63, note.
quoit the sledge] throw the hammer.

45. *carries coals*] a proverbial phrase, = 'do any dirty work' or 'submit to
indignity' (cf. *O.E.D.*, *coal*, 12). Here, after 'strong thigh'd', 'quoit the
sledge' and 'toss the bar', and, in association with 'privy' and 'lodgings' (cf.
III.ii.2–6), the phrase carries a similar innuendo in the assumption that the
'lovely squire' is not literally blackened by coals but arrives prepared for the
fire of sexual encounter.

47. *wild-fire*] i.e., raging passion (see III.ii.115–16).

Card. How idly shows this rage! which carries you,
    As men convey'd by witches through the air,   50
    On violent whirlwinds – this intemperate noise
    Fitly resembles deaf men's shrill discourse,
    Who talk aloud, thinking all other men
    To have their imperfection.
Ferd.   Have not you
    My palsy?
Card.   Yes – I can be angry   55
    Without this rupture: there is not in nature
    A thing that makes man so deform'd, so beastly,
    As doth intemperate anger: – chide yourself.
    You have divers men who never yet express'd
    Their strong desire of rest, but by unrest,   60
    By vexing of themselves: – come, put yourself
    In tune.
Ferd.   So; I will only study to seem
    The thing I am not. I could kill her now,
    In you, or in myself, for I do think
    It is some sin in us, heaven doth revenge   65
    By her.
Card.   Are you stark mad?
Ferd.   I would have their bodies
    Burnt in a coal-pit, with the ventage stopp'd,
    That their curs'd smoke might not ascend to heaven:
    Or dip the sheets they lie in, in pitch or sulphur,
    Wrap them in't, and then light them like a match;   70
    Or else to boil their bastard to a cullis,

49–50.] *so Dyce i;* . . . rage? / Which . . . *Q.*   55. Yes –] *Luc i;* Yes, *Q;* Yes, but *Dyce ii;* Yes; *Haz;* Yet *conj. Samp;* Yes, yet *McIl.*   56. rupture] *Q;* rapture *conj. Dyce ii.*

---

55. *palsy*] paralysis; involuntary shaking.

56. *rupture*] Dyce's 'rapture' is followed by several editors and supported by Compositor B's setting of 'distruction' for 'distraction' (I.i.381); but 'palsy' of the previous line and 'deform'd' of the following suggest a sequence of word-play on physical disabilities.

62–6. *So . . . her*] See Intro., p. 36.

67. *coal-pit*] a pit for making charcoal.

69–70.] Cf. Painter's account of Otho's 'butcherly' cruelty (App. I, p. 279).

And give 't his lecherous father, to renew
The sin of his back.
Card.   I'll leave you.
Ferd.   Nay, I have done –
I am confident, had I been damn'd in hell
And should have heard of this, it would have put me   75
Into a cold sweat: – In, in; I'll go sleep –
Till I know who leaps my sister, I'll not stir:
That known, I'll find scorpions to string my whips,
And fix her in a general eclipse.   *Exeunt.*

76–7. *I'll ... stir*] This is echoed and, perhaps, revalued at the beginning
of the next Act (III.i.21–2). Webster has been taken to task for allowing
Ferdinand to be inactive for two or three years following the discovery of
the Duchess's child. But his response to this news is both wild and paralysed
(cf. 'palsy', l. 55): while he wants to act (and does act in fantasy), he is unable
to bring himself to do so. Such a state of being is consistently portrayed in
this scene and later: his talk of a husband (an absurd one) for his sister may
be both a probe and a self-indulgence; his silence on coming into her
chamber in III.ii and his subsequent questions, generalizations, cruelty and
refusal to act are best understood as a mixture of passion and paralysis. 'I
will never see thee more' (ll. 136 and 141) is followed by rapid action, in
riding away (cf. ll. 161–2).
    78. *scorpions ... whips*] Cf. *W.D.*, II.i.245. The idea derives from I *Kings*,
xii.II: my father hath chastised you with whips, but I will chastise you with
scorpions' – where 'scorpions' is thought to mean knotted or barbed scourges
(so *O.E.D.*).
    79. *general*] total.

Act III

ACTUS III, SCENA I.

Enter ANTONIO *and* DELIO.

Ant. Our noble friend, my most beloved Delio!
　　O, you have been a stranger long at court –
　　Came you along with the Lord Ferdinand?
Delio. I did sir; and how fares your noble duchess?
Ant. Right fortunately well: she's an excellent　　　　　5
　　Feeder of pedigrees; since you last saw her,
　　She hath had two children more, a son and daughter.
Delio. Methinks 'twas yesterday: let me but wink,
　　And not behold your face, which to mine eye
　　Is somewhat leaner, verily I should dream　　　　　10
　　It were within this half-hour.
Ant. You have not been in law, friend Delio,
　　Nor in prison, nor a suitor at the court,
　　Nor begg'd the reversion of some great man's place,
　　Nor troubled with an old wife, which doth make　　　15
　　Your time so insensibly hasten.
Delio.　　　　　　　　　　Pray sir, tell me,
　　Hath not this news arriv'd yet to the ear
　　Of the Lord Cardinal?
Ant.　　　　　　　　　　I fear it hath –
　　The Lord Ferdinand, that's newly come to court,
　　Doth bear himself right dangerously.
Delio.　　　　　　　　　　Pray why?　　　　　20
Ant. He is so quiet, that he seems to sleep
　　The tempest out, as dormice do in winter:

III.i.0.1.] *Q4; Antonio, and Delio, Duchesse, Ferdinand, Bosola Q.*

III.i.5–11.] Antonio jokes confidently or unfeelingly about his wife's child-bearing, as if unaware of the growing dangers of their secret marriage; Delio catches his boastful and playful tone.

16.] *insensibly*] (1) imperceptibly; (2) foolishly.

22. *dormice*] Cf. I.i.282, and note. 'To sleep like a dormouse' was a proverb (Tilley D568).

Those houses that are haunted are most still,
Till the devil be up.
Delio.   What say the common people?
Ant. The common rabble do directly say   25
She is a strumpet.
Delio.   And your graver heads,
Which would be politic, what censure they?
Ant. They do observe I grow to infinite purchase
The left-hand way, and all suppose the duchess
Would amend it, if she could: for, say they,   30
Great princes, though they grudge their officers
Should have such large and unconfined means
To get wealth under them, will not complain
Lest thereby they should make them odious
Unto the people – for other obligation   35
Of love, or marriage, between her and me,
They never dream of.

Enter FERDINAND *and* Duchess.

Delio.   The Lord Ferdinand
Is going to bed.
Ferd.   I'll instantly to bed,
For I am weary: – I am to bespeak
A husband for you.
Duch.   For me, sir! pray who is't?   40
Ferd. The great Count Malateste.
Duch.   Fie upon him, –
A count! he's a mere stick of sugar-candy,

37. S.D.] *so Luc i; at l. o.i Q; at end of line Q4; after* going to bed, *l. 38, Dyce
i.* Duchess] *This ed.; Dutchess, and Bosola Q4; Duchess and Attendants Dyce
ii subs.*   39. to] *Q2; to be Q.*

25. *directly*] plainly, simply.
27. *censure*] judge.
28. *purchase*] acquisitions, wealth.
31–5. *Great...people*] from Donne, *Ignatius His Conclave* (1611), p. 92:
'...Princes, who though they enuy and grudge, that their great Officers
should haue such immoderate meanes to get wealth; yet they dare not com-
plaine of it, least thereby they should make them odious and contemptible
to the people' (so Marcia Anderson, *ap.* Dent).
42. *sugar-candy*] Cf. *D.L.C.*, ii.i.153–5: 'You are a foole, a precious
one – you are a meere sticke of Sugar Candy, a man may looke quite
thorow you'.

You may look quite thorough him: when I choose
A husband, I will marry for your honour.

Ferd. You shall do well in't: – how is't, worthy Antonio?   45

Duch. But sir, I am to have private conference with you
About a scandalous report, is spread
Touching mine honour.

Ferd.   Let me be ever deaf to't:
One of Pasquil's paper bullets, court-calumny,
A pestilent air which princes' palaces   50
Are seldom purg'd of: yet, say that it were true, –
I pour it in your bosom – my fix'd love
Would strongly excuse, extenuate, nay, deny
Faults, were they apparent in you: go be safe
In your own innocency.

Duch.   O bless'd comfort!   55
This deadly air is purg'd.

                              Exeunt [*all except* FERDINAND].

Ferd.   . Her guilt treads on
Hot-burning coulters: –

---

54. were] *Q3*; where *Q.*   55. *Duch.*] *Q; Duch. (aside) Dyce ii.*   56. *all
except Ferdinand*] *Dyce ii subs.; manent Ferd. Bosola Q4.*   57. S.D.] *so Dyce
ii; at l. o.1 Q; at l. 37 Q4.*

---

45. *how . . . Antonio*] Ferdinand supposes him to be the Duchess's pander,
and here tries to make him betray his complicity; the Duchess immediately
tries to divert attention.

49. *Pasquil's . . . bullets*] Pasquil was, reputedly, a schoolmaster (some
authorities say a cobbler) who lived in Rome in the 15th century and had a
bitter tongue; his name was transferred to an old statue placed in Piazza
Navona to which it was a custom to attach topical lampoons. The original
Latin pasquinades were collected and published in 1544; the form had its
greatest vogue in Italy in 1585–90.

For *bullets*, cf. *Ado*, II.iii.249–50: 'quips and sentences and these paper
bullets of the brain'.

52. *pour . . . bosom*] assure you, confide in you; as Dent has shown, this
is a common phrase, but it may have retained a special implication of ardour
and intimacy for Webster; he used it for Bracciano's first appeal to Vittoria
(*W.D.*, I.ii.205).

52–4. *my . . . you*] from *A.T.*, IV.i.1994–6: 'Loue cannot finde an imper-
fection forth: / But doth excuse, extenuate, or denie / Faults where it likes,
with shaddowes of no woorth'.

56–7. *Her . . . coulters*] Ordeal by red-hot *coulters*, or ploughshares, was
known in Old English law. Emma, the mother of Edward the Confessor,
walked 'barefoot upon nine culters red hote in Winchester Church without

Enter BOSOLA.

Now Bosola,

How thrives our intelligence?

Bos.   Sir, uncertainly:
'Tis rumour'd she hath had three bastards, but
By whom, we may go read i'th' stars.

Ferd.   Why some   60
Hold opinion, all things are written there.

Bos. Yes, if we could find spectacles to read them –
I do suspect there hath been some sorcery
Us'd on the duchess.

Ferd.   Sorcery! to what purpose?

Bos. To make her dote on some desertless fellow   65
She shames to acknowledge.

Ferd.   Can your faith give way
To think there's pow'r in potions, or in charms,
To make us love, whether we will or no?

Bos. Most certainly.

Ferd. Away, these are mere gulleries, horrid things   70
Invented by some cheating mountebanks
To abuse us: – do you think that herbs or charms
Can force the will? Some trials have been made
In this foolish practice; but the ingredients
Were lenitive poisons, such as are of force   75
To make the patient mad; and straight the witch

---

harme (an usuall kind of triall in those daies and then called *Ordalium*) and
so cleered her selfe of that imputation, that she made her chastitie by so
great a miracle more famous to posterity' (Camden's *Britain* (tr. 1610), p.
211). In the course of discussing 'Symptoms of Jealousy', Burton (*Anatomy*,
III.iii.2) lists numerous women who vindicated their chastity in this way.

66–79. *Can . . . her*] The many details and energetic phrasing of this
digression show how readily Ferdinand is drawn to question the sources of
sensual longing.

73. *will*] In view of 'force To make . . . mad' (ll. 75–6) and 'rank blood'
(l. 78 below), *will* here means 'carnal desire, appetite' (*O.E.D.*, 2), rather
than 'wish, intention, power of choice', etc. Cf. Whigham, 1996, pp. 191 etc.
And see, also, III.ii.116–18, note.

75. *lenitive*] soothing. Lucas considered the epithet 'forced' and suggested
that Q's 'lenative' was derived from L. *lenare*, to prostitute. But Webster
used 'lenative' in its ordinary sense in *A.Q.L.*, I.i.91, and often showed particular interest in poisons that work secretly (cf. *W.D.*, II.i.285–7 and note,
and v.i.69–75). Ferdinand means that these potions were sweet to take, but
poisonous in that they rendered the takers crazy.

Swears, by equivocation, they are in love.
The witchcraft lies in her rank blood: this night
I will force confession from her. You told me
You had got, within these two days, a false key   80
Into her bedchamber.
Bos.   I have.
Ferd.   As I would wish.
Bos. What do you intend to do?
Ferd.   Can you guess?
Bos.   No: –
Ferd. Do not ask then:
He that can compass me, and know my drifts,
May say he hath put a girdle 'bout the world   85
And sounded all her quicksands.
Bos.   I do not
Think so.
Ferd.   What do you think then? pray?
Bos.   That you
Are your own chronicle too much; and grossly
Flatter yourself.
Ferd.   Give me thy hand, I thank thee:
I never gave pension but to flatterers,   90
Till I entertained thee. Farewell:
That friend a great man's ruin strongly checks
Who rails into his belief all his defects.   *Exeunt.*

SCENA II.

Enter Duchess, ANTONIO *and* CARIOLA.

Duch. Bring me the casket hither, and the glass: –
You get no lodging here tonight, my lord.

87–8. That . . .] *so Samp*; . . . are / Your . . . *Q.*   92–3.] *italicized Q.*

III.ii.0.1] *Q4 subs.; Dutchesse, Antonio, Cariola, Ferdinand, Bosola, Officers Q.*

82.] Probably the metre stresses 'Can *you* guess'.

85. *put . . . world*] a proverbial phrase often used of Drake's circum-
navigation: see, e.g., G. Whitney, *Emblems* (1586), p. 203, or the ambitious
Bussy's opening speech (*Bussy*, I.i.23).

87–8. *you . . . much*] Cf. *W.D.*, v.i.100–1: "Tis a ridiculous thing for a
man to be his own chronicle', and *Troil.*, II.iii.165–6: 'pride is his own glass,
his own trumpet, his own chronicle'.

III.ii.2. *lodging*] See II.v.45, note.

Ant. Indeed, I must persuade one: –
Duch.   Very good:
    I hope in time 'twill grow into a custom
    That noblemen shall come with cap and knee,   5
    To purchase a night's lodging of their wives.
Ant. I must lie here.
Duch.   Must? you are a lord of mis-rule.
Ant. Indeed, my rule is only in the night.
Duch. To what use will you put me?
Ant.   We'll sleep together: –
Duch. Alas, what pleasure can two lovers find in sleep?   10
Cari. My lord, I lie with her often; and I know
    She'll much disquiet you: –
Ant.   See, you are complain'd of.
Cari. For she's the sprawling'st bedfellow.
Ant. I shall like her the better for that.
Cari. Sir, shall I ask you a question?   15
Ant. I pray thee, Cariola.
Cari. Wherefore still when you lie with my lady
    Do you rise so early?
Ant.   Labouring men
    Count the clock oft'nest Cariola,
    Are glad when their task's ended.
Duch.   I'll stop your mouth.   20
                                   [*Kisses him.*]

10.] *so Q*; Alas, / What...*Dyce i.*   14.] *so Q*;...her / The...*McIl.*
16.1] *Q*; Ay, *Dyce i.*   20.1.] *Dyce ii.*

---

5. *with ... knee*] an informal way of saying 'with cap in hand and bended
knee'.

7. *lord of mis-rule*] one chosen to preside over feasts and revels at Court,
universities, great houses, etc.; he was very young or of low degree, and so
reversed the usual hierarchies. See E. K. Chambers, *Medieval Stage* (1903),
I.403–19, and E. Welsford, *The Fool* (1935), ch. ix.
    Q's hyphen is retained to point the quibble on 'mistress'.

8. *my ... night*] probably suggested by Painter; App. I, p. 263.

9. *use*] with sexual innuendo, which is continued and varied in the following lines.

17. *still*] always.

20. *I'll ... mouth*] The phrase was proverbial (Tilley M1264), and its
application to a kiss common; cf. *W.D.*, IV.ii.192–3, and *Ado*, II.i.321–3.

Ant. Nay, that's but one – Venus had two soft doves
        To draw her chariot: I must have another.   [*Kisses her.*]
        When wilt thou marry, Cariola?
Cari.   Never, my lord.
Ant. O fie upon this single life! forgo it!
        We read how Daphne, for her peevish flight,   25
        Became a fruitless bay-tree; Syrinx turn'd
        To the pale empty reed; Anaxarete
        Was frozen into marble: whereas those
        Which marry'd, or prov'd kind unto their friends,
        Were, by a gracious influence, transshap'd   30
        Into the olive, pomegranate, mulberry;
        Became flow'rs, precious stones, or eminent stars.

---

22. S.D.] *Luc i; She kisses him again Dyce ii.*   25. flight] *Dyce i;* slight *Q.*

24–32.] from Whetstone, *Heptameron* (1582), C4: 'And where Ismarito, attributes such Glorie unto a Single lyfe, because that Daphne was metamorphosed into a Bay tree, whose Branches are always greene: In my opinion, his reason is fayre like the Bay Tree; for the Bay Tree is barren of pleasant fruict, & his pleasing words of weighty matter. Furthermore, what remembrance is theare of faire Sirinx coynesse, refusing to be God Pans wife? other then that she was metamorphosed into a fewe unprofitable Reedes: Or of Anaxaretes chaste crueltie towardes Iphis, [other] then that she remaineth an Image of Stone in Samarin . . . But in the behalf of Mariage, thousands haue ben changed into Olyue, Pomegranate, Mulberie, and other fruictfull trees, sweete flowers, Starres, and precious stones, by whom the worlde is beautified, directed and noorished' (so Dent, who noted that in the 1593 edn, titled *Aurelia*, 'Pans' was misprinted 'Paris' and so may have led Webster on to consider 'Paris' case', ll. 33–42).

Daphne was wooed by Apollo (Ovid, *Met.*, i.452, etc.). Pan made his pipe from the reed into which *Syrinx* was changed (*Met.*, i.691, etc.). Iphis hanged himself at *Anaxarete*'s door and then Venus changed her to stone for being unaffected as his body was taken to its grave (*Met.*, xiv.74, etc.).

The *olive* and *pomegranate* are not associated with any well-known or appropriate metamorphosis: the *mulberry*'s fruit was turned to red from the blood of Pyramus, who slew himself because he thought Thisbe was dead (*Met.*, iv.55–165).

25. *fight*] Dent suggested that Q's 'slight' might be correct because 'Webster's source refers only to Daphne's refusal'. But, according to *O.E.D.*, 'slight' was not used for 'display of contemptuous indifference or disregard' etc. until 1701; in Webster's day it meant a 'small matter, trifle'. Moreover, '*peevish* slight' would be unusefully tautologous. There are other misprints in the following lines.

29. *friends*] often used of lovers, or 'paramours', of either sex; see, for example, *Meas.*, i.iv.29, and *Wint.*, i.ii.108–9.

Cari. This is a vain poetry: but I pray you tell me,
    If there were propos'd me, wisdom, riches, and beauty,
    In three several young men, which should I choose?   35
Ant. 'Tis a hard question: this was Paris' case
    And he was blind in't, and there was great cause;
    For how was't possible he could judge right,
    Having three amorous goddesses in view,
    And they stark naked? 'twas a motion   40
    Were able to benight the apprehension
    Of the severest counsellor of Europe.
    Now I look on both your faces so well form'd,
    It puts me in mind of a question I would ask.
Cari. What is't?
Ant.   I do wonder why hard-favour'd ladies,   45
    For the most part, keep worse-favour'd waiting-women
    To attend them, and cannot endure fair ones.
Duch. O, that's soon answer'd.
    Did you ever in your life know an ill painter
    Desire to have his dwelling next door to the shop   50
    Of an excellent picture-maker? 'twould disgrace
    His face-making, and undo him: – I prithee,
    When were we so merry? – my hair tangles.
Ant. Pray thee, Cariola, let's steal forth the room
    And let her talk to herself; I have divers times   55

---

33. is a] *Q*; is *conj. Samp.*   41. apprehension] *Q*ᵇ (apprehention); approbation *Q*ᵃ.   50. his] *Q*ᵇ; the *Q*ᵃ.

---

33. *vain*] worthless, foolish.
34–42]. Cf. Alexander, *J.G.*, I.i.59–60, where Juno complains of the
judgement of Paris: 'No wonder too though one all iudgement lost, / That
had three naked goddesses in sight'.
40. *motion*] Lucas glossed 'puppet-show', quoting (after *O.E.D.*) Jonson;
but 'proposal' or 'incitement' (cf. *O.E.D.*, 9 and 10) is possibly more
apposite.
50. *his*] Press-corrections in this forme may be authorial; see Intro.,
pp. 43–5.
53. *When ... merry*] 'A lightening' of the spirits was said to precede death
(Tilley L277): cf. *W.D.*, I.ii.269: 'Woe to light hearts – they still forerun our
fall', and *Rom.*, v.iii.88–90.
my hair tangles] The Duchess becomes intent on her hair and her own
image in the 'glass' (l. 1).

Serv'd her the like, when she hath chaf'd extremely:
I love to see her angry: – softly, Cariola.

Exit with CARIOLA.

Duch. Doth not the colour of my hair 'gin to change?
When I wax gray, I shall have all the court
Powder their hair with arras, to be like me: –   60
You have cause to love me; I enter'd you into my heart
Before you would vouchsafe to call for the keys.

Enter FERDINAND [behind].

We shall one day have my brothers take you napping:
Methinks his presence, being now in court,
Should make you keep your own bed: but you'll say   65
Love mix'd with fear is sweetest. I'll assure you
You shall get no more children till my brothers
Consent to be your gossips: – have you lost your tongue?

[Turns and sees Ferdinand.]

'Tis welcome:
For know, whether I am doom'd to live or die,   70
I can do both like a prince. *Ferdinand gives her a poniard.*

---

57. S.D.] *Dyce i subs.; Exeunt Q.*   62.1.] *so Dyce i; at l. o.1 Q; after l. 61*
(*... unseen*) *Q4.* 68–9.] *so Q4; one line Q.* 68.1.] *Luc i subs.*   71. S.D.]
Q^b (to right of two lines of type for l. 71); not in Q^a.

60. *Powder ... arras*] Powdered orris or iris root was used for whitening
and perfuming hair. In England in the 17th century, orris was often called
arras (properly, a rich tapestry fabric) as in *W.D.*, v.iii.117, and that form is
kept in this text for its luxurious associations.
    61–2.] Cf. Sidney, *Arcadia*, I.XI (*Wks*, I.69): '... his fame had so framed
the way to my mind, that his presence, so full of beauty, sweetnes, and
noble conversation, had entred there before he vouchsafed to call for the
keyes'.
    68. *gossips*] godfathers (to your child).
    68. S.D.] Alternatively, she sees him in her mirror (see l. 53, note).
    69.] At once she knows that her brother's presence threatens her life; her
words express no surprise.
    70–1. *know ... prince*] from *Arcadia*, I.iv (*Wks*, I.25): 'Lastly, whether
your time call you to live or die, doo both like a prince'.
    71. *poniard*] presumably his father's (cf.I.i.331–2); it has been presented
with a strange formality before, and is so now (cf. ll. 149–54). The Duchess
knows her life is threathened and expresses no surprise, seeing the poniard
(in the mirror?) before it is given to her.

Ferd.   Die then, quickly!
Virtue, where art thou hid? what hideous thing
Is it that doth eclipse thee?
Duch.   Pray sir, hear me: –
Ferd. Or is it true, thou art but a bare name,
And no essential thing?
Duch.   Sir: –
Ferd.   Do not speak.
Duch.   No sir: 75
I will plant my soul in mine ears to hear you.
Ferd. O most imperfect light of human reason,
That mak'st us so unhappy, to foresee
What we can least prevent! Pursue thy wishes,
And glory in them: there's in shame no comfort   80
But to be past all bounds, and sense of shame.
Duch. I pray sir, hear me: I am married.
Ferd.   So: –
Duch. Happily, not to your liking: but for that,
Alas, your shears do come untimely now
To clip the bird's wings that's already flown!   85
Will you see my husband?
Ferd.   Yes, if I could change
Eyes with a basilisk: –

75–6. No . . .] *so Q; one line McIl.*   78. us] *Q4; not in Q.*   86–7. Yes . . .
basilisk] *so Dyce i; . . . I / Could . . . Q.*

72–5. *Virtue . . . thing*] from *Arcadia*, ii.i (*Wks*, 1.146): 'O Vertue, where
doost thou hide thy selfe? or what hideous thing is this which doth eclips
thee? or is it true that thou weart never but a vaine name, and no essentiall
thing . . . ?' *essential* = real.
77–81.] from the same soliloquy in *Arcadia* as Ferdinand's previous
speech: 'O imperfect proportion of reason, which can too much forsee, &
too little prevent . . . In shame there is no comfort, but to be beyond all
bounds of shame.' See, also, *W.D.*, v.vi.180, and note.
83. *Happily*] haply, perhaps.
84–5.] from *Arcadia*, ii.v (*Wks*, 1.177), where Philoclea is warned not to
fall in love: 'Alas thought Philoclea to here selfe, your sheeres come to late
to clip the birds wings that already is flowne away'. To *clip . . . wings* was a
proverbial saying (Tilley W498).
86–7. *if . . . basilisk*] For the repartee, Lucas compared *R3*, i.ii.150–1: '–
Thine eyes, sweet lady, have infected mine. – Would they were basilisks, to
strike thee dead!'
A *basilisk*, or cockatrice, was a fabled reptile 'brought forth of a Cockes
egge' and hatched by a Snake or Toad (Topsell, *Serpents* (1608), p. 119).

Duch.   Sure, you came hither
      By his confederacy.
Ferd.   The howling of a wolf
      Is music to thee, screech-owl, prithee peace!
      Whate'er thou art, that hast enjoy'd my sister, –   90
      For I am sure thou hear'st me – for thine own sake
      Let me not know thee: I came hither prepar'd
      To work thy discovery, yet am now persuaded
      It would beget such violent effects
      As would damn us both: – I would not for ten millions   95
      I had beheld thee; therefore use all means
      I never may have knowledge of thy name;
      Enjoy thy lust still, and a wretched life,
      On that condition. – And for thee, vile woman,
      If thou do wish thy lecher may grow old   100
      In thy embracements, I would have thee build
      Such a room for him as our anchorites
      To holier use inhabit: let not the sun
      Shine on him, till he's dead; let dogs and monkeys
      Only converse with him, and such dumb things   105
      To whom nature denies use to sound his name;
      Do not keep a paraquito, lest she learn it.
      If thou do love him, cut out thine own tongue
      Lest it bewray him.
Duch.   Why might not I marry?
      I have not gone about, in this, to create   110
      Any new world, or custom.
Ferd.   Thou art undone:
      And thou hast ta'en that massy sheet of lead
      That hid thy husband's bones, and folded it
      About my heart.

---

88. confederacy] *Q3*; consideracy *Q*.   89. thee] *Q4*; the *Q*.   95. damn] *Q2*
(damne); dampe *Q*.

According to Pliny (*Nat. History* (tr. 1601), XXIX.iv) 'all other serpents doe
flie from and are afraid of [it] . . . and (by report) if he do but set his eye on
a man, it is enough to take away his life'.
      89. *to thee*] i.e., 'compared to thee'.
      90–9] Spoken so that her (unseen) lover shall hear.
      106. *use*] ability.

Duch.   Mind bleeds for't.
Ferd.   Thine? thy heart?
    What should I name 't, unless a hollow bullet   115
    Fill'd with unquenchable wild-fire?
Duch.   You are, in this,
    Too strict: and were you not my princely brother
    I would say too willful: my reputation
    Is safe.
Ferd.   Dost thou know what reputation is?
    I'll tell thee – to small purpose, since th' instruction   120
    Comes now too late:
    Upon a time, Reputation, Love, and Death
    Would travel o'er the world; and it was concluded
    That they should part, and take three several ways:
    Death told them, they should find him in great battles,   125
    Or cities plagu'd with plagues; Love gives them counsel
    To inquire for him 'mongst unambitious shepherds,
    Where dowries were not talk'd of, and sometimes
    'Mongst quiet kindred that had nothing left
    By their dead parents: 'Stay', quoth Reputation,   130
    'Do not forsake me; for it is my nature
    If once I part from any man I meet
    I am never found again'. And so, for you:
    You have shook hands with Reputation,

---

115. *bullet*] cannon-ball: explosive shells were introduced in the place of solid ones during the 16th century.

116. *wild-fire*] used of explosives; but cf. II.v.47.

116–18. *Your . . . wilful*] Cf. Cesario to Clarissa in *Fair Maid of the Inn*, I.i, after counselling her not to marry without his approval: '*Clarissa*. You haue my hand for't; – *Cesario*. Which were it not my sisters, I should kisse / With too much heate'. The Duchess's *wilful* probably means 'passionate'; cf. the '*wilful* shipwreck' of Bracciano's 'lascivious dream' (*W.D.*, II.i.32–42). See also III.i.73, and note.

122–33. *Upon . . . again*] based on P. Matthieu, *Henry IV* (tr. 1612), Ss1^v: 'Reputation . . . the goddesse of great courages is so delicate, as the least excesse doth blemish it, an vniust enterprise dishonoreth it . . . It is a spirit that goes and returnes no more. They report that water, fire, and reputation, vndertooke to goe throughout the world, and fearing they should goe astray, they gaue signes one vnto another: Water said that they should find her where as they sawe reeds, and fire whereas the smoke appeared, loose me not said reputation, for if I get from you, you will neuer finde mee againe.' *upon* = once upon.

And made him invisible: – so fare you well.   135
I will never see you more.
Duch.   Why should only I,
   Of all the other princes of the world,
   Be cas'd up, like a holy relic? I have youth,
   And a little beauty.
Ferd.   So you have some virgins   140
   That are witches: – I will never see thee more.   *Exit.*

              Enter ANTONIO *with a pistol*[, *and* CARIOLA].

Duch. You saw this apparition?
Ant.   Yes: we are
   Betray'd; how came he hither? I should turn
   This to thee, for that.
Cari.   Pray sir, do: and when
   That you have cleft my heart, you shall read there   145
   Mine innocence.
Duch.   That gallery gave him entrance.
Ant. I would this terrible thing would come again,
   That, standing on my guard, I might relate
   My warrantable love: –   *She shews the poniard.*
                    ha, what means this?
Duch. He left this with me: –
Ant.   And it seems did wish   150
   You would use it on yourself?

141.1] *so Q4 (subs.); after* apparition, *l. 142 Q; ... and Cariola Dyce i.*
149. S.D.] *so Dyce ii; to right of two lines of type of l. 150 Q.*

137–9. *Why ... relic*] possibly from Pettie, II.75: '... not to suffer a
mayde to go abrode but once or twise in the yeare, and to keepe her inclosed
like a holy relique, is the way to make her ... more easie to bee caught in
a net'.
   140–1. *virgins ... witches*] Cf. III.i.78, and Intro., p. 34.
   141. *I ... more*] preparing for IV.i (see esp. ll. 23–8). The repetition (from
l. 136) gives force to the words; IV.i.23 suggests that they were meant to be
both 'solemn' and 'rash'. Perhaps this is a response to his sister's 'beauty'
(l. 140), or to a 'wilful' attraction to her (l. 118). In Fletcher's *King and No
King* (1611), when Arbaces believes he lusts after his sister, he tells her: 'thy
dwelling must be dark and close / Where I may never see thee' (IV.iv.77–8).
For the effect of this line in performance, see Intro., p. 59.
   142. *apparition*] Meanings ranged from 'spectre' and 'illusion', to 'phe-
nomenon' and 'appearance'.
   144. *This ... that*] i.e., the pistol to Cariola for betrayal.

Duch. His action seem'd
  To intend so much.
Ant. This hath a handle to't
  As well as a point – turn it towards him,
  And so fasten the keen edge in his rank gall: –
  [*Knocking within*]
  How now! who knocks? more earthquakes?
Duch. I stand   155
  As if a mine, beneath my feet, were ready
  To be blown up.
Cari. 'Tis Bosola: –
Duch. Away!
  O misery! methinks unjust actions
  Should wear these masks and curtains, and not we: –
  You must instantly part hence: I have fashion'd it already.   160
  Exit ANTONIO.

Enter BOSOLA.

Bos. The duke your brother is ta'en up in a whirlwind,
  Hath took horse, and's rid post to Rome.
Duch. So late?
Bos. He told me, as he mounted into th' saddle,
  You were undone.
Duch. Indeed, I am very near it.
Bos. What's the matter?   165
Duch. Antonio, the master of our household,
  Hath dealt so falsely with me, in's accounts:
  My brother stood engag'd with me for money
  Ta'en up of certain Neapolitan Jews,
  And Antonio lets the bonds be forfeit.   170
Bos. Strange! – [*Aside*] This is cunning: –

151–2. His . . . much] *so Samp;* . . . Action / Seem'd . . . *Q.*   153–4.] *so Q;*
. . . and / So . . . *Samp.*   154.1.] *Dyce ii.*   160.2] *so Q4; at l. o.1 Q.*
171. *Aside*] *Dyce ii.*

158. *unjust*] faithless, dishonest (cf. *O.E.D.*, 2).
168–70.] i.e., Ferdinand was security (*stood engaged*) for money that the
duchess (*with me*) had borrowed (*ta'en up*), and Antonio, by some breach of
contract (as a failure to pay due interest) causes, or allows (*lets*), Ferdinand
to become liable for the sum borrowed (*bonds be forfeit*).

Duch.   And hereupon
  My brother's bills at Naples are protested
  Against: – call up our officers.
Bos.   I shall.   *Exit.*

                    [*Enter* ANTONIO.]

Duch. The place that you must fly to is Ancona,
  Hire a house there. I'll send after you   175
  My treasure and my jewels: our weak safety
  Runs upon enginous wheels; short syllables
  Must stand for periods. I must now accuse you
  Of such a feigned crime as Tasso calls
  Magnanima menzogna: a noble lie   180
  'Cause it must shield our honours: – hark! they are
    coming.

                Enter [BOSOLA *and*] Officers.

Ant. Will your grace hear me?
Duch. I have got well by you: you have yielded me
  A million of loss; I am like to inherit

173.1.] *Q4.*   177. enginous] *Dyce i*; engenous *Q*; ingenious *Q2.*   181.1.] *Q4*
subs.; *Officers (at l. o.1) Q.*

  172–3. *My . . . Against*] i.e., it has been formally declared (*protested*) that
his bills of exchange, or promissory notes (*bills*), are not acceptable.
  176–7. *our . . . wheels*] 'The world runs on wheels' was a proverb (Tilley
W893), implying haste and impermanence. Perhaps *enginous* is, simply, 'like
an engine'; for which Dyce quoted Dekker, *Whore of Babylon* (1607),
I.ii.165–6: 'For that one Acte giues like an enginous wheele, / Motion to all.'
But it was also used for 'clever, crafty, cunning' (cf. *O.E.D.*, 1).
  178. *periods*] complete sentences.
  179–80. *feigned . . . menzogna*] from *Gerus. Lib.*, 11.22; Soprina takes the
blame for rescuing a statue of the Virgin from a mosque, in order to prevent
wholesale persecution of Christians.
  183. *I . . . by you*] The first of a series of *doubles entendres*, comparable to
those in II.i.118 ff. At l. 187, 'quietus' echoes the 'Quietus est' of I.i.464.
Other quibbling phrases are: 'I pray let him' (i.e., 'be an example for ill'
or 'for good'; or, possibly, *let him* = 'let him go' *or* 'let him remain' – see
O.E.D. 9, 10, and 1, and *1H4*, I.i.91 and *Wint.*, I.ii.41); 'h'as done that . . . I
mean not to publish'; 'use your fortune elsewhere' (cf. I.i.495 and, possibly,
use = 'have intercourse with' – see *O.E.D.*, 10b); 'brook' ('profit from' *or*
'bear with' – see *O.E.D.*, 1 and 3); 'I am all yours, . . . All mine should be
so'; 'your pass' ('permission to go' *or* 'approval' – see *O.E.D.*, 8 and 3); and
'what 'tis to serve . . . with body, and soul'.

The people's curses for your stewardship.   185
You had the trick in audit-time to be sick,
Till I had sign'd your *quietus*; and that cur'd you
Without help of a doctor. – Gentlemen,
I would have this man be an example to you all:
So shall you hold my favour; I pray let him,   190
For h'as done that, alas, you would not think of,
And, because I intend to be rid of him,
I mean not to publish: – use your fortune elsewhere.

Ant. I am strongly arm'd to brook my overthrow,
As commonly men bear with a hard year: 195
I will not blame the cause on't; but do think
The necessity of my malevolent star
Procures this, not her humour. O the inconstant
And rotten ground of service! – you may see:
'Tis ev'n like him, that in a winter night   200
Takes a long slumber o'er a dying fire,
As loth to part from't; yet parts thence as cold
As when he first sat down.

Duch.   We do confiscate,
Towards the satisfying of your accounts,
All that you have.   205

Ant. I am all yours: and 'tis very fit
All mine should be so.

Duch.   So, sir; you have your pass.

Ant. You may see, gentlemen, what 'tis to serve
A prince with body, and soul.   *Exit.*

Bos. Here's an example, for extortion: what moisture is drawn   210
out of the sea, when foul weather comes, pours down and
runs into the sea again.

Duch. I would know what are your opinions of this Antonio.

---

202. As loth] *Q^c*; A-loth *Q^a*.   213.] *so this ed.*; ... opinions / Of ... *Q.*

194. *brook*] endure.
207. *pass*] permission to leave.
210–12.] a commonplace: cf. Cotgrave, *Dictionary* (1611), *s.v.* Mer: 'Les
Rivieres retournent en la mer. Prov. (Said when Princes doe squeeze out of
their spungie Officers the moisture which they haue purloyned from them.)'
(so Dent).

2nd. Off. He could not abide to see a pig's head gaping: I
    thought your grace would find him a Jew.   215
3rd. Off. I would you had been his officer, for your own sake.
4th. Off. You would have had more money.
1st. Off. He stopp'd his ears with black wool; and to those
    came to him for money, said he was thick of hearing.
2nd. Off. Some said he was an hermaphrodite, for he could   220
    not abide a woman.
4th. Off. How scurvy proud he would look, when the treasury
    was full! Well, let him go: –
1st. Off. Yes, and the chippings of the buttery fly after him, to
    scour his gold chain.   225
Duch. Leave us.   *Exeunt* Officers.
    What do you think of these?
Bos. That these are rogues, that in's prosperity,
    But to have waited on his fortune, could have wish'd
    His dirty stirrup riveted through their noses,   230
    And follow'd after's mule, like a bear in a ring;
    Would have prostituted their daughters to his lust;
    Made their first-born intelligencers; thought none happy
    But such as were born under his bless'd planet,
    And wore his livery: and do these lice drop off now?   235
    Well, never look to have the like again:
    He hath left a sort of flatt'ring rougues behind him –

226–7.] *so Dyce i; one lne Q.*   226. S.D.] *so Dyce i; after l. 225 Q subs.; after
l. 227 Q4.*   233. first-born] *Q^c*; first-borne and *Q^a*.

214–15.] a conflation of two proverbs: 'Some cannot abide to see a pig's
head gaping' (of irrational fads, as at *Mer. V.,* IV.i.47), and 'Invite not a Jew
either to pig or pork' (Tilley P310 and J50).
    218. *black wool*] An old cure for deafness was said to be 'take the gall of
an Hare, mixe it with the greace of a Foxe, and with blacke wooll, instill this
into the eare' (Bartholomeus, *De Prop. Rerum* (tr. 1582), VII.xxi).
    224. *chippings . . . buttery*] 'parings of the crust of a loaf' (*O.E.D.*, 2) from
the larder.
    225. *gold chain*] a steward's badge of office; cf. *Tw.N.,* II.iii.128–9: 'Go,
Sir, rub your chain with crumbs'.
    231. *in a ring*] i.e., led on a ring (cf. Abbott §160).
    235. *lice . . . now*] a common image for flatterers: lice were supposed to
leave a body as soon as the blood failed.
    237. *sort*] set, gang.

Their doom must follow: princes pay flatterers
In their own money; flatterers dissemble their vices
And they dissemble their lies: that's justice –   240
Alas, poor gentleman!

Duch. Poor? he hath amply fill'd his coffers.

Bos.   Sure
He was too honest: Pluto, the god of riches,
When he's sent by Jupiter to any man
He goes limping, to signify that wealth   245
That comes on god's name comes slowly: but when
     he's sent
On the devil's errand, he rides post and comes in by
     scuttles.
Let me show you what a most unvalu'd jewel
You have, in a wanton humour, thrown away,
To bless the man shall find him: he was an excellent   250
Courtier, and most faithful, a soldier that thought it
As beastly to know his own value too little
As devilish to acknowledge it too much:
Both his virtue and form deserv'd a far better fortune.

242–3. Sure . . .] *so this ed.; one line* Q.   247. On] *Q2; One Q.*

238–40. *princes . . .*] from Matthieu, *Henry IV* (1612), Cc3: 'Princes pay flatterers, in their owne money: Flatterers dissmble their vices, and they dissemble their lies, that's Justice'.

243–7. *Pluto . . .*] derived, probably through some intermediary, from Lucian, *Timon*, 20 (so Dent).
The *god of riches* was properly called Plutus, but he was sometimes given the name of the god of the underworld. In their original forms the names are related, and *Pluto* may have been transferred to the other god as a propitiatory euphemism or as a mark of the 'devil' (so Bacon, 'Of Riches'), or because wealth comes from underground (so Lucas).

247. *scuttles*] *O.E.D.* glosses 'short hurried runs', but this passage is the only illustration before Addison (1712): moreover 'scuttling' hardly agrees with riding *post* (i.e., express, in haste). Perhaps Webster drops the personification and *scuttles* = 'large baskets' (as used for vegetables, etc.).

248. *unvalu'd*] (1) 'invaluable', and (2) 'not regarded as of value'.

254.] from Jonson's dedication to Prince Henry of *The Masque of Queens* (1609): ' . . . both yor vertue, & yor forme did deserue yor fortune'. Webster drew on this dedication in *Monumental Column* (1613), and on the masque in *W.D.*, III.ii.135.

His discourse rather delighted to judge itself, than show
    itself.   255
His breast was fill'd with all perfection,
And yet it seem'd a private whisp'ring-room,
It made so little noise of 't.
Duch.   But he was basely descended.
Bos. Will you make yourself a mercenary herald,
Rather to examine men's pedigrees than virtues?   260
You shall want him,
For know an honest statesman to a prince
Is like a cedar, planted by a spring:
The spring bathes the tree's root, the grateful tree
Rewards it with his shadow: you have not done so –   265
I would sooner swim to the Bermudas on
Two politicians' rotten bladders, tied
Together with an intelligencer's heart-string,
Than depend on so changeable a prince's favour.
Fare thee well, Antonio; since the malice of the world   270
Would needs down with thee, it cannot be said yet
That any ill happened unto thee,
Considering thy fall was accompanied with virtue.

---

258. It] *Q*; he *conj. Samp.*   266–9.] *so* Dyce i;... Politicians / Rotten ...
-string / Then ... *Q.*   272–3.] *so Samp;* ... fall, / Was ... *Q.*

255.] from *Arcadia*, i.v (*Wks*, 1.32), describing Parthenia: 'a wit which
delighted more to judge it selfe, then to showe it selfe'. *discourse* = 'wit, faculty
of resoning'.

256–8. *His ... of 't*] Cf. *Monumental Column*, ll. 78–9: 'Who had his
breast insteated with the choice / Of vertues, though they made no ambitious
noise'. For *whisp'ring-room* see note at 1.i.334.

259–60.] from *Arcadia*, i.ii (*Wks*, 1.15): '... I am no herald to enquire of
mens pedigrees, it sufficeth me if I know their vertues'.

262–5. *For ... shadow*] probably indebted to *Arcadia*, i.xv (*Wks*, 1.96):
'... a little River neere hand, which for the moisture it bestowed upon rootes
of some flourishing Trees, was rewarded with their shadowe'.

know] i.e., take note that.

266. *Bermudas*] Especially after a wreck in 1609, these 'still-vexed' islands
were famous for wild noises and strange creatures, as for storms (cf. *A.Q.L.*,
v.i.350–67, and *Tempest*, ed. F. Kermode (1954), Intro.).

270–3. *since ...*] a Senecan theme and commonplace, which Webster
found in *Arcadia*, i.iv (*Wks*, 1.24): '... if the wickedness of the world should
oppresse it [prosperity], it can never be said, that evil hapneth to him, who
falles accompanied with vertue'.

down with] overthrow.

Duch. O, you render me excellent music.
Bos.   Say you?
Duch. This good one that you speak of, is my husband.   275
Bos. Do I not dream? can this ambitious age
    Have so much goodness in't, as to prefer
    A man merely for worth, without these shadows
    Of wealth, and painted honours? possible?
Duch. I have had three children by him.
Bos.   Fortunate lady!   280
    For you have made your private nuptial bed
    The humble and fair seminary of peace:
    No question but many an unbenefic'd scholar
    Shall pray for you for this deed, and rejoice
    That some preferment in the world can yet   285
    Arise from merit. The virgins of your land
    That have no dowries, shall hope your example
    Will raise them to rich husbands: should you want
    Soldiers, 'twould make the very Turks and Moors
    Turn Christians, and serve you for this act.   290
    Last, the neglected poets of your time,
    In honour of this trophy of a man,
    Rais'd by that curious engine, your white hand,
    Shall thank you, in your grave, for't; and make that
    More reverend than all the cabinets   295
    Of living princes. For Antonio,
    His fame shall likewise flow from many a pen,
    When heralds shall want coats to sell to men.

282–3. peace:... but] *Q3;* peace,... but: *Q;* peace,... but *Q2.*

---

277. *prefer*] advance; choose.
279. *painted*] false, specious; cf. *W.D.*, i.i.51: 'Leave your painted
comforts'.
282. *seminary*] seed-bed, breeding-place, nursery.
293. *curious*] skilfully or beautifully made, exquisite; cf. Venus of Adonis
(*Ven.*, l. 734): 'the curious workmanship of nature'.
  engine] instrument, device (cf. *O.E.D.*, 10b).
294. *thank... for't*] i.e., write commemorative poems in your honour.
295. *reverend*] venerated.
  cabinets] private rooms.
298. *heralds...*] The granting of arms by the Heralds' College was
subject to abuse; in 1619, a Royal Commission was set up to inquire into
the sale of pedigrees, etc. The wealthy clown Sogliardo in *Every Man Out
of His Humour* buys his arms for £30.

Duch. As I taste comfort in this friendly speech,
　　So would I find concealment.   300
Bos. O, the secret of my prince,
　　Which I will wear on th' inside of my heart.
Duch. You shall take charge of all my coin and jewels,
　　And follow him; for he retires himself
　　To Ancona.
Bos.　　　　　So.
Duch.　　　　　　　Whither, within few days,   305
　　I mean to follow thee.
Bos.　　　　　　　Let me think:
　　I would wish your grace to feign a pilgrimage
　　To Our Lady of Loretto, scarce seven leagues
　　From fair Ancona; so may you depart
　　Your country with more honour, and your flight   310
　　Will seem a princely progress, retaining
　　Your usual train about you.
Duch.　　　　　　　Sir, your direction
　　Shall lead me by the hand.
Cari.　　　　　　　In my opinion,
　　She were better progress to the baths
　　At Lucca, or go visit the Spa   315
　　In Germany, for, if you will believe me,
　　I do not like this jesting with religion,
　　This feigned pilgrimage.

313–15. In...] *so Q;*... opinion, / She ... Lucca, / Or ... *Dyce i;*...
progresse / To ... (*2 lines*) *Samp.*

---

302. *wear ... heart*] Cf. *Ham.*, III.ii.77–8: 'I will wear him / In my heart's
core, ay, in my heart of heart'.
307–12. *I ... you*] By seeming to aid her escape Bosola may aim at enter-
ing the Duchess's confidence more deeply or, as Lucas suggested, aim at
dishonouring her still more by encouraging her to 'jest with religion' and
desert her Duchy (as Francisco 'instructs' Bracciano to 'marry a whore'; see
W.D., IV.iii.52–6).
308. *Our Lady of Loretto*] See Intro., pp. 31–2.
315–16. *Lucca ... Germany*] The spas are mentioned in Florio, in a
passage (II.xv) also speaking of Loretto and Ancona (so Lucas). *Spa* is in
Belgium, some 16 miles south of Liège; the Belgians were often known by
the more general term of Germans.
317–18.] Cariola voices a serious objection: cf. III.iii.60–2, and Marston,
Malcontent (1604), IV.iii: 'A fellow that makes Religion his stawking horse,/
He breedes a plague'.

Duch. Thou art a superstitious fool –
　　Prepare us instantly for our departure:　　　　320
　　Past sorrows, let us moderately lament them,
　　For those to come, seek wisely to prevent them.
　　　　　　　　　　　　　Exit [with CARIOLA].
Bos. A politician is the devil's quilted anvil –
　　He fashions all sins on him, and the blows
　　Are never heard: he may work in a lady's chamber,　　325
　　As here for proof. What rests, but I reveal
　　All to my lord? O, this base quality
　　Of intelligencer! why, every quality i'th' world
　　Prefers but gain or commendation:
　　Now, for this act I am certain to be rais'd,　　　　330
　　And men that paint weeds to the life are prais'd.　　*Exit.*

SCENA III.

Enter Cardinal *with* MALATESTE, FERDINAND *with* DELIO
and SILVIO, *and* PESCARA.

Card. Must we turn soldier then?
Mal.　　　　　　　　The Emperor,
　　Hearing your worth that way, ere you attain'd

322.1. *with Cariola*] *Q4 subs.*
331.] *italicized Q4;* 'And ... *Q.*

III.iii.0.1–2.] *Q4 subs.; Cardinall, Ferdinand, Mallateste, Pescara, Siluio, Delio, Bosola Q.*

321–2.] from Alexander, *Croesus,* III.i.1019–22: 'we should such past mis-fortunes pretermit, / At least no more immoderately lament them, / And as for those which are but comming yet, / Vse ordinary meanes for to preuent them'.
323–5. *A ... heard*] Cf. Chapman, *Byron's Tragedy* (1608), I.ii.53–4: '... great affairs will not be forg'd / But upon anvils that are lin'd with wool', and T. Adams, *Gallant's Burden* (1612), C1ᵛ–2: 'an insensible Heart is the Deuils Anuile, he fashioneth all sinnes on it, and the blowes are not felt'.
325. *lady's chamber*] Cf. *Characters,* 'A Jesuit': 'No place in our Climate hides him so well as a Ladyes Chamber' (Lucas).
326. *rests*] remains.
329. *Prefers*] assists in bringing about, promotes (cf. *O.E.D.,* 2).
330. *quality*] profession.
III.iii.0, S.D.] The location is at Rome again, in a room of a palace which is probably an Aragonian family possession. A conference is taking place

This reverend garment, joins you in commission
With the right fortunate soldier, the Marquis of
    Pescara,
And the famous Lannoy.

Card.   He that had the honour   5
Of taking the French king prisoner?

Mal.   The same –
Here's a plot drawn for a new fortification
At Naples.

Ferd. This great Count Malateste, I perceive,
Hath got employment?

Delio.   No employment, my lord;   10
A marginal note in the muster-book, that he is
A voluntary lord.

Ferd.   He's no soldier?

Delio. He has worn gunpowder in's hollow tooth,
For the toothache.

Sil. He comes to the leaguer with a full intent   15
To eat fresh beef and garlic, means to stay
Till the scent be gone, and straight return to court.

Delio. He hath read all the late service
As the City Chronicle relates it,
And keeps two painters going, only to express   20
Battles in model.

Sil.   Then he'll fight by the book.

13–14.] *so Luc* i; *one line Q.*   20. painters] *Q*ᶜ; Pewterers *Q*ᵃ.   21. he'll] *Q2;*
hel; *Q.*

---

about military and political operations. The two brothers might be sitting at
the head of a large table, the other persons standing around (or possibly
sitting at the far end of the table), in attendance but out of earshot unless
addressed specifically.

    1–3.] For possible sources of these details, see Boklund., 1962. The
Emperor was Charles V.

    7. *plot*] plan.

    12. *voluntary*] volunteer.

    15. *leaguer*] military camp.

    16. *fresh . . . garlic*] food supposed to increase fighting ardour.

    18. *late service*] recent military operations.

    20. *painters*] Press-corrections in this forme are probably authorial.

    21. *model*] scale drawing, ground-plan (cf. *O.E.D.*, 1).

    by the book] a common phrase for 'according to rule, in set phrase or manner';
but here, also, 'theoretically, rather than practically' (cf. *W.D.*, v.iii.21).

Delio. By the almanac, I think –
    To choose good days, and shun the critical.
    That's his mistress' scarf.
Sil.   Yes, he protests
    He would do much for that taffeta –   25
Delio. I think he would run away from a battle
    To save it from taking prisoner.
Sil.   He is horribly afraid
    Gunpowder will spoil the perfume on't –
Delio. I saw a Dutchman break his pate once
    For calling him pot-gun; he made his head   30
    Have a bore in't, like a musket.
Sil. I would he had made a touch-hole to't.
Delio. He is indeed a guarded sumpter-cloth,
    Only for the remove of the court.

Enter BOSOLA.

Pes. Bosola arriv'd! what should be the business?   35
    Some falling out amongst the cardinals.

---

32. to't.] to 't. / *Del.* (= *Catchword*) Q.   33. *Delio.* He] *Brown iii;* He Q.
34.1.] *so Q4; at ll. 0.1–2 Q.*

22–3.] Cf. C. Dariot, *Introduction to Astrological Judgement* (1598), R2:
'I will shew you how in the beginning of any matter the constitution and
due disposition of the Heauens and heauenly bodyes is to bee obserued
and marked, for euery houre of the day is not apt or fit for the beginning of
euery work . . .'
    25. *taffeta*] 'plain-wove, glossy silk' (*O.E.D.*).
    30. *pot-gun*] a child's toy, made of elder (sometimes called a 'pop-gun'),
and hence used contemptuously of a braggart or boaster; this passage is the
first occurrence recorded in *O.E.D.* Cf. *H5*, IV.i.209–10 (Williams to the
disguised king): 'That's a perilous shot out of an elder-gun . . . 'tis a foolish
saying'.
    30, 32. *he*] i.e., the Dutchman.
    33. *He*] Q's catch-word (on G4ᵛ), its full-stop after l. 32, and the intro-
duction of a fresh notion with 'indeed', all suggest either that ll. 33–4 should
be Delio's or that some lines are missing. Compositor B probably omitted
a speech-prefix at 1.i.116. Here, *He* is Malateste.
    33–4. *guarded . . .*] ornamented (*guarded*) cloth covering a pack-horse
when the beast is employed in changing the place of residence of the Court;
cf. *W.D.*, 1.ii.50–1, where Camillo's wit is said to be 'Merely an ass in's
foot-cloth'.

These factions amongst great men, they are like
Foxes: when their heads are divided
They carry fire in their tails, and all the country
About them goes to wreck for't.
Sil.   What's that Bosola?   40
Delio. I knew him in Padua – a fantastical scholar, like such
who study to know how many knots was in Hercules'
club, of what colour Achilles' beard was, or whether
Hector were not troubled with the toothache; he hath
studied himself half blear-eyed to know the true symme-   45
try of Caesar's nose by a shoeing-horn; and this he did
to gain the name of a speculative man.

41–7.] *so Dyce i;* . . . scholler, / Like . . . in / Hercules . . . was, / Or . . . -ach,
/ He . . . the / True . . . this / He . . . *Q;* . . . scholler, / Like . . . knots / Was . . .
was, / Or . . . -ach – / He . . . know / The . . . -horne, / And . . . did / To . . . *Luc*
i.

37–40. *These . . . for't*] an allusion to Samson who tied pairs of foxes
together by their tails and attached firebrands to them, so that they destroyed
the Philistines' harvest (cf. *Judges*, xv.4–5); this was a popular story in moralizing writings of the time.
    41–7.] from Matthieu, *Henry IV* (1612), Qq3ᵛ: 'The study of vaine things
is a toilsome idlenesse, and a painful folly. The spirits beeing once stroken
with this disease . . . spend whole nights to finde how many knots were in
Hercules club, and of what colour Achilles beard was . . .' Florio also provides a slight parallel (I.xxxviii): 'This man, whom about mid-night, when
others take their rest, thou seest come out of his studie meagre-looking, with
eyes-trilling, fleugmatike, squalide, and spauling, doost thou thinke, that
plodding on his bookes he doth seek how he shal become an honester man;
or more wise, or more content? There is no such matter. Hee will either die
in his pursute, or teach posterity the measure of Plautus verses, and the true
Orthography of a Latine worde.'
    Dent called this a 'lamentable intrusion', inconsistent with what we know
of both Delio and Bosola. But young, ambitious men, like Gabriel Harvey,
or Thomas Overbury, or Flamineo (see *W.D.*, I.ii.319–27), came from the
universities to seek preferment with 'great men'; to gain a reputation for
'speculation' would be a recommendation for attention at court. Chapman's
Bussy called himself a 'scholar' in his encounter with Maffé (*Bussy*, Q1,
I.i.183).
    41. *Padua*] This 'nursery of Arts' (*Shr.*, I.i.2) was one of the most famed
universities of the time, being founded in 1238.
    47. *speculative*] 'theorizing', and also 'deeply searching'; *O.E.D.* cites
Bacon, *Advancement* (1605), I.iii.7: 'To be speculative into another man, to
the end to know how to worke him, . . . proceedeth from a heart that is
double'.

Pes. Mark Prince Ferdinand:
  A very salamander lives in's eye,
  To mock the eager violence of fire.   50
Sil. That cardinal hath made more bad faces with his oppres-
  sion than ever Michael Angelo made good ones; he lifts
  up's nose, like a foul porpoise before a storm –
Pes. The Lord Ferdinand laughs.
Delio.   Like a deadly cannon
  That lightens ere it smokes.   55
Pes. These are your true pangs of death,
  The pangs of life that struggle with great statesmen –
Delio. In such a deformed silence, witches whisper
  Their charms.
Card. Doth she make religion her riding-hood   60
  To keep her from the sun and tempest?
Ferd.   That!
  That damns her: – methinks her fault and beauty,
  Blended together, show like leprosy,
  The whiter, the fouler: – I make it a question
  Whether her beggarly brats were ever christen'd.   65

51–3.] *so Dyce i;* . . . oppression / Then . . . ones, / He . . . *Q, Luc i* (. . . before
/ A . . .). 58–9.] *so Samp; one line Q.* 61–3. That . . .] *so Dyce i;* . . . and /
Beauty . . . (*two lines*) *Q.*

49–50.] Salamanders were supposed to live in *fire*, and *fire* was emblematic of passion, destruction, or torment; cf. R.C., *Time's Whistle* (1616;
E.E.T.S. ed., 1871), 119: 'Yet he can live no moe without desire, / Then can
the salamandra without fire'.

51–2. *made . . . ones*] Dent compared Dallington, *View of France* (1604),
N2: 'when I was in Italy, ye should heare them say in derision, that the King
of Spayne [by failing to pay his debts] had made more ill faces vpon the
Exchange, in one day, then Michael Angelo, . . . had euer made good faces
in all his life'.
  The *bad faces* are those of the victims of the cardinal's oppressive acts.

52–3. *lifts . . . storm*] Cf. the proverb, 'The porpoise plays before a storm'
(Tilley P483). The primary sense of *lifts up's nose* is illustrated by *Tp.*,
IV.i.177–8: 'lifted up their noses As they smelt music', but there may also be
an allusion to 'to hold up one's nose' = 'to be proud or haughty' (*O.E.D.*,
nose, 8d).

62–4. *methinks . . . fouler*] Crawford compared Chapman, *Penitential
Psalms* (1612), 'A Great Man', ll. 17–19; 'Ill vpon ill he layes: th' embroderie
/ Wrought on his state, is like a leprosie, / The whiter, still the fouler'.

65. *beggarly brats*] 'beggar's brats' was a proverbial, contemptuous phrase
(so *O.E.D.*).

Card. I will instantly solicit the state of Ancona
        To have them banish'd.
Ferd.   You are for Loretto?
        I shall not be at your ceremony: fare you well.
                                    [*Exit Cardinal.*]
        [*To Bosola*] Write to the Duke of Malfi, my young
            nephew
        She had by her first husband, and acquaint him   70
        With's mother's honesty.
Bos.   I will.
Ferd.   Antonio!
        A slave, that only smell'd of ink and counters,
        And ne'er in's life look'd like a gentleman,
        But in the audit-time – go, go presently,
        Draw me out an hundred and fifty of our horse,   75
        And meet me at the fort-bridge.   *Exeunt.*

SCENA IV.

Enter Two Pilgrims *to the Shrine of Our Lady of Loretto.*

1st. Pil. I have not seen a goodlier shrine than this,
        Yet I have visited many.
2nd. Pil. The Cardinal of Arragon
        Is this day to resign his cardinal's hat;
        His sister duchess likewise is arriv'd   5
        To pay her vow of pilgrimage – I expect
        A noble ceremony.
1st. Pil.   No question: – they come.

68, 69. S.D.] *Cam.*   73. life] *Q2*; like *Q.*
III.iv.o.1.]   *Dyce i; Two . . . Q.*

69–70. *Duke . . . husband*] The only reference to this son; he is ignored in
Ferdinand's hope of treasure (IV.ii.281–3) and Delio's assertion of the rights
of Antonio's son whose survival is Webster's alteration to Painter's account
(V.vi.107–8 and 112–13).
    72. *counters*] small tokens used as an aid in counting.

III.iv.o.1] See Intro. pp. 31–2 for significance of this scene's location and
spectacle. This scene is often cut in performance and may be, in the words
of Q's title page, one of the 'diverse things printed, that the length of the
play would not bear in the presentment'. It is omitted in Q4 of 1678, which
was published 'as it is now acted at the Duke's Theatre'.
    7. S.D. State of Ancona] i.e., its ruling body (cf. 'They are . . .', l. 30).

Here the ceremony of the Cardinal's *instalment in the habit of a soldier,*
performed in delivering up his cross, hat, robes and ring at the shrine,
and investing him with sword, helmet, shield and spurs; then ANTONIO,
the Duchess *and their* Children, *having presented themselves at the*
shrine, are (by a form of banishment in dumb-show expressed towards
them by the cardinal and the State of Ancona) banished: during all which
ceremony, this ditty is sung, to very solemn music, by divers Churchmen;
and then exeunt [all, except the Two Pilgrims].

Arms and honours deck thy story	The author
To thy fame's eternal glory!	disclaims
Adverse fortune ever fly thee,	this ditty 10
No disastrous fate come nigh thee!	to be his.

I alone will sing thy praises,
Whom to honour virtue raises,
And thy study, that divine is,
Bent to martial discipline is: 15
Lay aside all those robes lie by thee;
Crown thy arts with arms, they'll beautify thee.

O worthy of worthiest name, adorn'd in this manner,
Lead bravely thy forces on under war's warlike banner!

7.1. *habit*] Q^b; *order* Q^a. *of* a] Q2; a Q. 7.5. *in dumb-show*] Q^b; *not in*
Q^a. 7.6. *State*] *so* Q. 7.7. *ditty*] Q^b; *Hymne* Q^a. 7.8–9. *all . . . Pilgrims*]
Dyce ii. 8. *Arms*] Q^b; *The Hymne. / Armes* Q^a. 8–11. *The . . . his*] Q^b (*to*
right of ll. 10–13, approx.); *not in* Q^a.

8–24.] Lumbering metre, repetitions, clumsy rhymes and phrasing are
reasons enough for Webster to add a disclaimer of authorship when he
visited the press during the printing of his play (see Intro., pp. 43–5); '*this*
ditty' is less dignified than '*The Hymn*', found only in the un-corrected Qa.
   If the verses were cobbled together by those providing music for the ceremonies, they wrote nothing to supplement either the vows of the Duchess
and her family or their banishment, a sequence of mimed performances that
formed the second and third parts of what is, in effect, a 'dumb-show'. Significant action is marked by similar means with the dumb-shows of *W.D.*
II.ii and the ceremonies of its IV.iii and V.i. The first part with its elaborate
disrobing and arming will take a considerable time to enact, the other two
being comparatively short and less in need of musical support. However the
violence (l. 36) with which the Cardinal takes the ring from the Duchess's
finger must be a sufficiently large action to be clearly seen and noted; the
noble ceremony (l. 7) is likely to be suddenly disrupted and awkward at this
moment.

O, mayst thou prove fortunate in all martial courses!   20
Guide thou still, by skill, in arts and forces!
Victory attend thee nigh whilst Fame sings loud thy pow'rs;
Triumphant conquest crown thy head, and blessings pour down
    show'rs!

1st. Pil. Here's a strange turn of state! who would have
    thought
  So great a lady would have match'd herself   25
  Unto so mean a person? yet the cardinal
  Bears himself much too cruel.
2nd. Pil.   They are banish'd.
1st. Pil. But I would ask what power hath this state
  Of Ancona to determine of a free prince?
2nd. Pil. They are a free state sir, and her brother show'd   30
  How that the Pope, fore-hearing of her looseness,
  Hath seiz'd into th' protection of the church
  The dukedom, which she held as dowager.
1st. Pil. But by what justice?
2nd. Pil.   Sure, I think by none,
  Only her brother's instigation.   35
1st. Pil. What was it with such violence he took
  Off from her finger?
2nd. Pil.   'Twas her wedding ring,
  Which he vow'd shortly he would sacrifice
  To his revenge.
1st. Pil.   Alas, Antonio!
  If that a man be thrust into a well,   40
  No matter who sets hand to't, his own weight
  Will bring him sooner to th' bottom: – come, let's
  hence.

30. sir] *Q*^b*; not in Q*^a.   32. Hath] *Q*^b*; Had Q*^a.

20. courses] encounters.
21. forces] military strength.
26. *mean*] low-born.
29. *determine of*] judge, decide concerning (cf. *O.E.D.*, 5).
30. *free state*] but Ancona was dependent on papal protection.
40–2. *If . . . bottom*] from Florio, II.xxxi: 'the mischiefe [of losing one's temper] is, that after you are once falne into the pit, it is no matter who thrusts you in, you never cease till you come to the bottome. The fall presseth, hasteneth, mooveth and furthereth it selfe.'

Fortune makes this conclusion general:
All things do help th' unhappy man to fall.   *Exeunt.*

SCENA V.

Enter ANTONIO, Duchess, Children, CARIOLA, Servants.

Duch. Banish'd Ancona!
Ant.   Yes, you see what pow'r
Lightens in great men's breath.
Duch.   Is all our train
Shrunk to this poor remainder?
Ant.   These poor men,
Which have got little in your service, vow
To take your fortune: but your wiser buntings,   5
Now they are fledg'd, are gone.
Duch.   They have done wisely –
This puts me in mind of death: physicians thus,
With their hands full of money, use to give o'er
Their patients.
Ant.   Right the fashion of the world:
From decay'd fortunes every flatterer shrinks;   10
Men cease to build where the foundation sinks.

44.] *italicized this ed.;* 'All ... Q.

III.V.0.1.] *Q4; Antonio, ... Seruants, Bosola, Souldiers, with Vizards Q.*
1. Ancona!] *Dyce i;* Ancona? *Q.*

43-4,] If *help* is emphasized, as suggested by the metre, this *conclusion* will not sound as trite as it would otherwise; *unhappy* = unfortunate, ill-fated.
44.] from *A.T.*, IV.i.1931: 'All things must help th' vnhappy man to fall'.

III.V.1. *Banish'd Ancona*] an echo of the opening word of *W.D.*
2. *Lightens*] lights up; flashes (like lightning).
breath] decree (see *O.E.D.* 9).
5. *buntings*] a kind of bird, allied to larks but without song; cf. Lafeu of the braggart Parolles: 'I took this lark for a bunting' (*All's W.*, II.v.6–7); this was proverbial (cf. Tilley B722).
7–9. *physicians ... patients*] Dent suggested this was proverbial; he quoted Painter, *Palace*, ii (1567), 'Lord of Virle', p. 277ᵛ: 'And therefore despairing of his helth [he was love-sick], with handes full of money they [his doctors] gaue him ouer'.
9. *Right*] just, exactly.

Duch. I had a very strange dream tonight.
Ant.   What was't?
Duch. Methought I wore my coronet of state,
    And on a sudden all the diamonds
    Were chang'd to pearls.
Ant.   My interpretation   15
    Is, you'll weep shortly, for to me, the pearls
    Do signify your tears: –
Duch. The birds that live i' th' field
    On the wild benefit of nature, live
    Happier than we; for they may choose their mates,   20
    And carol their sweet pleasures to the spring: –

                Enter BOSOLA [*with a letter*].

Bos. You are happily o'erta'en.
Duch.   From my brother?
Bos. Yes, from the Lord Ferdinand, your brother,
    All love and safety –
Duch.   Thou dost blanch mischief,
    Wouldst make it white: – see, see, like to calm weather   25
    At sea, before a tempest, false hearts speak fair
    To those they intend most mischief.

21.1.] *Q4*; *Bosola Q (at l. o.1)*.

12–17.] from Mathieu, *Henry IV* (1612), H3: 'Some few daies before this
fatall accident shee [the queen] had two dreames, the which were true pre-
dictions, when as the Iewelers and Lapidaries prepared her crowne she
drempt that the great diamonds and all the goodly stones which shee had
giuen them to inrich it were turned into Pearles, the which the interpreters
of dreames take for teares'.
    18–19. *live . . . nature*] perhaps from *Arcadia*, IV (*Wks*, II.119): 'to have for
foode the wilde benefites of nature'; the phrase is repeated in *A.Q.L.*,
IV.i.81–2, a strong indication of its being taken from Webster's commonplace
book.
    benefit] gift; advantages, right.
    21. *carol*] sing joyfully.
    22. *happily*] fortunately: unintentionally, Bosola echoes the concluding
lines of the previous scene.
    24. *blanch*] blanch over, 'whitewash' (cf. *O.E.D.*, v^1., 5); *mischief* = ill
fortune, harm.
    25–6. *calm . . . tempest*] Cf. the proverb, 'After a calm comes a storm'
(Tilley C24).

(Reads) Send Antonio to me; I want his head in a business: –
A politic equivocation!
He doth not want your counsel, but your head;   30
That is, he cannot sleep till you be dead.
And here's another pitfall, that's strew'd o'er
With roses; mark it, 'tis a cunning one:
[*Reads*] *I stand engaged for your husband, for several debts*
   at Naples: let not that trouble him, I had rather have his   35
   heart than his money.
And I believe so too.

Bos.   What do you believe?

Duch. That he so much distrusts my husband's love,
He will by no means believe his heart is with him
Until he see it: the devil is not cunning enough   40
To circumvent us in riddles.

Bos. Will you reject that noble and free league
Of amity and love which I present you?

Duch. Their league is like that of some politic kings,
Only to make themselves of strength and pow'r   45
To be our after-ruin: tell them so.

Bos. And what from you?

Ant.   Thus tell him: I will not come.

Bos. And what of this?

Ant.   My brothers have dispers'd
Bloodhounds abroad; which till I hear are muzzled,

---

28. Reads] *Q4; A Letter. (rom. and inset) Q.*   28–9.] *so Dyce i; one line Q.*
28.] *italicized Q.*   34. Reads] *Dyce ii.*   34–6.] *italicized Q.*

28–31.] Louis XI played this trick on Louis of Luxembourg, Constable
of France, sending a letter saying he 'wanted his head', and so being able to
kill him (so Dent).

32. *pitfall*] concealed pit, used to capture animals or men.

35–6. I . . . money] See Camden's *Remains* (1605), Ee4^v (of Richard III):
'. . . when diverse shires of England offered him a benevolence, hee refused
it, saying, I know not in what sence: "I had rather have your hearts, than
your money"' (so Dent).

39–40. *believe . . . it*] from Donne, *Ignatius His Conclave* (1611), p. 89:
'wee consider not the entrails of Beasts, but the entrails of souls, in confes-
sions, and the entrails of Princes, in treasons; whose hearts wee do not
beleeue to be with vs, till we see them' (so Dent).

42. *league*] covenant.

44. *league*] alliance, treaty.

48. *this*] i.e., the letter.

No truce, though hatch'd with ne'er such politic skill   50
Is safe, that hangs upon our enemies' will.
I'll not come at them.
Bos.   This proclaims your breeding.
Every small thing draws a base mind to fear,
As the adamant draws iron; fare you well sir,
You shall shortly hear from's.   *Exit.*   55
Duch. I suspect some ambush:
Therefore by all my love, I do conjure you
To take your eldest son, and fly towards Milan:
Let us not venture all this poor remainder
In one unlucky bottom.
Ant.   You counsel safely: –   60
Best of my life, farewell: since we must part
Heaven hath a hand in't; but no otherwise
Than as some curious artist takes in sunder
A clock or watch when it is out of frame,
To bring 't in better order.   65
Duch. I know not which is best,
To see you dead, or part with you: – farewell boy;
Thou art happy, that thou hast not understanding
To know thy misery, for all our wit
And reading brings us to a truer sense   70

51–2.] *so Q; after l. 47 conj. Craik; after l. 46 (spoken by Duch.) conj. this ed.*
61. farewell: . . . part] *Q;* farewell, . . . part: *Dyce i.*

50–1.] from *A.T.,* v.iii.3250–3: 'For all the fauour that she could procure, / Was leaue to liue a priuate person still; / And yet of that she could not be made sure, / Which did depend vpon her enemies will'.

T. W. Craik suggested (quoted in Lucas, ii) that these lines should follow l. 47; but 'at them' of l. 52 is then a little awkward referring to the 'brothers' rather than 'bloodhounds'. If the lines are misplaced, they might be moved to follow l. 46, to become part of the Duchess's speech which in Q ends with a semi-colon.

54. *adamant*] lodestone.

59–60. *venture . . . bottom*] Cf. the proverb, 'Venture not all in one bottom' (Tilley A209); *bottom* = 'hold, ship'; *remainder*, i.e., all we have left, with pun on 'residue of a deceased person's estate'.

68–71. *happy . . . sorrow*] Cf. *Ecclesiastes,* i.18: 'For in much wisdom is much grief: and he that increaseth knowledge, increaseth sorrow'.

Of sorrow: – in the eternal church, sir,
I do hope we shall not part thus.
Ant.   O, be of comfort!
Make patience a noble fortitude,
And think not how unkindly we are us'd:
Man, like to cassia, is prov'd best, being bruis'd.   75
Duch. Must I, like to a slave-born Russian,
Account it praise to suffer tyranny?
And yet, O Heaven, thy heavy hand is in't.
I have seen my little boy oft scourge his top
And compar'd myself to't: naught made me e'er   80
Go right but heaven's scourge-stick.
Ant.   Do not weep:
Heaven fashion'd us of nothing; and we strive
To bring ourselves to nothing: – farewell Cariola,
And thy sweet armful: if I do never see thee more,
Be a good mother to your little ones,   85
And save them from the tiger: fare you well.
Duch. Let me look upon you once more; for that speech
Came from a dying father: your kiss is colder

75.] *italicized this ed.;* 'Man ... *Q^b*. 80–1.] *so Dyce i;* ... right, / But,
... *Q*.

71–2. *in ... thus*] Cf. *Arcadia*, II.xiii (*Wks*, i.233): 'when she thought him
dead, she sought all meanes (as well by poyson as by knife) to send her soule,
at least, to be maried in the eternall church with him'.
    eternal church] i.e., congregation of the blessed in heaven.
    74. *unkindly*] with unnatural cruelty.
    75.] a form of the proverb, 'If you beat spice it will smell the sweeter'
(Tilley S746); for the force of *prov'd*, see *W.D.*, I.i.48–51: 'Perfumes the more
they are chaf'd the more they render / Their pleasing scents, and so affliction
/ Expresseth virtue, fully, whether true, / Or else adulterate'.
    76–7.] from Sidney, *Astrophel & Stella*, ii: 'and now like slave-borne
Muscovite: / I call it praise to suffer tyrannie'.
    78–81. *Heaven ... stick*] Lucas suggested this was from *Arcadia*, II.xii
(*Wks*, I.227f.): 'Griefe onely makes his wretched state to see / (Even like a
toppe which nought but whipping moves) / ... / But still our dazeled eyes
their way do misse, / While that we do at his sweete scourge repine, / The
kindly way to beate us to our blisse'.
    82–3. *Heaven ... nothing*] from Donne, *First Ann.*, ll. 155–7: 'Wee seeme
ambitious, Gods whole worke t'undoe; / Of nothing hee made us, and we
strive too, / To bring our selves to nothing backe'.
    84. *sweet armful*] Cariola is holding his youngest child.

Than that I have seen an holy anchorite
Give to a dead man's skull.   90
Ant. My heart is turn'd to a heavy lump of lead,
With which I sound my danger: fare you well.
                Exit[, *with his elder* Son].
Duch. My laurel is all withered.
Cari. Look, madam, what a troop of armed men
Make toward us.

        Enter BOSOLA *with a* Guard, *with visards.*

Duch.   O, they are very welcome: 95
When Fortune's wheel is overcharg'd with princes,
The weight makes it move swift. I would have my ruin
Be sudden: – I am your adventure, am I not?
Bos. You are, you must see your husband no more –

92.1. *with . . . Son*] Dyce i subs.   94. a] *Q^b^; not in Q^a^.*   95. *Enter . . . Guard*]
Q^b^; not in Q^a^; Souldiers (at *l. o. 1*) *Q; after* sudden, *l. 98 Dyce ii.*   *with visards*]
Q (at *l. o. 1*); *disguis'd Q4; vizarded* (after '*Bosola*') *Dyce ii.*   97. move] *Q^b^;*
more *Q^a^.*

93.] Although *laurel* was, proverbially, 'ever green' (Tilley L95), it was
supposed to wither on the death of a king. Lucas suggested an echo of
Cleopatra's cry on the death of Antony: 'O, wither'd is the garland of the
war' (*Ant.*, IV.XV.64). Alison Findlay suggests word play on *Loretto*-laurel.
    95. S.D. *with visards*] Q's entry-direction at the head of this scene is
ambiguous. Probably the soldiers and Bosola wear visards, for 'What devil
art thou . . .' (l. 100) suggests that the Duchess does not recognize Bosola
at first, and 'I'd beat that counterfeit face into thy other' (l. 118) might imply
that she has seen through a disguise. But possibly none wear visards, or only
the soldiers, for the simple '*Enter Bosola with a Guard*' was probably Webster's own direction (added as a press-correction), and 'counterfeit' of l. 118
could refer simply to Bosola's apparent change of sides already evident from
his earlier, undisguised entry.
    96–7. *When . . . swift*] from *A. T.*, v.i.2836–8: 'The wheele of Forture still
must slippery proue, / And chiefly when it burdend is with kings, / Whose
states as weightiest most must make it moue'.
    97–8. *I . . . sudden*] Cf. Jonson, *Sejanus*, IV.3–4: 'O, my fortune, / Let it
be sodaine thou prepar'st against me'; Webster probably borrowed the retort
immediately preceding for *W.D.*, III.ii.270.
    98. *I . . . adventure*] The usage is unusual: perhaps, ironically, 'You
wished to meet me by chance', or 'I am what matters to you, what is going
to be perilous for you' (cf. *O.E.D.*, 1 and 2 and 3–8). Sykes glossed 'quarry',
a sense not quoted in *O.E.D.*; he compared Marmion, *Holland's Leaguer*
(1632): 'I have a bird i' th' wind, I'll fly thee on him: He shall be thy adventure, thy first quarry'.

Duch. What devil art thou, that counterfeits heaven's
    thunder?   100
Bos. Is that terrible? I would have you tell me
    Whether is that note worse that frights the silly birds
    Out of the corn, or that which doth allure them
    To the nets? you have hearken'd to the last too much.
Duch. O misery! like to a rusty o'ercharg'd cannon,   105
    Shall I never fly in pieces? come: to what prison?
Bos. To none: –
Duch.   Whither then?
Bos.   To your palace.
Duch.   I have heard
    That Charon's boat serves to convey all o'er
    The dismal lake, but brings none back again.
Bos. Your brothers mean you safety, and pity.
Duch.   Pity!   110
    With such a pity men preserve alive
    Pheasants and quails, when they are not fat enough
    To be eaten.
Bos. These are your children?
Duch.   Yes: –
Bos.   Can they prattle?

---

101. *Bos.*] *Q^b*; *not in Q^a*. 101–2.] *so Q*;...whether / Is...*Dyce i*.
105. *Duch.*] *Q^b*; *Ant. Q^a*. o'ercharg'd] *Q2 subs.*; ore-char'd *Q*. 107–9. I...
again] *so Dyce i*;...conuay / All...(*two lines*) *Q*. 110–11. Pity...] *so
Dyce i; one line Q*. 111. a] *Q^b*; *not in Q^a*.

102. *silly*] ignorant, lowly (see l. 132, below); but there may be an instinctive or ironic sympathy in Bosola's speech, for *silly* also = 'frail, defenceless,
innocent, deserving of pity'.
105–6. *like...pieces*] Cf. Donne, *Of the Progress of the Soul*, ll. 181–2, of
the soul leaving the body at death: 'Thinke that a rustie Peece, discharg'd
is flowne / In peeces...'
108–9. from Alexander, *J.G.*, v.i.2577–8: 'Ah, th' vnrelenting Charons
restlesse barge / Stands to transport all ouer, but brings none backe'.
   dismal (from L. *dies mali*) retained its original senses of 'fatal, disastrous,
terrible'; *O.E.D.* does not cite the modern senses of 'dark' or 'cheerless' until
1617.
111–13.] from *Arcadia*, III.xxiii (*Wks*, I.488f.): 'with the same pittie as
folkes keepe foule, when they are not fatte inough for their eating'.

Duch.   No:
    But I intend, since they were born accurs'd,   115
    Curses shall be their first language.
Bos.   Fie, madam,
    Forget this base, low fellow.
Duch.   Were I a man
    I'd beat that counterfeit face into thy other.
Bos. One of no birth –
Duch.   Say that he was born mean:
    Man is most happy when's own actions   120
    Be arguments and examples of his virtue.
Bos. A barren, beggarly virtue.
Duch. I prithee, who is greatest? can you tell?
    Sad tales befit my woe: I'll tell you one.
    A salmon, as the swam unto the sea,   125
    Met with a dog-fish, who encounters her
    With this rough language: 'Why art thou so bold
    To mix thyself with our high state of floods,
    Being no eminent courtier, but one
    That for the calmest and fresh time o'th' year   130
    Dost live in shallow rivers, rank'st thyself
    With silly smelts and shrimps? and darest thou
    Pass by our dog-ship, without reverence?'
    'O', quoth the salmon, 'sister, be at peace:
    Thank Jupiter we both have pass'd the net!   135
    Our value never can be truly known

115–16. Cf. Caliban, another accursed (illegitimate) character: 'You taught me language . . . I know how to curse (*Tp.*, I.ii.363–4).

118. *counterfeit*] See l. 95 S.D., note, above.

120–1.] Cf. Dedication, ll. 14–15; Dent compared Hall, *Epistles*, VI.ix: 'It is an happy thing when our owne actions may be either examples, or arguments of good'.

arguments] evidence, proof.

126. *dog-fish*] 'a name given to various small sharks' (*O.E.D.*, I); it was also applied opprobriously to persons.

128. *floods*] water (as opposed to land). Cf. *2H4*, V.ii.129–33: 'The tide of blood in me / Hath proudly flow'd in vanity till now: / Now doth it turn and ebb back to the sea, / Where it shall mingle with the state of floods / And flow henceforth in formal majesty'.

132. *smelts*] small fish, sparlings; used by Jonson, Dekker, etc. for 'simpletons'.

Till in the fisher's basket we be shown;
I'th' market then my price may be the higher,
Even when I am nearest to the cook and fire.'
So, to great men, the moral may be stretched: 140
Men oft are valued high, when th'are most wretched.
But come; whither you please: I am arm'd 'gainst
    misery;
Bent to all sways of the oppressor's will.
There's no deep valley, but near some great hill.   *Exeunt.*

---

140. stretched] *Q, Scott;* stretch'd *Dyce ii.*   141.] *italicized this ed.;* „Men
... *Q.*   wretched] *Q4;* wretch'd *Q, Dyce ii.*   144.] *italicized Q.*

143–4.] Cf. the proverb, 'There is no hill without its valley' (Tilley
H467).
    The last of these two lines is ambiguous: it might be a counsel of 'safety-
first' (cf. *W.D.*, IV.i.23–5) or yielding acceptance; but cf. the *Character* of 'A
Noble ... Housekeeper': 'His *thoughts have a high aime,* though their dwelling bee in the Vale of an *humble heart;* whence, as by an Engin (that raises
water to fall, that it may rise the higher) he is *heightned in his humility*' (italics
ed.). An impression of pride is ensured in the play by l. 141, above, and by
the Duchess taking her own time (stopping to tell a tale and leaving before
she is commanded to do so); humility is suggested by 'silly smelts ...
market ... cook', and 'Bent to all sways'. So the last line of Act III prepares
for Bosola's first speech in the following scene (especially l. 6).

Act IV

ACTUS IV, SCENA I.

Enter FERDINAND *and* BOSOLA.

Ferd. How doth our sister duchess bear herself
    In her imprisonment?
Bos.   Nobly; I'll describe her:
    She's sad, as one long us'd to't; and she seems
    Rather to welcome the end of misery
    Than shun it: – a behaviour so noble   5
    As gives a majesty to adversity;
    You may discern the shape of loveliness
    More perfect in her tears, than in her smiles;
    She will muse four hours together, and her silence,
    Methinks, expresseth more than if she spake.   10
Ferd. Her melancholy seems to be fortify'd
    With a strange disdain.

IV.i.0.1.] *Q4 subs.; Ferdinand, Bosola, Dutchesse, Cariola, Seruants Q.*   9. four]
Q; for *conj. Collier, Haz.*

IV.i.] Bosola's promise to convey the duchess to her 'palace' (III.v.107)
and talk of her 'chamber' and 'lodging' (IV.i.26 and 128, and IV.ii.3) could
imply that he has done so (cf. 'lodgings', II.iii.3). Thus 'imprisonment'
(l. 2) could mean 'house-arrest'.

But (1) Webster makes no dramatic point of such a return, (2) '*This* is a
prison?' (IV.ii.11) can hardly refer to familiar surroundings.

Perhaps the Duchess was right to assume that she was to be taken to some
unknown prison (III.v.106).

3–8.] from *Arcadia*: 'But Erona sadde indeede, yet like one rather used,
then new fallen to sadnesse ... seemed rather to welcome then to shunne
that ende of miserie' (II.xxix; *Wks*, I.332); 'a behaviour so noble, as gave a
majestie to adversitie' (I.ii; *Wks*, I.16); of Erona's sadness, in which Plangus
may 'perceyve the shape of lovelinesse more perfectly in wo, then in joyful-
nesse' (II.xxix; *Wks*, I.333).

shape = 'image, picture'.

11–12. *Her ... disdain*] from Alexander, *Croesus*, IV.i.1431–2: '... with a
silent pittie-pleading looke, / Wich shewes with sorrow mixt a high
disdaine'.

179

Bos.   'Tis so: and this restraint
        (Like English mastiffs, that grow fierce with tying)
        Makes her too passionately apprehend
        Those pleasures she's kept from.
Ferd.   Curse upon her!   15
        I will no longer study in the book
        Of another's heart: inform her what I told you.   *Exit.*

                    Enter Duchess.

Bos. All comfort to your grace!
Duch.   I will have none: –
        Pray thee, why dost thou wrap thy poison'd pills
        In gold and sugar?   20
Bos. Your elder brother, the Lord Ferdinand,
        Is come to visit you: and sends you word,
        'Cause once he rashly made a solemn vow
        Never to see you more, he comes i'th' night;
        And prays you, gently, neither torch nor taper   25
        Shine in your chamber: he will kiss your hand,
        And reconcile himself; but, for his vow,
        He dares not see you: –
Duch.   At his pleasure;
        Take hence the lights: [*Bosola removes lights.*]

17.1.] *so Q4; at l. 0.1 Q;... and Attendants Samp.* 29. *Bosola ... lights*] This
ed.; *Exeunt Attendants with ... Samp. Enter Ferdinand*] *Q4 subs. (after
come).*

12–15. *restraint ... from*] Cf. *Arcadis*, I.iv (*Wks*, I.25): 'Leave womens
minds, the most untamed that way of any: see whether ... a dogge growe
not fiercer with tying? What dooth ielousie [of a father for his daughters],
but stirre up the mind to thinke, what it is from which they are restrayned?'
See, also, *W.D.*, I.ii.198–201, and note.
    16–17. *I ... heart*] from P. Matthieu's supplement to de Serres, *General
Inventory* (tr. 1607), p. 1033: 'the King of Spaine resolued not to studie any
more in the Bookes of an others heart, hauing so good Intelligence with the
King of France, as he desired not to vnderstand his affaires by any other
Instrument then his Ambassadors'.
    19–20.] Cf. *W.D.*, III.ii.190–i: 'I discern poison, / Under your gilded
pills'; the notion was proverbial (see Tilley P325: 'To sugar [gild] the
pill').
    29. *Take ... lights*] See Intro., p. 54.

[*Enter* FERDINAND.]

he's come.

Ferd.   Where are you?

Duch.   Here sir: –

Ferd. This darkness suits you well.   30

Duch. I would ask you pardon: –

Ferd.   You have it;
For I account it the honourabl'st revenge,
Where I may kill, to pardon: – where are your cubs?

Duch. Whom?

Ferd. Call them your children;   35
For though our national law distinguish bastards
From true legitimate issue, compassionate nature
Makes them all equal.

Duch.   Do you visit me for this?
You violate a sacrament o'th' church
Shall make you howl in hell for't.

Ferd.   It had been well   40
Could you have liv'd thus always; for indeed
You were too much i' th' light: – but no more –

---

30. *This ... well*] See III.ii.141, note; esp. quotation from *King and No King*.

32–3. *I ... pardon*] Cf. the proverb, 'To pardon is divine revenge' (Tilley R92) and Hall, *Characters* (1608), 'Valiant Man': 'he holds it the noblest reuenge, that he might hurt and doth not'. Ferdinand's next words show that he does not offer acceptance, understanding or love; in effect, he threatens her with a lifetime of being ostracized and left to suffer her loss and shame. See also l. 110, below.

33. *cubs*] Cf. IV.ii.259. Dent suggested an allusion to Raleigh's 1603 trial, in which the conspirators were charged with saying: 'there would never be a good world in England, till the King and his Cubs (meaning his Royall issue) were taken away'.

36–8. *though ... equal*] Cf. Matthieu's de Serres, *General Inventory* (tr. 1607), p. 1027: 'A father ... cannot think too soone nor to often, to breed vp the youth of his child in vertue, nor to assure his fortune: I say a child without distinction, for although the Law doth distinguish Bastards from them that are lawfully begotten, yet nature makes no difference'. Cf. *D.L.C.*, IV.ii.278–80.

42. *too ... light*] i.e., too exposed, not sufficiently sheltered; but *too much* suggests also a very common quibble, as in *Mer. V.*, v.i.129–30: 'Let me give light, but let me not be light [i.e., wanton]; / For a light wife doth make a heavy husband'. Webster varied the word-play in *D.L.C.*, I.ii.51–2.

I come to seal my peace with you: here's a hand
                Gives her a dead man's hand.
To which you have vow'd much love; the ring upon't
You gave.
Duch.   I affectionately kiss it.   45
Ferd. Pray do: and bury the print of it in your heart:
I will leave this ring with you for a love-token;
And the hand, as sure as the ring; and do not doubt
But you shall have the heart too; when you need a
    friend
Send it to him that ow'd it; you shall see   50
Whether he can aid you.
Duch.   You are very cold.
I fear you are not well after your travel: –
Hah! lights! – O, horrible!
Ferd.   Let her have lights enough.   *Exit.*
Duch. What witchcraft doth he practise that he hath left
A dead man's hand here? –   55

*Here is discovered, behind a traverse, the artificial figures of Antonio
and his children, appearing as if they were dead.*

43.1.] *so Q4; to right of ll. 43–5, approx. Q.*   53. *Exit] Q; Ex. / Enter Bosola
Q4; Exit. Re-enter Seruants with lights Luc i.*   55.2. *children] Q; child conj.
Luc ii.*

43.1.] For the source of this incident, see Boklund (1962), pp. 28–9.
50. *ow'd*] owned.
55.1. Here . . . traverse] 'discover' was often used in 17th-century stage-directions for indicating the opening of some curtained acting area: 'traverse' was used of curtains or screens across a room, hall or stage. See *W.D.*, v.iv.64 and 65.1–3. If Bosola left the stage at line 29, he may return here to effect the discovery.
55.2. children] Lucas (2nd ed.) argued that only the elder son who rode off with Antonio should be shown: the Duchess would not leave instructions for their care (IV.ii.203–5) if she thought they were dead, and 'why should an avaricious Duke go to the cost and trouble of wax corpses for two children who were in a few minutes to be real ones?' But common sense is not a true measure for such a scene in a play (or in life); the stage-direction is probably authorial (see Intro., pp. 46–7) and we may suppose that Webster aimed at maximum horror and cruelty. There may be dramatic point in the Duchess reacting only to 'it' (ll. 62–3) and 'that . . . trunk' (l. 68) as if she saw Antonio only; and there may be more pathos if she forgets that she has seen her children dead when she remembers them before her own death.

Bos. Look you: here's the piece from which 'twas ta'en:
　　He doth present you this sad spectacle
　　That now you know directly they are dead –
　　Hereafter you may wisely cease to grieve
　　For that which cannot be recovered.   60
Duch. There is not between heaven and earth one wish
　　I stay for after this: it wastes me more
　　Than were't my picture, fashion'd out of wax,
　　Stuck with a magical needle and then buried
　　In some foul dunghill; and yon's an excellent property   65
　　For a tyrant, which I would account mercy.
Bos. What's that?
Duch. If they would bind me to that lifeless trunk,
　　And let me freeze to death.
Bos.　　　　　　　　　　　Come, you must live.
Duch. That's the greatest torture souls feel in hell –   70
　　In hell: that they must live, and cannot die.
　　Portia, I'll new-kindle thy coals again,

---

58. That] *Q; That, Dyce i. dead –] This ed.;* dead, *Q, Dyce i.*

---

58. *directly*] 'plainly' or 'immediately'.
59–60.] Dent compared Petrarch, *Physic against Fortune* (tr. 1579), Kk3ᵛ:
'Admit death be euyll, whiche the learned denye, truely no man wyl denie
but that weepyng is in vayne, for that which cannot be recouered'.
62–5. *wastes . . . dunghill*] Dekker's *Whore of Babylon,* II.ii.168–80 illustrates this superstition: 'This virgin waxe, / Burie I will in slimie putred
ground, / Where it may peece-meale rot: As this consumes, / So shall shee
pine, and (after languor) die. / These pinnes shall sticke like daggers to her
heart, / And eating through her breast, turne there to gripings, / Cramp-like
Convulsions, shrinking vp her nerues, / As into this they eate. / – . . . Where
wilt thou burie it? – On this dunghill' (so Dent).
65. *property*] 'device' or 'instrument', with perhaps an allusion to a stage
property.
68–9. *bind . . . death*] Anderson (*ap.* Dent) noted that this punishment is
illustrated in emblem books (e.g. Whitney (1586), p. 99) to symbolize ill-
matched marriages.
69. *Come . . . live*] Bosola may physically prevent her from approaching
the wax figures, to maintain the deception.
72–4. *Portia . . . wife*] Plutarch's *Livers of the Noble Grecians and Romans,*
tr. North (1579), told how Brutus's wife killed herself by putting hot coals
in her mouth, 'choosing to die, rather than languish in pain'. Brutus praised
her inner strength: 'the weake constitution of her body doth not suffer her

And revive the rare and almost dead example
Of a loving wife.
Bos.   O fie! despair? remember
You are a Christian.
Duch.   The chuch enjoins fasting: 75
I'll starve myself to death.
Bos.   Leave this vain sorrow:
Things being at the worst begin to mend;
The bee when he hath shot his sting into your hand
May then play with your eyelid.
Duch. Good comfortable fellow   80
Persuade a wretch that's broke upon the wheel
To have all his bones new set; entreat him live
To be executed again: – who must despatch me?
I account this world a tedious theatre,
For I do play a part in't 'gainst my will.   85
Bos. Come, be of comfort, I will save your life.
Duch. Indeed I have not leisure to tend so small a business.
Bos. Now, by my life, I pity you.
Duch.   Thou art a fool then,
To waste thy pity on a thing so wretch'd

77–8.] *so Q;* ... bee / When ... *Dyce i.*   87.] *so Q;* ... tend / So ... *Dyce i.*

to performe in shew the valiant acts that we are able to doe; but for corage
and constant minde, she shewed herself as stowt in the defence of her contry,
as any of us' (ed. W. E. Henly (1896), vi.236 and 204).

76. *starve ... death*] Lucas noted that the legitimacy of this kind of suicide
is discussed in Donne, *Biathanatos*, II.6.5.

77–9.] The common proverb and the image are found together in Whetstone, *Heptameron* (1582), U3: 'let this comfort you: that thinges when they
are at the worst, begin againe to amend ... The Bee, when he hath lefte his
stinge in your hande without dainger may playe with your eye lidde.'

81. *wheel*] an instrument of torture.

84–90. *I ... itself*] from *Arcadia*, II.xxix (*Wks*, I.333), and, like the borrowings at ll. 3–8 above, about Erona: 'But she (as if he had spoken of a
small matter, when he mencioned her life, to which she had not leisure to
attend) desired him if he loved her, to shew it, in finding some way to save
Antiphilus. For her, she found the world but a wearisom stage unto her,
where she played a part against her will: and therefore besought him, not to
cast his love in so unfruitful a place, as could not love it selfe.'

As cannot pity itself: – I am full of daggers: 90
Puff: let me blow these vipers from me.

              Enter Servant.

What are you?
Serv.   One that wishes you long life.
Duch. I would thou wert hang'd for the horrible curse
    Thou hast given me: [*Exit Servant.*]
              I shall shortly grow one

---

90. itself] *Q4 subs.; it Q.* 91. vipers] *Q; vapours conj. this ed.* 91.1.] *so
Q4; at l. o.1 Q (Seruants).* 94. S.D.] *Samp.*

---

90. *daggers*] The first record in *O.E.D.* of this figurative use (= 'mental
pain or affliction') is *Mer. V.,* III.i.115: 'Thou stickest a dagger in me'; see also
Ham., III.iv.95.
    91.] The sense is obscure. Jacobean writers usually alluded to the poison
of *vipers*, or to the belief that their young gnawed their way out of the womb,
so killing the mother; they also echoed the biblical usage = 'wicked men'
(see, e.g., *Matthew,* xxiii.33). Along these lines, Webster might imply that
the Duchess wished to loose the stings within her and without her (cf.
'daggers', l. 90).
    But '*Puff:* let me *blow*' is also strange with reference to '*vipers*'. Of course,
the Duchess is under strain that would lead to irrationality and fantasy, but
Webster is normally exact in his use of natural history and fable (see notes
at II.v.38–9, v.v.45, etc.), and in 'distracted' scenes in *W.D.* (v.iii.82–126 and
v.iv.82–90) he maintains an exact 'reason in madness', not least in allusions
to fables and natural history.
    The text may be corrupt here, *vipers* being printed in error for '*vapours*';
if the MS. from which Crane worked read 'vapors' (a common 17th-century
spelling), the corruption could easily occur through misreading. Here
'vapours' would be a variation of 'mist' (cf. *O.E.D., vapour,* 2b), a word
Webster used of perplexities at the time of death (see IV.ii.188 and
note). He used 'vapours' = 'insubstantial things' (cf. *O.E.D.,* 2c) in *A Monumental Column* (1613), a poem with many echoes of *D.M.*: '. . . while men
rotten vapours do persue, / They could not be thy friends, and flatterers
too'.
    92–4. *What . . . me*] from *Arcadia,* III.xxiii (*Wks,* 1.485): 'he heard one
stirre in his chamber, by the motion of garments; and he with an angry voice
asked, Who was there? A poore Gentlewoman (answered the partie) that
wish long life unto you. And I soone death to you (said he) for the horrible
curse you have given me.'
    94.] The servant probably slips away when least noticeable. In this Act
and the next several entrances are without the 'realistic' motivation that
Webster usually contrived, and thus occur as if timed by 'Fate': so this

Of the miracles of pity: – I'll go pray: no,   95
I'll go curse: –
Bos.   O fie!
Duch.   I could curse the stars.
Bos.   O fearful!
Duch. And those three smiling seasons of the year
    Into a Russian winter, nay the world
    To its first chaos.
Bos. Look you, the stars shine still: –
Duch.   O, but you must   100
    Remember, my curse hath a great way to go. –
    Plagues, that make lanes through largest families,
    Consume them! –
Bos.   Fie lady!
Duch.   Let them, like tyrants,
    Never be remember'd, but for the ill they have done;
    Let all the zealous prayers of mortified   105
    Churchmen forget them! –
Bos.   O, uncharitable!
Duch. Let heaven, a little while, cease crowning martyrs,
    To punish them!
    Go howl them this: and say I long to bleed:
    It is some mercy, when men kill with speed.   *Exit.*   110

95–6. Of ... curse] *so Q; ... pray; / No ... Dyce i.* 100–1. O ... go] *so Dyce i; one line Q.* 108–9.] *so Dyce i; one line Q.* 110.] *italicized this ed.; ,, it ... Q. Exit] Q; Exit, with Servants Luc i.* 110.1.] *Q4.*

servant enters at l. 91, and Bosola at IV.ii.114; other examples are at V.i.25 and V.iv.33 and 41.

100. *Look ... still*] The Bible tells how God set the stars in the firmament when he created the world out of primal chaos (*Genesis*, i.14–19).

102–3. *Plagues ... them*] probably from Chapman, writing of cannon shot, *Penitential Psalms*, 'A Fragment', l. 44: 'Wars that make lanes thro whole posterities', and *Bussy*, III.ii.382: 'a mudering piece, making lanes in armies' (so Lucas).

103 (twice), 106, 108, 109. *them*] hatred and/or misery may prevent her from naming the Aragonian brothers, her persecutors.

110.] Cf. *W.D.*, I.i.56–8: 'I thank them, / And would account them nobly merciful / Would they dispatch me quickly'. This was a Senecan commonplace; *De Beneficiis*, ii.5.3: '*Misericordiae genus est cito occidere*'.

S.D.] Ferdinand has been listening from offstage (as at III.ii.62).

[*Enter* FERDINAND.]

Ferd. Excellent: as I would wish; she's plagu'd in art.
These presentations are but fram'd in wax,
By the curious master in that quality,
Vincentio Lauriola, and she takes them
For true substantial bodies.   115
Bos. Why do you do this?
Ferd.   To bring her to despair.
Bos. Faith, end here:
And go no farther in your cruelty –
Send her a penitential garment to put on
Next to her delicate skin, and furnish her   120
With beads and prayer-books.
Ferd.   Damn her! that body of hers,
While that my blood ran pure in't, was more worth
Than that which thou wouldst comfort, call'd a soul –
I will send her masques of common courtesans,
Have her meat serv'd up by bawds and ruffians,   125
And, 'cause she'll needs be mad, I am resolv'd
To remove forth the common hospital
All the mad-folk, and place them near her lodging;
There let them practise together, sing, and dance,
And act their gambols to the full o'th' moon: 130

112–14. *These . . . Lauriola*] Wax effigies of the dead were familiar to
Webster's audience, being placed on coffins in funeral processions of the
great; there was a collection of them in Westminster Abbey (so Lucas).

curious = 'expert, ingenious, scrupulous'. *quality* = 'craft'.

Vincentio Lauriola seems to be a name invented by Webster, perhaps with
pun on Loretto and laurel (see III.v.93, note).

116. *despair*] the ultimate sin.

121–3. *body . . . soul*] for Webster's contemporaries a starkly (or obsessively) irreligious statement. The *body* was only a temporary house for the
soul while on earth; sometimes it was called the soul's prison or cage (see
IV.ii.124–32).

129–30.] This continues the line of reaction from 'delicate skin . . . Damn
her! that body of hers . . . common courtesans . . . bawds and ruffians'.
Bedlam's representation in plays was usually bawdy or obscene (cf. *N.Ho*,
IV.iii, and Fletcher's *Pilgrim* (1621), III.vi). The sexual connotation is obvious
in *practise together* (cf. *W.D.*, II.i.110), *act*, *gambols*, and *moon*.

130. *full o'th' moon*] Ferdinand alludes to the popular superstition that
madness was influenced by the moon, its effect being strongest when it was
full.

           If she can sleep the better for it, let her –
           Your work is almost ended.
Bos. Must I see her again?
Ferd.   Yes.
Bos.   Never.
Ferd.   You must.
Bos. Never in mine own shape,
           That's forfeited by my intelligence,   135
           And this last cruel lie: when you send me next,
           The business shall be comfort.
Ferd.   Very likely –
           Thy pity is nothing of kin to thee: – Antonio
           Lurks about Milan; thou shalt shortly thither
           To feed a fire, as great as my revenge,   140
           Which ne'er will slack, till it have spent his fuel:
           Intemperate agues make physicians cruel.   *Exeunt.*

Scena II.

Enter Duchess *and* CARIOLA.

Duch. What hideous noise was that?
Cari.   'Tis the wild consort
           Of madmen, lady, which your tyrant brother
           Hath plac'd about your lodging: – this tyranny,
           I think, was never practis'd till this hour.
Duch. Indeed I thank him: nothing but noise and folly   5
           Can keep me in my right wits, whereas reason
           And silence make me stark mad: – sit down;
           Discourse to me some dismal tragedy.
Cari. O, 'twill increase your melancholy.

142.] *italicized Q4;* 'Intemperate . . . *Q.*

IV.ii.0.1.] *Q4 subs.; Duchesse, Cariola, Seruant, Mad-men, Bosola, Executioners,
Ferdinand Q.*

    142.] 'Crudelem medicum intemperans aeger facit'; a Latin proverb of
some currency in English (see Dent).

    IV.ii.1. *consort*] company; but there might be an ironical quibble on *consort*
= 'group of musicians', for 'noise' of the same line was often used for 'music'
or 'band of musicians'.
    8–10.] from Alexander, *Croesus*, III.i.853–4: 'Tell on at length th' originall
of all, / To heare of greater griefe, 'twill make mine lesse'.

Duch.   Thou art deceiv'd,
  To hear of greater grief would lessen mine –   10
  This is a prison?
Cari.   Yes, but you shall live
  To shake this durance off.
Duch.   Thou art a fool;
  The robin-redbreast, and the nightingale,
  Never live long in cages.
Cari.   Pray dry your eyes.
  What think you of, madam?
Duch.   Of nothing: 15
  When I muse thus, I sleep.
Cari. Like a madman, with your eyes open?
Duch. Dost thou think we shall know one another,
  In th'other world?
Cari.   Yes, out of question.
Duch. O that it were possible we might   20
  But hold some two days' conference with the dead,
  From them I should learn somewhat, I am sure
  I never shall know here: – I'll tell thee a miracle –
  I am not mad yet, to my cause of sorrow.
  Th' heaven o'er my head seems made of molten brass,   25
  The earth of flaming sulphur, yet I am not mad:

---

22. sure] *Q;* sure, *Dyce i.*

---

12. *durance*] (1) imprisonment, (2) duration, (3) endurance.
13–14. *robin ... cages*] Cf. Ariosto, *Satires* (tr. 1608), III: 'The cage is to
the Nightingale a hell, / The Thrush and Black-bird both do loue it well, /
The Robin red-brest rob'd of libertie, / Growes sad and dies with inward
melancholy'.
18–19. *Dost ... world*] Cf. Marston, *Dutch Courtezan* (1605), IV.iv.72–5:
'– shall we know one another in the other world? ... I would fain see him
again! O my tortured mind!' The Duchess betrays no such doubts at ll.
208–10, below.
24.] Cf. *Jn*, III.iv.48–9 and 59–60: 'I am not mad: / I would to heaven I
were! / For then, 'tis like I should forget myself: / ... / ... too well, too well
I feel / The different plague of each calamity'.
25–6. *Th' heaven ... sulphur*] Cf. one of the curses in *Deut.*, upon those
who 'will not hearken unto the voice of the Lord thy God': 'the heaven that
is over thy head shall be brass, and the earth that is under thee shall be iron'
(so Bradbrook, *M.L.R.*, 1947). Dekker or Webster associated *sulphur* with
God's judgement in *N.Ho*, I.iii.100–4: 'if euer I had thought vncleane, / ... /
Let Sulpher drop from Heauen, and naile may body / Dead to this earth'.

    I am acquainted with sad misery,
    As the tann'd galley-slave is with his oar;
    Necessity makes me suffer constantly,
    And custom makes it easy – who do I look like now?   30
Cari. Like to your picture in the gallery,
    A deal of life in show, but none in practice;
    Or rather like some reverend monument
    Whose ruins are even pitied.
Duch.   Very proper:
    And Fortune seems only to have her eyesight   35
    To behold my tragedy: – How now!
    What noise is that?

Enter Servant.

Serv.   I am come to tell you
    Your brother hath intended you some sport:
    A great physician, when the Pope was sick
    Of a deep melancholy, presented him   40
    With several sorts of madmen, which wild object,
    Being full of change and sport, forc'd him to laugh,
    And so th' imposthume broke: the self-same cure
    The duke intends on you.

---

30. who] *Q;* Whom *Haz.*   37. S.D.] *so Q4; at l. o.1 Q.*

27–30. *I ... easy*] from Matthieu's continuation of de Serres, *Inventory,*
p. 817: 'I am inured to my afflictions, as a Galley slaue to his oare. Necessity
teacheth me to suffer constantly, and custome makes my suffrance easie'; so
Dent, who also quoted Seneca, *De Tranquil.,* x.i. 'To tan' was not yet used
= 'to thrash'.
    31–2.] from *Arcadia,* i.xiii (*Wks,* i.90): he 'stood like a well wrought
image, with some life in shew, but none in practise'.
    33. *monument*] statue, effigy.
    34. *pitied*] with wordplay on 'pitted' = disfigured with scars, worn away.
    proper] appropriate; and also, ironically, 'excellent'.
    35–6. *Fortune ... tragedy*] In Act i she had spoken of 'blind' Fortune
(i.i.494–5); this idea is possibly from *Arcadia,* ii.xxix (*Wks,* i.331) of Antiphilus
in prosperity: 'as if fortune had only gotten eies to cherish him'.
    39–43. *A ... broke*] Lucas compared Donne, *Of the Progress of the Soul,*
ll. 477–9: 'When no Physitian of redresse can speake, / A joyfull casuall violence may breake / A dangerous Apostem in thy breast'. *imposthume =*
'abscess'.

Duch.   Let them come in.

Serv. There's a mad lawyer, and a secular priest,   45
    A doctor that hath forfeited his wits
    By jealousy; an astrologian
    That in his works said such a day o'th' month
    Should be the day of doom, and failing of't,
    Ran mad; an English tailor, craz'd i'th' brain   50
    With the study of new fashion; a gentleman usher
    Quite beside himself, with care to keep in mind
    The number of his lady's salutations,
    Or 'How do you', she employ'd him in each morning;
    A farmer too, an excellent knave in grain,   55
    Mad 'cause he was hinder'd transportation:
    And let one broker that's mad loose to these,
    You'd think the devil were among them.

Duch. Sit Cariola: let them loose when you please,
    For I am chain'd to endure all your tyranny.   60

---

51. fashion] *Q;* fashions *Q2.*   60.1.] *so Dyce ii; at l. o.1 Q; after l. 44 Q4.*

---

45. *secular*] 'living "in the world", not in monastic seclusion'.

50–1. *English . . . fashion*] a common jibe: cf. Nashe, *Unfortunate Traveller*, *Wks*, II.281: 'I, being a youth of the English cut, . . . imitated foure or fiue sundry nations in my attire at once', and *Fair Maid of the Inn*, IV.ii, where the man in the moon is said to be 'an Englishman that stands there starke naked, with a paire of sheires in one hand, and a great bundle of broad cloath in the other . . . cutting out of new fashions' (ll. 152–5).

55. *knave in grain*] a common phrase for a thorough rogue (*in grain* = 'dyed fast'); with a quibble on *grain* = 'corn'.

56. *hinder'd transportation*] probably an allusion to regulations allowing the export of grain when its price fell below a certain level; on 18 Jan. 1613, there was a special proclamation against export (*transportation*) of grain because of a peculiar shortage (so Lucas, quoting *Cal. State Papers, Dom. (1611–18)*, p. 168). Cf. *Characters* (1615), 'An Ingrosser of Corne'.

57. *broker*] used of pedlars, second-hand dealers, pawnbrokers, procurers, etc.; here, probably, a marriage *broker*, or go-between in quarrels, whose madness would set them all at odds rather than bring about peace.

60. *chain'd*] in apposition to 'loose' of the previous line: madmen were frequently controlled by being bound (cf. *N.Ho*, IV.iii.164ff.), and the most violent *chain'd*.

60.1.] For the masque-like elements of this incident, see Intro., pp. 12, 49 and 66.

60.2.] For the setting of this song, see App. II.

Enter Madmen.

Here, by a Madman, *this song is sung, to a dismal kind of music.*

> *O, let us howl, some heavy note,*
> *Some deadly dogged howl,*
> *Sounding as from the threat'ning throat*
> *Of beasts, and fatal fowl!*
> *As ravens, screech-owls, bulls, and bears,*   65
> *We'll bill and bawl our parts,*
> *Till irksome noise have cloy'd your ears*
> *And corrosiv'd your hearts.*
> *At last when as our choir wants breath,*
> *Our bodies being blest,*   70
> *We'll sing like swans, to welcome death,*
> *And die in love and rest.*

1st. Madman. Doomsday not come yet? I'll draw it nearer by
a perspective, or make a glass that shall set all the world
on fire upon an instant: I cannot sleep; my pillow is   75
stuffed with a litter of porcupines.

61–72.] *italicized Q.* 66. *bill*] *Q; bell Q2.*

---

66. bill] Q2's '*bell*' = 'to bellow', and is an attractive reading; but, like
'bawl', it is appropriate to animals rather than birds. *bill* may be a nonce-
usage, meaning 'to utter through the bill or beak' (on the analogy of 'to
mouth' = 'to declaim'); so the repeated opposition between birds and beasts
would be suitably sustained in the words of the song.

68. corrosiv'd] corroded, fretted, vexed.

71–2.] A veiled premonition of the Duchess's death: kneeling she will ask
death to 'Come' and foresee a time of 'quiet' for her brothers (ll. 232–5,
below). That swans exchanged their harsh cries for song at the moment of
death was a common idea (see Tilley S1028).

73. 1st. Madman] His first speech characterizes him as the Astrologer,
but at l. 93 he sounds like the Lawyer, and at l. 100 he might be any of the
eight. The 2nd Madman is nowhere clearly characterized; the 3rd is the
Priest for his first three or four speeches; and the 4th is consistently
the Doctor. Probably Webster numbered the speeches 1 to 4 in order to
show where they begin and end, expecting the uncharacterized speeches to
be allocated among the eight Madmen as the scene was elaborated in
rehearsals. Or Crane may have tried to simplify Webster's arrangement when
he prepared the printer's copy.

74. *perspective*] optical instrument, magnifying glass.

75–6. *my pillow* . . .] Camillo's pillow was said to be stuffed with 'horn-
shavings', appropriate to a cuckold (*W.D.*, I.ii.76–7), and a sleepless 'Law-
bound' man's with 'Lawyers penknifes' (*Characters*, 'Franklin', ll. 11–13).

2nd. Madman. Hell is a mere glass-house, where the devils are continually blowing up women's souls, on hollow irons, and the fire never goes out.

3rd. Madman. I will lie with every woman in my parish the   80
tenth night: I will tythe them over, like hay-cocks.

4th. Madman. Shall my pothecary outgo me, because I am a cuckold? I have found out his roguery: he makes alum of his wife's urine, and sells it to puritans that have sore throats with over-straining.   85

1st. Madman. I have skill in heraldry.

2nd. Madman. Hast?

1st. Madman. You do give for your crest a woodcock's head, with the brains picked out on't – you are a very ancient gentleman.   90

3rd. Madman. Greek is turned Turk; we are only to be saved by the Helvetian translation.

1st. Madman. Come on sir, I will lay the law to you.

This madman is tormented by thoughts of combat: *porcupines* were said to defend themselves by shooting their quills (or spines) at enemies.

77–9.] Cf. Dekker, *A Knight's Conjuring* (1607), C4ᵛ, of hell: 'for like the Glasse-house Furnace in Blacke-friers, the bone fires that are kept there, neuer goe out'. Blown glass interested Webster, with a Bosch-like fascination: at II.ii.6–13, its shape is likened to a woman's pregnant belly and in *W.D.*, I.ii.136–9, the fire of a glass-factory is associated with lust. In the present passage he probably imagined a soul as a naked body, as in pictorial representations of hell.

80–1.] i.e., I will take them to my bed, claiming a priest's rights to a tenth of the produce of a parishioner's land.

84–5.] Puritans were ridiculed for their long sermons and for singing psalms in a very high-pitched voice.

88–90.] For the granting of arms, see III.ii.298, note: *ancient* implies that there was no need to invent the coat of arms or pay for the honour. Sogliardo's crest in *Every Man Out* is 'your boar without head, rampant'.

woodcock was often used of a fool or dupe; the bird is reputed to be easily caught in snares or nets.

91–2.] The Geneva, or 'Breeches', Bibie of 1560 had a strong Puritan bias in the translation and notes; the Authorized Version of 1611 aimed at greater accuracy and eradication of 'seditious' material.

The title page of the Geneva New Testament had *Exodus*, xiv.13, as a prominent motto: 'Feare ye not, stand stil, and behold the saluacion of the Lord, which he wil shewe to you this day': cf. *only . . . saved* (l. 91).

93. *lay*] (1) expound, (2) apply (i.e., bring a charge against you).

2nd. Madman. O, rather lay a corrosive; the law will eat to
the bone.   95
3rd. Madman. He that drinks but to satisfy nature is
damned.
4th. Madman. If I had my glass here, I would show a sight
should make all the women her call me mad doctor.
1st. Madman. What's he, a rope-maker?   100
                    [*Points at 3rd. Madman.*]
2nd. Madman. No, no, no, a snuffling knave, that while he
shows the tombs, will have his hand in a wench's
placket.
3rd. Madman. Woe to the caroche, that brought home my
wife from the masque, at three o'clock in the morning! it   105
had a large featherbed in it.
4th. Madman. I have pared the devil's nails forty times,
roasted them in raven's eggs, and cured agues with
them.
3rd. Madman. Get me three hundred milch-bats to make   110
possets, to procure sleep.

---

100. S.D.] *Luc i subs.*

---

94. *corrosive*] corrosive, or caustic, medicine; often used figuratively, =
'grief, annoyance', or 'sharp remedy'.

96–7.] i.e., only drunks are blessed.

98. *glass*] either a glass vessel used for alchemical or medicinal experi-
ments (so in *A.Q.L.*, 1.i.332), or a perspective glass, like the 'spectacles'
Flamineo describes to Camillo (*W.D.*, 1.ii.100–6), in which the mad Doctor
would show some indecent illusion. Or perhaps the Astrologer is speaking
(cf. 'perspective', l. 74).

100. *rope-maker*] a trade closely allied to the hangman's in *Characters*,
'Sexton', ll. 14–17.

101. *snuffling*] speaking through the nose; hence, here, hypocritically.

103. *placket*] petticoat, or, possibly, 'opening in a skirt'; cf. *Lr*, III.iv.99–
100: 'keep thy foot out of brothels, thy hand out of plackets . . .'

106. *featherbed*] fantasy mixed with the fact that coaches were sometimes
luxuriously equipped: cf. *Fair Maid of the Inn*, IV.ii.27–31: 'we shall haue
em come hurrying hither in Fetherbeds . . . that moue vpon 4 wheeles, in
Spanish caroches'.

107. *pared . . . nails*] a proverbial saying, similar to 'clipping his wings' (cf.
Tilley N12).

111. *possets*] drinks of hot milk curdled with ale or wine and spiced.

4th. Madman. All the college may throw their caps at me,
     I have made a soap-boiler costive – it was my master-
     piece: –

Here the dance, consisting of 8 Madmen, *with music answerable*
     thereunto; after which BOSOLA, *like an old man, enters*
                    [*and the* Madmen *leave*].

Duch. Is he mad too?
Serv.   Pray question him: I'll leave you.   [*Exit.*]   115
Bos. I am come to make thy tomb.
Duch.   Hah, my tomb!
     Thou speak'st as if I lay upon my death-bed,
     Gasping for breath: dost thou perceive me sick?
Bos. Yes, and the more dangerously, since thy sickness is
     insensible.   120
Duch. Thou art not mad, sure – dost know me?
Bos. Yes.
Duch. Who am I?

114.2. *man*] *Q; Bell-Man Q4.*   114.3. *and . . . leave*] *This ed.*   115. *Exit*]
This ed.; Exeunt Servant and Madmen Dyce i.

112. *throw . . . me*] a common phrase of variable meaning (cf. Tilley C62):
either 'give pursuit' or 'give over the race'.
    113. *made . . . costive*] making a soap-maker (*soap-boiler*) constipated was
a difficult feat, for diarrhoea was an occupational hazard: cf. *A.Q.L.*, v.i.64:
'I may turn Soap-boyler, I haue a loose body'.
    114. S.D.] At the end of a Jacobean Court masque, the dancers would
'take out' members of the audience to dance with them but this dance is not
a stately celebration and Bosola is directed to enter *after* its conclusion. The
Duchess does not recognize him and so, almost certainly, neither will the
audience. He might be taken as an allegorical representation of death (as in
a traditional 'dance of death') but her question (l. 115) implies that she is
unaware that the *old man* has this significance.
    116. *I . . . tomb*] After an initial silence that intensifies the moment of
encounter, Bosola directs the attention of the Duchess and audience to the
reality of the dramatic situation and takes it one step further than might be
expected.
    118–20. *dost . . .*] Cf. Florio, II.xxv: 'Let us not seeke our euell out of us;
it is within us, it is rooted in our entrailes. And onely because we perceiue
not to be sicke, makes our recouerie to proue more difficult.'
    insensible] imperceptible.

Bos. Thou art a box of worm-seed, at best, but a salvatory of
green mummy: – what's this flesh? a little crudded milk,   125
fantastical puff-paste; our bodies are weaker than those
paper prisons boys use to keep flies in; more contemptible, since ours is to preserve earth-worms. Didst thou
ever see a lark in a cage? such is the soul in the body: this
world is like her little turf of grass, and the heaven o'er   130
our heads, like her looking-glass, only gives us a miserable knowledge of the small compass of our prison.

Duch. Am not I thy duchess?

Bos. Thou art some great woman, sure, for riot begins to sit
on thy forehead, clad in grey hairs, twenty years sooner   135
than on a merry milkmaid's. Thou sleepest worse than if
a mouse should be forced to take up her lodging in a cat's
ear: a little infant that breeds its teeth, should it lie with
thee, would cry out, as if thou wert the more unquiet
bedfellow.   140

---

124. best,] *Q; best Dyce i.*

124. *worm-seed*] The dried flower heads of this plant were a medicine
used against intestinal worms. There is a quibble on *seed* = 'origin, germ'.
salvatory] box for holding ointment.
125. *green mummy*] a medicine was prepared from mummies; *green* is
presumably a quibble to suggest a 'living' corpse, or flesh that is not 'ripe'
enough to be mummy.
125. *crudded milk*] Crawford compared Donne, *Of the Progress of the Soul*,
ll. 165–6: 'This curded milke, this poore unlittered whelpe, / My body'. The
ultimate source is probably *Job*, x.9–10.
126. *fantastical*] eccentric, grotesque: *O.E.D.* first records 'puff-paste'
in Marston, *Antonio and Mellida* (1602), III, used figuratively of a dandy
(Cotgrave's *Dictionary* (1611) is its first literal usage).
127. *prisons*] 'The body is the prison of the soul' was a common proverb
(Tilley B497); see, e.g., *A. V.*, IV.ii.89–91: 'My mighty soule might rush out
of this prison . . .'
129. *lark in a cage*] echoing ll. 13–14, above.
133.] The question may signal that she has recognized Bosola or that she
assumes the unknown old man is one of her subjects. More simply, she is
supplying the answer she had expected to her questions (ll. 121, 123).
134. *riot*] disorder or, possibly, 'signs of extravagant or loose living'; an
echo of III.ii.58–60.
136. *merry milkmaid's*] proverbially fair, innocent, and carefree; cf. *Char-*
acters, 'A Fair and Happy Milkmaid'.
137–8. *mouse . . . ear*] Cf. the proverb, 'It is a bold mouse that breeds
(nestles) in a cat's ear' (Tilley M1231).
139–40. *thou . . .*] another echo of Act III, scene ii; see ll. 11–14.

Duch. I am Duchess of Malfi still.

Bos. That makes thy sleeps so broken:

Glories, like glow-worms, afar off shine bright,

But look'd to near, have neither heat, nor light.

Duch. Thou art very plain.   145

Bos. My trade is to flatter the dead, not the living – I am a
tomb-maker.

Duch. And thou comest to make my tomb?

Bos. Yes.

Duch. Let me be a little merry – of what stuff wilt thou make   150
it?

Bos. Nay, resolve me first, of what fashion?

Duch. Why, do we grow fantastical in our death-bed? do we
affect fashion in the grave?

Bos. Most ambitiously: princes' images on their tombs do not   155
lie, as they were wont, seeming to pray up to heaven, but
with their hands under their cheeks, as if they died of the
tooth-ache; they are not carved with their eyes fixed upon
the stars, but as their minds were wholly bent upon the
world, the selfsame way they seem to turn their faces.   160

Duch. Let me know fully therefore the effect

Of this thy dismal preparation,

This talk fit for a charnel.

Bos.   Now I shall:

143–4.] *italicized this ed.;* 'Glories . . . *Q.* 146–7.] *so Dyce i; . . .* liuing / I
. . . *Q.* 150–1.] *so Dyce i; . . .* merry, / Of . . . *Q.* 153–60.] *so Dyce i; . . .*
bed? / Do . . . graue? / *Bos.* . . . tombes, / Do . . . pray, / Vp . . . cheekes, / (As
. . . carued / With . . . their / Mindes . . . world, / The . . . *Q.* 163.1. *Enter*
Executioners] *so Dyce i; at l. 0.1 Q; after l. 166 Q4.* with . . . bell] *Dyce i; A*
Coffin . . . Bell (to right of ll. 164–6) Q; A Coffin, brought in (after l. 164) Q4.

143–4.] repeated from *W.D.*, v.i.41–2; taken from *A.T.*, v.iii.3428–9:
'Some things afarre doe like the Glow-worme shine, / Which look't too neere,
have of that light no signe'.

155–60.] This fashion in tomb-making had started in England by the
1560s (cf. tomb of the Hobys, illustrated in E. Mercer, *English Art, 1553–1625*
(1962), plate 83b); but a full freedom in the choice of pose dates from the
early 17th century (cf. Mercer, pp. 239–52).

161. *effect*] purpose.

163.1. cords] These may represent, as symbols in a masque (see Ewbank,
1958, 1969), both a wedding ring (cf. l. 247, below and I.i.87, note) and
'love knot' (cf. *W.D.*, v.iii.174–5, as Bracciano is strangled: 'This is a true-
love knot / Sent from the Duke of Florence').

Enter Executioners[, *with*] *a coffin, cords and a bell.*

Here is a present from your princely brothers,
And may it arrive welcome, for it brings   165
Last benefit, last sorrow.
Duch.   Let me see it –
I have so much obedience in my blood,
I wish it in their veins, to do them good.
Bos. This is your last presence-chamber.
Cari. O my sweet lady!
Duch.   Peace, it affrights not me.   170
Bos. I am the common bellman
That usually is sent to condemn'd persons
The night before they suffer: –
Duch.   Even now thou said'st
Thou wast a tomb-maker.
Bos.   'Twas to bring you
By degrees to mortification. Listen: 175

---

175. Listen] *Q;* Listen. / *Rings his Bell Q4;* Listen: (*dirge Haz.*)

164–9.] A new authoritative tone and formality imply that Bosola has
dropped his disguise of an old man; he assumes another, at line 171.
    171. *common bellman*] Stowe's *Survey of London,* continued and enlarged
by Anthony Munday in 1618, entered into the Stationers' Register in 1612,
records how Robert Dove, a 'Citizen and Merchant Taylor of *London*', 'gave
to the Parish of S[t] *Sepulchres* the summe of fifty pounds, that after the
severall Sessions in *London,* when the prisoners remaine in the Gaole, as
condemned men to death, expecting execution on the morrow following, the
Clerke of the Church should come in the night time, and likewise early in
the morning, to the window of the prison where they lye, and there ringing
certain toules with a hand-bell, appointed for the purpose, he doth afterward
(in most Christian manner) put them in minde of their present condition,
and ensuing execution, desiring them to be prepared therefore as they ought
to bee' (London, 1633, p. 102). The prayer and tolling bell were repeated
when the prisoners were in the cart and brought by the church on their way
to execution: the people watching were then asked to pray for the condemned. John Webster, the dramatist's father, as a member of the Common
Council of the Merchant Taylors, was a witness to the deed that established
the charity in 1605.
    172–3.] implying that the Duchess is already condemned to die as a
criminal.
    175. *mortification* (1) state of torpor and insensibility preceding death; (2)
a religious exercise to subdue the appetites and passions of the flesh.
    Listen] Bosola probably sounds his bell here, and possibly before each new
sentence in his dirge. Something of the stage-effect desired by Webster may

Hark, now everything is still,
The screech-owl, and the whistler shrill
Call upon our dame, aloud,
And bid her quickly don her shroud.
Much you had of land and rent,   180
Your length in clay's now competent.
A long war disturb'd your mind
Here your perfect peace is sign'd.
Of what is't fools make such vain keeping?
Sin their conception, their birth weeping;   185
Their life a general mist of error,
Their death a hideous storm of terror.
Strew your hair with powders sweet,
Don clean linen, bathe your feet,
And (the foul fiend more to check)   190
A crucifix let bless your neck.

176–93.] *italicized Q.*

be gathered from *D.L.C.*, II.iii, where a 'dismall' sounding bell is heard and
then two bell-men enter asking for prayers for the newly dead.

177.] A catalogue of 'fatal birds' in *The Faerie Queene* (II.xii.36) includes:
'The ruefull strich, still waiting on the bere. / The whistler shrill, that who
so heares doth dy'.

whistler was applied to various species, as the widgeon, ring ouzel and
lapwing.

At this point the dirge is antithetical to an epithalamium, which customar-
ily bade such creatures be silent on the wedding night: cf. *Two Noble Kinsmen*,
I.i and Spenser, *Epith.*, ll. 345–6 (so Ekeblad, *R.E.S.*, n.s., ix (1958),
pp. 253–67).

178. our dame] i.e., night.

181. competent] appropriate, sufficient.

183.] An echo of I.i.464 and III.ii.187.

184–7.] traditional sentiments and largely conventional expression: cf.
Misfortunes of Arthur, Epilogus, 13–15: 'Whereof (alas) should wretched man
be proude, / Whose first conception is but Sinne, whose birth / But paine,
whose life but toyle, and needes must dye?' (so Dent).

186. mist] often used by Webster for 'uncertainty' or 'confused knowledge', as v.vi.94: 'In a mist: I know not how – / Such a *mistake* . . .', and
W.D., v.vi.259–60: 'we confound / Knowledge with knowledge. O I am in
a mist'.

188.] In requiring the Duchess to prepare herself to be laid out, the dirge
echoes epithalamiums, for a bride might strew her flowing hair with powder
(so Ekeblad, who quoted Donne's *Epithalamium* for the Earl of Somerset in
1613, iv: see also Jonson, *Hymenaei* (1606), ll. 57 and 184).

The powdered 'hair' is another echo of III.ii.58–60.

> 'Tis now full tide,'tween night and day:
> End your groan, and come away.

Cari. Hence villains, tyrants, murderers! alas!
    What will you do with my lady? call for help.   195
Duch. To whom? to our next neighbours? they are
    mad-folks.
Bos. Remove that noise.
Duch.   Farewell Cariola:
    In my last will I have not much to give;
    A many hungry guests have fed upon me,
    Thine will be a poor reversion.
Cari.   I will die with her.   200
Duch. I pray thee, look thou giv'st my little boy
    Some syrup for his cold, and let the girl
    Say her prayers, ere she sleep.
                    [*Executioners force* CARIOLA *off.*]
                Now what you please –
    What death?
Bos.   Strangling: here are your executioners.
Duch. I forgive them: 205
    The apoplexy, catarrh, or cough o'th' lungs
    Would do as much as they do.
Bos. Doth not death fright you?
Duch.   Who would be afraid on't?
    Knowing to meet such excellent company
    In th' other world.   210

---

203. S.D.] *Q4 subs. (after l. 204).*   208. on't?] *Q; on't, Q3.*

192–3] This 'strongly suggests the traditional exhortation at the end of the epithalamium, referring to the impatiently awaited night of the bridal bed . . . And so the Duchess goes, not to ardent bridegroom, but to "violent death"' (Ekeblad).

    200. *reversion*] right of future possession, bequest (a legal term).

    205.] Executioners customarily knelt to ask forgiveness of their victim (see *W.D.*, v.vi.211–12) and probably do so here (so Cambridge ed.).

    206. *catarrh*] formerly a name for cerebral haemorrhage.

    208–13.] Cf. *W.D.*, v.vi.219–26: 'Are you so brave? . . . Methinks fear should dissolve thee into air . . .', and Florio, I.xxv: 'So many thousands of men, lowe-layde in their graves afore-vs, may encourage-vs, not to fear, or be dismayed to goe meete so good company in the other world . . .'. Lines 211–12 echo III.v.71–2.

Bos. Yet, methinks,
    The manner of your death should much afflict you,
    This cord should terrify you?
Duch.   Not a whit:
    What would it pleasure me to have my throat cut
    With diamonds? or to be smothered   215
    With cassia? or to be shot to death with pearls?
    I know death hath ten thousand several doors
    For men to take their exits; and 'tis found
    They go on such strange geometrical hinges,
    You may open them both ways: – any way, for
       heaven-sake,   220
    So I were out of your whispering: – tell my brothers
    That I perceive death, now I am well awake,
    Best gift is they can give, or I can take.
    I would fain put off my last woman's fault,
    I'd not be tedious to you.
Execut.   We are ready.   225
Duch. Dispose my breath how please you, but my body
    Bestow upon my women, will you?
Execut.   Yes.
Duch. Pull, and pull strongly, for your able strength
    Must pull down heaven upon me: –
    Yet stay; heaven-gates are not so highly arch'd   230
    As princes' palaces, they that enter there

---

213. you?] *Q; you. Dyce i.*

217–8. *I . . . exits*] a Senecan commonplace; Tilley (D140) quoted from Greville, Marston, Florio, Fletcher, etc.
219–20. *go . . . ways*] obscure: perhaps, (1) 'lead to heaven or hell', or (2) 'open by an act of will (i.e. suicide) or of acceptance (i.e., of murder or accident)'. C. Leech suggests that *geometrical* gives a nightmarish impression of swinging doors; cf. I.i.59–65 (*Webster: The Duchess of Malfi* (1963), pp. 43–6).
223.] In Alexander, *A.T.*, IV.ii.2163–4, a queen grieving over her murdered husband welcomes a sword, cord and poison given to aid her own suicide: 'Fit gifts for her to giue, for me to take, / Since she exceeds in hate, and I in griefe'.
224–5. *I . . . you*] Cf. the proverbs that a woman's tongue 'is the last thing about her that dies' and 'is always in motion' (Tilley W676–7).
230–2. *heaven . . . knees*] a commonplace: Webster might have derived it from *Cymbeline* (III.iii.2–7), for Belarius speaks of 'the gates of monarchs . . . arch'd so high' (so Lucas).

Must go upon their knees. – [*Kneels.*] Come violent
   death,
Serve for mandragora to make me sleep!
Go tell my brothers, when I am laid out,
They then may feed in quiet.   *They strangle her.*   235
Bos. Where's the waiting woman?
Fetch her: some other strangle the children.

[Executioners *fetch* CARIOLA, *and one goes to strangle the children.*]

    Look you, there sleeps your mistress.
Cari.   O, you are damn'd
Perpetually for this: – my turn is next,
Is't not so order'd?
Bos.   Yes, and I am glad   240
You are so well prepar'd for't.
Cari.   You are deceiv'd sir,
I am not prepar'd for't, I will not die;
I will first come to my answer, and know
How I have offended.
Bos.   Come, dispatch her: –
You kept her counsel, now you shall keep ours.   245
Cari. I will not die, I must not, I am contracted
To a young gentleman.

---

232. *Kneels*] *Dyce ii; after l. 233 Q4.*   235. S.D.] *so Q4; to right of ll. 234–5*
Q.   237.1.] *This ed.; Enter Cariola Q4 (after* mistress, *l. 239); Cariola and*
Children are brought in by the Executioners; who presently strangle the Children
Dyce ii.

---

235. *mandragora*] mandrake; this is the only occasion Webster used this
form or alluded to the plant's narcotic properties; possibly he was influenced,
as other writers have been, by *Oth.*, III.iii.330.

236–7. Vittoria's heightened consciousness at her death was shown by
word-play (*W.D.*, v.vi.224 and 240–1), and so may the Duchess's: *laid out*
= (1) 'prepared for burial', and (2) 'spent, expended' (usually of money; but
cf. *Tw.N.*, III.iv.222); and, in view of *feed*, there may be a further pun on
'*laying* a table'. *Feed in quiet* may allude to the proverbs 'A little with quiet
is the only diet', and 'Better enjoy a little with quietness than possess much
with trouble' (Tilley L361 and L350). See, also, l. 199, above.

237.1] Probably the children are strangled off-stage: cf. 'this' of l. 254
below, and Q's S.D. two lines later.

243. *come . . . answer*] make a legal defence.

Execut.   Here's your wedding ring.

Cari. Let me but speak with the duke: I'll discover
    Treason to his person.

Bos.   Delays: – throttle her.

Execut. She bites, and scratches: –

Cari.   If you kill me now   250
    I am damn'd: I have not been at confession
    This two years: –

Bos.   When?

Cari.   I am quick with child.

Bos.   Why then,
    Your credit's sav'd: – [*The Executioners strangle Cariola.*]
                     bear her into th' next room;
    Let this lie still.

        [*Exeunt* Executioners *with the body of Cariola.*]

           Enter FERDINAND.

Ferd.   Is she dead?

Bos.   She is what
    You'd have her: but here begin you pity –   255
               Shows the Children strangled.
    Alas, how have these offended?

Ferd.   The death
    Of young wolves is never to be pitied.

Bos. Fix your eye here: –

Ferd.   Constantly.

---

253. S.D.] *Dyce ii.*   254. this] *Q; these Dyce ii.*   254. Exeunt . . . Cariola]
Dyce ii.   Enter Ferdinand] *Q4* (*after l. 253*); *at l. O.1 Q.*   255.1.] *so Dyce i;
to right of ll. 255–6 Q.*

    249. *Here's . . . ring*] Cf. Painter; App. I, p. ••: 'in stead of a carcanet
placed a roape . . .'
    254. *Is she dead?*] Bosola's reply may imply an element of reproach in this
question (see ll. 291–309, below). If Ferdinand has been watching out of
sight and so enters at just the right moment (as he has before; see note at
IV.i.100), his unnecessary question may be motivated by some deep-seated,
unspoken unease, such as fear, disbelief or guilt.
    256–7. *The . . .*] Cf. the proverbs, 'The death of a young wolf does never
come too soon', and 'The death of wolves is the safety of the sheep' (Tilley
D145 and D146).

Bos.   Do you not weep?
Other sins only speak; murder shrieks out:
The element of water moistens the earth,   260
But blood flies upwards, and bedews the heavens.
Ferd. Cover her face: mine eyes dazzle: she died young.
Bos. I think not so: her infelicity
Seem'd to have years too many.
Ferd. She and I were twins: 265
And should I die this instant, I had liv'd
Her time to a minute.
Bos.   It seems she was born first:
You have bloodily approv'd the ancient truth,
That kindred commonly do worse agree
Than remote strangers.
Ferd.   Let me see her face again: –   270
Why didst not thou pity her? what an excellent
Honest man mightst thou have been
If thou hadst borne her to some sanctuary!
Or, bold in a good cause, oppos'd thyself
With thy advanced sword above thy head,   275
Between her innocence and my revenge!

270–2. Let...] *so Q;...* face / Again ... what / An ... *Dyce i.*

259.] Cf. Hall, *Epistles*, VI.viii: 'Other sinnes speake, this crieth, and will neuer be silent, till it be answered with it selfe'.
260–1.] probably from Nashe, *Unfortunate Traveller* (*Wks*, II.320): 'water powred forth sinkes downe quietly into the earth, but bloud spilt on the ground sprinkles vp to the firmament;' see also the biblical story of Cain and Abel, *Genesis*, iv.10: 'the voice of thy brother's blood crieth unto me from the ground'.
264. *Cover her face*] Cf. 'He dares not see you' (IV.i.28).
She...young] There may be an allusion to the well-known proberb, 'The good die young' (Tilley G251); so Ferdinand's reaction to her death would include a response to her 'innocence' (l. 276) from the very beginning (see also 'good cause', l. 274). The other form of the proverb, 'Those that God loves do not live long', suggests an acceptance of Fate, or Providence; but this idea is not reflected elsewhere in the scene. Possibly both reactions are implied in Ferdinand's three words: they are mingled, for example, in Nashe's 'Beauty is but a flowre, / ... / Queenes haue *died yong* and faire, / Dust hath closde Helens eye. / I am sick, I must dye: / Lord, haue mercy on vs' (*Summer's Last Will*, ll. 1588–94).
268–70. *You...strangers*] Cf. More, *Richard III*; *Works* (1557), p. 50: 'As though ... children could not play but wᵗ their kyndred, wit whom for the more part they agree much worse then wyth straungers' (so Dent).

I bade thee, when I was distracted of my wits,
Go kill my dearest friend, and thou hast done't.
For let me but examine well the cause:
What was the meanness of her match to me?   280
Only I must confess, I had a hope,
Had she continu'd widow, to have gain'd
An infinite mass of treasure by her death:
And that was the main cause: . . . her marriage! –
That drew a stream of gall, quite through my heart.   285
For thee, (as we observe in tragedies
That a good actor many times is curs'd
For playing a villain's part) I hate thee for 't:
And for my sake say thou hast done much ill well.
Bos. Let me quicken your memory; for I perceive   290
You are falling into ingratitude: I challenge
The reward due to my service.
Ferd.   I'll tell thee
What I'll give thee –
Bos.   Do: –
Ferd.   I'll give thee a pardon
For this murder: –
Bos.   Hah?
Ferd.   Yes: and 'tis
The largest bounty I can study to do thee.   295
By what authority didst thou execute
This bloody sentence?
Bos.   By yours –

---

283. death:] *Q.*   284. that] *Q*; what *Q2, Q3.*   cause: . . . her marriage! –]
This ed., cause; her Marriage, *Q;* cause? her Marriage, *Q3;* cause, her marriage, *Haz; cause;* her Marriage – *Luc i.*   297. Mine?] *Q;* Mine! *Dyce i.*

279–85.] A break in sense (and the actor's delivery) seems inevitable
before and after *her marriage;* the alternative is emendation. (For comparable
abrupt changes in the course of a speech, cf. *W.D.,* II.i.78, note). The hope
of 'infinite' treasure is a spurious explanation: the Duchess's son by her first
husband (see III.iii.69–70) will inherit her estate and wealth. His words are
either to deceive Bosola (cf. *Rom.,* V.iii.28–32, where Romeo deceives
Balthasar) or an instinctive attempt to 'cover up' the deep feelings exposed
by 'dearest friend' of l. 278. (The speech does not read like self-questioning;
the context is too impassioned.) After the confession of l. 285, Ferdinand
again veers, to attack the only person he can.

Ferd.   Mine? was I her judge?
    Did any ceremonial form of law
    Doom her to not-being? did a complete jury
    Deliver her conviction up i'th' court?   300
    Where shalt thou find this judgement register'd
    Unless in hell? See: like a bloody fool
    Th' hast forfeited thy life, and thou shalt die for't.
Bos. The office of justice is perverted quite
    When one thief hangs another: – who shall dare   305
    To reveal this?
Ferd.   O, I'll tell thee:
    The wolf shall find her grave, and scrape it up:
    Not to devour the corpse, but to discover
    The horrid murder.
Bos.   You, not I, shall quake for't
Ferd. Leave me: –
Bos.   I will first receive my pension.   310
Ferd. You are a villain: –
Bos.   When your ingratitude
    Is judge, I am so.
Ferd.   O horror!
    That not the fear of him which binds the devils
    Can prescribe man obedience!
    Never look upon me more.
Bos.   Why fare thee well: 315
    You brother and yourself are worthy men;
    You have a pair of hearts are hollow graves,
    Rotten, and rotting others: and your vengeance,

304–5. *The ... another*] perhaps from Guevera, *Dial of Princes* (1557), III.ix; H6ᵛ: 'For much is the office of iustice peruerted, when one thiefe hangeth another on the galouse' (so Dent, noting that this book is echoed sereral times in *A. V.*).

307–9. *The ... murder*] The superstitious believed that wolves uncovered the bodies of murdered men and left them exposed; cf. *W.D.*, v.iv.103–4. Here and at l. 277, above, Ferdinand is moving towards his later lycanthropic state (see v.ii.5–10).

312. *binds*] probably 'confines, controls' and *him* = God. Here and at IV.ii.61, Webster may have been influenced by Psalm 149. where, to execute vengeance on the heathen, God is said to 'bind the Kings with chains and their nobles with fetters of iron' (v. 8).

317. *hollow*] shallow (*O.E.D.*, I. c) or, possibly, open.

Like two chain'd bullets, still goes arm in arm –
You may be brothers; for treason, like the plague,   320
Doth take much in a blood. I stand like one
That long hath ta'en a sweet and golden dream:
I am angry with myself, now that I wake.
Ferd. Get thee into some unknown part o'th' world
That I may never see thee.
Bos.   Let me know   325
Wherefore I should be thus neglected? sir,
I serv'd your tyranny; and rather strove
To satisfy yourself, than all the world;
And though I loath'd the evil, yet I lov'd
You that did counsel it; and rather sought   330
To appear a true servant, than an honest man.
Ferd. I'll go hunt the badger; by owl-light:
'Tis a deed of darkness.   *Exit.*
Bos. He's much distracted: – off my painted honour:
While with vain hopes our faculties we tire,   335
We seem to sweat in ice, and freeze in fire.
What would I do, were this to do again?
I would not change my peace of conscience
For all the wealth of Europe: – she stirs; here's life:
Return, fair soul, from darkness, and lead mine   340

319.] Cf. Chapman, *Revenge*, v.i.7–9: '. . . who in th' act itself / Includes
th' infliction, which like chained shot / Batter together still'. *chain'd bullets* =
cannon balls (or half-balls) linked by a chain, and used chiefly in naval
warfare for destroying masts, rigging etc.

321. *take . . . blood*] catch a strong hold on a family; see *O.E.D.*, *take*, 7f.

324–5. *Get . . . there*] so King John requites his hit-man, Hubert: 'Out of
my sight, and never see me more' (*Jn*, IV.ii.203ff.).

327–31.] from *Arcadia*, II.x (*Wks*, I.211–12), of a villain's assistants who
'willingly held out the course, rather to satisfie him, then al the world; and
rather to be good friendes, then good men: so as though they did not like
the evill he did, yet they liked him that did the evill; and though not councel-
lors of the offence, yet protectors of the offender'.

332–3.] A *badger* 'is hardlie taken, but by devises and ginnes' (Topsell,
Four-Footed Beasts (1607), p. 34); Turberville's *Book of Hunting* (1576)
recommends 'a fayre moonshine night' (ed. 1908, p. 190).

The *Character* of the 'Franklin' (ll. 15–16) may show something of the
associations in Webster's mind: 'He neuer sits vp late, but when he hunts
the Badger, the vowed foe of his Lambs'.

owl-light was a fairly common phrase for twilight or evening.

334. *painted*] false, specious; cf. III.ii.279.

Out of this sensible hell: – she's warm, she breathes: –
Upon thy pale lips I will melt my heart
To store them with fresh colour: – who's there?
Some cordial drink! – Alas! I dare not call:
So pity would destroy pity: – her eye opes,   345
And heaven in it seems to ope, that late was shut,
To take me up to mercy.
Duch. Antonio!
Bos.   Yes, madam, he is living –
The dead bodies you saw were but feign'd statues;
He's reconcil'd to your brothers; the Pope hath
    wrought   350
The atonement.
Duch.   Mercy!   *She dies.*
Bos. O, she's gone again: there the cords of life broke.
O sacred innocence, that sweetly sleeps
On turtles' feathers, whilst a guilty conscience
Is a black register, wherein is writ   355
All our good deeds and bad, a perspective
That shows us hell! That we cannot be suffer'd
To do good when we have a mind to it!
This is manly sorrow:
These tears, I am very certain, never grew   360
In my mother's milk. My estate is sunk
Below the degree of fear: where were
These penitent fountains while she was living?
O, they were frozen up! Here is a sight
As direful to my soul as is the sword   365

363–4.] so *Q;* . . . fountaines, / While . . . *Luc i.*

---

345. *pity . . . pity*] i.e., calling for help would bring back Ferdinand.
348–51.] On the Duchess's last words, see Intro., p. 32.
351. *atonement*] reconciliation.
352. *cords of life*] sinews or nerves. 'Heart-strings' were often spoken of as
if they were tangible; cf. *Jn,* v.vii.52–5, and *Lr,* v.iii.216–17: 'the strings of
life / Began to crack'.
354–6. *guilty . . . bad*] a variation of the more usual idea that *bad* deeds
are recorded.
356. *perspective*] 'optical glass', or 'aspect'.
361–2. *My . . . fear*] i.e., I am past fear; from *Arcadia,* II.x (*Wks,* I.208):
'our state is soncke below the degree of feare'.
estate = 'condition' (moral, bodily or mental), 'fortune', and 'status'.

Unto a wretch hath slaim his father. Come,
I'll bear thee hence:
And execute thy last will; that's deliver
Thy body to the reverent dispose
Of some good women: that the cruel tyrant   370
Shall not deny me. Then I'll post to Milan
Where somewhat I will speedily enact
Worth my dejection.

Exit[, *with the body of the* Duchess].

366–7.] *so Dyce i; one line Q;* . . . Father: / Come . . . *Q4.*   373.1. *with . . .*
Duchess] *Q4 subs.*

---

369. *dispose*] This was the usual form; 'disposal' is first recorded by
O.E.D. in 1630.

373. *dejection*] 'overthrow, humiliation', the usual senses in Webster's day.

Act V

Enter ANTONIO *and* DELIO.

Ant. What think you of my hope of reconcilement
    To the Aragonian brethren?
Delio.   I misdoubt it,
    For though they have sent their letters of safe conduct
    For your repair to Milan, they appear
    But nets to entrap you: the Marquis of Pescara,   5
    Under whom you hold certain land in cheat,
    Much 'gainst his noble nature, hath been mov'd
    To seize those lands, and some of his dependants
    Are at this instant making it their suit
    To be invested in your revenues.   10
    I cannot think they mean well to your life
    That do deprive you of your means of life,
    Your living.
Ant.   You are still an heretic
    To any safety I can shape myself.

Enter PESCARA.

Delio. Here comes the Marquis: I will make myself   15
    Petitioner for some part of your land,
    To know whither it is flying.
Ant.   I pray do.   *[He retires.]*

---

v.i.0.1.] *Q4; Antonio, Delio, Pescara, Iulia Q.*   14.1.] *so this ed.; at l. 0.1 Q;
after l. 17 Q4.*   17. S.D.] *Samp subs.*

v.i.3–4. *sent . . . Milan*] identifying both the new location of the play's
action and the risk Antonio has taken.
    6. *in cheat*] 'subject to escheat'; Anotonio possessed land on condition
that if he died intestate without heirs or committed treason, felony, etc., it
would revert to Pescara.
    11–13. *I . . . living*] Cf. *Mer.V.*, iv.i.374–7: ' . . . you take my life / When
you do take the means whereby I live', and *Ecclesiasticus*, xxxiv.22: 'He that
taketh away his neighbour's living, slayeth him'.

Delio. Sir, I have a suit to you.
Pes.   To me?
Delio.   An easy one:
    There is the Citadel of Saint Bennet,
    With some demesnes, of late in the possession   20
    Of Antonio Bologna – please you bestow them on me?
Pes. You are my friend: but this is such a suit,
    Nor fit for me to give, nor you to take.
Delio. No sir?
Pes.   I will give you ample reason for 't
    Soon in private: –

                   Enter JULIA.

                     here's the cardinal's mistress.   25
Julia. My lord, I am grown your poor petitioner,
    And should be an ill beggar, had I not
    A great man's letter here, the cardinal's,
    To court you in my favour.   [*Gives letter.*]
Pes.   He entreats for you
    The Citadel of Saint Bennet, that belong'd   30
    To the banish'd Bologna.
Julia.   Yes.
Pes. I could not have thought of a friend I could
    Rather pleasure with it: 'tis yours.
Julia.   Sir, I thank you:
    And he shall know how doubly I am engag'd
    Both in you gift, and speediness of giving,   35
    Which makes your grant the greater.   *Exit.*
Ant. [*Aside*]   How they fortify
    Themselves with my ruin!
Delio.   Sir, I am
    Little bound to you.
Pes.   Why?

25. S.D.] *so this ed.; at l. o.1 Q; at end of line Q4.* 29. S.D.] *Dyce ii.*
32–3. I . . . yours] *so Q; . . . rather / Pleasure . . . Dyce i.* 32. could] *Q;*
would *Q4.* 36. *Aside*] *Samp.*

---

19. *Bennet*] Benedict.
23.] Cf. the passages from *A.T.* quoted at 1.i.264–6 and IV.ii.253, above.
34–6. *how . . . greater*] Cf. the old and common proverb, 'He that gives
quickly gives twice' (Tilley G125).

Delio. Because you deny'd this suit to me, and gave't
   To such a creature.
Pes.   Do you know what it was?   40
   It was Antonio's land: not forfeited
   By course of law, but ravish'd from his throat
   By the cardinal's entreaty: it were not fit
   I should bestow so main a piece of wrong
   Upon my friend; 'tis a gratification   45
   Only due to a strumpet, for it is injustice.
   Shall I sprinkle the pure blood of innocents
   To make those followers I call my friends
   Look ruddier upon me? I am glad
   This land, ta'en from the owner by such wrong,   50
   Returns again unto so foul an use
   As salary for his lust. Learn, good Delio,
   To ask noble things of me, and you shall find
   I'll be a noble giver.
Delio.   You instruct me well.
Ant. [*Aside*] Why, here's a man now, would fright
      impudence   55
   From sauciest beggars.
Pes. Prince Ferdinand's come to Milan
   Sick, as they give out, of an apoplexy;
   But some say 'tis a frenzy: I am going
   To visit him.   *Exit.*
Ant.   'Tis a noble old fellow.   [*He advances.*]   60

55. *Aside*] *Samp.*   60. *He advances*] *McIl subs.*

47–8.] Another acknowledgement of dangerous and violent times: see lines 75–6, below, and note on lines 3–4.
43–6. *it . . . injustice*] The whole episode, as well as these words, may derive from Florio, I.xxix: 'Epaminondas had caused a dissolute yoong man to be imprisoned: Pelopidas entreated him, that for his sake he would set-him at libertie, but he refused him, and yeelded to free-him at the request of an harlot of his, which likewise sued for his enlargement; saying, it was a gratification due unto a Courtizan, and not to a Captaine'.
59. *frenzy*] Frenzy was said to be an inflammation of the brain due to an invasion of choler: its symptoms were like those of melancholic madness, but continuous rather than cyclic. Men so afflicted 'swarue from al sense, in any thing they vtter, being inconstant, and so intricating themselues, that another Sphinx should haue work enough to explane their conceits, & Oedipus himself would sweate, to apprehend the meaning of their words . . . ' (T. Garzoni, *Incurable Fools* (1600), C1ᵛ).

Delio. What course do you mean to take, Antonio?

Ant. This night I mean to venture all my fortune
　　(Which is no more than a poor ling'ring life)
　　To the cardinal's worst of malice: I have got
　　Private access to his chamber, and intend　　　　　　65
　　To visit him, about the mid of night,
　　As once his brother did our noble duchess.
　　It may be that the sudden apprehension
　　Of danger – for I'll go in mine own shape –
　　When he shall see it fraught with love and duty,　　70
　　May draw the poison out of him, and work
　　A friendly reconcilement: if it fail,
　　Yet it shall rid me of this infamous calling;
　　For better fall once, than be ever falling.

Delio. I'll second you in all danger: and how e'er,　　75
　　My life keeps rank with yours.

Ant. You are still my lov'd, and best friend.　　　*Exeunt.*

SCENA II.

Enter PESCARA *and a* Doctor.

Pes. Now doctor, may I visit your patient?

Doc. If't please your lordship: but he's instantly
　　To take the air here in the gallery,
　　By my direction.

Pes.　　　　　　　Pray thee, what's his disease?

Doc. A very pestilent disease, my lord,　　　　　　5
　　They call lycanthropia.

---

v.ii.0.1.] *Q4 subs.; Pescara, a Doctor, Ferdinand, Cardinall, Malateste, Bosola, Iulia Q.*　6. call] *Q;* can it *conj. Samp.*

---

64. *malice*] (1) power to harm, (2) ill-will.

73. *calling*] position in life, means of livelihood.

74.] Cf. Florio, I.xxxii: 'There is no man so base-minded, that loveth not rather to fall once, than ever to remaine in feare of falling'; this derives from Seneca, *Epistles,* xxii.3.

75. *how e'er*] whatever happens.

v.ii.3–4. *take . . . direction*] Doctors recommended that melancholic patients should expose themselves only to warm, moist air, and take only moderate exercise (cf. L. Babb, *Eliz. Malady* (1951), p. 39).

5–19. *A . . . try*] from Goulart, *Admirable and Memorable Histories* (tr. 1607), pp. 386–7: 'For there be Licanthropes in whom the melancholike

Pes.   What's that?
        I need a dictionary to't.
Doc.   I'll tell you:
        In those that are possess'd with't there o'erflows
        Such melancholy humour, they imagine
        Themselves to be transformed into wolves,   10
        Steal forth to churchyards in the dead of night,
        And dig dead bodies up: as two nights since
        One met the duke, 'bout midnight in a lane
        Behind Saint Mark's church, with the leg of a man
        Upon his shoulder; and he howl'd fearfully;   15
        Said he was a wolf, only the difference
        Was, a wolf's skin was hairy on the outside,
        His on the inside; bade them take their swords,
        Rip up his flesh, and try: straight I was sent for,
        And having minister'd to him, found his grace   20
        Very well recovered.
Pes.   I am glad on't.
Doc. Yet not without some fear
        Of a relapse. If he grow to his fit again
        I'll go a nearer way to work with him

---

humor doth so rule, as they imagine themselues to be transformed into
Wolues . . . and all night doe nothing but runne into Church-yardes, and
about graues . . . One of these melancholike Licanthropes . . . carried then
vpon his shoulders the whole thigh and legge of a dead man . . . A Coun-
triman neere unto Pauia, in the yeare 1541 . . . did constantlye affirme that
hee was a Wolfe, and that there was no other difference, but that Wolues
were commonlie hayrie without, and hee was betwixt the skinne and the
flesh. Some (too barbarous and cruell Wolues in effect) desiring to trie the
truth thereof, gaue him manie wounds vpon the armes and legges [from
which the man died].'
    Some authorities called the disease a form of melancholy (as the Doctor
may acknowledge at l. 9) but Robert Burton insists that it is madness which
he defined as 'a vehement dotage, or raving without a fever, far more violent
than melancholy, full of anger and clamour, horrible looks, actions, gestures,
troubling the patients with far greater vehemency both of body and mind,
without all fear and sorrow, with such impetuous force and boldness that
sometimes three or four men cannot hold them' (*Anatomy of Melancholy*
[1621], I.i.I.iv).
    24. *nearer*] 'more direct', or, possibly, 'more intimate, familiar'.

Than ever Paracelsus dream'd of: if   25
They'll give me leave I'll buffet his madness out of him.

Enter FERDINAND, MALATESTE, *and* Cardinal; BOSOLA
[*follows and watches, apart*].

Stand aside: he comes.

Ferd. Leave me.

Mal. Why doth your lordship love this solitariness?

Ferd. Eagles commonly fly alone: they are crows, daws, and   30
starlings that flock together: – look, what's that follows
me?

Mal. Nothing, my lord.

Ferd. Yes: –

Mal. 'Tis your shadow.   35

Ferd. Stay it, let it not haunt me.

Mal. Impossible: if you move, and the sun shine: –

Ferd. I will throttle it.   [*Throws himself down on his shadow.*]

Mal. O, my lord; you are angry with nothing.

Ferd. You are a fool: how is't possible I should catch my   40
shadow unless I fall upon't? When I go to hell, I mean

26.1.] *so Q4; at l.o.1 Q; after l. 27 Dyce i; . . . Ferdinand, with Attendants at a
distance, Malateste . . . conj. this ed.*   26.2.] *This ed.*   30–2.] *so Dyce i; . . .*
and / Sterlings . . . that, / Followes . . . *Q; . . .* crows, / Daws, . . . Look, /
What's . . . *Haz.*   38. S.D.] *Q4 subs.*   40–3.] *so Dyce i; . . .* foole: / How . . .
shadow / Vnlesse . . . Hell, / I . . . you / Good . . . *Q.*

---

25. *Paracelsus*] a noted physician-magician (1493–1541): he combined the
studies of chemistry and medicine, and classified animal and vegetable
bodies together; many strange stories were told of him.

26. *buffet*] Whipping was a usual and authoritatively recommended
remedy, as well as a means of control.

28–9.] Pleasant company was recommended by doctors as a cure for
melancholy; *solitariness* was forbidden.

30–1. *Eagles . . . together*] from *Arcadia*, I.ix (*Wks*, 1.56): 'Eagles we see
fly alone; and they are but sheepe, which alwaies heard togther': this is the
first occurrence of the proverb noted by Tilley (E7 and S314). See also *Troil.*,
I.ii.265–6: 'The eagles are gone: crows and daws, crows and daws!' *daws* =
jackdaws.

31–41. *look . . . upon't*] 'To be afraid of one's own shadow' was a proverbial expression for causeless fear (cf. 'haunt', l. 36) and 'to fight with one's
own shadow', for a vain or useless act (Tilley S261–2).

41. *When . . . hell*] a sudden and explicit admission of the guilt that has
been obscured by expressions of his fear and madness.

to carry a bribe; for look you, good gifts evermore make
way for the worst persons.

Pes. Rise, good my lord.

Ferd. I am studying the art of patience.   45

Pes. 'Tis a noble virtue: –

Ferd. To drive six snails before me, from this town to Moscow;
neither use goad nor whip to them, but let them take their
own time: – the patientest man i'th' world match me for
an experiment – and I'll crawl after like a sheep-biter.   50

Card. Force him up.   [*They raise him.*]

Ferd. Use me well, you were best: what I have done, I have
done: I'll confess nothing.

Doc. Now let me come to him: – are you mad, my lord? are
you out of your princely wits?   55

Ferd. What's he?

Pes. Your doctor.

Ferd. Let me have his beard sawed off, and his eyebrows filed
more civil.

Doc. I must do mad tricks with him, for that's the only way   60
on't. I have brought your grace a salamander's skin, to
keep you from sun-burning.

47–50.] *so Dyce i;* . . . towne / To . . . them, / But . . . world / Match . . . after
/ Like . . . *Q.*   51. S.D.] *Dyce ii.*   52–3.] *so Dyce i;* . . . best: / What . . . *Q.*
54–5.] *so Dyce i;* . . . mad / (My . . . *Q;* . . . Lord? / Are . . . *Samp.*   58–9.] *so
Dyce i;* . . . eye / Browes . . . *Q;* . . . off, / And . . . *Haz;* . . . browes / Fil'd . . .
Samp.   60–2.] *so Dyce i;* . . . him, / For . . . brought / Your . . . you / From
. . . *Q.*

42–3. *good . . . persons*] an allusion to the practice of bribing a gaoler in
the more usual kind of prison (so Clifford Leech).

45–6.] Cf. the common proverb, 'Patience is a virtue' (Tilley P109).

47–9. *To . . . time*] For the proverb, 'You drive a snail to Rome', Tilley
cited only one MS. collection before the date of *D.M.* (S582).

50. *sheep-biter*] dog that worries sheep.

52–3. *what . . . nothing*] The common proverb was 'I know what I know'
(Tilley K173). Shakespeare had come close to Webster's usage, for Iago in
Oth., v.ii. 306–7: 'What you know, you know. / From this time forth I never
will speak word.'

59. *civil*] decent, becoming.

60. *mad tricks*] Burton disapproved of this treatment (II.ii.6.ii); it is
enacted, however, by Corax in Ford's *Lover's Melancholy*, IV.ii.

61. *salamander's skin*] The skin of this lizard-like creature was supposed
to resist fire, as the *salamander* itself was said to live in it, or to quench it.

Ferd. I have cruel sore eyes.

Doc. The white of a cockatrix's egg is present remedy.

Ferd. Let it be a new-laid one, you were best: –   65
Hide me from him; physicians are like kings,
They brook no contradiction.

Doc. Now he begins to fear me, now let me alone with him.

Card. How now, put off your gown!

Doc. Let me have some forty urinals filled with rose-water: 70
he and I'll go pelt one another with them – now he begins
to fear me: – can you fetch a frisk, sir? – Let him go, let
him go upon my peril: I find by his eye, he stands in awe
of me; I'll make him as tame as a dormouse.

Ferd. Can you fetch your frisks, sir? – I will stamp him into   75
a cullis, flay off his skin, to cover one of the anatomies
this rogue hath set i'th' cold yonder, in Barber-
Chirurgeons' Hall. Hence, hence, you are all of you like

68.] *so Dyce i;* ... me, / Now ... *Q;* ... begins / To ... *Samp.* him] *Q;*
him. / *puts off his four Cloaks one after another Q4.* 70–4.] *so Dyce i;* ...
water: / He ... them, / Now ... sir? / Let ... perill: / I ... me, / I'll ... *Q.*
75–80.] *so Dyce i;* ... Cullice: / Flea ... Anotomies, / This ... hall: / Hence
... sacrifice, / There's ... belly, / Flattery ... *Q.*

---

63. *I ... eyes*] 'In the eyen is seene and knowne the disturbaunce
and gladnesse of the Soule. And also loue and wrath, and other passions'
(Bartholomeus, *De Prop. Rerum* (tr. 1582), v.v).

64–5.] See III.ii.86–7, note. *Isaiah,* lix.4–8, says that wicked and violent
men 'hatch cockatrice' eggs ...: [and] he that eateth of their eggs dieth'.

present = 'instant, immediate'.

69.] The business with four gowns in Q4 is reminiscent of the many
waistcoats of the Gravedigger in *Hamlet* in the 18–19th centuries; but
for Shakespeare's play this comic business was not introduced until after
Garrick's death in 1779 (see A. C. Sprague, *Shakespeare and the Actors*
(1944), pp. 175–6 and note).

72. *fetch a frisk*] cut a caper, dance.

75–6. *stamp ... cullis*] The original use of *stamp* = 'pound, crush' (as in a
mortar) was still common, along with the primary mod. sense.

cullis = 'broth' (often made from pulverized ingredients).

76–8. *one ... Hall*] Dead bodies, especially of executed criminals, were
brought to the Barber-Surgeons' Hall, in Monkswell Street, near Cripple-
gate, London, to be dissected or preserved and displayed as specimens
(*anatomies*) in the museum of the Hall.

78–9. *Hence ... sacrifice*] If the actor's actions suit his words and Ferdinand starts to pummel and tear at the Doctor, physically strong as well as
wolf-like in feeling, his victim will already be on the floor, as Q4 directs a

beasts for sacrifice; there's nothing left of you, but tongue,
and belly, flattery, and lechery.   [*Exit.*]   80
Pes. Doctor, he did not fear you throughly.
Doc. True, I was somewhat too forward.   [*Exit.*]
Bos. Mercy upon me, what a fatal judgement
        Hath fall'n upon this Ferdinand!
Pes.   Knows your grace
        What accident hath brought unto the prince   85
        This strange distraction?
Card. [*Aside*] I must feign somewhat: – [*To them*] Thus they
        say it grew:
        You have heard it rumour'd for these many years,

---

79. sacrifice] *Q;* sacrifice. / *Throws the Doctor down and beats him Q4.*
80. *Exit*] *Q4; Exit, followed by Attendants conj. this ed.*   82. *Exit*] *This ed.*
83. *Bos.*] *Q; Bos.* [*Aside*] *conj. this ed.*   87. S.D.s] *Dyce ii subs.*

---

few lines later. However that may be, the madman's focus of attention will
change as he subjects those standing by to his anger and denunciation. The
actor is likely to keep the climax of his performance in this scene until now
and may well include the theatre audience in Ferdinand's denunciation of
beasts for sacrifice.

For *beasts for sacrifice* see North's Plutarch, 'Phocion' (ed. 1612), p. 751:
'Demades . . . liued so insolently, and gouerned so lewdly . . . as Antipater
sayd of him, after he was very old: that there was nothing left of him, no
more then of a beast sacrificed, but the tongue and belly'; the idea was fairly
common, appearing for example in *Arcadia*, 2nd Eclogue (*Wks*, II.230; so
Dent).

81. *throughly*] thoroughly.

80. Exit] An immediate exit will accentuate the accompanying laugh-line;
in *W.D.*, the lawyer's words imply an exit at a similar moment (III.ii.50).

83–4. *Mercy . . . Ferdinand*] This brief speech marks Bosola's return to
the stage and the change in his involvement with the play's action. His entry
is marked at the beginning of the scene, as are others throughout Q, but he
must have been on stage long enough to witness the extent of Ferdinand's
madness and suffering. If he entered at line 25, at the same time as his
'master' (see l. 113, below) but at some distance from him, he has again been
the 'politic dormouse' of the first Act (l. 282); until now he has watched
events silently but remains unnoticed by the Cardinal until line 103. The
sympathy with Ferdinand, expressed in the opening *Mercy upon me*, is,
however, new: such sensitivity was first expressed towards the Duchess at
IV.ii.347–54. Bosola relapses into silence until he makes himself known at
line 100.

88–92. *You . . . riches*] as ll. 5–19 above, from Goulart, *Histories* (tr. 1607),
p. 620: 'There is a Noble and ancient familie at Parma, called Tortelles,
hauing a Castell, in the which there is a great Hall, vnder the Chimney
wher-of there doth some-times appeare an ancient Woman, seeming to be

None of our family dies, but there is seen
The shape of an old woman, which is given   90
By tradition to us to have been murder'd
By her nephews, for her riches; such a figure
One night, as the prince sat up late at's book,
Appear'd to him; when crying out for help,
The gentlemen of's chamber found his grace   95
All on a cold sweat, alter'd much in face
And language; since which apparition,
He hath grown worse and worse, and I much fear
He cannot live.
Bos. Sir, I would speak with you.
Pes.   We'll leave your grace,   100
Wishing to the sick prince, our noble lord,
All health of mind and body.
Card.   You are most welcome.
[*Exeunt all except* Cardinal *and* BOSOLA.]
[*Aside*] Are you come? so: – this fellow must not know
By any means I had intelligence
In our duchess' death; for, though I counsell'd it,   105
The full of all th' engagement seem'd to grow
From Ferdinand. [*To him*] Now sir, how fares our
    sister?
I do not think but sorrow makes her look
Like to an oft-dy'd garment: she shall now

102.1.] *Q4 subs.*   103. *Aside*] *This ed.; after* so *Dyce ii.*   107. *To him*] *Dyce
ii subs.*

---

a 100. yeares old. This signifieth that some one of the familie shall dye soone
after . . . They say this old woman whose shadow appeares, was some-times
a riche Lady, who for her money was slaine by her Nephews, which cutte
her body in peeces, and cast it into the Priuies'.

91. *shape*] used of both spectral and imaginary forms.

99–100. *He . . . live*] By inventing a 'tradition' that implies his brother is
incurable, the Cardinal tries to frighten off those who might try to see or
help him. He may also be preparing them for news of a death he will arrange
himself: he was the one who 'counselled' his sister's death and he has reason
for this other murder (see ll. 224–5). Bosola sees death 'in's eyes', as if he
were 'nothing else but murder' (ll. 144–5, below).

109. *Like . . . garment*] Crawford compared Donne, *Anat. of the World*, ll.
355–6: 'And colour is decai'd: summers robe growes / Duskie, and like an
oft dyed garment showes'.

Taste comfort from me – why do you look so wildly?   110
O, the fortune of your master here, the prince,
Dejects you – but be you of happy comfort:
If you'll do one thing for me I'll entreat,
Though he had a cold tomb-stone o'er his bones,
I'd make you what you would be.
Bos.   Any thing –   115
Give it me in a breath, and let me fly to 't:
They that think long, small expedition win,
For musing much o'th' end, cannot begin.

Enter JULIA.

Julia. Sir, will you come in to supper?
Card.   I am busy, leave me.
Julia. [*Aside*] What an excellent shape hath that fellow!   120
                                              Exit.
Card. 'Tis thus: Antonio lurks here in Milan;
Inquire him out, and kill him: – while he lives
Our sister cannot marry, and I have thought
Of an excellent match for her: – do this, and style me
Thy advancement.   125
Bos. But by what means shall I find him out?
Card. There is a gentleman, call'd Delio,
Here in the camp, that hath been long approv'd
His loyal friend: set eye upon that fellow,
Follow him to mass – may be Antonio,   130
Although he do account religion

---

115. I'd] Q (I'll'd); I'll *Luc i.*   118.1.] so Q4; at l. o.1 Q.   120. Aside] Dyce
ii.

116. *Give . . . breath*] i.e., 'say what you want in a word'. With wordplay
on *breath* = 'power of breathing, life', Bosola may take satisfaction from a
hidden meaning, 'bring your sister back to life and I would want nothing
more'.
117–8.] Cf. Alexander, *J.C.*, IV.i.1803–4: 'Who muse of many things,
resolue of none, / And thinking of the end, cannot beginne'.
124–5. *style . . .*] name your reward to me.
128. *camp*] military encampment. The Cardinal is still involved as a
soldier, following III.iii.1, etc.
131–2. *he . . . name*] Cf. *Arcadia*, IV (*Wks*, II.133): 'As for vertue, hee
counted it but a schoole name'. *O.E.D.* first records *school-name* in this
passage of *Arcadia*: the allusion is to the 'Schoolmen' of 9–14th centuries;
according to Bacon (*Advancement*, 1) they brought forth 'cobwebs of

But a school-name, for fashion of the world
May accompany him; or else go inquire out
Delio's confessor, and see if you can bribe
Him to reveal it; there are a thousand ways   135
A man might find to trace him; as to know
What fellows haunt the Jews for taking up
Great sums of money, for sure he's in want;
Or else to go to th' picture-makers and learn
Who bought her picture lately – some of these   140
Happily may take –

Bos.   Well, I'll not freeze i'th' business;
I would see that wretched thing, Antonio,
Above all sights i'th' world.

Card.   Do, and be happy.   *Exit.*

Bos. This fellow doth breed basilisks in's eyes,
He's nothing else but murder: yet he seems   145
Not to have notice of the duchess' death –
'Tis his cunning: I must follow his example;
There cannot be a surer way to trace
Than that of an old fox.

---

140. bought] *Dyce i,* brought *Q.*   149. S.D.] *conj. Samp, Luc i; Enter Julia*
Q4.

---

learning, admirable for the fineness of thread and work, but of no substance
or profit'.

137. *haunt*] frequent, visit.
taking up] borrowing.

140. *bought her picture*] suggesting that Antonio will want some substitute
for the presence of his wife, as Isabella kisses her absent husband's picture
every night before bed (see *W.D.,* II.ii.25–8).

141. *freeze*] *O.E.D.* does not record a similar figurative use.

143. *Do . . . happy*] As with 'happily' (l. 141), 'fortunate' is the primary of
two meanings. After his rapid and wary aside (ll. 103–7) and the direct and
heartless 'kill him', the Cardinal has relaxed and is almost playful when
thinking of ways to find Antonio and encouraging Bosola to kill the man he
calls a *wretched thing* (l. 142). In this easier mood, he very wrongly takes
Bosola's words to mean that he is eager to be the assassin as, earlier, he had
asked Ferdinand 'Whose throat must I cut?' (I.i.249). This entire duologue
confirms Bosola's change of mind and heart and, for the first time, reveals
the Cardinal's uncertainty in preparation for his soliloquy at the start of the
play's last scene.

144. *basilisks*] Cf. III.ii.86–7 and note.

148–9. *There . . . fox*] proverbial, although Tilley quoted only one MS.
source before *D.M.* (W164).

[*Enter* JULIA *pointing a pistol at him.*]

Julia.   So, sir, you are well met.
Bos. How now?
Julia.   Nay, the doors are fast enough: –   150
Now sir, I will make you confess your treachery.
Bos. Treachery?
Julia.   Yes, confess to me
Which of my women 'twas you hir'd, to put
Love-powder into my drink?
Bos.   Love-powder!
Julia.   Yes,
When I was at Malfi –   155
Why should I fall in love with such a face else?
I have already suffer'd for thee so much pain,
The only remedy to do me good
Is to kill my longing.
Bos.   Sure your pistol holds
Nothing but perfumes, or kissing-comfits.   160
Excellent lady,
You have a pretty way on't to discover
Your longing: come, come, I'll disarm you,
And arm you thus – yet this is wondrous strange.
Julia. Compare thy form, and my eyes together,   165
You'll find my love no such great miracle.
Now you'll say
I am wanton: this nice modesty in ladies

154–5. Yes . . .] *so McIl; one line Q.*   160–1.] *so Dyce i; one line Q.*   166–7.] *so Dyce i; one line Q.*

154. *Love-powder*] Cf. III.i.63–77.
160. *kissing-comfits*] sweetmeats to perfume the breath.
164. *arm*] embrace (a sense first recorded by *O.E.D.* a few years before *D.M.*, in *Cym.*, IV.ii.400). After 'disarm' of the previous line (i.e., 'remove the pistol'), *arm* may carry the secondary meaning of 'provide you with a weapon (to use on me)'.
165–6.] from *Arcadia*, v (*Wks*, II.186): 'Let her beawtie be compared to my yeares, and such effectes will be found no miracles'; Webster rephrased this again in *D.L.C.*, II.i.258–60: 'Compare her beauty and my youth together, / And you will find the faire effects of loue / No myracle at all'.
168–70. *this* . . .] suggested by *Arcadia*, III (*Wks*, II.31); see ll. 216–19, note below. *nice* had a range of meanings, as 'shy, delicate, fastidious; reluctant, trivial'; perhaps 'shy' is most appropriate here, giving a quibble on 'familiar' (cf. l. 183, below). For *familiar*, see I.i.259, note.

Is but a troublesome familiar
That haunts them.   170
Bos. Know you me, I am a blunt soldier.
Julia.   The better –
Sure, there wants fire where there are no lively sparks
Of roughness.
Bos.   And I want compliment.
Julia.   Why ignorance
In courtship cannot make you do amiss,
If you have a heart to do well.
Bos.   You are very fair.   175
Julia. Nay, if you lay beauty to my charge,
I must plead unguilty.
Bos.   Your bright eyes
Carry a quiver of darts in them, sharper
Than sunbeams.
Julia.   You will mar me with commendation,
Put yourself to the charge of courting me   180
Whereas now I woo you.
Bos. [*Aside*] I have it, I will work upon this creature –
[*To her*] Let us grow most amorously familiar:
If the great cardinal now should see me thus,
Would he not count me a villain?   185
Julia. No: he might count me a wanton,
Not lay a scruple of offence on you;
For if I see and steal a diamond,
The fault is not i'th' stone, but in me the thief
That purloins it: – I am sudden with you;   190
We that are great women of pleasure use to cut off

---

171. me,] *Q*; me? *Q3*.   173–4. Why . . .] *so Dyce i; one line Q*.   182. *Aside*]
Dyce ii.   183. *To her*] *Dyce ii subs.*

172–3. *Sure . . . roughness*] from *Arcadia*; see ll. 191–4, note below.
173–5. *Why . . . well*] from *Arcadia*, I.xvii (*Wks*, I.106): '. . . doing all
things with so pretie grace, that it seemed ignorance could not make him do
amisse, because he had a hart to do well'; this is based on the common
proverb, 'Nothing is impossible to the willing heart' (Tilley N299).
177–9. *Your . . . sunbeams*] two commonplaces linked together; for the
first part cf., e.g., *Arcadia*, I.xvii (*Wks*, I.107): 'what a quiver of arrowes her
eyes caried'.
191–4. *We . . . together*] with ll. 172–3 above, from *Arcadia*, III.xvii (*Wks*,
I.452–3), of the pleasures of being raped: 'For what can be more agreable,
then upon force to lay the fault of desire, and in one instant to joyne a deare

These uncertain wishes, and unquiet longings,
And in an instant join the sweet delight
And the pretty excuse together; had you been i'th'
    street,
Under my chamber window, even there   195
I should have courted you.
Bos.   O, you are an excellent lady.
Julia. Bid me do somewhat for you presently,
    To express I love you.
Bos.   I will, and if you love me,
Fail not to effect it.
The cardinal is grown wondrous melancholy;   200
Demand the cause; let him not put you off
With feign'd excuse, discover the main ground on't.
Julia. Why would you know this?
Bos.   I have depended on him,
And I hear that he is fall'n in some disgrace
With the Emperor – if he be, like the mice   205
That forsake falling houses, I would shift
To other dependence.
Julia. You shall not need follow the wars;
    I'll be your maintenance.
Bos.   And I your loyal servant –
But I cannot leave my calling.
Julia.   Not leave   210
An ungrateful general, for the love of a sweet lady?
You are like some, cannot sleep in feather-beds,
But must have blocks for their pillows.
Bos.   Will you do this?
Julia. Cunningly.
Bos.   Tomorrow I'll expect th' intelligence.

199–200.] *so Dyce i; one line Q.* 208–210. You . . . calling] *so Q;* . . . need
/ Follow . . . maintenance / *Bos.* . . . cannot / Leave . . . *Dyce i.* 210–11. Not
. . .] *so Haz;* . . . an / Vngratefull . . . *Q;* . . . ungrateful / General . . . *Dyce i.*

delight with a just excuse? or rather the true cause is . . . we thinke there
wants fire, where we find no sparkles at lest of furie'.
   196. *courted*] with allusion to a *courtesan's* customary way of attracting
attention by sitting at a window in a public place.
   197. *presently*] immediately.
   205–6. *mice . . . houses*] so Pliny and others; the saying became proverbial
(see Tilley M1243).

Julia. Tomorrow? get you into my cabinet,   215
  You shall have it with you: do not delay me,
  No more than I do you; I am like one
  That is condemn'd – I have my pardon promis'd,
  But I would see it seal'd: – go, get you in,
  You shall see me wind my tongue about his heart,   220
  Like a skein of silk.   [*Exit* BOSOLA.]

    [*Enter* Cardinal, *followed by* Servants.]

Card. Where are you?
Serv.   Here.
Card.   Let none upon your lives
  Have conference with the Prince Ferdinand,
  Unless I know it: [*Exeunt* Servants.]
    – [*Aside*] in this distraction
  He may reveal the murder.   225

---

221. *Exit Bosola*] *Q4.* 221.1.] *Dyce i subs.; Enter Cardinal Q4.* 222–6.] *so*
Q; . . . conference / With . . . it: – / In . . . reveal / The . . . *(4 lines) Dyce i;* . . .
lives / Have . . . Ferdinand, / Unless . . . it: – / In . . . murder. / Yond's . . .
Haz. 224. *Exeunt Servants*] *so Haz; after l. 225 Dyce ii. Aside*] *Dyce ii.*

216–9. *do . . . seal'd*] from *Arcadia*, III (*Wks*, II.31): 'But in deede this
direct promise of a short space [of time before her longing is satisfied],
joyned with the cumbersome familiar of womankinde, I meane modestie,
stayed so Gynecias minde, . . . not unlike to the condemned prisoner, whose
minde still running uppon the violent arrivall of his cruell death, heares that
his pardon is promised, but not yet signed'.
 221. *like a skein of silk*] Cf. Chapman, *Gentleman Usher* (pl. 1606): 'For
he that cannot turn and wind a woman / Like silk about his finger, is no
man' (III.ii.361–2).
 223. S.Ds.] Julia may have heard the Cardinal approaching but the scene
would be staged more easily and effectively if, at 'get you into my cabinet',
she were to direct Bosola to hide within an on-stage door and, at line 221,
'discover' the Cardinal in his study by drawing a traverse curtain. Such an
arrangement would explain the confidence with which Julia promises to give
Bosola immediate 'intelligence', since this would not depend on the Cardinal's entrance at just this moment and when he is evidently engaged in other
urgent business. It would also allow the Cardinal to pick up the poisoned
book at line 273 so that the actor need not find a credible way of bringing
such a dangerous article on stage when he enters at line 222. An appropriate
stage direction might have been lost when the entry, along with others, was
moved to the beginning of the scene (see Intro. p. 45). Webster had used a
discovery to reveal action taking place at *W.D.*, v.iv.64–5, and the use of
curtains to reveal a person in a study or private chamber was a common
device in plays of the period.

Yon's my ling'ring consumption:
I am weary of her; and by any means
Would be quit of.
Julia.   How now, my lord?
What ails you?
Card.   Nothing.
Julia.   O, you are much alter'd:
Come, I must be your secretary, and remove   230
This lead from off your bosom – what's the matter?
Card. I may not tell you.
Julia. Are you so far in love with sorrow,
You cannot part with part of it? or think you
I cannot love your grace when you are sad,   235
As well as merry? or do you suspect
I, that have been a secret to your heart
These many winters, cannot be the same
Unto your tongue?
Card.   Satisfy thy longing –
The only way to make thee keep my counsel   240
Is not to tell thee.
Julia.   Tell your echo this,
Or flatterers that like echoes still report
What they hear though most imperfect, and not me:
For, if that you be true unto yourself,
I'll know.
Card.   Will you rack me?
Julia.   No, judgement shall   245
Draw it from you: it is an equal fault
To tell one's secrets unto all, or none.

---

226. *ling'ring consumption*] Cf. Overbury, *Characters*, 'A Very Woman':
'She is Salomon's cruell creature and a man's walking-consumption.'
   228. *quit of*] rid of (see *O.E.D., v.,* 1 b).
   231. *secretary*] confidant (see *O.E.D.*, 1).
   233–9. *Are . . . tongue*] from *Arcadia,* II.v (*Wks,* 1.176): 'Do you love your
sorrowe so well, as to grudge me part of it? Or doo you thinke I shall not
love a sadde Pamela, so well as a joyfull? Or be my eares unwoorthie, or my
tongue suspected?'
   240–1. *The . . . thee*] a proverbial charge against women (see Tilley W649
and S196).
   244. *if . . . yourself*] i.e., if you will keep faith with me, your 'other self'.

Card. The first argues folly.
Julia.   But the last tyranny.
Card. Very well – why imagine I have committed
　　Some secret deed, which I desire the world   250
　　May never hear of.
Julia.   Therefore may not I know it?
　　You have conceal'd for me as great a sin
　　As adultery: – sir, never was occasion
　　For perfect trial of my constancy
　　Till now: sir, I beseech you.
Card.   You'll repent it.
Julia.   Never.   255
Card. It hurries thee to ruin: I'll not tell thee –
　　Be well advis'd, and think what danger 'tis
　　To receive a prince's secrets: they that do,
　　Had need have their breasts hoop'd with adamant
　　To contain them: I pray thee yet be satisfy'd;   260
　　Examine thine own frailty; 'tis more easy
　　To tie knots, than unloose them: – 'tis a secret
　　That, like a ling'ring poison, may chance lie
　　Spread in thy veins, and kill thee seven year hence.
Julia. Now you dally with me.
Card.   No more; thou shalt know it.   265
　　By my appointment, the great Duchess of Malfi,
　　And two of her young children, four nights since,
　　Were strangled.
Julia.   O heaven! sir, what have you done?
Card. How now? how settles this? think you your bosom
　　Will be a grave, dark and obscure enough,   270
　　For such a secret?

269–70.] *so Dyce i;* ... your / Bosome ... *Q.*

---

259. *breasts ... adamant*] a common phrase; cf. Marston, *Antonio and Mellida*, v.i: 'And 'twere not hoopt with steele, my brest wold break' and Chapman, *Bussy*, III.ii.213–14: 'if my heart were not hooped with adamant, the conceit of this would have burst it.' *adamant*, usually = 'lodestone' or 'diamond', was used poetically (as in Latin) for the hardest iron or steel.

261–2. *'tis ... them*] This sounds proverbial, yet Dent reported he had not found it except in *Arcadia*, II.xxvi (*Wks*, I.318), of rebels who cannot halt their rebellion: 'finding it far easier to tie th[a]n to loose knots'.

269. *settles*] either 'sinks deeply' (i.e., into the mind; see *O.E.D.*, 13b), or 'settles down, becomes still'.

Julia.   You have undone yourself, sir.
Card. Why?
Julia.   It lies not in me to conceal it.
Card.   No?
   Come, I will swear you to't upon this book.
Julia. Most religiously.
Card.   Kiss it.   [*She kisses the book.*]
   Now you shall never utter it; thy curiosity   275
   Hath undone thee: thou'rt poison'd with that book;
   Because I knew thou couldst not keep my counsel,
   I have bound thee to't by death.

               [*Enter* BOSOLA.]

Bos. For pity-sake, hold!
Card.   Ha, Bosola!
Julia.   I forgive you –
   This equal piece of justice you have done,   280
   For I betray'd your counsel to that fellow:
   He overheard it; that was the cause I said
   It lay not in me to conceal it.
Bos. O foolish woman,
   Couldst not thou have poison'd him?
Julia.   'Tis weakness,   285
   Too much to think what should have been done – I go,
   I know not whither.   [*Dies.*]
Card.   Wherefore com'st thou hither?

272–3. No...] *so Dyce i; one line Q.* 275. S.D.] *Dyce ii.* 278.1.] *Q4.*
279. Bosola!] *Dyce i; Bosola? Q.* 286–7. Too...whither] *so Dyce i;...*
done, / I ... Q. 287. whither] *Q2; whether Q.* 287. Dies] *Q4.*

   279. *I forgive you*] an echo of the Duchess forgiving the Executioners who
were obeying orders (IV.ii.205); Julia forgives the Cardinal who has murdered
her.
   280. *equal*] equitable.
   285. *Couldst ... him?*] probably a return of Bosola's wry and obtruding
sense of humour; it is clearly present al ll. 310–11, 313–17 and 324 below.
   285–6. *'Tis ... done*] from *Arcadia,* I.iv (*Wks,* I.24): '. . . it is weakenes too
much to remember what should have beene done'.
   286–7. *I ... whither*] Dent has shown that devotional writers often applied
this phrase to death as a journey to an unknown destination; Webster
used it in *W.D.,* v.vi.107 (in Flamineo's parody of dying) and 249 (for
Vittoria's penultimate speech), and *D.L.C.,* v.v.10.

Bos. That I might find a great man, like yourself,
     Not out of his wits as the Lord Ferdinand,
     To remember my service.
Card.   I'll have thee hew'd in pieces.   290
Bos. Make not yourself such a promise of that life
     Which is not yours to dispose of.
Card.   Who plac'd thee here?
Bos. Her lust, as she intended.
Card.   Very well,
     Now you know me for your fellow murderer.
Bos. And wherefore should you lay fair marble colours   295
     Upon your rotten purposes to me?
     Unless you imitate some that do plot great treasons,
     And when they have done, go hide themselves i'th'
        graves
     Of those were actors in't?
Card. No more, there is a fortune attends thee.   300
Bos. Shall I go sue to Fortune any longer?
     'Tis the fool's pilgrimage.
Card.   I have honours in store for thee.
Bos. There are a many ways that conduct to seeming
     Honour, and some of them very dirty ones.
Card. Throw to the devil   305
     Thy melancholy: the fire burns well,

293–4. Very ...] *so Dyce i; one line Q;* ... me / For ... *Haz.* 300.] *so this
ed.;* ... more, / There ... *Q;* ... is / A ... *Dyce i.* 303–4.] *so Q; as prose
conj. Leech.*

295–6.] i.e., like painting rotten wood to simulate marble; cf. *Arcadia*,
II.xvii (*Wks*, I.260): 'Shall I labour to lay marble coulours over my ruinous
thoughts?'
   297–9.] i.e., the Cardinal has spoken fairly in order to allay suspicion
before covering his tracks by slaying Bosola; from Chapman, *Penitential
Psalms*, 'A Great Man', l. 62: 'Plots treason, and lies hid in th' actors
graue'.
   302. *'Tis ... pilgrimage*] Cf. the proverbs, 'Fortune favours fools', and
'God sends fortune to fools' (Tilley F600 and G220).
   303–4.] Cf. Hall, *Epistles*, I.iii: 'I care not how many thousand ways there
are to seeming honour, besides this of vertue: they all (if more) still leade to
shame'.
   306–8. *the fire ... smother*] i.e., the 'devil' (l. 305) is doing his own work
well enough, without more help.

What need we keep a stirring of 't, and make
A greater smother? thou wilt kill Antonio?
Bos. Yes.
Card.   Take up that body.
Bos.   I think I shall
Shortly grow the common bier for churchyards.   310
Card. I will allow thee some dozen of attendants
To aid thee in the murder.
Bos.   O, by no means:
Physicians that apply horse-leeches to any rank swelling
use to cut off their tails, that the blood may run through
them the faster; let me have no train when I go to shed   315
blood, lest it make me have a greater when I ride to the
gallows.
Card. Come to me after midnight, to help to remove that
body to her own lodging: I'll give out she died o'th'
plague; 'twill breed the less inquiry after her death.   320
Bos. Where's Castruchio, her husband?
Card. He's rode to Naples to take possession
Of Antonio's citadel.
Bos. Believe me, you have done a very happy turn.
Card. Fail not to come: – there is the master-key   325
Of our lodgings; and by that you may conceive
What trust I plant in you.
Bos.   You shall find me ready.
                                        Exit Cardinal.
O poor Antonio, though nothing be so needful
To thy estate as pity, yet I find
Nothing so dangerous. I must look to my footing: 330
In such slippery ice-pavements, men had need
To be frost-nail'd well; they may break their necks else.

---

312. O . . .] *separate line Q; as prose Dyce i.*   318–20.] *so this ed.;* . . . body /
To . . . Plague; / 'Twill . . . *(3 lines) Q;* . . . remove / That . . . out / She . . .
enquiry / After . . . *Dyce i;* . . . me / After body / To . . . Plague; / 'Twill . . .
Luc i.   327.1.] *so Dyce i; after* you *Q (Exit).*

328–30. *O . . . dangerous*] from *Arcadia,* II.x (*Wks,* I.207): 'In deede our
state is such, as though nothing is so needfull unto us as pittie, yet nothing
is more daungerous unto us, then to make our selves so knowne as may
stirre pittie'. *estate* = condition, fortune.
    331–2.] *frost-nail'd* is recorded in *O.E.D.* (1594), but not *ice-pavements*
(although similar compounds were common).

The precedent's here afore me: how this man
Bears up in blood! seems fearless! Why, 'tis well:
Security some men call the suburbs of hell,   335
Only a dead wall between. Well, good Antonio,
I'll seek thee out, and all my care shall be
To put thee into safety from the reach
Of these most cruel biters, that have got
Some of thy blood already. It may be   340
I'll join with thee, in a most just revenge.
The weakest arm is strong enough, that strikes
With the sword of justice: – still methinks the duchess
Haunts me: there, there! –
'Tis nothing but my melancholy.   345

343.] *so Q; . . .* Justice. / Still . . . *Q4.*   duchess] *Q;* Dutchess *Starts* [S.D.]
Q4. 344–5.] *so this ed.; one line Q.*   344.] *The Duchess appears to him (at
end of line) conj. this ed.*

334. *Bears . . . blood*] probably, 'persists, or drives forward, in shedding
blood'; but the phrase is obscure. *O.E.D.* first cites *bears up* = 'to maintain
one's ground' in 1656 (21c; but see, also, 19, 20 and 29a and b), and, while
blood commonly = 'bloodshed, manslaughter' etc., the phrase *in blood* is also
a technical hunting term = 'full of life' (*O.E.D.*, 7).

335.] Cf. Hecate in *Mac.*, III.v.32–3: 'security / Is mortals' chiefest enemy',
and Tilley W152.

security = 'confidence that one is secure'.

suburbs of hell was a common phrase among preachers (so Dent, who
quoted Adams, *Gallant's Burden* (1612), Ci^{v}: 'Securitie is the very suburbes
of Hell . . .', in a passage probably used for III.ii.323–5).

336. *dead*] unbroken, continuous (cf. *O.E.D.*, 25); the same sense is
implied at v.v.97, with a similar quibble by association with 'graves'.

339. *biters*] blood-suckers (cf. *O.E.D.*, *bite*, *v*, 3); Webster used *horseleech*
thus in *W.D.*, v.vi.166. Or, perhaps, short for 'sheep-biters' (cf. v.ii.50, and
note).

340. *blood*] i.e., Antonio's children.

344–5. *The . . . justice*] from *Arcadia*, III.xii (*Wks*, 1.422): 'think not lightly
of never so weake an arme, which strikes with the sword of justice'.

343–5.] Perhaps a S.D. should be added to indicate that the Duchess
appears to Bosola; in *W.D.*, IV.i.102, '*Enter Isabella's Ghost*' accompanies
'. . . I'll close mine eyes, / And in a melancholic thought I'll frame / Her
figure 'fore me . . . methinks she stands afore me . . . 'Tis my melancholy . . .'
Certainly Bosola should act as if *he* actually sees her.

A melancholy person may imagine 'a thousand chimeras and visions,
which to his thinking he certainly sees, bugbears, talks with black men,
ghosts, goblins, &c' (Burton, *Anatomy*, I.iii.I.ii.).

Bosola's *melancholy* is now a true melancholy of remorse, not the affectation of a malcontent (cf. I.i.75, note).

O Penitence, let me truly taste thy cup,
That throws men down, only to raise them up.

Exit [with Julia's body].

Scena III.

Enter ANTONIO *and* DELIO.
[There is an] ECHO *from the* Duchess' *grave.*

Delio. Yon's the cardinal's window: – this fortification
        Grew from the ruins of an ancient abbey;
        And to yon side o'th' river, lies a wall,
        Piece of a cloister, which in my opinion
        Gives the best echo that you ever heard,   5
        So hollow, and so dismal, and withal
        So plain in the distinction of our words,
        That many have suppos'd it is a spirit
        That answers.
Ant.   I do love these ancient ruins:
        We never tread upon them but we set   10
        Our foot upon some reverend history.
        And questionless, here in this open court,
        Which now lies naked to the injuries
        Of stormy weather, some men lie interr'd
        Lov'd the church so well, and gave so largely to't,   15
        They thought it should have canopy'd their bones

---

347. *with Julia's body*] *Cam; not in* Q.

v.iii.0.1–2.] *Samp subs.; Antonio, Delio, Eccho, (from . . . Graue.)* Q.

348–9.] possibly influenced by Alexander, *Croesus*, v.i.2774–6: 'Though I
haue tasted of afflictions cup, / Yet it may be, the gods for a good cause /
Haue cast me downe to raise a thousand vp'.
349. S.D.] a visual echo of the end of iv.ii (Cambridge ed.).

v.iii.0.2. Echo . . . grave] See Intro., pp. 54–5.
9–11. *I do . . .*] from Florio, iii.ix, of the ruins of ancient Rome: 'Is it by
Nature or by the errour of fantasie, that the seeing of places, wee know to
have bin frequented or inhabited by men, whose memorie is esteemed or
mencioned in stories, doeth in some sorte moove and stirre vs vp as much
or more, than the hearing of their noble deedes, or reading of their composi-
tions? . . . So great a power of admonition is in the verie place: And that in
this Citty is most infinite; for which way soeuer wee walke, wee sette our
foote upon some Historie' (from Cicero, *De Finibus*, v.1–2).

Till doomsday; but all things have their end:
Churches and cities, which have diseases like to men,
Must have like death that we have.
Echo.   *Like death that we have.*
Delio. Now the echo hath caught you: –
Ant.   It groan'd methought, and gave   20
A very deadly accent.
Echo.   *Deadly accent.*
Delio. I told you 'twas a pretty one: you may make it
A huntsman, or a falconer, a musician,
Or a thing of sorrow.
Echo.   *A thing of sorrow.*
Ant. Ay sure: that suits it best.
Echo.   *That suits it best.*   25
Ant. 'Tis very like my wife's voice.
Echo.   *Ay, wife's voice.*
Delio. Come, let's walk farther from't: –
I would not have you go to th' cardinal's tonight:
Do not.
Echo.   *Do not.*
Delio. Wisdom doth not more moderate wasting sorrow   30
Than time: take time for't; be mindful of thy safety.
Echo. Be mindful of thy safety.
Ant.   Necessity compels me:
Make scrutiny throughout the passes
Of your own life, you'll find it impossible
To fly your fate.
Echo.   *O, fly your fate!*   35

19ff *Like . . . have. etc.*] *italicized Q.*   27. let's] *Q4*; let's vs Q.   28. go] *Q^b*;
too *Q^a; not in Q2.*   33. passes] *Q*; passages *Q4.*   35. Echo.] *Q4 sub.; not in
Q (speech inset).*

17–19. *all . . . we have*] The idea is common and found, for example, in
Florio, II.xxiii. *diseases* is used quibblingly, for, as well as in its modern sense,
disease was often used = 'absence of ease, trouble, disturbance' (*O.E.D.*, I).

27. *let's*] This seems the better emendation on metrical grounds, especially in view of the elided 'from't'. Compositor A's error might be due to
an uncertainty like that which led him to print 'lets's' at v.v.28, where the
right reading is clearly 'let's'.

33. *passes*] events (cf. *O.E.D.*, 5); however, Q4's emendation gains some
support from *D.L.C.*, v.v.67–8: 'you haue met both / In these seuerall
passages . . .'

34–5. *impossible . . . fate*] proverbial; cf. Tilley F83.

Delio. Hark: the dead stones seem to have pity on you
    And give you good counsel.
Ant. Echo, I will not talk with thee,
    For thou art a dead thing.
Echo.   *Thou art a dead thing.*
Ant. My duchess is asleep now,   40
    And her little ones, I hope sweetly: O heaven,
    Shall I never see her more?
Echo.   *Never see her more.*
Ant. I mark'd not one repetition of the echo
    But that: and on the sudden, a clear light
    Presented me a face folded in sorrow.   45
Delio. Your fancy, merely.
Ant. Come: I'll be out of this ague;
    For to live thus is not indeed to live:
    It is a mockery, and abuse of life –
    I will not henceforth save myself by halves;   50
    Lose all, or nothing.
Delio.   Your own virtue save you!
    I'll fetch your eldest son, and second you:
    It may be that the sight of his own blood
    Spread in so sweet a figure may beget
    The more compassion.
Ant.   How ever, fare you well: 55
    Though in our miseries Fortune have a part,
    Yet in our noble suff'rings she hath none –
    Comtempt of pain, that we may call our own.   *Exeunt.*

55.] *so Dyce i; . . . compassion. / How . . . Q. Ant.] conj. Samp, Luc i; not in Q, Dyce i.*

  44–5. *on . . . sorrow*] See Intro., pp. 54–5.
  47. *ague*] Cf. v.iv.67–9.
  48–9.] Cf. Matthieu, *Inventory*, p. 1050: 'But it shall be an incomparable miserie to bee alwayes depriued of the Kings grace and fauour, without the which the best conditions are most lamentable, and a life of this manner how short soeuer, is a tedious and a languishing Life, it is no Life, it is to languish and to abuse Life'.
  50.] Cf. Florio, ii.xv: 'I will neither feare, nor save my selfe by halfes'.
  53. *his*] i.e., the Cardinal's.
  54. *Spread*] (1) displayed, (2) disseminated.
  56–8.] from Alexander, *A.T.*, iv.ii.2455–7: 'For in our actions Fortune hath a part, / But in our suffrings, all things are our owne: / Loe now I loath the world . . .'.

SCENA IV.

Enter Cardinal, PESCARA, MALATESTE, RODERIGO,
and GRISOLAN.

Card. You shall not watch tonight by the sick prince,
  His grace is very well recover'd.
Mal. Good my lord, suffer us.
Card.   O, by no means;
  The noise, and change of object in his eye,
  Doth more distract him: I pray, all to bed,   15
  And though you hear him in his violent fit,
  Do not rise, I entreat you.
Pes. So sir, we shall not –
Card.   Nay, I must have you promise
  Upon your honours, for I was enjoin'd to't
  By himself; and he seem'd to urge it sensibly.   10
Pes. Let our honours bind this trifle.
Card. Nor any of your followers.
Mal.   Neither.
Card. It may be to make trial of your promise
  When he's asleep, myself will rise, and feign
  Some of his mad tricks, and cry out for help,   15
  And feign myself in danger.
Mal.   If your throat were cutting,
  I'd not come at you, now I have protested against it.
Card. Why, I thank you.   [*Withdraws.*]

---

v.IV.0.1–2.] *Dyce i; Cardinall . . . Rodorigo, Grisolan. Bosola, Ferdinand,
Antonio, Seruant Q. 18. Withdraws] Luc i subs.*

---

v.iv.17. *protested*] sworn on oath.
  18, 21, S.D.s.] With entries grouped together at the beginning of the scene
(see Intro., p. 45), Webster's handling of on-stage action has been lost. In
this text the Cardinal is directed to move apart from others on stage so that
his subsequent soliloquy has a stronger impact when he returns to hold
attention alone. Within ten lines, he must explain his action, confess his
inner thoughts and announce his intention to kill Bosola. These disclosures
follow each other abruptly, setting a new and swift dramatic idiom which
will then be sustained by the numerous entrances, exits and further surprises
that occur within the next twenty lines. By these means, Webster has ensured
that 'fate moves swift' (l. 78; see also v.v.42–4).
  So rapid are these events that some present-day productions encourage
an outbreak of grotesque or horrific comedy. Ironic comedy and mocking
laughter are certainly intended in lines 20–34 of the following scene.

Gris.   'Twas a foul storm tonight.
Rod. The Lord Ferdinand's chamber shook like an osier.
Mal. 'Twas nothing but pure kindness in the devil   20
　　To rock his own child.   *Exeunt [all except the* Cardinal].
Card. The reason why I would not suffer these
　　About my brother, is because at midnight
　　I may with better privacy convey
　　Julia's body to her own lodging: –   25
　　O, my conscience!
　　I would pray now: but the devil takes away my heart
　　For having any confidence in prayer.
　　About this hour I appointed Bosola
　　To fetch the body: when he hath serv'd my turn,   30
　　He dies.   *Exit.*

Enter BOSOLA.

Bos. Hah? 'twas the cardinal's voice: I heard him name
　　Bosola, and my death: listen, I hear one's footing.

Enter FERDINAND.

Ferd. Strangling is a very quiet death.
Bos. [*Aside*] Nay then, I see I must stand upon my guard. 35
Ferd. What say' to that? whisper, softly: do you agree to't?
　　So it must be done i'th' dark: the cardinal
　　Would not for a thousand pounds the doctor should
　　　　see it.   *Exit.*
Bos. My death is plotted; here's the consequence of murder:
　　We value not desert, nor Christian breath,   40
　　When we know black deeds must be cur'd with death.

---

21. all...Cardinal] *Dyce i subs.*   25–6.] *so this ed.; one line Q.*   31.1.] *so
Dyce i; at ll. 0.1–2 Q; after l. 28 Cam.*   33.1.] *so Dyce i; at ll. 0.1–2. Q.*
34. quiet] *Q2;* quiein *Q.*   35. Aside] *Dyce ii.*   then, I see] *Q3 (subs.);* then
I see, *Q.*   36–8.] *so Q; as prose Dyce i.*   36. say'] *Q;* say *Q2;* say you *Q3.*
37. So] *Q;* So; *Dyce ii.*   40–1.] *italicized Q (,,We...).*   41.1.] *so Q4 subs.;
at ll. 0.1–2 Q.*

---

19. *osier*] willow tree, wicker basket.
27–8.] from *Arcadia,* III.xiii (*Wks,* I.432), of a coward: 'Faine he would
have prayed, but he had not harte inough to have confidence in praier'.   *For*
= 'from'.
41. black...death] a rehandling of the proverb found in Seneca and, for
example, *W.D.,* II.i.319: 'Small mischiefs are by greater made secure' (cf.
Tilley C826).

Enter ANTONIO *and* Servant.

Serv. Here stay sir, and be confident, I pray:
   I'll fetch you a dark lantern.   *Exit.*
Ant. Could I take him at his prayers,
   There were hope of pardon.
Bos.   Fall right my sword! [*Stabs him.*]   45
   I'll not give thee so much leisure as to pray.
Ant. O, I am gone! Thou hast ended a long suit
   In a minute.
Bos.   What art thou?
Ant.   A most wretched thing,
   That only have thy benefit in death,
   To appear myself.

[*Enter* Servant *with a light.*]

Serv.   Where are you, sir?   50
Ant. Very near my home: – Bosola!
Serv.   O, misfortune!
Bos. Smother thy pity, thou art dead else: – Antonio!
   The man I would have sav'd 'bove mine own life!
   We are merely the stars' tennis-balls, struck and
     banded
   Which way please them – O good Antonio,   55
   I'll whisper one thing in thy dying ear
   Shall make thy heart break quickly: Thy fair duchess
   And two sweet children –
Ant.   Their very names
   Kindle a little life in me.

---

45. S.D.] *Dyce ii.*   49. thy] *Q;* this *Q4.*   50. S.D.] *Q4.*   51. Bosola!] *Dyce i;*
Bosola? *Q.*

---

43. *dark lantern*] Cf. II.iii.o.1 and note. By leaving on these words, the
Servant reminds the audience that it is night time and this, in turn, explains
why Bosola does not see whom he has killed.

47. *suit*] (1) 'petition', and (2) 'quest, chase'; i.e., punning on 'pray' of
the previous line.

49. *benefit*] good deed, favour.

50. *To ... myself*] i.e., he has only his mere self to show; this is a quibbling answer to Bosola's 'What art thou?' (l. 48).

51. *home*] last resting place; destination; death.

54–5. *We ... them*] a familiar conceit; it is found in *Arcadia* (*Wks*, 1.330
and II.177), Florio (III.ix) and Plautus, *Captivi*, Prol. 22 (so Sykes and
Lucas). *banded* = 'bandied'. Cf. v.v.100–2, note.

Bos.   Are murder'd!
Ant. Some men have wish'd to die   60
    At the hearing of sad tidings: I am glad
    That I shall do't in sadness; I would not now
    Wish my wounds balm'd, nor heal'd, for I have no use
    To put my life to. In all our quest of greatness,
    Like wanton boys whose pastime is their care,   65
    We follow after bubbles, blown in th' air.
    Pleasure of life, what is't? only the good hours
    Of an ague; merely a preparative to rest,
    To endure vexation: – I do not ask
    The process of my death; only commend me   70
    To Delio.
Bos. Break heart! –
Ant.   And let my son fly the courts of princes.
                                              [*Dies.*]
Bos. Thou seem'st to have lov'd Antonio?
Serv.   I brought him hither,
    To have reconcil'd him to the cardinal.
Bos. I do not ask thee that: –   75
    Take him up, if thou tender thine own life,
    And bear him, where the Lady Julia
    Was wont to lodge. – O, my fate moves swift!
    I have this cardinal in the forge already,
    Now I'll bring him to th' hammer: – O direful
    misprision!   80

---

61. sad] *Q;* glad *conj. Brereton (ap. Luc i).*   72.1] *Dyce i.*

62. *in sadness*] 'in earnest'; i.e., punning on *sad* of l. 61.
65–6.] Alexander, Parsons, and Drummond are among the moralizing authors in whose works Dent has found this idea.
67–8. *Pleasure . . . ague*] Cf. Hall, *Epistles*, i.ii: 'All these earthly delights . . . are but as a good day betweene two agues . . .'
68–9. *merely . . . vexation*] Cf. almost the last words of Flamineo, in *W.D.*, v.vi.273–4: '. . . rest breeds rest, where all seek pain by pain', and *D.M.*, ii.v.59–61.
72. *And . . . princes*] Cf. the last words of Vittoria, in *W.D.*, v.vi.261–2: 'O happy they that never saw the court, / Nor ever knew great man but by report.'
80. *misprision*] perhaps a quibble: (1) 'mistake', and (2) 'failure to recognize value' (cf. *O.E.D., sb.*[1] and *sb.*[2]).

I will not imitate things glorious,
No more than base: I'll be mine own example.
On, on: and look thou represent, for silence,
The thing thou bear'st.   *Exeunt.*

SCENA V.

Enter Cardinal, with a book.

Card. I am puzzled in a question about hell:
He says, in hell there's one material fire,
And yet it shall not burn all men alike.
Lay him by: – how tedious is a guilty conscience!
When I look into the fish-ponds, in my garden,   5
Methinks I see a thing, arm'd with a rake
That seems to strike at me: –

Enter BOSOLA, *and* Servant *with* ANTONIO'S *body.*

Now! art thou come?

---

v.v.o.1.] *Q4; Cardinall (with a Booke) Bosola, Pescara, Malateste, Rodorigo,
Ferdinand, Delio, Seruant with Antonio's body Q. 7–8.] so Dyce ii; one line
Q;...me: / Now...Har. 7. S.D.] so Dyce ii; at l. o.1 Q.*

81–2.] Cf. the words of the dying Flamineo, in *W.D.*, v.vi.256–7: 'I do not
look / Who went before, nor who shall follow me . . .' and also *W.D.*, v.i.75–7.

v.v.o.1. with a book] an old stage-device for indicating melancholy or
introspection: see for example, *Spanish Tragedy*, III.xiii, *Hamlet*, II.ii,
Marston's *Antonio's Revenge*, II.iii, '*Second Maiden's Tragedy*', IV.iv, etc.
2–3.] Dent quoted two accounts, Luis de Granada (tr. 1598) and *Dialogues of S. Gregory* (tr. 1608): 'The fire of hell is but one: yet doth it not in
one manner torment all sinners . . .'
4. *Lay him by*] to be echoed later, at ll. 89–90.
tedious] besides the modern senses, this could mean 'painful, troublesome'
(*O.E.D.*, 2); the latter sense is found in *A.V.*, III.i.73: 'the tediousness of
his importunate suit'.
5–7. *When . . . me*] The ultimate source is an account of Pertinax by Julius
Capitolanus; it was several times repeated, as in Lavater, *Of Ghosts* (1572),
Shakespeare Ass. Rep., p. 61: 'for ye space of three dayes before he was
slayne by a thrust, [he] sawe a certayne shaddowe in one of his fishepondes,
which with a sword ready drawen threatened to slay him, & therby much
disquieted him'. See Dent for further occurrences.
The *rake* may be a version of the tenterhooks with which devils were
depicted as they drove damned souls into hell.
7. Enter Bosola] The timing of this entry, on the talk of striking, accentu-
ates its menace and the sense of Fate moving swiftly and inexorably.

Thou look'st ghastly:
There sits in thy face some great determination,
Mix'd with some fear.

Bos.   Thus it lightens into action: 10
I am come to kill thee.

Card.   Hah? help! our guard!

Bos. Thou art deceiv'd:
They are out of thy howling.

Card. Hold: and I will faithfully divide
Revenues with thee.

Bos.   Thy prayers and proffers   15
Are both unseasonable.

Card.   Raise the watch!
We are betray'd!

Bos.   I have confin'd your flight:
I'll suffer your retreat to Julia's chamber,
But no further.

Card.   Help! we are betray'd!

Enter[*, above,*] PESCARA, MALATESTE, RODERIGO[*, and*
GRISOLAN].

Mal.   Listen: –

Card. My dukedom for rescue!

Rod.   Fie upon his counterfeiting!   20

Mal. Why, 'tis not the cardinal.

Rod.   Yes, yes, 'tis he:
But I'll see him hang'd, ere I'll go down to him.

Card. Here's a plot upon me, I am assaulted! I am lost,
Unless some rescue!

Gris.   He doth this pretty well:
But it will not serve to laugh me out of mine honour.   25

16–17. Raise . . . betray'd] *so Luc i; one line Q.*   19. S.D.] *so Dyce i; at l. o.1
Q; at end of line Q4.   above*] *Q4.   and Grisolan*] *Dyce i.*   25. serve] *Q3;
serue; Q.*

8. *ghastly*] Meanings ranged from 'causing terror' to 'ghost-like' and 'full
of fear'.

9–10. *There . . . fear*] Cf. *Arcadia*, i.ix (*Wks*, 1.57): 'he might see in his countenance some great determination mixed with feare'. *sits* = is settled, fixed.

13. *howling*] For Webster *howling* often implied wailing and, even, tears;
cf. *W.D.*, v.iii.35–7; v.iv.65; v.vi.156; and *D.L.C.*, v.iv.183.

20. *My . . . rescue*] See note l. 47 below.

Card. The sword's at my throat: –
Rod.   You would not bawl so loud then.
Mal. Come, come:
    Let's go to bed: he told us thus much aforehand.
Pes. He wish'd you should not come at him: but believe't,
    The accent of the voice sounds not in jest.   30
    I'll down to him, howsoever, and with engines
    Force ope the doors.   [*Exit above.*]
Rod.   Let's follow him aloof,
    And note how the cardinal will laugh at him.
        [*Exeunt, above,* MALATESTE, RODERIGO, *and* GRISOLAN.]
Bos. There's for you first –   *He kills the Servant.*
    'Cause you shall not unbarricade the door   35
    To let in rescue.
Card. What cause hast thou to pursue my life?
Bos.   Look there: –
Card. Antonio!
Bos.   Slain by my hand unwittingly: –
    Pray, and be sudden; when thou kill'd'st thy sister,
    Thou took'st from Justice her most equal balance,   40
    And left her naught but her sword.
Card.   O, mercy!
Bos. Now it seems thy greatness was only outward;
    For thou fall'st faster of thyself, than calamity
    Can drive thee. I'll not waste longer time: there!
                        [*Stabs him.*]

27–8.] *so McIl; one line Q;* . . . go / To . . . *Dyce ii.* 32. S.D.] *Dyce i.*
33.1] *Dyce i.* 34–6.] *so Dyce i;* . . . doore / To . . . (*2 lines*) *Q;* . . . unbarra-
cade / The . . . (*two lines*) *Luc i.* 34. S.D.] *so this ed.; after l. 36 Q.* 37. What
. . . life] *so Q;* . . . thou / To . . . *Luc i.* 44. S.D.] *Q4.*

---

34. *There's* . . . *first*] Perhaps the Servant was about to leave (so Cambridge ed.).

40. *equal*] just, impartial.

42–4. *thy* . . . *thee*] from *Arcadia,* II.xxix (*Wks,* I.332): 'For Antiphilus that
had no greatnesse but outwarde, that taken away, was readie to fall faster than
calamitie could thrust him'. Unlike Ferdinand and Bosola, the Cardinal changes
in a moment to a grovelling and panicky suppliant. See l. 13, note, above.

Webster used similar words for the *Character,* 'An Intruder into Favour':
'all this gay glitter shewes on him, as if the Sunne shone in a puddle . . . : and
when hee is falling, hee goes himselfe faster then misery can driue him'.

When the Cardinal is wounded by his brother, however, he recognizes the
demands of Justice and regains control of himself (ll. 53–5ff.).

Card. Thou hast hurt me: –
Bos.   Again!   [*Stabs him again.*]
Card.   Shall I die like a leveret   45
    Without any resistance? help, help, help!
    I am slain!

                    Enter FERDINAND.

Ferd.   Th' alarum! give me a fresh horse:
    Rally the vaunt-guard, or the day is lost:
    Yield, yield! I give you the honour of arms,
    Shake my sword over you – will you yield?   50
Card. Help me, I am your brother.
Ferd.   The devil!
    My brother fight upon the adverse party?
    There flies your ransom.
                    He wounds the Cardinal, and in the scuffle gives
                                Bosola his death-wound.
Card.   O Justice!
    I suffer now, for what hath former been:
    Sorrow is held the eldest child of sin.   55
Ferd. Now you're brave fellows: – Caesar's fortune was harder
    than Pompey's; Caesar died in the arms of prosperity,

45. S.D.] *Dyce ii.*   47. S.D.] *so Q4; at l. o.1 Q.*   51. devil!] *Dyce i;* diuell?
Q.   53. S.D.] *so this ed.; to right of ll. 52–3 Q.*   54. been] *Q4;* bin *Q.*
55.] *italicized this ed.;* "Sorrow ... *Q.*

    45. *leveret*] young hare; Turbeville considered a *leveret* too 'feeble' to be
worth hunting (*Hunting* (1576), p. 170).
    47. *give ... horse*] Cf. *R3*, v.iv.7 and 13: 'my kingdom for a horse'; con-
trast the Cardinal's cry at l. 20, above.
    48. *vaunt-guard*] vanguard; the obsolete form is kept in this edition
because of associations with 'vaunt', *sb.* = 'boast'.
    49. *I ... arms*] either 'I salute you as soldiers' (so Sampson), or 'I, as a
soldier, honour you as if you were dead' ('Military honours' = 'marks of
respect paid by troops at burials etc.'; see *O.E.D., honour, sb.,* 5d).
    53. *There ... ransom*] Being killed, he cannot be held for ransom.
    55. Cf. Giovanni's warning to Flamineo, *W.D.,* v.iv.21–3: 'Study your
prayers, sir, and be penitent, / ... I have heard grief nam'd the eldest child
of sin'.
    56–8. *Caesar's ... disgrace*] from Whetstone, *Heptameron* (1582), H2:
'What difference was there between the Fortunes of Cesar and Pompey,
when their endes were both violent: saue that I hould Cesars to be the
harder: for that, he was murthered in the Armes of Prosperytie, and Pompey,
at the feete of Disgrace'.

Pompey at the feet of disgrace: – you both died in the
field. The pain's nothing: pain many times is taken away
with the apprehension of greater, as the toothache with   60
the sight of a barber that comes to pull it out – there's
philosophy for you.

Bos. Now my revenge is perfect: *He kills Ferdinand.*
                                              sink, thou main cause
Of my undoing! – The last part of my life
Hath done me best service.   65

Ferd. Give me some wet hay, I am broken-winded –
I do account this world but a dog-kennel:
I will vault credit, and affect high pleasures,
Beyond death.

Bos.   He seems to come to himself,
Now he's so near the bottom.   70

Ferd. My sister! O! my sister! there's the cause on't:
Whether we fall by ambition, blood, or lust,
Like diamonds, we are cut with our own dust.   [*Dies.*]

Card. Thou hast thy payment too.

---

63. S.D.] *so this ed.; to right of l. 65 Q; after* cause *Dyce i.*   69–70. He . . .] *so
Dyce i; one line Q.*   71. O!] *Q;* O *Dyce i.*   my sister!] *Q3;* my sister, *Q.*
72–3. *italicized this ed.;* "Whether . . . / "Like . . . *Q.*   73. *Dies*] *Dyce i.*

59–61. *pain . . . pull it out*] Possibly from Phillip de Mornay, *Discourse of
Life and Death*: 'We does as . . . they who all the weeke long runne vp and
downe the sreetes with payne of the teeth, and seeing the Barber coming to
pull them out, feele no more payne' (so Dent).

63. S.D.] Compositor B probably placed this direction as he did because
there was most space to the right of the text at that point; he clearly misplaced IV.ii.235 S.D. for such a reason.

66.] Markham recommended 'Grass in Summer, and Hay sprinkled with
water in Winter' for a horse the was broken-winded (quoted by Lucas from
Masterpiece Revived, ed. 1688, p. 72).

68. *vault credit*] overleap expectation, or belief.

70. *near the bottom*] near death. Perhaps a reference to the turning of
Fortune's wheel that draws him down (see 'come', l. 69) from the '*high
pleasures*' (l. 68) of life.

72–3.] Cf. Nashe, *Christ's Tears* (1593), Dedic.: 'An easie matter is it for
anie man to cutte me (like a Diamond) with mine own dust'; the phrase was
probably proverbial, a variant of 'Diamonds cut diamonds' (Tilley D323).
Ferdinand seems to imply that each man is his own worst enemy; but,
in view of l. 71, he might mean that his sister was his *own* dust. See, also,
I.i.299–301 and note.

Bos. Yes, I hold my weary soul in my teeth,   75
    'Tis ready to part from me: – I do glory
    That thou, which stood'st like a huge pyramid
    Begun upon a large and ample base,
    Shalt end in a little point, a kind of nothing.

    [*Enter* PESCARA, MALATESTE, RODERIGO, *and* GRISOLAN.]

Pes. How now, my lord?
Mal.   O, sad disaster!
Rod.   How comes this?   80
Bos. Revenge, for the Duchess of Malfi, murdered
    By th' Aragonian brethren; for Antonio,
    Slain by this hand; for lustful Julia,
    Poison'd by this man; and lastly, for myself,
    That was an actor in the main of all   85
    Much 'gainst mine own good nature, yet i'th' end
    Neglected.
Pes.   How now, my lord?
Card.   Look to my brother:
    He gave us these large wounds, as we were struggling
    Here i'th' rushes: – and now, I pray, let me
    Be laid by, and never thought of.   [*Dies.*]   90
Pes. How fatally, it seems, he did withstand
    His own rescue.
Mal.   Thou wretched thing of blood,
    How came Antonio by his death?
Bos. In a mist: I know not how –
    Such a mistake as I have often seen   95
    In a play: – O, I am gone! –

79.1.] *Q4 subs.*   83. this] *Q4;* his *Q.*   90. *Dies*] *Q4.*

75. *hold* . . .] Cf. Florio, ii.xxxv: 'The soule must be held fast with ones teeth, since the lawe to liue in honest men, is not to liue as long as they please, but so long as they ought'; this is based on Seneca, *Epist.*, civ.3. In death the *soul* was commonly depicted leaving the body through the mouth.

77–9. *thou* . . . *nothing*] A *pyramid* was a famous example of great labour used in the service of pride.

89. *rushes*] Green rushes were commonly strewed on the floors of apartments and on the stages of public theatres.

94. *mist*] Cf. IV.ii.188, and note.

We are only like dead walls, or vaulted graves,
That ruin'd, yields no echo: – Fare you well –
It may be pain, but no harm to me to die
In so good a quarrel. O, this gloomy world!   100
In what a shadow, or deep pit of darkness,
Doth womanish and fearful mankind live!
Let worthy minds ne'er stagger in distrust
To suffer death, or shame for what is just –
Mine is another voyage.   [*Dies.*]   105
Pes. The noble Delio, as I came to th' palace,
Told me of Antonio's being here, and show'd me
A pretty gentleman, his son and heir.

                Enter DELIO [*with* Antonio's Son].

Mal. O Sir, you come too late!
Delio.   I heard so, and
Was arm'd for't ere I came. Let us make noble use   110
Of this great ruin; and join all our force
To establish this young, hopeful gentleman
In's mother's right. These wretched eminent things
Leave no more fame behind 'em than should one
Fall in a frost, and leave his print in snow;   115
As soon as the sun shines, it ever melts,

---

98. yields] Q (yieldes); yield *Dyce i.*   105. Dies] *Q4.*   108.1.] *so Q4; at
l. o.1 Q.   with . . . Son] Dyce i subs.*

97. *dead*] continuous, unbroken; see v.ii.336, and note.
99–100. *It . . . quarrel*] probably proverbial (so Dent): cf. *Arcadia*, III.ix
(*Wks*, I.400): 'thinking it wrong, but no harme to him that shoulde die in
so good a cause.'
100–2. *O . . .*] from *Arcadia*, v (*Wks*, II.177): 'in such a shadowe, or
rather pit of darkness, the wormish mankinde lives, that neither they knowe
how to foresee, nor what to feare: and are but like tenisballs, tossed by the
racket of hyer powers'.
113. *In's mother's right*] The Duchess held the dukedom of Malfi as
'dowager' (see III.iv.31–3); on her death it would revert to the son of her first
marriage. Here *right* could refer to personal possessions, entitlement to
justice and vindication of her 'truth' (see l. 119). The last is likely to be the
most significant in this context. Citing Lawrence Stone's *Road to Divorce*,
p. 69, the Cambridge editors note that a contract of marriage *per verba de
presenti* (see I.i.478–9), while valid in the eyes of the church, had no validity
in common law and, therefore, conferred no rights with regard to
property.

Both form, and matter: – I have ever thought
Nature doth nothing so great, for great men,
As when she's pleas'd to make them lords of truth:
Integrity of life is fame's best friend,   120
Which nobly, beyond death, shall crown the ends.   *Exeunt.*

FINIS.

120–1.] *italicized Q* (*"Integrity . . ."*).

118–19.] from *Arcadia*, ii.vii (*Wks*, 1.190): 'Nature having done so much
for them in nothing, as that it made them Lords of truth, whereon all the
other goods were builded'.

120. Integrity] Among current meanings were 'wholeness', 'soundness,
freedom from moral corruption' and 'innocence, honesty, sincerity' (so
O.E.D.).

121.] Cf. the proverb, 'The end crowns (or tries) all' (Tilley E116).

The Source of *The Duchess of Malfi*, from William Painter's *The Palace of Pleasure*, Volume ii (1567)

Editorial Note

The first edition of Painter is here reprinted from the copy in the Folger Library. A very few changes in punctuation and capitalization and some minor corrections have been introduced; abbreviations have been expanded.

Footnotes indicate passages verbally echoed in *The Duchess*. A collation follows, recording all 'substantive' editorial changes, usually in favour of the second quarto of 1575 (?); it also list a selection of further readings from the second quarto which significantly modify or clarify the sense. A = first quarto; B = second quarto.

Modern editions of the complete *Palace of Pleasure*, by J. Haslewood (1813), J. Jacobs (1890) and H. Miles (1929), follow the second edition, which was 'corrected and augmented' by Painter. But the original text may be preferred as a less 'varnished' tale; Painter's changes on almost every page aimed at elegance and clarity, and so a direct phrase was often replaced with one more studied or decorous, and sometimes strictures upon the Duchess's behaviour were toned down.

If an editor's taste did not encourage him to choose the first quarto, the need to provide students of Webster with a version of the source of *The Duchess* which has not been reprinted since the sixteenth century will dictate its adoption in the present context. Not only is the tone different but, at times, characterization as well: so Bosola was an 'assured manqueller' before becoming a 'pestilent' one, and Delio had 'small acquaintance' with Antonio before the second edition said he had none. We cannot be sure that we have read Webster's main source until both editions have been studied. And if we could have one only, it should probably be the first: while in emphasis or idea *The Duchess* once seems closer to the first and once to the second edition (III.ii.276–9 and III.ii.60–1; see footnotes,

p. 269), on one occasion Webster seems to echo the words of the
first and not of the second (III.i.24–7; see footnote, p. 259).

THE DUCHESSE OF MALFI

The Infortunate mariage of a Gentleman, called *ANTONIO
BOLOGNA*, with the Duchesse of *MALFI*, and the pitifull death
of them bothe.

The xxiij. Nouel.

The greater Honor and authoritie men haue in this world, and
the greater their estimation is, the more sensible and notorious are
the faultes by them committed, and the greater is their slander. In
lyke manner more difficult it is for that man to tolerate and sustaine
Fortune, which all the dayes of his life hathe liued at his ease, if by
chaunce hee fall into any great necessitie, than for hym which neuer
felt but woe, mishappe, and aduersitie. *Dyonisius* the Tyrant of
Sicilia, felte greater payne when hee was expelled his kingdome, than
Milo did, being banished from *Rome*. For so muche as the one was
a Soueraigne Lord, the sonne of a King, a Justiciarie on earth, and
the other but a simple Citizen of a Citie, wherein the people had
Lawes, and the lawes of Magistrates had in reuerence. So likewyse
the fall of a high and loftie Tree, maketh a greater noyse, than that
whiche is lowe and little. Highe Towers and stately Palaces of
Princes be seene further off, than the poore Cabans and homely
shephierds Sheepecotes. The Walles of loftie Cities salute the
viewers of the same farther of, than the simple caues, which the
poore doe dig belowe the Mountaine rocks. Wherefore it behoueth
the Noble, and such as haue charge of Common wealth, to liue an
honest lyfe, and beare their port vpryght, that none haue cause to
take ill example vpon dyscourse of their deedes and naughtie life.[1]
And aboue all, that modestie ought to be kept by women, whome
as their race, Noble birth, authoritie and name, maketh them more
famous, euen so their vertue, honestie, chastitie, and continencie
more praiseworthy. And behouefull it is, that like as they wishe to
be honoured aboue all other, so their life do make them worthy of
that honour, without disgracing their name by deede or woorde, or
blemishing that brightnesse which may commende the same. I
greatly feare that all the Princely factes, the exploits and conquests

1. Wherefore . . . : I.i.11–15.

done by the *Babylonian* Queene *Semyramis*, neuer was recommended
with such praise, as hir vice had shame in records by those which
left remembrance of ancient acts. Thus I say, bicause a woman
being as it were the Image of sweetenesse, curtesie and shamefastnesse, so soone as she steppeth out of the right tracte, and leaueth
the smel of hir duetie and modestie, bisides the denigration of hir
honor, thrusteth hir self into infinite troubles and causeth the ruine
of such which should be honored and praised, if womens allurement
solicited them not to follie. I wil not here indeuor my self to seeke
for examples of *Samson*, *Salomon* or other, which suffred themselues
fondly to be abused by women: and who by meane of them be
tumbled into great faults, and haue incurred greater perils. Contenting my self to recite a right pitifull Historie done almost in our time,
when the French vnder the leading of that notable captaine *Gaston
de Foix*, vanquished the force of *Spaine* and *Naples* at the iourney of
Rauenna in the time of the French king called *Levves* the twelfth,[2]
who married the Lady *Marie*, daughter to king *Henry* the seuenth,
and sister to the victorious Prince of worthy memory king *Henry* the
eight, wife (after the death of the sayd *Levves*) to the puissant Gentleman *Charles*, late Duke of *Suffolke*.

In that very time then liued a Gentleman of *Naples*, called *Antonio
Bologna*, who hauing bene Master of houshold to *Fredericke* of
Aragon, sometime King of *Naples*, after the French had expelled
those of *Aragon* out of that Citie, the sayde *Bologna* retired into
Fraunce, and thereby recouered the goods, which hee possessed
in his countrey. The Gentleman bisides that he was valient of his
persone, a good man of warre, and wel estemed amongs the best,
had a passing numbre of good graces, which made him to be
beloued and cherished of euery wight: and for riding and managing
of great horse, he had not his fellow in *Italy*:[3] he could also play
exceeding well and trim vpon the Lute, whose faining voyce so well
agreed therunto, that the most melancholike persons wold forget
their heauinesse, vpon hearing of his heauenly noise: and besides
these qualities, hee was of personage comely, and of good proportion. To be short, Nature hauing trauailed and dispoyled hir Treasure house for inriching of him, he had by Arte gotten that, which
made him most happy and worthy of praise, which was, the knowledge of good letters, wherin hee was so well trained, as by talke and
dispute thereof, he made those to blush that were of that state and

2. when . . . : I.i.72–3.   3. for . . . : I.i.139–41.

profession. *Antonio Bologna* hauing left *Fredericke* of *Aragon* in
Fraunce, who expulsed out of *Naples* was retired to king *Levves*,
went home to his house to liue at rest and to auoyd trouble, forgetting the delicates of Courtes and houses of great men, to be the only
husband of his owne reuenue. But what? It is impossible to eschue
that which the heauens haue determined vpon us: and lesse the
vnhappe, whych seemeth to follow vs, as it were naturally proceed-
ing from our mothers wombe: In such wise as many times, he which
seemeth the wisest man, guided by misfortune, hasteth himself wyth
stouping head to fall headlong into his deathe and ruine. Euen so
it chaunced to this *Neapolitane* Gentleman: for in the very same
place where he attained his aduancement, he receiued also his dimi-
nution and decay, and by that house which preferred hym to what
he had, he was depriued, both of his estate and life: the discourse
whereof you shall vnderstand. I haue tolde you already, that this
Gentleman was Maister of the King of *Naples* houshold, and being
a gentle person, a good Courtier, wel trained vp, and wise for
gouernment of himself in the Court and in the service of Princes,
the Duchesse of *Malfi* thought to intreat him that hee would serue
hir, in that office which he serued the king. This Duchesse was of
the house of *Aragon*, and sister to the Cardinal of *Aragon* which then
was a rich and puissant personage. Being thus resolued, was wel
assured that she was not deceiued: for so much as she was persuaded, that *Bologna* was deuoutly affected to the house of *Aragon*,
as one brought vp there from a child. Wherfore sending for him
home to his house, she vsed vnto him these, or like words: 'Master
Bologna, sith your ill fortune, nay rather the vnhap of our whole
house is such, as your good Lord and master hath forgon his state
and dignitie, and that you therwithall haue lost a good Master,
wythout other recompence but the praise which euery man giueth
you for your good seruice, I haue thought good to intreat you to do
me the honor, as to take charge of the gouernment of my house,
and to vse the same, as you did that of the king your master. I know
well that the office is to vnworthy for your calling: notwithstanding
you be not ignoraunt what I am, and how neere to him in bloud,
to whom you be so faithfull and louing a seruaunt: and albeit that
I am no Queene, endued with great reuenue, yet with that little I
haue, I bear a Princely heart: and such as you by experience do
knowe what I haue done, and daily do to those which depart my
seruice, recompensing them according to their paine and trauaile:
magnificence is obserued as well in the Courts of poore Princes, as

in the stately Palaces of great Kings and monarches. I do remembre that I haue red of a certain noble gentleman, a *Persian* borne, called *Ariobarzanes*, who vsed great examples of curtesie and stoutness towards king *Artaxerxes*, wherwith the king wondred at his magnificence, and confessed himself to be vanquished: you shall take aduise of this request, and I in the mean time do think you will not refuse the same, as well for that my demaund is iust, as also being assured, that our house and race is so well imprinted in your heart, as it is impossible that the memory therof can be defaced.' The gentleman hearing the courteous demaund of the Duchesse, knowing himself how deeply bound he was to the name of *Aragon*, and led by some vnknowen prouocation to his great yll luck, answered hir in this wise: 'I wold to god madame, that with so good reason and equitie I were able to make denial of your commaundement, as iustly you require the same: wherfore for the bounden duety which I owe to the name and memorie of the house of *Aragon*, I make promise that I shall not only sustain the trauail, but also the daunger of my life, daily ready to be offred for your seruice: but I feele in minde I know not what, which commaundeth me to withdraw my self to liue alone at home at my house, and to be content with the little I haue, forgoing the sumptuouse charge of Princes houses, which life would be wel liked of my self, were it not for the feare that you madame shold be discontented with my refusal, and that you shold conceiue, that I disdained your offred charge, or contempne your Court for respect of the great Office I bare in the Court of the Kyng, my Lord and Master. For I cannot receiue more honor, than to serue hir, which is of that stock and royall race. Therefore at all aduentures I am resolued to obey your wil, and humbly to satisfy the duty of the charge wherin it pleaseth you to imploy me, more to pleasure you for auoiding of displeasure: then for desire I haue to liue an honorable life in the greatest princes house of the world, sith I am discharged from him in whose name resteth my comfort and only stay, thinking to have liued a solitary life, and to passe my yeres in rest, except it were in the pore abilitie of my seruice to the house, wherunto I am bound continually to be a faithful seruaunt. Thus Madame, you see me to be the rediest man of the world, to fulfill the request, and accomplish such other seruice wherin it shall please you to imploy me.' The Duchesse thanked him very heartily, and gaue him charge of all hir householde traine, commaunding eche person to do him such reuerence as to hir self, and to obey him as the chief of all hir familie. This Lady was a widow, but a passing faire Gentlewoman, fine and very yong, hauing a yong sonne vnder hir guard and keping, left by the deceased Duke hir husband, togither with the Duchie, the inheritaunce of hir childe. Now consider hir personage being such, hir easy life and delicate bringing vp, and daily seeing the youthely trade and maner of Courtiers life, whether she felt hir self prickt with any desire, which burned hir heart the more incessantly, as the flames were hidden and couert: from the outward shew whereof she stayd hir self so well as she could. But she following best aduise, rather esteemed the proofe of mariage, than to burne with so little fire, or to incurre the exchange of louers, as many vnshamefast strumpets do, which be rather giuen ouer, than satisfied with pleasure of loue. And to say the truthe, they be not guided by wisdomes lore, which suffer a maiden ripe for mariage to be long vnwedded, or yong wife long to liue in widdowes state, what assurance so euer they make of their chaste and stayed life. For bookes be so full of such enterprises, and houses stored with examples of such stolne and secrete practises, as there neede no further proofe for assurance of our cause, the same of it self being so plaine and manifest. And a great follie it is to build the fantasies of chastitie, amid the follies of worldly pleasures. I will not goe about to make those matters impossible, ne yet wil iudge at large, but that there be some maidens and wiues, which wisely can conteine themselues amongs the troupe of amorous sutors. But what? the experience is very hard, and the proofe no lesse daungerous, and perchaunce in a moment the minde of some peruerted, whych all their liuing dayes haue closed their eares from the wordes of those that haue made offer of louing seruice, we neede not run to forayne Histories, ne yet to seeke records that be auncient, sith we may see the daily effects of the like, practized in Noble houses, and Courtes of Kings and Princes. That this is true, example of this fair Duchesse, who was moued with that desire which pricketh others that be of Flesh and bone.[4] This Lady waxed very weary of lying alone, and grieued hir heart to be without a match, specially in the night, when the secrete silence and darknesse of the same presented before the eies of hir minde, the Image of the pleasure which she felt in the life time of hir deceased Lord and husband,[5] whereof now feeling hir selfe despoiled, she felt a continuall combat, and durst not attempte that which she desired most, but eschued the thing wherof hir minde liked best. 'Alas (said she) is it possible after the taste of

4. moued . . . : I.i.453.   5. when . . . : IV.i.12–15.

the value of honest obedience which the wife oweth vnto hir husband, that I should desire to suffer the heat which burneth and altereth the martired minds of those that subdue them selues to loue? Can such attempt pierce the heart of me to become amorous by forgetting and straying from the limittes of honest life? But what desire is this? I haue a certaine vnacquainted lust, and yet very well know not what it is that moueth me, and to whome I shall vow the spoile thereof. I am truely more fonde and foolish than euer *Narcissus* was, for there is neither shadow nor voyce vpon which I can well stay my sight, nor yet simple Imagination of any worldly man, whereupon I can arrest the conceipt of my vnstayed heart, and the desires which prouoke my mind. *Pygmalion* loued once a Marble piller, and I haue but one desire, the coloure wherof is more pale than death.[6] There is nothyng which can giue the same so much as one spot of vermilion rud. If I do discouer these appetites to any wight, perhaps they will mock me for my labor, and for all the beautie and Noble birth that is in me, they wil make no conscience to deeme me for their iesting stock, and to solace themselues with rehersall of my fond conceits. But sith there is no enimie in the field, and that but simple suspition doth assaile vs, we must breake of the same, and deface the entier remembrance of the lightnesse of my braine. It appertaineth vnto me to shew my self, as issued forth of the Noble house of *Aragon*. To me it doeth belong to take heede how I erre or degenerate from the royall bloud wherof I came.' In this sort that fair widow and yong Princesse fantasied in the nyght vpon the discourse of hir appetites. But when the day was come, seeing the great multitude of the *Neapolitan* Lords and gentlemen which marched vp and downe the Citie, eying and beholding their best beloued, or vsing talk of mirth with them whose seruaunts they were, al that which she thought vpon in the night, vanished so sone as the flame of burned straw, or the pouder of the Canon shot, and purposed for any respect to liue no longer in that sort, but promised the conquest of some friend that was lustie and discreete. But the difficultie rested in that she knew not vpon whom to fixe hir loue, fearing to be slaundered, and also that the light disposition and maner of most part of youth wer to be suspected, in such wise as giuing ouer all them whych vauted vpon their Gennets, Turkey Palfreis, and other Coursers along the Citie of *Naples*, she purposed to take repast of other Venison, than of that fond and wanton troupe. So hir mishap

6. *Pygmalion* . . . : I.i.454–5.

began already to spin the threede which choked the aire and breath
of hir vnhappie life. Ye haue heard before that M. *Bologna* was one
of the wisest and most perfect gentlemen that the land of *Naples*
that tyme brought forth, and for his beautie, proportion, galant-
nesse, valiance, and good grace, without comparison. His fauor was
so sweete and pleasant, as they which kept him companie, had
somwhat to do to abstain their affection. Who then could blame this
faire Princesse, if (pressed with desire of matche, to remoue the
ticklish instigations of hir wanton flesh, and hauing in hir presence
a man so wise) she did set hir minde on him, or fantasie to mary
him? wold not that partie for calming of his thirst and hunger, being
set at the table before sundry sorts of delicate viands, ease his
hunger? Me think the person doth greatly forget himself, which
hauing handfast vpon occasion, suffreth the same to vanish and flie
away, sith it is wel knowne that she being bald behinde, hath no
place to sease vpon, when desire moueth vs to lay hold vpon hir.
Which was the cause that the Duchesse becam extremely in loue
with the master of hir house. In such wise as before al men, she
spared not to praise the great perfections wherwith he was enriched,
whom she desired to be altogether hirs. And so she was inamored,
that it was as possible to see the night to be void of darknesse, as
the Duchesse without the presence of hir *Bologna*, or else by talk of
words to set forth his praise, the continual remembrance of whome
(for that she loued him as hir self) was hir only minds repast. The
gentleman that was ful wise, and had at other times felt the great
force of the passion which procedeth from extreme loue, immediatly
did mark the countenance of the Duchesse, and perceiued the same
so nere, as unfainedly he knew that very ardently the Ladie was in
loue with him: and albeit he saw the inequality and difference
betwene them both, she being sorted out of the royal bloud, yet
knowing loue to haue no respect to state or dignity, determined to
folow his fortune, and to serue hir which so louingly shewed hir self
to him. Then sodainly reprouing his fonde conceit, hee sayd vnto
himself: 'What follie is that I enterprise, to the great preiudice and
perill of mine honor and life? Ought the wisdom of a Gentleman to
straie and wandre through the assaults of an appetite rising of sensuality, and that reason giue place to that which doeth participate
with brute beastes depriued of all reason by subduing the mynde to
the affections of the body? No no, a vertuous man ought to let shine
in him self the force of the generositie of his mynde. This is not to
liue according to the spirite, when pleasure shall make vs forget our

APPENDIX I 255

duetie and sauegard of our Conscience. The reputation of a wise
Gentleman resteth not onely to be valiant, and skilfull in feates of
armes, or in seruice of the Noble: But nedefull it is for him by discretion to make himselfe prayse worthy, and by vanquishing of him
self to open the gate to fame, whereby he may euerlastingly make
himselfe glorious to all posteritie. Loue pricketh and prouoketh the
spirit to do wel, I do confesse, but that affection ought to be
addressed to some vertuous end, tending to mariage, for otherwise
that vertuous image shall be soyled with the villanie of beastly pleasure. Alas (said he,) how easie it is to dispute, when the thing is
absent, which can bothe force and violently assaile the bulwarks of
most constant hearts. I full well doe see the trothe, and doe feele
the thing that is good, and know what behoueth me to follow: but
when I view that diuine beautie of my Ladie, hir graces, wisdome,
behauior and curtesie, when I see hir to cast so louing an eie vpon
me, that she vseth so great familiaritie, that she forgetteth the greatnesse of hir house to abase hir self for my respect: how is it possible
that I should be so foolish to dispise a duetie so rare and precious,
and to set light by that which the Noblest would pursue with all
reuerence and indeuor? Shall I be so much voide of wisedome to
suffer the yong Princesse to see hir self contempned of me, to
conuert hir loue to teares, by setting hir mynde vpon an other, to
seeke mine ouerthrow? Who knoweth not the furie of a woman?
specially of the Noble dame, by seeing hir self despised? No, no,
she loueth me, and I will be hir seruaunt, and vse the fortune prof-
fred. Shal I be the first simple Gentleman that hath married or loued
a Princesse? Is it not more honourable for me to settle my minde
vpon a place so highe, than vpon some simple wenche by whome I
shall neither attaine profit, or aduauncement? *Baldouine* of *Flaun-
ders*, did not hee a Noble enterprise when he caried away *Iudith* the
daughter of the *French* King, as she was passing vpon the seas into
England, to be married to the king of that Countrey? I am neither
Pirat nor aduenturer, for that the Ladie loueth me. What wrong doe
I then to any person by yelding loue againe? Is not she at libertie?
To whome ought she to make accompt of hir dedes and doings, but
to God alone and to hir owne conscience? I will loue hir, and cary
like affection for the loue which I know and see that she beareth
vnto me, being assured that the same is directed to good end, and
that a woman so wise as she is, will not commit a fault so filthy, as
to blemish and spot hir honor.' Thus *Bologna* framed the plot to
intertaine the Duchesse (albeit hir loue alredy was fully bent vpon

him) and fortified him self against all mishap and perillous chaunce that might succeede, as ordinarily you see that louers conceiue all things for their aduauntage, and fantasie dreames agreable to that which they most desire, resembling the mad and Bedlem persons, which haue before their eies, the figured fansies which cause the conceit of their furie, and stay themselues vpon the vision of that, which most troubleth their offended brain. On the other side, the Duchesse was in no lesse care of hir louer, the wil of whom was hid and secrete, which more did vexe and torment hir, than the fire of loue that burned hir so feruently. She could not tell what way to hold, to do him vnderstand hir heart and affection. She feared to discouer the same vnto him, doubting either of some fond and rigorous answer, or of reueling of hir mind to him, whose presence pleased hir more than all the men of the world. 'Alas (said she,) am I happed into so strange misery, that with mine own mouth I must make request to him, which with al humilitie ought to offer me his seruice? Shall a Ladie of such bloud as I am, be constrained to sue, wher all other be required by importunat instance of their suters?[7] Ah loue, loue, what so euer he was that clothed thee with such puissance, I dare say he was the cruel enimie of mans fredom. It is impossible that thou hadst thy being in heauen, sith the clemencie and courteous influence of the same inuesteth man with better benefits, than to suffer hir nourse children to be intreated with such rigor. He lieth which sayth that *Venus* is thy mother, for the sweetenesse and good grace that resteth in that pitifull Goddesse, who taketh no pleasure to see louers perced with so egre trauails as that which afflicteth my heart. It was some fierce cogitation of *Saturne* that brought thee forth, and sent thee into the world to breake the ease of them which liue at rest without any passion or grief. Pardon me Loue, if I blaspheme thy maiestie, for the stresse and endlesse grief wherein I am plunged, maketh me thus to roue at large, and the doubts which I conceiue, do take away the health and soundnesse of my mind, the little experience in thy schole causeth this amaze in me, to be solicited with desire that countersayeth the duetie, honor, and reputation of my state: the partie whome I loue, is a Gentleman, vertuous, valiant, sage, and of good grace. In this there is no cause to blame Loue of blindnesse, for all the inequalitie of our houses, apparant vpon the first sight and shew of the same. But from whence issue the Monarches, Princes and greater Lords,

7. Alas . . . : I.i.441–2.

but from the naturall and common masse of earth, whereof other men doe come? what maketh these differences betwene those that loue eche other, if not the sottish opinion which we conceiue of greatnesse, and preheminence: as though naturall affections be like to that ordained by the fantasie of men in their lawes extreme.[8] And what greater right haue Princes to ioyn with a simple gentlewoman, than the Princesse to mary a Gentleman, and such as *Anthonio Bologna* is, in whome heauen and nature haue forgotten nothing to make him equall with them which marche amongs the greatest. I thinke we be the daily slaues of the fond and cruell fantasie of those Tyraunts, which say they haue puissance ouer vs: and that straining our will to their tirannie, we be still bound to the chaine like the galley slaue.[9] No no, *Bologna* shall be my husband, for of a friend I purpose to make him my loyall and lawfull husband, meaning therby not to offend God and men togither, and pretend to liue without offense of conscience, whereby my soule shall not be hindred for anything I do, by marying him whom I so straungely loue. I am sure not to be deceiued in Loue. He loueth me so much or more as I do him, but he dareth not disclose the same, fearing to be refused and cast off with shame. Thus two vnited wils, and two hearts tied togither with equal knot cannot choose but bring forth fruites worthie of such societie.[10] Let men say what they list, I will do none otherwise than my head and mind haue already framed. Semblably I neede not make accompt to any persone for my fact, my body, and reputation being in full libertie and freedome. The bond of mariage made, shall couer the fault which men would deeme, and leauing mine estate, I shall do no wrong but to the greatnesse of my house, which maketh me amongs men right honorable. But these honors be nothing worth, where the minde is voide of contentation, and where the heart prickt forward by desire leaueth the body and mind restlesse without quiet.' Thus the Duchesse founded hir enterprise, determining to mary hir housholde Maister, seeking for occasion and time, meete for disclosing of the same, and albeit that a certaine naturall shamefastnesse, which of custome accompanieth Ladies, did close hir mouth, and made hir to deferre for a certaine time the effect of hir resolued minde, yet in the end vanquished with loue and impacience, she was forced to breake of silence, and to assure hir self in him, reiecting feare

8. But . . . : II.i.101–4. 9. we . . . : IV.ii.27–8.
10. Thus . . . : I.i.480 and 487.

conceiued of shame, to make hir waie to pleasure, which she lusted more than marriage, the same seruing hir, but for a Maske and couerture to hide her follies and shamelesse lusts, for which she did the penance that hir follie deserued. For no colorable dede or deceitful trompery can serue the excuse of any notable wickednesse. She then throughly persuaded in hir intent, dreamyng and thinking of nought else, but vpon the imbracement of hir *Bologna*, ended and determined hir conceits and pretended follies: and vpon a time sent for him vp into hir chamber, as commonly she did for the affaires and matters of hir house, and taking him aside vnto a window, hauing prospect into a garden, she knew not how to begin hir talk: (for the heart being seased, the minde troubled, and the wittes out of course, the tongue failed to doe his office,) in such wise, as of long time she was vnable to speake one onely woord. Hee surprised with like affection, was more astonned by seeing the alteration of his Ladie. So the two Louers stoode still like Images beholding one another, without any mouing at all, vntil the Ladie the hardiest of them bothe, as feeling the most vehement and greatest grief, tooke *Bologna* by the hand, and dissembling what she thought, vsed this or such like language: 'If any other besides your self, Gentleman, should vnderstand the secretes which now I purpose to disclose, I doubt what speeche were necessary to colour my woords: But being assured of your discretion and wisdom, and with what perfection nature hath indued you, and Arte, hauing accomplished that in you which nature did begin to work, as one bred and brought vp in the royall Court of the second *Alphonse*, of *Ferdinando* and *Frederick* of *Aragon* my cousins, I wil make no doubt at all to manifest to you the hidden secretes of my heart, being well persuaded that when you shall both heare and sauor my reasons, and tast the light which I bring forthe for me, easily you may iudge that mine aduise cannot be other, than iust and reasonable. But if your conceits shall straye from that which I shal speak, and deeme not good of that which I determine, I shall be forced to thinke and say that they which esteeme you wise and sage, and to be a man of good and ready wit, be maruelously deceiued. Notwithstanding my heart foretelleth that it is impossible for maister *Bologna* to wandre so farre from equitie, but that by and by he wil enter the lystes, and discerne the white from black, and the wrong from that which is iust and right. For so much as hitherto I neuer saw thing done by you, which preposterated or peruerted the good iudgement that all the world esteemeth to shine in you, the same well manifested and declared by your

tongue, the right iudge of the mind: you know and see how I am a
widow through the death of the noble Gentleman of good remembrance, the Duke my Lord and husband: you be not ignoraunt also,
that I haue liued and gouerned my self in such wise in my widow
state, as there is no man so hard and seuere of iudgement, that can
blason reproche of me in that which appertaineth to the honesty
and reputation of such a Ladie as I am, bearing my port so right,
as my conscience yeldeth no remorse, supposing that no man hath
wherewith to bite and accuse me. Touching the order of the goods
of the Duke my sonne, I have vsed them with such diligence and
discretion, as bisides the dettes which I haue discharged sithens the
death of my Lord, I haue purchased a goodly Manor in *Calabria*,
and haue annexed the same to the Dukedom of his heire: and at
this day doe not owe one pennie to any creditor that lent mony to
the Duke, which he toke vp to furnish the charges in the warres,
which he sustained in the seruice of the Kings our soueraine Lords
in the late warres for the kingdome of *Naples*. I haue as I suppose
by this meanes stopped the slaunderous mouth, and giuen cause
vnto my sonne, during his life to accompt himself bound vnto his
mother. Now hauing till this time liued for other, and made my self
subiect more than Nature could beare, I am entended to chaunge
both my life and condition. I haue till thys time run, trauailed, and
remoued to the Castels and Lordships of the Dukedome, to *Naples*
and other places, being in mind to tary as I am a widow. But what?
new affaires and new councel hath possest my mind. I haue trauailed
and pained my self inough, I haue too long abidden a widowes life,
I am determined therefore to prouide a husband,[11] who by louing
me, shal honor and cherish me, according to the loue which I shal
bear to him, and my desert. For to loue a man without mariage,
God defend my heart should euer think, and shall rather die a
hundred thousand deathes, than a desire so wicked shold soile my
conscience, knowing well that a woman which setteth hir honor to
sale, is lesse than nothing, and deserueth not that the common aire
shold breathe vpon hir, for all the reuerence that men do beare or
make them. I accuse no person, albeit that many noble women haue
their forheds marked, with the blame of dishonest life, and being
honored of some, be neuerthelesse the common fable of the people.[12]
To the intent then that such mishap happen not to me, and perceiuing my self vnable stil thus to liue, being yong as I am, and (God

11. I . . . : I.i.387. 12. many . . . : III.i.24–7.

be thanked) neither deformed nor yet painted, I had rather be the louing wife of a simple feere, than the Concubine of a king or great Prince. And what? is the mightie Monarche able to wash away the fault of his wife which hath abandoned him contrary to the duty and honesty which the vndefiled bed requireth? no les than Princesses that whilom trespassed with those which wer of baser stuffe than themselues. *Mesalina* with her imperial robe could not so wel couer hir faultes, but that the Historians do defame hir with the name and title of a common woman. *Faustina* the wife of the sage Monarch *Marcus Aurelius*, gained lyke report by rendring hir self to others pleasure, bisides hir lawful spouse. To mary my self to one that is mine equall, it is impossible, for so much as there is no Lord in all this Countrey meete for my degree, but is to olde of age, the rest being dead in these later warres. To mary a husband that yet is but a child, is follie extreeme, for the inconueniences which daily chaunce thereby, and the euil intreatie that Ladies do receiue when they come to age, and their nature waxe cold, by reason whereof, imbracements be not so fauorable, and their husbands glutted with ordinary meat vse to run in exchange. Wherefore I am resolued without respite or delay, to choose some wel qualited and renoumed Gentleman, that hath more vertue than richesse, of good Fame and brute, to the intent I may make him my Lord, espouse and husband. For I cannot imploy my loue vpon treasure, which may be taken away, where richesse of the minde do faile, and shall be better content to see an honest Gentleman with little reuenue to be praised and commended of euery man for his good deedes, than a rich carle curssed and detested of all the world. Thus much I say, and it is the summe of all my secretes, wherein I pray your Councell and aduise. I know that some wil be offended wyth my choise, and the Lords my brothers, specially the Cardinall will think it straunge, and receiue the same with ill digesture, that muche a do shall I haue to be agreed with them and to remoue the grief which they shall conceiue against me for this mine enterprise: wherefore I would the same should secretely be kept, vntil without perill and daunger either of my self or of him, whome I pretende to mary, I may publish and manifest, not my loue but the mariage which I hope in God shall soon be consummate and accomplished with one, whome I doe loue better than my self, and who as I full well do know, doeth loue me better than his owne proper life.' Maister *Bologna*, which till then harkned to the Oration of the Duchesse without mouing, feeling himself touched so neere, and hearing that his Ladie had made hir approche for mariage, stode stil astonned, his tongue not able to frame one word,[13] only fantasied a thousand *Chimeraes* in the aire, and formed like numbre of imaginations in his minde, not able to coniecture what hee was, to whome the Duchesse had vowed hir loue, and the possession of hir beauty. He could not thinke that this ioy was prepared for himself for that his Ladie spake no woord of him, and he lesse durst open his mouth, and yet was wel assured that she loued him beyond measure. Notwithstanding knowing the ficklenesse and vnstable heart of women, he sayd vnto himself that she would chaunge hir minde, for seing him to be so great a Cowarde, as not to offer hys service to a Ladie by whome he saw himself so manie times bothe wantonly looked vpon, and intertained with some secresie more than familiar.[14] The Duchesse which was a fine and subtile dame, seeing hir friend rapt with the passion, and standing stil vnmoueable through feare, pale and amazed, as if hee had bene accused and condempned to die, knew by that countenaunce and astonishment of *Bologna*, that she was perfectly beloued of him: and so meaning not to suffer hym any longer to continue in that amaze, ne yet to further fear him, wyth hir dissembled and fained mariage of any other but with him, she toke him by the hand, and beholding him with a wanton and luring eye, (in such sort as the curious Philosophers themselues would awake,[15] if such a Lampe and torch did shine within their studies), she sayde thus vnto hym: 'Seignor *Anthonio*, I pray you be of good cheere, and torment not your self for any thing that I haue said: I know well, and of long time haue perceyued what good and faithfull loue you beare me, and with what affection you haue serued me, sithens first you vsed my companie. Thinke me not to be so ignorant, but that I know ful wel by outward signes, what secretes be hid in the inner heart: and that coniectures many times doe giue me true and certaine knowledge of concealed things. And am not so foolish to thinke you to be so vndiscrete, but that you haue marked my countenaunce and maner, and therby haue knowen that I haue bene more affectioned to you, than to any other. For that cause (sayd she, straining him by the hand very louingly, and with cherefull coloure in hir face) I swear vnto you, and doe promise that if you so thinke meete, it shall be none other but your self whom I wil haue, and desire to take to husband and lawfull spouse, assuring my self so much of you, as the loue which so long time hath ben hidden and couered in our hearts, shal appeare by so

13. Maister . . . : I.i.450–5.   14. he sayd . . . : I.i.425–6.   15. in . . . : III.ii.40–2.

euident proofe, as only death shal end and vndoe the same.' The
gentleman hearing such sodain talk, and the assurance of that which
he most wished for, albeit he saw the daunger extreeme wherunto
he launched himself by espousing this great Ladie, and the enimies
he shold get by entring such aliance: notwithstanding building vpon
vaine hope, and thinking at length that the choler of the *Aragon*
brothers would passe away if they understoode the mariage, determined to pursue the purpose, and not to refuse that great preferment, being so prodigally offred, for which cause he answered his
Lady in this maner. 'If it were in my power madame, to bring to
passe that, which I desire for your seruice by acknowledging of the
benifits and fauors which you depart vnto me, as my mind presen-
teth thanks for the same, I wold think my self the happiest Gentleman that lyueth, and you the best serued Princesse of the world.
For one better beloued (I dare presume to say, and so long as I liue
wil affirm) is not to be found. If til this time I delayed to open that
which now I discouer vnto you, I beseeche you Madame to impute
it to the greatnesse of your estate, and to the duetie of my calling
and office in your house, being not seemely for a seruant to talk of
such secretes with his Ladie and mistresse. And truely the pain which
I haue indured to holde my peace, and to hide my griefe, hath bene
more noysome to me than one hundred thousand like sorowes
together, although it had ben lawfull to haue reuealed them to some
trusty friend: I do not deny madame, but of long time you did perceiue my follie and presumption, by addressing my minde so high,
as to the *Aragon* bloud, and to such a Princesse as you be. And who
can beguile the eye of a Louer, specially of hir, whose Paragon for
good minde, wisedom and gentlenesse is not? And I confesse to you
bisides, that I haue most euidently perceiued how certain loue hath
lodged in your gracious heart, wherwith you bare me greater affection than you did to any other within the compasse of your familie.
But what? Great Ladies hearts be fraught with secretes and conceits
of other effects than the minds of simple women, which caused me
to hope for none other guerdon of my loyal and faithfull affection,
than death, and the same very short, sith that litle hope accompanied with great, nay rather extreme passion, is not able to giue sufficient force, both to suffer and to stablish my heart with constancie.
Now for so much as of your motion, grace, curtesie and liberalitie
the same is offred, and that it pleaseth you to accept me for yours,
I humbly beseche you to dispose of me not as husband, but of one
which is, and shalbe your seruaunt for euer, and such as is more

ready to obey, than you to commaund. It resteth now Madame, to consider how, and in what wise our affairs are to be directed, that things being in assurance, you may so liue without peril and brute of slaunderous tongues, as your good fame and honest report may continue without spot or blemish.'

Beholde the first Acte of the Tragedie, and the prouision of the fare which afterwardes sent them bothe to their graue, who immediately gaue their mutuall Faith: and the houre was assigned the next day, that the fair Princesse shold be in hir chamber alone, attended vpon with one only Gentlewoman which had ben brought vp with the Duchesse from hir cradle, and was made priuie to the heauy mariage of those two louers which was consummate in hir presence. And for the present time they passed the same in words, for ratification wherof they went to bed togither. But the pain in the end was greater than the pleasure, and had ben better for them bothe, yea and also for the third, that they had shewed them selues so wyse in the deede, as discrete in keping silence of that which was done. For albeit their mariage was secrete, and therby politikely gouerned them selues in their stelthes and robberies of loue, and that *Bologna* more oft held the state of the steward of the house by day, than of Lord of the same, and by night supplied that place,[16] yet in the end, the thing was perceiued which they desired to be closely kept. And as it is impossible to till and culture a fertile ground, but that the same must yelde some frute, euen so the Duchesse after many pleasures (being ripe and plentiful) became with child, which at the first astonned the maried couple: neuerthelesse the same so well was prouided for, as the first childbedde was kept secrete, and none did know thereof. The childe was nourced in the towne, and the father desired to haue him named *Frederick*, for remembraunce of the parents of his wife. Now fortune which lieth in daily waite and ambushment, and liketh not that men shold long loiter in pleasure and passetime, being enuious of such prosperity, cramped so the legges of our two louers, as they must needes change their game, and learne some other practise: for so much as the Duchesse being great with childe again, and deliuered of a girle, the businesse of the same was not so secretely done, but that it was discouered. And it suffised not that the brute was noised through *Naples*, but that the sound flew further off. As eche man doth know that rumor hath many mouthes, who with the multitude of his

16. *Bologna* . . . : III.ii.7–8.

264 THE DUCHESS OF MALFI

tongues and Trumps, proclaimeth in diuers and sundry places, the
things which chaunce in al the regions of the earth, euen so that
babling foole caried the newes of that second childbed to the eares
of the Cardinall of *Aragon* the Duchesse brother, being then at
Rome. Think what ioy and pleasure the *Aragon* brothers had, by
hearing the report of their sisters facte. I dare presume to say, that
albeit they were extremely wroth with this happened slaunder, and
with the dishonest fame whych the Duchesse had gotten throughout
Italie, yet farre greater was their sorrow and grief, for that they did
not know what hee was that so courteously was allied to their house,
and in their loue had increased their ligneage. And therfore swelling
wyth despite, and rapt with furie to see themselues so defamed by
one of their bloud, they purposed by all meanes whatsoever it cost
them, to know the lucky louer that had so wel tilled the Duchesse
their sisters field.[17] Thus desirous to remoue that shame from before
their eyes, and to be reuenged of a wrong so notable, they sent
espials round about, and scoutes to *Naples*, to view and spy the
behauior and talk of the Duchesse, to settle some certaine iudgement of him, whych stealingly was become their brother in law. The
Duchesse Court being in thys trouble, shee dyd continually perceiue
in hir house, hir brothers men to mark hir countenance, and to note
those that came thither to visite hir, and to whom she vsed greatest
familiaritie,[18] bicause it is impossible but that the fire, although it
be raked vnder the ashes, must give some heat. And albeit the two
louers vsed eche others companie, without shewing any signe of
their affection, yet they purposed to chaunge their estate for a time,
by yelding truce to their pleasures. Yea, and although *Bologna* was
a wise and prouident personage, fearing to be surprised vpon the
fact, or that the Gentlewoman of the Chamber corrupted with
Money, or forced by feare, shold pronounce any matter to his hin-
derance or disauantage, determined to absent himself from *Naples*,
yet not so sodainly but that hee made the Duchesse his faithfull
Ladie and companion priuie of his intent. And as they were secretely
in their chamber togither, hee vsed these or such like woords:
"Madame, albeit the right good intent and vnstained conscience, is
free from fault, yet the iudgement of men hath further relation to
the exterior apparance, than to vertues force and innocencie it self,
as ignorant of the secrets of the thought: and so in things that be
wel done, we must of necessitie fall into the sentence of those, whom

17. tilled . . . : II.v.19.   18. mark . . . : I.i.252–5.

beastly affection rauisheth more, than ruled reason. You see the
solempne watch and garde which the seruaunts of the Lords your
brothers do within your house, and the suspicion which they haue
conceiued by reason of your second childbed, and by what meanes
they labor truely to know how your affaires proceede, and things do
passe. I feare not death where your seruice may be aduaunced, but
if herein the maiden of your chamber be not secrete, if she be corrupted, and if she kepe not close that which she ought to do, it is
not ignorant to you that it is the losse of my life, and shall die suspected to be a whoremonger and varlet, even I, (I say) shall incurre
that perill, which am your true and lawfull husband. Thys separation
chaunceth not by Iustice or desert, sith the cause is too righteous
for vs: but rather your brethren will procure my death, when I shall
thinke the same in greatest assurance. If I had to do but with one
or two, I wold not change the place, ne march one step from *Naples*,
but be assured, that a great band, and the same wel armed will set
vpon me. I pray you madame suffer me to retire for a time, for I
am assured that when I am absent, they will neuer soile their hands,
or imbrue their sweards in your bloud. If I doubted any thing at al
of perill touching your owne person, I had rather a hundred hundred
times die in your companie, than liue to see you no more. But out
of doubt I am, that if the things were discouered, and they knew
you to be begotten with childe by me, you should be safe, where I
shold sustaine the penaunce of the fact, committed without fault or
sinne. And therfore I am determined to goe from *Naples*, to order
mine affaires, and to cause my Reuenue to be brought to the place
of mine abode, and from thence to *Ancona*, vntil it pleaseth God to
mitigate the rage of your brethren, and recouer their good wils to
consent to our mariage. But I meane not to doe or conclude any
thing without your aduise. And if this intent doe not like you, giue
me councell Madame, what I were best to doe, that both in life and
death you may knowe your faithfull seruaunt and louing husband
is ready to obey and please you.'

This good Ladie hearing hir husbands discourse, vncertain what
to doe, wept bitterly, as wel for grief to lose his presence, as for that
she felt hir self with child the third time. The sighes and teares, the
sobbes and heauie lookes, which she threwe forth vpon hir sorowfull
husband, gaue sufficient witnesse of hir paine and grief. And if none
had heard hir, I thinke hir playntes woulde haue well expressed hir
inwarde smarte of minde. But like a wise Ladie, seeing the alleaged
reasons of hir husband, licensed him, although against hir minde,

not without vtterance of these few words, before hee went out of hir Chamber: 'Deare husband, if I were so well assured of the affection of my brethren, as I am of my maids fidelitie, I would entreat you not to leaue me alone: specially in the case I am, being with childe. But knowing that to be iust and true which you haue sayd, I am content to force my wil for a certaine time, that hereafter we may liue at rest together, ioyning our selues in the companie of our children and familie, voide of those troubles, which great Courts ordinarily beare within the compasse of their Palaces. Of one thing I must intreat you, that so often as you can by trustie messenger, you send me word and intelligence of your health and state, bicause the same shal bryng vnto me greater pleasure and contentation, than the welfare of mine owne: and bicause also, vpon such occurrentes as shall chaunce, I may prouyde for mine owne affaires, the suretie of my self, and of our children.' In saying so, she embraced him very amorously, and he kissed hir wyth so great sorrow and grief of heart, as the soule thought in that extasie out of his body to take hir flight, sorowful beyond mesure so to leue hir whome he loued,[19] for the great curtesies and honor which he had receiued at hir hands. In the end, fearing that the *Aragon* espials wold come and perceiue them in those priuities, *Bologna* tooke his leaue, and bad hys Ladie and spouse Farewell.

And this was the second Acte of this Tragicall Historie, to see a fugitife husband secretely to mary, especially hir, vpon whom he ought not so much as to loke but with feare and reuerence. Beholde here (O ye foolish louers) a Glasse of your lightnesse, and ye women, the course of your fonde behauior. It behoueth not the wise sodainly to execute their first motions and desires of their heart, for so much as they may be assured that pleasure is pursued so neare with a repentance so sharp to be suffred, and hard to be digested, as their voluptuousnesse shall vtterly discontent them. True it is, that mariages be done in Heauen, and performed in earth, but that saying may not be applied to fooles, which gouerne themselues by carnall desires, whose scope is but pleasure, and the reward many times equal to their follie. Shall I be of opinion that a housholde seruaunt ought to sollicite, nay rather suborne the daughter his Lord without punishment, or that a vile and abiect person dare to mount vpon a Princes bed? No no, pollicie requireth order in all, and eche wight ought to matched according to their qualitie, without making a

19. kissed . . . : III.v.88–90.

pastime of it to couer our follies, and know not of what force loue
and desteny be, except the same be resisted. A goodly thing it is to
loue, but where reason loseth his place, loue is without his effect,
and the sequele rage and madnesse. Leaue we the discourse of those
which beleue that they be constrained to folowe the force of their
minde, and may easily subdue themselues to the lawes of vertue and
honesty, like one that thrusteth his head into a sack, and thinks he
can not get out, such people do please themselues in their losse, and
think all well that is noisom to their health, daily following their
contrarie. Come we again then to sir *Bologna*, who after he had left
his wife in hir Castell, went to *Naples*, and hauing sessed a rent vpon
hir landes, and leuied a good summe of money, he repaired to
Ancona, a Citie of the patrimonie of the *Romane* Church, whither
he caried his two children, which he had of the Duchesse, causing
the same to be brought vp with such diligence and care, as is to be
thought a father wel affectioned to his wife would doe, and who
delighted to see a braunche of the tree, that to him was the best
beloued fruit of the world. There he hired a house for his train, and
for those that waited vpon his wife, who in the meane time was in
great care, and could not tell of what woode to make hir arowes,
perceiuing that hir belly began to swell, and grow to the time of hir
deliuerie, seeing that from day to day, hir brothers seruaunts were
at hir back, voide of councel and aduise, if one euening she had not
spoken to the Gentlewoman of hir chamber, touching the douts and
peril wherin she was, not knowing how she might be deliuered from
the same. That maiden was gentle and of a good minde and stomake,
and loued hir mistresse very derely, and seeing hir so amazed and
tormenting hir self to death, minding to fray hir no further, ne to
reproue hir of hir fault, which could not be amended, but rather to
prouide for the daunger whereunto she had hedlong cast hir self,
gaue hir this aduise: 'How now Madame (said she,) is that wisdom
which from your childhode hath bene so familiar in you, dislodged
from your brest in time, when it ought chiefly to rest for incountring
of those mishaps that are comming vpon vs? Thinke you to auoid
the dangers, by thus tormenting your self, except you set your hands
to the work, thereby to giue the repulse to aduerse fortune? I haue
heard you many times speake of the constancie and force of minde,
which ought to shine in the dedes of Princesses, more clerely than
amongs those dames of baser house, and which ought to make
them appere like the sunne amid the little starres. And yet I see you
now astonned, as though you had neuer forseene that aduersitie

chaunceth so wel to catch the great within his clouches, as the base
and simple sort. Is it but now, that you haue called to remembraunce, that which might insue your mariage with sir *Bologna*? Did
hys only presence assure you against the waits of fortune, and is it
the thought of paines, feares and frights, which now turmoileth your
dolorous mind? Ought you thus to vexe your self, when nede it is
to think how to saue both your honor, and the frute within your
intrailes? If your sorow be so great ouer sir *Bologna*, and if you feare
your childbed wil be descried, why seeke you not meanes to attempt
some voyage, for couering of the fact, to beguile the eyes of them
which so diligently do watch you? Doth your heart faile you in that
matter? Whereof do you dreame? Why sweat and freat you before
you make me answer?' 'Ah sweete heart (answered the Duchesse,)
if thou feltest the paine which I do suffer, thy tongue wold not be
so much at will, as thou shewest it now to be for reprofe of my smal
constancie. I do sorow specially for the causes which thou alleagest,
and aboue all, for that I know wel, that if my brethren had neuer
so litle intelligence of my being with child, I were vndone and
my life at an end,[20] and peraduenture poore wench, thou shouldest
beare the penaunce for my sinne. But what way can I take, that stil
these candles may not giue light, and I may be voided of the traine
which ought to wayt vpon my brethren? I thinke if I should descend
into Hel, they would know, whither any shadowe there were in loue
with me. Now gesse if I should trauaile the Realme, or retire to any
other place, whither they wold leaue me at peace? Nothing lesse,
sith they would sodainly suspect that the cause of my departure
proceeded of desire to liue at libertie, to dallie wyth him, whome
they suspect to be other than my lawfull husbande. And it may be
as they be wicked and suspicious, and will doubt of my greatnesses,
so shall I be farre more infortunate by trauailyng than here in miserie
amidde myne anguishe: and you the rest that be keepers of my
Councell, shall fal into greater daunger, vpon whome no doubt they
wil be reuenged, and flesh themselues for your vnhappy waiting and
attendance vpon vs.' 'Madame (said the bolde maiden,) be not
afraide, and follow mine aduise. For I hope that it shall be the
meanes both to see your spouse, and to rid those troublesome verlets
out of your house, and in like manner safely to deliuer you into good
assuraunce.' 'Say your minde (sayd the Ladie,) for it may be that I
will gouerne my self according to the same.' 'Mine aduise is then,

20. I . . . : III.ii.111 and 164.

(sayd the Gentlewoman,) to let your household vnderstand, that
you haue made a vow to visite the holy Temple of our Lady of
Loretto, (a famous place of Pilgrimage in *Italie*) and that you commaund your traine to make themselues ready to waite vpon you for
accomplishment of your deuotion, and from thence you shall take
your iourney to soiorne at *Ancona*, whither before you depart, you
shall send your moueables and plate, with such money as you shall
think necessarie. And afterwardes God will performe the rest, and
through his holy mercy will guide and direct all your affaires.' The
Duchesse hearing the mayden speake those woords, and amazed of
hir sodaine inuention, could not forbeare to embrace and kisse hir,
blessing the houre wherin she was borne, and that euer she chaunced
into hir companie, to whome afterwardes she sayd: 'My wench, I
had well determined to giue ouer mine estate and noble porte, ioy-
fully to liue like a simple Gentlewoman with my deare and welbeloued husband, but I could not deuise how I should conueniently
departe this Countrey wythout suspition of some follie: and sith that
thou hast so well instructed me for bringing the same to passe, I
promise thee that so diligently thy councel shal be performed, as
I see the same to be right good and necessarie. For rather had I see
my husband, being alone without title of Duchesse or great Lady,
than to liue without him beautified with the graces and foolish
names of honor and preheminence.'[21] This deuised plot was no
soner grounded, but she gaue such order for execution of the same,
and brought it to passe wyth such dexteritie, as the Ladie in lesse
than viij. dayes had conueyed and sent the most part of hir moueables, and specially the chiefest and best to *Ancona*, taking in the
meane time hir way towards *Loretto* after she had bruted hir solempne
vow made for that Pilgrimage. It was not sufficient for this foolish
woman to take a husband, more to glut hir libidinous appetite, than
for other occasion, except she added to hir sinne, an other execrable
impietie, making holy places and dueties of deuotion, to be as it
were the ministers of hir follie.[22] But let vs consider the force of
Louers rage, which so soone as it hath seased vpon the minds of
men, we see how maruellous be the effects thereof, and with what
straint and puissaunce that madnesse subdueth the wise and strongest worldings. Who wold think that a great Ladie wold haue abandoned hir estate, hir goods and childe, would haue misprised hir
honor and reputation, to folow like a vagabond, a pore and simple

21. rather . . . : III.ii.276–9. 22. added . . . : III.ii.317–18 and III.iii.60–1.

Gentleman,[23] and him bisides that was the houshold seruaunt of hir
Court? And yet you see this great and mightie Duchesse trot and
run after the male, like a female Wolfe or Lionesse (when they goe
to sault,) and forget the Noble bloud of *Aragon*[24] wherof she was
descended, to couple hir self almost with the simplest person of all
the trimmest Gentlemen of *Naples*. But turne we not the example
of follies, to be a matter of consequence: for if one or two become
bankrupt of their honor, it foloweth not good Ladies, that their facte
should serue for a matche to your deserts, and much lesse a patron
for you to follow.[25] These Histories be not written to train and trap
you, to pursue the thousand thousand slippery sleightes of Loues
gallantise, but rather carefully to warn you to behold the semblable
faultes, and to serue for a drugge to discharge the poyson which
gnaweth and fretteth the integritie and soundnesse of the soule.
The wise and skilfull Apothecary or compositor of drugges, dresseth
Vipers flesh to purge the patient from hote corrupted bloude, which
conceiueth and engendreth Leprosie within his body. In like manner,
the fonde loue, and wicked ribauldrie of *Semiramis, Pasiphae, Mes-
salina, Faustina* and *Romida* is shewed in wryt, that euery of you
should feare to be numbered and recorded amongs such common
and dishonorable women. You Princes and great Lordes read the
follies of *Paris*, the adulteries of *Hercules*, the daintie and effeminate
life of *Sardanapalus*, the tirannie of *Phalaris, Busiris* or *Dionysius* of
Scicile, and see the History of *Tiberius, Nero, Caligula, Domitian* and
Heliogabalus, and spare not to numbre them amongs our wanton
youthes which soile themselues with such villanies more filthily than
the swine do in the durt. Al this intendeth it an instruction for your
youth to follow the infection and whoredome of those monsters?
Better it were all those bokes were drenched in bottomlesse depth
of seas, than christian life by their meanes shold be corrupted: but
the example of the wicked is induced for to eschue and auoid them
as the life of the good and honest is remembred to frame and
addresse our behauior in this world to be praise worthy and commended. Otherwise the holinesse of sacred writ shold serue for an
argument to the vnthrifty and luxurious to confirm and approue
their beastly and licencious wickednesse. Come we again then to
our purpose: the good Pilgrime of *Loretto* went forth hir voyage to
atchieue hir deuotions, and to visite the Saint for whose Reliques
she was departed the Countrey of the Duke hir sonne. When she

23. Who . . . : III.iv.24–6.   24. Noble . . . : II.v.21–3.   25. it . . . : III.ii.286–8.

had done hir suffrages at *Loretto*, hir people thought that the voyage was at an end, and that she wold haue returned again into hir Countrey. But she said vnto them, that sith she was so neere *Ancona*, being but xv. miles off, she would not returne before she had seen the auncient and goodly city, which diuers Histories do greatly recommend, as wel for the antiquitie, as for the pleasant seat therof. All were of hir aduise, and went to see the antiquities of *Ancona*, and she to renue the pleasures which she had before begon with hir *Bologna*, who was aduertised of all hir determination, resting now like a God, possessed with the iewels and richesse of the Duchesse, and had taken a faire palace in the great streat of the Citie, by the gate wherof the train of his Ladie must passe. The Harbinger of the Duchesse posted before to take vp lodging for the traine: but *Bologna* offred vnto him his Palace for the Lady. So *Bologna* which was already welbeloued in *Ancona*, and entred new amitie and great acquaintance with the Gentlemen of the Citie, with a goodly troupe of them, went forth to meete his wife, to whome he presented his house, and besought hir that she and hir traine would vouchsafe to lodge with him. She receiued the same very thankfully, and withdrew hir self vnto his house, who conducted hir thither, not as a Husband, but like hym that was hir humble and affectionate seruaunt. But what needeth much discourse of woordes? The Duchesse knowing that it was impossible but eche man must be priuie to hir facte, and know what secretes hath passed betweene hir and hir Husband, to the ende that no other opinion of hir Childebed should be conceyued, but that which was good and honest, and done since the accomplishment of the mariage, the morrowe after hir arriuall to *Ancona*, assembled all hir traine in the Hall, of purpose no longer to keepe secrete that syr *Bologna* was hir Husbande, and that already she had had two Children by him, and againe was great with childe. And when they were come together after dinner, in the presence of hir husband, she spake vnto them these words: 'Gentlemen, and al ye my trusty and louing seruants, highe time it is to manifest to euery of you, the thing which hath ben done before the face, and in the presence of him who knoweth the most obscure and hydden secrets of our thoughts. And needefull it is not to kepe silent that which is neither euill done ne hurtfull to any person. If things could be kept secrete and still remaine vnknown, except they were declared by the doers of them, yet would not I commit the wrong in concealing that, which to discouer vnto you doth greatly delite me, and deliuereth my mind from exceeding grief, in such wise as if the

flames of my desire could breake out with such violence, as the fire
hath taken heat within my mind, ye shold see the smoke mount vp
with greater smoulder than that which the mount *Gibel* doeth vomit
forth at certaine seasons of the yeare. And to the intent I may not
keepe you long in this suspect, this secrete fire within my heart, and
that which I will cause to flame in open aire, is a certain opinion
which I conceiue for a marriage by me made certaine yeares past,
at what time I chose and wedded a husband to my fantasie and
liking, desirous no longer to liue in widow state, and vnwilling to
doe the thing that should preiudice and hurt my conscience. The
same is done, and yet in one thing I haue offended, which is by
long keeping secrete the performed mariage: for the wicked brute
dispearsed through the realme by reason of my childbed, one yere
past, hath displeased some, howbeit my conscience receiueth
comfort, for that the same is free from fault or blot. Now know ye
therfore what he is, whome I acknowledge for my Lord and spouse,
and who it is that lawfully hath me espoused in the presence of this
Gentlewoman whom you see, which is the witnesse of our Nuptials
and accorde of mariage. This gentleman here present *Antonio
Bologna*, is he to whom I haue sworn and giuen my faith, and hee
againe to me hath ingaged his owne. He it is whom I accompt for
my spouse and husband, and with whome henceforth I meane to
rest and continue. In consideration wherof, if there be any heere
amongs you all, that shall mislike of my choise, and is willing to wait
vpon my sonne the Duke, I meane not to let them of their intent,
praying them faithfully to serue him and to be carefull of his person,
and to be vnto him so honest and loyall, as they haue bene to me
so long as I was their mistresse. But if any of you desire stil to make
your abode with me, and to be partakers of my wealth and woe, I
wil so entertain him, as hee shall haue good cause to be contented,
if not, depart ye hence to *Malfi*, and the steward shall prouide for
either of you according to your degree: for touching my self I do
minde no more to be termed an infamous Duchesse: rather had I
be honored with the title of a simple Gentlewoman, or with that
estate which she can haue that hath an honest husband, and with
whom she holdeth faithfull and loyall companie, than reuerenced
with the glory of a Princesse, subiect to the despite of slanderous
tongues. Ye know (said she to *Bologna*) what hath passed betwene
vs, and God is the witnesse of the integritie of my Conscience,
wherefore I pray you bring forth our children, that each man may
beholde the fruites raised of our alliance.' Hauing spoken those

words, and the children brought forth into the hall, all the companie stode stil so astonned with that new success and tale, as though hornes sodainely had started forth their heads, and rested vnmoueable and amazed, like the great marble piller of *Rome* called *Pasquile*, for so much as they neuer thought, ne coniectured that *Bologna* was the successor of the Duke of *Malfi* in his mariage bed.

This was the preparatiue of the *Catastrophe* and bloudie end of this Tragedie. For of all the Duchesse seruaunts, there was not one that was willing to continue with their auncient mistresse, who with the faithful maiden of hir chamber remained at *Ancona*, enioying the ioyful embracements of hir husband, in al such pleasure and delights as they doe, which hauing liued in feare, be set at liberty, and out of al suspition, plunged in a sea of ioy, and fleting in the quiet calme of al passetime, where *Bologna* had none other care, but how to please his best beloued, and she studied nothing else but how to loue and obey him, as the wife ought to do hir husband. But this faire weather lasted not long, for although the ioyes of men do not long endure, and wast in litle time, yet delights of louers be lesse firme and stedfast, and pases away almost in one moment of an hour. Now the seruaunts of the Duchesse which were retired, and durst tary no longer with hir, fearing the fury of the Cardinal of *Aragon* brother to the Ladie, the very day they departed from *Ancona*, deuised amongs themselues that one of them shold ride in post to *Rome*, to aduertise the Cardinal of the Ladies mariage, to the intent that the *Aragon* brethren shold conceiue no cause to accuse them of felonie and treason. That determination spedily was accomplished, one posting towards *Rome*, and the rest galloping to the Countrey and Castels of the Duke. These newes reported to the Cardinal and his brother, it may be coniectured how grieuously they toke the same, and for that they were not able to digest them with modestie, the yongest of the brethren, yelled forth a thousand cursses and despites, against the simple sexe of womankind.[26] 'Ha (said the Prince, transported with choler,[27] and driuen in to deadly furie,) what law is able to punish or restrain the foolish indiscretion of a woman, that yeldeth hir self to hir own desires? What shame is able to bridle and withdrawe hir from hir minde and madnesse? Or with what feare is it possible to snaffle them from execution of their filthinesse? There is no beast be he neuer so wilde, but man sometime may tame, and bring to his lure and order. The force and

26. yelled . . . : II.v.31–6.   27. transported . . . : II.v.12–13.

diligence of man is able to make milde the strong and proud, and
to ouertake the swiftest beast and foule, or otherwise to attaine the
highest and deepest things of the world: but this incarnate diuelish
beast the woman, no force can surmount hir, no swiftnesse can
approche hir mobilitie, no good mind can preuent hir sleights and
deceites, they seeme to be procreated and borne against all order of
nature, and to liue without law, which gouerneth all other things
indued wyth some reason and vnderstanding. But what a great
abhomination is this, that a Gentlewoman of such a house as ours
is, hath forgotten hir estate, and the greatnesse of hir aliance, besides
the nobilitie of hir deceased husband, with the hope of the towarde
youth of the Duke hir sonne and our Nephew. Ah false and vile
bitch, I sweare by the almightie God and by his blessed wounds,
that if I can catch thee, and that wicked knaue thy chosen mate, I
will pipe ye both such a galiarde, as ye neuer felt the lyke ioy and
mirthe. I will make ye daunce such a bloudy bargenet, as your
whorish heate for euer shall be cooled. What abuse haue they committed vnder title of mariage, which was so secretely done, as their
Children do witnesse their filthy embracements, but their promise
of faith was made in open aire, and serueth for a cloke and visarde
for their most filthy whoredome.[28] And what if mariage was con-
cluded, be we of so little respect, as the carion beast would not
vouchsafe to aduertise vs of hir entent? Or is *Bologna* a man worthy
to be allied or mingled with the royall bloud of *Aragon* and *Castille?*[29]
No no, be hee neuer so good a Gentleman, his race agreeth not
with kingly state. But I make to God a vowe, that neuer will I take
one sound and restfull sleepe,[30] vntill I haue dispatched that infamous fact from our bloud, and that the caitife whoremonger be
vsed according to his desert.' The Cardinall also was out of quiet,
grinding his teeth togither, chattering forthe Jacke and Apes *Pater
noster*, promising no better vsage to their *Bologna* than his younger
brother did. And the better to intrap them both (without further
sturre for that time) they sent to the Lord *Gismondo Gonsago*, the
Cardinal of *Mantua*, then Legate for Pope *Iulius* the second at
Ancona, at whose hands they enioyed such friendship, as *Bologna*
and all his familie were commaunded spedily to auoide the Citie.
But for al that the Legate was able to do, of long time he could not
preuaile. *Bologna* had so great intelligence within *Ancona*. Neuer-

28. serueth . . . : III.iii.60–1.   29. royall . . . : II.v.21–3.
30. But . . . : II.v.76–9 and IV.i.23–4.

thelesse whiles he differred his departure, hee caused the most part
of his train, his children and goods to be conueyed to *Siena*, an
auncient Citie of *Thoscane*, which for the state and liberties, had
long time bene at warres with the *Florentines*, in such wise as the
very same day that newes came to *Bologna* that he shold departe the
Citie within xv. dayes, hee was ready, and mounted on horseback
to take his flight to *Siena*, which brake for sorrow the hearts of the
Aragon brethren, seeing that they were deceiued and frustrate of
their intent, bicause they purposed by the way to apprehend *Bologna*,
and to cut him in pieces. But what? the time of his hard luck was
not yet expired, and so the marche from *Ancona* serued not for the
Theatre of those two infortunate louers ouerthrow, who certain
moneths liued in peace in *Thoscane*. The Cardinal night nor day did
sleepe, and his brother stil did wayt to performe his othe of reuenge.
And seeing their enimie out of feare, they dispatched a post to
Alfonso Castruccio, the Cardinal of *Siena*, that he might entreat the
Lord *Borghese*, chief of the seignorie there, that their sister and
Bologna should be banished the Countrey and limits of that Citie,
which with small sute was brought to passe. These two infortunate,
husband and wife, were chased from al places, and so vnlucky as
whilom *Acasta* was, or *Oedipus*, after his fathers death and incestuous mariage with his mother, vncertain to what Saint to vow themselues, and to what place to take their flight. In the end they
determined to goe to *Venice*, and to take their flight to *Ramagna*,
there to imbarke themselues for to retire to the sauegarde of the
Citie, enuironned with the sea *Adriaticum*, the richest in *Europa*. But
the poore soules made their reconing there without their hoste,
failing half the price of their banket. For being vpon the territorie
of *Forly*, one of the train a farre off, did see a troupe of horsemen
galloping towardes their company, which by their countenaunce
shewed no signe of peace or amitie at all, which made them consider
that it was some ambush[31] of their enimies. The *Neapolitan* Gentleman seeing the onset bending vpon them, began to fear death, not
for that he cared at all for his mishap and ruine, but his heart began
to cleaue for heauinesse to see his wife and litle children ready to
be murdered, and serue for the passetime of the *Aragon* brethrens
eyes, for whose sakes he knew himself already predestinate to die,
and that for despite of him, and to accelerate his death by the ouerthrow of his, he was assured that they wold kil his children before

31. consider . . . : III.v.56.

his face and presence. But what is there to be done, where counsell and meanes to escape do faile? Ful of teares therfore, astonishment and fear, he expected death so cruel as man could deuise, and was alredy determined to suffer the same with good corage, for any thing that the Duchesse could say vnto him. He might well haue saued himself and his eldest sonne by flight, being both wel mounted vpon two good Turkey horsses, which ran so fast, as the quarrel discharged forth of a crosbow. But he loued too much his wife and children, and wold keepe them companie both in life and death. In the end the good Ladie sayd vnto him: 'Sir for all the ioyes and pleasures which you can doe me, for Gods sake saue your self and the little infant next you, who can wel indure the galloping of the horse. For sure I am, that you being out of our companie, we shal not need to fear any hurt. But if you do tary, you wil be the cause of the ruine and ouerthrow of vs all, and receiue therby no profit or aduantage: take this purse therfore, and saue your self, attending better Fortune in time to come.' The poore gentleman *Bologna* knowing that his wife had pronounced reason, and perceiuing that it was impossible from that time forth that she or hir traine could escape their hands, taking leaue of hir, and kissing his children not forgetting the money which she offred vnto him, willed his seruants to saue themselues by such meanes as they thought best. So giuing spurrs vnto his horse, he began to flee amaine, and his eldest sonne seeing his father gone, began to followe in like sorte. And so for that time they two were saued by breaking of the intended yll luck like to light vpon them. And in a place to rescue himself at *Venice*, hee turned another way, and in great iourneys arriued at *Millan*. In the meane time the horsemen were approched neere the Duchesse, who seeing that *Bologna* had saued himself, very courteously began to speake vnto the Ladie, were it that the *Aragon* brethren had giuen them that charge, or feared that the Ladie wold trouble them with hir importunate cries and lamentations. One therfore amongs them sayd vnto hir: 'Madame, we be commaunded by the Lordes your brethren, to conducte you home vnto your house, that you may receiue again the gouernment of the Duchie, and the order of the Duke your sonne, and doe maruell very much at your folly, for giuing your self thus to wander the Countrey after a man of so small reputation as *Bologna* is, who when he hath glutted his lusting lecherous mind with the comelinesse of your Noble personage, wil despoil you of your goods and honor, and then take his legs into some strange countrey.' The simple Ladie, albeit grieuous it was vnto hir to heare such speech of hir husband, yet held hir peace and dissembled what she thought, glad and well contented with the curtesy done vnto hir, fearing before that they came to kill hir, and thought hir self already discharged, hoping vpon their courteous dealings, that she and hir Children from that time forth should liue in good assuraunce. But she was greatly deceyued, and knew within shorte space after, the good will hir brethren bare vnto hir. For so soone as these gallants had conducted hir into the kingdome of *Naples*, to one of the Castels of hir sonne, she was committed to prison with hir children, and she also that was the secretarie of hir infortunate mariage. Till this time Fortune was contented to proceede with indifferent quiet against those Louers, but henceforth ye shall heare the issue of their little prosperous loue, and how pleasure hauing blinded them, neuer forsoke them vntill it had giuen them the ouerthrow.

It booteth not heere to recite fables or histories, contenting my self that ladies do read without too many weeping teares, the pitiful end of that miserable princesse, who seeing hir self a prisoner in the companie of hir litle children and welbeloued Maiden, paciently liued in hope to see hir brethren appaised, comforting hir self for the escape of hir husband out of the hands of his mortal foes. But hir assurance was changed into an horrible feare, and hir hope to no expectation of suretie, when certain dayes after hir imprisonment, hir Gaoler came in, and sayd vnto hir: 'Madame I do aduise you henceforth to consider vpon your conscience, for so much as I suppose that euen this very day your life shall be taken from you.' I leaue for you to thinke what horrour and traunce assailed the feeble heart of this pore Lady, and with what eares she receiued those cruell newes, but hir cries and mones together with hir sighes and lamentations, declared with what cheere she receiued that aduertisement. 'Alas (sayd she) is it possible that my brethren should so farre forget themselues, as for a fact nothing preiudiciall vnto them, cruelly to put to death their innocent sister, and to imbrue the memory of their fact, in the bloud of one which neuer did offend them? Must I against all right and equitie be put to death before the Iudge or Magistrate haue made trial of my life, and known the vnrighteousnesse of my cause? Ah God most righteous, and bountiful father, beholde the malice of my brethren, and the tyrannous crueltie of those which wrongfully doe seeke my bloud. Is it a sinne to mary?[32] Is it a fault to file and auoide the sinne of whoredome? What lawes be these, where mariage bed and ioyned matrimony is

32. Is . . . : III.ii.109–11.

pursued with like seueritie as murder, theft and aduoutrie? And
what Christianitie in a Cardinall, to shed the bloud which he ought
to defend? What profession is this, to assaile the innocent by the hie
way side and to reue them of lyfe, in place to punish theeues and
murderers? O Lord God thou art iust, and dost al things righteousty,
I see well that I haue trespassed against thy Maiestie in some other
notorious crime than by mariage: I most humbly therfore beseeche
thee to haue compassion vpon me, and to pardon mine offences,
accepting the confession and repentance of me thine humble
seruaunt for satisfaction of my sinnes, which it pleased thee to wash
away in the precious bloud of thy sonne our Sauior, that being so
purified, I might appere at the holy banket in thy glorious kingdome.' When she had thus finished hir prayer, two or three of the
ministers which had taken hir bisides *Forly*, came in, and sayd vnto
hir: 'Now Madame make ready your self to goe to God, for beholde
your houre is come.' 'Praised be that God (sayd she) for the wealth
and woe which it pleaseth him to send vs. But I beseeche you my
friends to haue pitie vpon these lyttle children and innocent creatures.[33] Let them not feele the smarte which I am assured my
brethren beare against their poore vnhappie father.' 'Well well
Madame (sayd they,) we will conuey them to such a place, as they
shal not want.' 'I also recommend vnto you (quod she) this poore
maiden, and entreat hir wel, in consideration of hir good seruice
done to the infortunate Duchesse of *Malfi*.' As she had ended those
woords, the two Ruffians did put a corde[34] about hir neck, and
strangled hir. The mayden seeing the piteous tragedie commensed
vpon hir mistresse, cried out amain, and cursed the cruell malice of
those tormenters, and besought God to be witnesse of the same,
and crying out vpon his diuine Maiestie, she besought him to bend
his iudgement against them which causelesse (being no Magistrates,)[35] hadde killed such innocent creatures. 'Reason it is (said
one of the tyrants) that thou be partaker of the ioy of thy mistresse
innocencie, sith thou hast bene so faithfull a minister, and mes-
sanger of hir follies.' And sodainly caught hir by the hair of the head,
and in stead of a carcanet[36] placed a roape about hir necke. 'How
now (quod she,) is this the promised faith which you made vnto my
Ladie?' But those woords flew into the air with hir soule, in companie of the miserable Duchesse.

33. I . . . : IV.ii.201–3.   34. corde: IV.ii.163.1.
35. causelesse . . . : IV.ii.296–302.   36. in . . . : IV.ii.247.

But hearken now the most sorowfull scene of all the tragedie. The litle children which had seen all the furious game done vpon their mother and hir maide, as nature prouoked them, or as same presage of their mishap led them therunto, kneled vpon their knees before those tyrants, and embracing their legs, wailed in such wise, as I think that any other, except a pitilesse heart spoiled of all humanitie, wold haue had compassion. And impossible it was for them to vnfold the embracements of those innocent creatures, which seemed to forethink their death by the wilde lokes and countenance of those roisters. Wherby I think that needes it must be confessed that nature hath in hir self, and vpon vs imprinted some signe of diuination, and specially at the hour and time of death, in such wise as the very beasts feele some conceits, although they see neither sword nor staffe, and indeuor to auoyde the cruell passage of a thing so fearful, as the separation of two things so neerely vnited, euen the body and soule, which for the motion that chaunceth at the very instant, sheweth how nature is constrained in that monstruous separation, and more than horrible ouerthrow. But who can appease a heart determined to do euil, and hath sworn the death of another forced therunto by some special commaundement? The *Aragon* brethren ment hereby nothing else, but to roote out the whole name and race of *Bologna*. And therfore the two ministers of iniquitie did like murder and slaughter vpon those two tender babes, as they committed vpon their mother, not without some motion of horror, for doing of an act so detestable. Behold here how far the crueltie of man extendeth, when it coueteth nothing else but vengeance, and marke what excessiue choler the minde of them produceth, which suffer themselues to be forced and ouerwhelmed with furie. Leaue we apart the crueltie of *Euchrates*, the sonne of the king of *Bactria*, and of *Phraates* the sonne of the *Persian* Prince, of *Timon* of *Athens*, and of an infinite number of those which were rulers and gouerners of the Empire of *Rome*: and let vs match with these *Aragon* brethren, one *Vitoldus*, Duke of *Lituania*, the crueltie of whom, constrained his own subiects to hang themselues, for fear least they shold fall into his furious and bloudy hands. We may confesse also these brutal brethren to be more butcherly than euer *Otho* erle of *Monferrato*, and prince of *Vrbin*, was, who caused a yeoman of his chamber to be wrapped in a sheete poudred with sulpher and brimston, and afterwards kindled with a candle, was scalded and consumed to death,[37] bicause only he waked not at

37. wrapped . . . : II.v.66–70.

an hour by him apointed. Let vs not excuse them also from some affinity with *Manfredus* the sonne of *Henry* the second Emperor, who smoldered his own father, being an old man, betwene ij. couerleds. These former furies might haue some excuse to couer their crueltie, but these had no other cause but a certain beastly madnesse which moued them to kil those litle children their neuews, who by no meanes could preiudice or anoy the Duke of *Malfi* or his title, in the succession of his Duchie, the mother hauing withdrawn hir goods, and was assigned hir dowry: but a wicked hart must needes bring forth semblable works according to his malice. In the time of these murders, the infortunate Louer kept himself at *Millan* wyth his sonne *Frederick*, and vowed himself to the Lord *Siluio Sauello*, who that time besieged the Castell of *Millan*, in the behalf of *Maximilian Sforcia*, which in the end he conquered and recouered by composition with the French within. But that charge being atchieued, the generall *Sauello* marched from thence to *Cremona* with his campe, whither *Bologna* durst not folow, but repaired to the Marquize of *Bitonte*, in which time the *Aragon* brethren so wrought, as his goods were confiscate at *Naples*, and he driuen to his shifts to vse the golden Duckates which the Duchesse gaue him to relieue him self at *Millan*, whose Death althoughe it was aduertised by many, yet hee coulde not be persuaded to beleue the same, for that diuers which went about to betray him, and feared he should flie from *Millan*, kept his beake in the water, (as the Prouerbe is,) and assured him both of the life and welfare of his spouse, and that shortly his brethren in law wold be reconciled, bicause that many Noble men fauored him well, and desired his returne home to his Countrey.[38] Fed and filled with that vaine hope, he remained more than a yeare at *Millan*, frequenting the companie, and well entertained of the richest Marchants and Gentlemen of the Citie: and aboue all other, he had familiar accesse to the house of the Ladie *Hippolita Bentiuoglia*, where vpon a day after dinner, taking his Lute in hand, wheron he could exceedingly wel play, he began to sing a certain Sonnet, which he had composed vpon the discourse of his misfortune, the tenor whereof is this.

The song of Antonio Bologna,
the husband of the Duchesse of Malfi.

If loue, the death, or tract of time, haue measured my distresse,
Or if my beating sorrowes may my languor well expresse:

38. diuers . . . : v.i.1–5 and 71–2.

Then loue come sone to visit me, which most my heart desires,
   And so my dolor findes some ease, through flames of fansies fires.
The time runnes out his rolling course, for to prolong mine ease,
   To thend I shall enioy my loue, and heart himself appease.
A cruell Darte brings happy death, my soule then rest shall finde:
   And sleping body vnder tombe, shall dreame time out of minde.
And yet the Loue, the time, nor Death, lokes not how I decrease:
   Nor giueth eare to any thing of this my wofull peace.
Full farre I am from my good happe, or halfe the ioy I craue,
   Wherby I change my state with teares, and draw full nere my graue.
The courteous Gods that giues me life, nowe moues the Planets all:
   For to arrest my groning ghost, and hence my sprite to call.
Yet from them still I am separd, by things unequall here,
   Not ment the Gods may be vniust, that bredes my changing chere.
For they prouide by their foresight, that none shall doe me harme:
   But she whose blasing beuty bright, hath brought me in a charm
My mistresse hath the powre alone, to rid me from this woe:
   Whose thrall I am, for whome I die, to whome my sprite shall goe.
Away my soule, go from the griefs, that thee oppresseth still,
   And let thy dolor witnesse beare, how much I want my will.
For since that loue and death himself, delights in guiltlesse bloud,
   Let time transport my troubled sprite, where dest'ny semeth good.

His song ended, the poore Gentleman could not forbeare from
pouring forth his luke warme teares, which aboundantly ran downe
his heauie face, and his panting sighes truely discouered the alteration of his mind, which moued eche wight of that assembly to pitie
his mournefull state: and one specially of small acquaintaunce, and
yet knew the deuises which the *Aragon* brethren had trained and
conspired against him: that unacquainted Gentleman his name was
Delio, one very well learned and of trimme inuention, and very
excellently hath endited in the *Italian* vulgar tongue. Who knowing
the Gentleman to be husbande to the deceased Duchesse of *Malfi*
came vnto him, and taking him aside, sayd: 'Sir, albeit I haue no
great acquaintance with you, this being the first time that euer I saw
you, to my remembrance, so it is, that vertue hath such force, and
maketh gentle mindes so amorous of their like, as when they doe
beholde eche other, they feele themselues coupled as it were in a
bande of minds, that impossible it is to diuide the same. Now
knowing what you be, and the good and commendable qualities in
you, I compte it my duetie to reueale that which may chaunce to
breede you damage. Know you then, that I of late was in companie
with a Noble man of *Naples*, which is in this Citie, banded with a

certaine companie of horsemen, who tolde me that hee had a spe-
ciall charge to kill you, and therfore prayed me (as he seemed) to
require you not to come in his sight, to the intent hee might not be
constrained to doe that, which should offende his Conscience, and
grieue the same all the dayes of his life. Moreouer I haue worse
tidings to tell you, which are, that the Duchesse your wife is deade
by violent hand in prison, and the moste parte of them that were in
hir companie. Besides this assure your self, that if you doe not take
heede to that which this *Neapolitane* captaine hathe differed, other
will doe and execute the same. This much I haue thought good to
tell you, bicause it would verie much grieue me, that a Gentleman
so excellent as you be, should be murdered in that miserable wise,
and would deeme my selfe vnworthy of life, if knowing these practises I should dissemble the same.' Wherunto *Bologna* answered:
'Syr *Delio* I am greatly bounde vnto you, and giue you heartie
thankes for the good will you beare me. But of the conspiracie of
the brethren of *Aragon*, and the death of my Ladie, you be deceyued,
and somme haue giuen you wrong intelligence. For within these two
dayes I receiued letters from *Naples*, wherein I am aduertised, that
the right honorable and reuerende Cardinall and his brother be
almost appeased, and that my goodes shall be rendred againe, and
my deare wife restored.' 'Ah syr (sayed *Delio*,) how you be beguiled
and fedde with follies, and nourished with sleights of Courte. Assure
your self that they which wryte these trifles, make such shamefull
sale of you, as the Butcher doeth of his flesh in the shambles, and
so wickedly betray you, as impossible it is to inuent a Treason more
detestable: but bethinke you well thereof.' When he had sayde so,
hee tooke his leaue, and ioyned himself in companie of fine and
pregnant wittes, there assembled togither. In the meane tyme, the
cruell spryte of the *Aragon* brethren were not yet appeased with the
former murders, but needes must finish the last acte of *Bologna* his
Tragedie by losse of his life, to keepe his wife and Children companie, so well in an other worlde,[39] as hee was vnited with them in
Loue in this fraile and transitorie passage. The *Neapolitan* gentleman
before spoken of by *Delio*, which had taken an enterprise to satisfie
the barbarous Cardinal, to berieue his Countreyman of life, hauing
changed his minde, and differing from day to day to sorte the same
to effect, which hee had taken in hande, it chaunced that a *Lombarde*
of larger conscience than the other, inuegled with Couetousnesse,

39. keepe . . . : III.v.71–2 and IV.ii.18–19 and 209-10.

and hired for readie money, practised th death of the Duchesse pore husband. This bloudy beast was called *Daniel de Bozola* that had charge of a certaine bande of footemen in *Millan*. This newe *Iudas* and assured manqueller, within certaine dayes after, knowing that *Bologna* oftentimes repaired to heare seruice at the Church[40] and couent of *S. Fraunces*, secretly conueyed himself in ambush, hard bisides the church of *S. Iames* whether he came, (being accompanied with a certaine troupe of souldioures) to assaile the infortunate *Bologna*, who was sooner slaine than hee was able to thinke vpon defense, and whose mishap was such, that he which killed him had good leisure to saue himself by reason of the little pursuite made after him. Beholde heere the Noble facte of a Cardinall, and what sauer it hath of Christian puritie, to commit a slaughter for a facte done many yeares past vpon a poore Gentleman which neuer thought him hurte. Is this the sweete obseruation of the Apostles, of whom they vaunt themselues to be the successors and folowers? And yet we cannot finde nor reade, that the Apostles, or those that stept in their trace, hired Ruffians and Murderers to cut the throtes of them which did them hurt. But what? It was in the time of *Iulius* the second, who was more marshall than christian, and loued better to shed bloud than giue blessing to the people. Such ende had the infortunate mariage of him, which ought to haue contented himself with that degree and honor that hee had acquired by his deedes and glory of his vertues, so much by eche wight recommended. We ought neuer to clime higher than our force permitteth, ne yet surmount the bounds of duety, and lesse suffer our selues to be haled fondly forth with desire of brutal sensualitie. The sinne being of such nature, that hee neuer giueth ouer the partie whome he mastereth, vntil he hath brought him to the shame of some Notable follie. You see the miserable discourse of a Princesse loue, that was not very wise, and of a gentleman that had forgotten his estate, which ought to serue for a loking glasse to them which be ouer hardie in making of enterprises, and doe not measure their abilitie with the greatnesse of their attemptes: where they ought to maintaine themselues in reputation, and beare the title of wel aduised: foreseeing their ruine to be example to all posteritie, as may be seene by the death of *Bologna*, and of all them which sprang of him, and of his infortunate spouse his Ladie and mistresse.

40. knowing . . . : v.ii.132–5.

But we haue discoursed inoughe hereof, sith diuersitie of other Histories doe call vs to bring the same in place, which were not much more happie than those, whose Historie ye haue already tasted.

Collation

p. 250, l. 26. she vsed] *A;* and vpon hys repaire vsed *B.*
p. 251, l. 27. is of that stock] *A;* is the paragon of . . . *B.*
p. 255, l. 9. vertuous image] *A;* vnspotted Image *B.*
p. 255, l. 14. diuine beautie] *A;* pereles beauty *B.*
p. 257, l. 1. masse of earth] *B;* mosse of . . . *A.*
p. 259, ll. 37. fable of the people] *A;* Fable of the Worlde *B.*
p. 262, ll. 6–7. *Aragon* brothers would] *B; Aragon* brother would *A.*
p. 263, l. 4. honest report] *B;* honest port *A.*
p. 264, l. 17. espials round about] *B;* espial round . . . *A.*
p. 265, l. 22. the things were discouered] *A;* our affaires were . . . *B.*
p. 266, l. 23. And this was] *B;* And thus was *A.*
p. 267, ll. 11–12. rent vpon hir landes] *B;* . . . his landes *A.*
p. 268, ll. 4–5. is it the thought] *B;* was it . . . *A.*
p. 268, l. 29. doubt of my greatnesse] *A;* . . . my beynge wyth Chylde *B.*
p. 269, ll. 22–23. foolish names of honor] *A;* Names . . . *B.*
p. 269, l. 33. ministers of hir follie] *A;* shadowes of . . . *B.*
p. 273, l. 29. coniectured how grieuously] *B;* considered how . . . *A.*
p. 273, l. 31. yelled forth] *A;* yalped forth *B.*
p. 274, l. 3. deepest things] *B;* deepest thing *A.*
p. 274, l. 19. filthy embracements] *A;* Lecherous loue *B.*
p. 276, l. 26. in a place to rescue] *A;* where he thought to . . . *B.*
p. 278, l. 4. and to reue them of lyfe] *B; not in A.*
p. 281, l. 27. small acquaintaunce] *A;* no acquaintace *B.*
p. 283, l. 4. assured manqueller] *A;* pestilent manqueller *B.*

APPENDIX II
'O, let us howl, some heavy note'
(IV.ii.61–72)
Commentary and Transcription by
David Greer

The music for this song survives in three seventeenth-century manuscripts:

- *A.* New York Public Library, Drexel MS. 4175, No. 42 (*c.* 1620–30; with lute accompaniment).[1]
- *B.* British Museum, Add. MS. 29481, ff. 5ᵛ–6 (*c.* 1630; vocal part only, with elaborate embellishments).
- *C.* New York Public Library, Drexel MS. 4041, Pt. II, No. 26 (*c.* 1650; with thorough-bass accompaniment).

In sources *A* and *B* it is unattributed, but in *C* Robert Johnson (*c.* 1582?–1633) is cited as the composer; this is almost certainly correct. The three sources present numerous variants in the music, but *A* and *B* are in substantial agreement, whereas *C* seems to be a later version, in which (amongst other revisions) the chromatic inflections on 'howl' have been eliminated. The lute part of *A* is rather unsatisfactory in that, besides containing several obvious scribal errors, it is extremely scanty in places. Nevertheless, because of its date, and because its vocal line is in general agreement with *B*, this version has been chosen for transcription here, as presenting the music as it was probably performed in the first productions of the play.[2]

In this transcription an E♭ has been added to the key-signature, the note-values have been halved, and slurs and regular barring

---

[1] According to the table of contents this manuscript originally contained another setting of 'O, let us howl' (No. 4), but this is now missing. See John P. Cutts, ' "Songs vnto the Violl and Lute" – Drexel MS. 4175', *Musica Disciplina*, xvi (1962), pp. 73–92.

[2] For other transcriptions see John P. Cutts, *La Musique de Scène de la Troupe de Shakespeare*, Paris, 1959, pp. 40–5 (versions *A*, *B*, & *C*), and Ian Spink, *Robert Johnson: Ayres, Songs and Dialogues* (*The English Lute-Songs*, 2nd Series, xvii), London, 1961, pp. 32–3 (version *C*).

O, let us howl ————— , some hea-vy note, Some deadly dogged howl-

Sounding as from the threat-'ning throat Of beasts, and fat-al

fowl! As ra-vens, screech-owls, bulls, and bears, We'll bill and bawl

our parts, Till irk-some noise have cloy'd your

EMENDATIONS TO *A*

The first number refers to the bar; V = voice, Au = accompaniment (upper stave), Al = accompaniment (lower stave); the second number indicates the note or chord within the bar, excluding rests and editorial additions. As in the transcription, note-values are halved.

3. Al. 5 and 4. Al. 2] tablature = C, not D.   4. Al. 6] [notation] in tablature.

5. Al. 3] [notation] in tablature.   5. Al. 4] G = F in tablature.   12. Al. 1] A♭ in tablature.   12. Au. 4] quaver C followed by quaver B♭ in tablature.   13. Al. 1] A♭ in tablature: rhythm sign = crotchet.   13. V. 4] G = A.   14. A. 1] C-minor chord has minim duration in tablature.   15. V. 3–4] rhythm = ♩. ♪   16. V. 9] E♭.   16. Al. 3–4 and 17. Al. 1–2] a course too low in tablature.   18. Al. 2] a course too low in tablature.   19. V. 4] E♮.   20. Al. 4–5] [notation] in tablature.

inserted. Some notes have been added to the original accompaniment to fill out the texture; such additions are indicated by small notation. All other alterations and corrections are listed below. The text of this Revels Plays edition is used here; the following variants occur in the three manuscripts:

> throat] throats *A*.   Of beasts, and] Of beasts or *C*.   fowl] fowls *A*.   bill]
> bell *A*, *B*.   have cloy'd your] hath cloy'd our *A*, *B*, *C*.   your hearts] our
> hearts *A*, *B*, *C*.   love] peace *A*, *B*.

Stylistically, 'O, let us howl, some heavy note' is an example of the declamatory type of song which developed in England in the second decade of the seventeenth century. Apart from the sinister inflections on 'howl' noted above, other features appropriate to a 'mad song' may be observed, such as the wayward harmonic twist in bars 5–6 and the wide leaps in bars 7–9.

APPENDIX III
Webster's imitation of other authors:
an index to passages cited in this edition

AUTHOR

CORRESPONDING PASSAGES IN
'THE DUCHESS OF MALFI'

Adams, Thomas
   The Gallant's Burden (1612)   (?) I.i.48–51; III.ii.323–5, V.ii.335.

Alexander, William
   The Alexandrean Tragedy   I.i.25–8, 173–7, 209, (?) 264–6;
      (1607)   III.i.52–4;   III.iv.44;   III.v.50–1,
         96–7; IV.ii.143–4, 223; (?) V.i.23;
         V.iii.56–8.
   Croesus (1604)   III.ii.321–2; IV.i.11–12; IV.ii.8–10;
         (?) V.ii.348–9.
   Julius Caesar (1607)   (?) III.ii.34–42; III.v.108–9;
         V.ii.117–8.

Ariosto, Ludovico
   Satires, tr. R. Tofte (1608)   (?) I.i.313; (?) II.i.34–7; (?) IV.ii.13–
         14.

Camden, William
   Remains of a Greater Work   (?) III.v.35–6.
      (1605)

Chapman, George
   Bussy D'Ambois (1604)   (?) I.i.157–8; (?) IV.i.102–3.
   Byron's Tragedy (1608)   (?) III.ii.323–5.
   Seven Penitential Psalms   I.i.181–2; III.iii.62–4; (?) IV.i.102–
      (1612)   3; V.ii.297–9.

Donne, John
   The First Anniversary (1611)   III.v.82–3; (?) v.ii.109.
   Ignatius his Conclave (1611)   (?) II.iv.16–19; III.i.31–5; III.v.39–
                                 40.
   Progress of the Soul (1612)   (?) I.i.201–3; III.v.105–6; (?)
                                 IV.ii.39–43.

Elyot, Sir Thomas
   The Image of Governance   (?) I.i.5–15, 398–403.
     (1541)

Goulart, Simon
   Admirable Histories, tr.   v.ii.5–19, 90–4.
     E. Grimeston (1607)

Guazzo, Stefano
   Civil Conversation, tr.   I.i.190–205; (?) III.ii.137–9.
     G. Pettie (1581)

Guevara, Antonio de
   The Dial of Princes, tr.   (?) IV.ii.304–5.
     T. North (1557)

Hall, Joseph
   Characters (1608)   I.i.(?) 162–5, (?) 171–2, 184–5,
                                 (?) 416, 438–40, (?) 451–2; (?)
                                 II.v.37–8; (?) IV.i.32–3.
   Epistles (1611)   I.i.(?) 37–8, (?) 242–3, (?) 438–40;
                                 III.v.120–1; IV.ii.259; v.ii.303–4;
                                 v.iv.67–8.

Jonson, Benjamin
   The Masque of Queens (1609)   III.ii.254.
   Sejanus (1605)   III.v.97–8.

Marston, John
   The Dutch Courtezan (1605)   (?) IV.ii.18–19.

Matthieu, Pierre
   Henry IV, tr. E. Grimeston   III.ii.122–33, 238–40; III.iii.41–7;
     (1612)   III.v.12–17.
   Louis XI, tr. E. Grimeston   (?) II.v.32–3
     (1614)

'Supplement', Jean de Serres,   IV.i.16–17, 36–8; IV.ii.27–30;
General Inventory, tr. E.   v.iii.48–9.
Grimeston (1607)

Montaigne, Michel de
Essays, tr. J. Florio (1603)   I.i.(?) 31–2, 41–3, (?) 58–9; II.i.(?)
26–8, 78–81, 89–90, (?) 99–101,
101–7, (?) 118–19, (?) 144–5; II.
ii.24–5, (?) 76–80; III.iv.40–2; (?)
IV.ii.118–20; v.i.(?) 43–6, (?) 74;
v.iii.9–11, 50; v.v.75.

Nashe, Thomas
Christ's Tears (1593)   v.v.72–3.
The Unfortunate Traveller   II.ii.37–49; (?) IV.ii.262–3.
(1594)

Overbury, Thomas
The Wife and Characters   Ded., 13–14; (?) I.i.339–40; (?)
(1614)   v.ii.226.

Painter, William
The Palace of Pleasure (1567)   I.i.16–22, (?) 92–103; (?) III.v.7–9.
[See also echoes noted in foot-
notes to App. I.]

Sidney, Sir Philip
Arcadia (1590)   III.ii.61–2, 70–1, 72–5, 77–81,
84–5, 255, 259–60, (?) 262–5,
270–3; III.v.(?) 18–19, (?) 71–2,
(?) 78–81, 111–13; IV.i.3–8, 12–15,
84–90, 92–4; IV.ii.31–2, (?) 35–6,
327–31, 360–1, v.ii.30–1, (?) 131–
2, 165–6, 168–70, 172–3, 173–5,
191–4, 216–9, 233–39, (?) 261–2,
285–6, (?) 295–6, 328–30, 344–5;
v.iv.27–8; v.v.9–10, 42–4, (?)
99–100, 100–2, 118–19.
Astrophel and Stella (1591)   III.v.76–7.

Whetstone, George
An Heptameron of Civil   I.i.55–6, (?) 298–9; III.ii.24–32; (?)
Discourses (1582)   IV.i.77–9; v.v.56–8.

Bibliography

The text makes reference to these books and articles by author's name and date as given below, with a few exceptions as noted.

Abbot, E. A., *A Shakespearian Grammar* (London, 1870, and many times reprinted).

Astington, John H., *English Court Theatre 1558–1642* (Cambridge, 1999).

Belsey, Catherine, *The Subject of Tragedy* (London, 1985).

Bentley, G. E., *The Jacobean and Caroline Stage*, 7 vols. (Oxford, 1941–68).

Bogard, Travis, *The Tragic Satire of John Webster* (Berkeley and Los Angeles, 1955).

Boklund, Gunnar, *'The Duchess of Malfi': Sources, Themes, Characters* (Cambridge, Mass., 1962).

Bradbrook, M. C., *John Webster: Citizen and Dramatist* (London and New York, 1980).

Brooke, Rupert, *John Webster & the Elizabethan Drama* (Toronto, 1926).

Brown, John Russell, 'The Printing of John Webster's Plays, I, II, and III', *Studies in Bibliography*, vi (1954), 117–40; viii (1956), 113–27; and xv (1962), 57–69.

'Representing sensuality in Shakespearean's Plays', *New Theatre Quarterly*, 51 (1997), 205–13.

'Techniques of Restoration: The Case of *The Duchess of Malfi*', in *Shakespearean Illuminations; Essays in Honor of Marvin Rosenberg*, ed. Jay L. Halio and Hugh Richmond (Newark and London, 1998), 317–35.

Burgess, John, 'Peter Gill', in *Directors' Shakespeare*, ed. John Russell Brown (London, 2008).

Callaghan, Dympna, ed., *'The Duchess of Malfi' [New Casebook]* (Basingstoke and New York, 2000).

Cave, Richard, *'The White Devil' and 'The Duchess of Malfi'; Text and Performance* (London, 1988).

Chambers, E. K., *The Elizabethan Stage*, 4 vols. (Oxford, 1923).

Cressy, David, *Birth, Marriage and Death: Ritual, Religion and the Life Cycle in Tudor and Stuart England* (Oxford, 1997).

Dent, R. W., *John Webster's Borrowing* (Berkeley and Los Angeles, 1960).

Dollimore, Jonathan, *Radical Tragedy: Religion, Ideology and Power in the Drama of Shakespeare and His Contemporaries* (Brighton, 1984).

Ekeblad [Ewbank], Inga-Stina, 'The Impure Art of John Webster', *Review of English Studies*, ix (1958); reprinted in Hunter (1969).

Ellis-Fermor, Una, *The Jacobean Drama* (London, 1936).

Foakes, R. A., *Henslowe's Diary*, 2nd ed. (Cambridge, 2002).

Forker, Charles R., *Skull Beneath the Skin: the Achievement of John Webster* (Carbondale and Edwardsville, 1986).

Goldberg, Dena, *Between Worlds: a Study of the Plays of John Webster* (Waterloo, Ontario, 1987).

Graves, R. B., *Lighting the Shakespearean Stage 1567–1642*, (Carbondale, Ill., 1999).

Griswold, Wendy, *Renaissance Revivals: City Comedy and Revenge Tragedy in the London Theatre, 1576–1980* (Chicago, 1986).

Gurr, Andrew, *The Shakespeare Company, 1594–1642* (Cambridge, 2004).

Holdsworth, R. V., *'The White Devil' and 'The Duchess of Malfi': A Casebook* (London, 1975).

Hunter, G. K. and S. K., edd., *John Webster [Penguin Critical Anthology]* (Harmondsworth, 1969).

Jackson, W. A., *Records of the Court of the Stationers' Company* (London, 1957).

Jardine, Lisa, *Still Harping on Daughters: Women and Drama in the Age of Shakespeare* (Brighton and New York, 1983).

Leech, Clifford., *John Webster* (London, 1951).

Webster: 'The Duchess of Malfi' (London, 1963).

Lindley, David, *The Trials of Frances Howard: Fact and Fiction at the Court of King James* (London, 1993).

Lomax, Marion, *Stage Images and Traditions: Shakespeare to Ford* (Cambridge, 1987).

Moore, Don D., *John Webster and His Critics, 1617–1964* (Baton Rouge, 1956).

Morris, Brian, ed., *John Webster [A Mermaid Critical Commentary]* (London, 1970).

Neill, Michael, *Issues of Death: Mortality and Identity in English Renaissance Tragedy* (Oxford, 1997).

Notes & Queries [*N&Q*].

Orgel, Stephen, *Impersonations: The Performance of Gender in Shakespeare's England* (Cambridge, 1996).

Ornstein, Robert, *The Moral Vision of Jacobean Tragedy* (Madison, Wisconsin, 1960).

Oxford English Dictionary [*O.E.D*].

Pearson, Jacqueline, *Tragedy and Tragicomedy in the Plays of John Webster* (Manchester, 1980).

Potter, Lois, 'Realism Versus Nightmare: Problems of Staging *The Duchess of Malfi*', in *The Triple Bond*, ed. Joseph G. Price (Philadelphia and London, 1975), 170–89.

Price, Hereward T., 'The Function of Imagery in Webster', *P.M.L.A.*, lxx (1955), 719–33.

Ribner, Irving, *Jacobean Tragedy: the Quest for Moral Order* (London, 1962).

Second Maiden's Tragedy [Anon.], ed. Anne Lancashire (Manchester, 1978).

Sturgess, Keith, *Jacobean Private Theatre* (London and New York, 1987).

Thomson, Peter, 'Webster and the Actor', in Brian Morris, *John Webster*, 23–44.

Tilley, M. P., *A Dictionary of the Proverbs in England in the Sixteenth and Seventeenth Centuries* (Ann Arbor, 1950).

Tricomi, Albert H., *Reading Tudor-Stuart Texts through Cultural Historicism* (Gainesville, Florida, 1996).

Whigham, Frank, 'Sexual and Social Mobility in *The Duchess of Malfi*', *P.M.L.A.*, 100 (1985), 167–86; reprinted in *Seizures of the Will in Early English Modern Drama* (Cambridge, 1996).

Index